Southwest Archaeology in the Twentieth Century

Southwest Archaeology in the Twentieth Century

EDITED BY

LINDA S. CORDELL AND DON D. FOWLER

THE UNIVERSITY OF UTAH PRESS
Salt Lake City

The Defiance House Man colophon is a registered trademark of The University of Utah Press. It is based upon a four-foot-tall, Ancient Puebloan pictograph (late PIII) near Glen Canyon, Utah.

10 09 08 07 06 05   5 4 3 2 1

LIBRARY OF CONGRESS CATALOGING-IN-PUBLICATION DATA

Southwest archaeology in the twentieth century / edited by Linda S. Cordell and Don D. Fowler.
    p. cm.
  Includes bibliographical references and index.
  ISBN-13: 978-0-87480-825-4 (cloth : alk. paper)
  ISBN-10: 0-87480-825-1
  1. Indians of North America—Southwest, New—Antiquities. 2. Archaeology—Southwest, New—History—20th century. 3. Southwest, New—Antiquities.
I. Cordell, Linda S. II. Fowler, Don D., 1936–
  E78.S7S563 2006
  979'.033—dc22   2005017157

Contents

Figures

Preface

The opportunity to develop this volume came from a symposium we organized for the 100th Annual Meeting of the American Anthropological Association (AAA) held November 28–December 2, 2001 at the Marriott Wardman Park Hotel in Washington, D.C. Cathy L. Costin, program editor for archaeology for the centennial meeting, requested that we develop a symposium that dealt in some way with the role of southwestern archaeology in the theoretical and methodological development of the discipline of anthropology. The overarching theme of the 100th Annual Meeting was the transformation of anthropology, including the changing relationship between archaeology and other subfields of anthropology. Costin recommended that we take a retrospective view of southwestern archaeology in the twentieth century. We thank her and the AAA program committee for challenging us to this task. We are grateful to all of those who participated in the symposium, and to those who attended that session and provided their comments, all of which were useful to us in moving from a symposium to an edited volume. We also thank the reviewers chosen by the University of Utah Press, whose cogent comments helped us, and some of our authors, focus the volume a bit better.

We thank all the authors who provided chapters for this volume, and, by extension, all the librarians and archivists who helped them. While the process of moving this project to publication was not as long or bumpy as similar ventures of which we have been part, it was not without its snags. We are grateful to all who stayed with it and with us. We thank June-el Piper for editorial assistance that went far beyond assembling the bibliography. And we thank Sarah Soliz for her eagle eye and author-friendly copyediting; her work made this a better book. We acknowledge the assistance as well of Marion (Bonnie) Salter, at the University of Nevada, Reno, and of Marcelyn Ritchie, marketing manager at the University of Utah Press. Last, though by no means least, we are grateful to Jeff Grathwohl, editor-in-chief of the University of Utah Press, for his assistance and willingness to work with two, often hard to reach, editors.

LINDA S. CORDELL, Boulder, Colorado
DON D. FOWLER, Reno, Nevada

I. The Contexts of Southwest Archaeology

I

Introduction

Don D. Fowler and Linda S. Cordell

This volume aims to give readers an overview of the historical development of archaeology as it is practiced in the American Southwest and
an introduction to some of the substantive contributions the archaeology of this region has made to understanding of the past. The Southwest is an anthropological culture area familiar to many Americans for
its archaeological treasures, such as the cliff dwellings of Mesa Verde,
Colorado, and Canyon de Chelly, Arizona; the impressive stone buildings of Chaco Canyon, New Mexico; and the massive multistory adobe
buildings, ball courts, and mounds of Paquimé in Chihuahua, Mexico.
The Southwest is equally well known for its vibrant indigenous peoples:
Apaches, Hopis, Maricopas, Navajos, Pimas, Rio Grande Pueblos, To-
hono O'Odham, Yumas, Yaquis, Zunis, and others. While establishing precise boundaries of any culture area is difficult, archaeologist
Erik K. Reed (1964) usefully and enduringly defined the Southwest as
the region of North America extending from Las Vegas, Nevada, to
Las Vegas, New Mexico, and from Durango, Colorado, to Durango,
Mexico. Other definitions expand or contract this area. Indeed, one
research question for over a century and a half has been how far south
the archaeological Southwest extends.

Whatever boundaries scholars agree upon, the Southwest is a region
seen from the eastern United States (Fowler 2000:ix). Mexican scholars define the region as the Northwest, as *seen from* Mexico City. However defined, the Southwest has been the scene of intense archaeological
investigation for more than 100 years, with more research being done

therein than in any other part of the United States. In pulling together the institutional contexts and histories of major topics of archaeological concern within the region during the twentieth century, we want to provide a useful reference for advanced students and professional archaeologists who work in the Southwest. We hope that archaeologists who work in other parts of the world also will find this information a useful entryway into the current literature of Southwest archaeology and as a case study to compare to other regions. Finally, while we admit to writing largely for our anthropological and archaeological colleagues, we would be pleased if others who live in or visit the Southwest find their experience of its archaeological bounty enhanced by the contributions provided here.

This project began with a request from the program committee for the 2001 American Anthropological Association (AAA) Annual Meeting in Washington, D.C., the meeting that marked the beginning of the organization's centennial year. We were invited to develop a session on Southwest archaeology, because it was thought that archaeologists working in the Southwest have had an extraordinary influence on the discipline of American anthropology in general. In keeping with the themes of the centennial meeting, we were asked to develop a retrospective view of how archaeological method and theory had been transformed throughout the twentieth century in the archaeology of our region. The timing of the request was fortunate, largely because it quickly followed the publication of two books that set the stage and tone for us. Don D. Fowler's (2000) *A Laboratory for Anthropology: Science and Romanticism in the American Southwest, 1846–1930* and James E. Snead's (2001) *Ruins and Rivals: The Making of Southwest Archaeology* explore the institutional settings, personalities, intellectual pursuits, and research agendas of southwestern archaeologists from roughly 1850 to 1950. Both volumes acknowledge the intellectual contributions of our region that we felt could be pursued in more depth and brought forward in time to include many of the changes in professional southwestern archaeology during the later decades of the twentieth century. In addition to a retrospective view of southwestern archaeology, we also wished to include perspectives on contemporary issues.

In organizing the AAA symposium and expanding it into this book, our focus has been on archaeologists and the institutional settings in which they work. Neither venue offers a history of archaeological theory or of archaeological contributions to anthropological theory. Rather, our concern has been with describing the interplay among individuals and the formal and informal institutions in which they work in carrying out national and regional agendas. The AAA symposium was held November 29, 2001, and included presentations by Fowler, Snead, Stephen E. Nash and Jeffrey S. Dean, Bruce B. Huckell, J. Jefferson Reid, Robert W. Preucel, Jane H. Kelley and Arthur C. MacWilliams, Catherine M. Cameron, James E. Ivey and David Hurst Thomas, Katherine A. Spielmann, William H. Doelle and David A. Phillips Jr., and Linda S. Cordell. Douglas W. Schwartz of the School of American Research and David R. Wilcox of the Museum of Northern Arizona served as thoughtful and helpful discussants. Following the symposium, with publication in mind, we asked Barbara J. Mills to contribute a chapter on the history of archaeological field schools in the Southwest, and Stephen H. Lekson to develop a chapter on complexity and social hierarchy, which they have done. Previous commitments prevented Cameron and Schwartz from providing chapters for the book. We are pleased that Stephanie M. Whittlesey joined as coauthor with Jeff Reid. We think that the present book preserves much of the spirit and content of the symposium from which it derived, while expanding and adding some themes. The volume has benefited from the thoughtful comments of four anonymous reviewers.

The organization of this volume departs from the AAA symposium from which it derived. The book is divided into two major sections. In the first, chapters by Fowler, Snead, Reid and Whittlesey, Mills, Kelley and MacWilliams, Doelle and Phillips, and Cordell examine lthe intellectual histories and institutional contexts of Southwest archaeology in the twentieth century. In the second section of the book, chapters by Nash and Dean, Huckell, Lekson, Spielmann, Preucel, and Ivey and Thomas address substantive contributions and continuing themes current among archeologists working in the Southwest today. Neither the historical context nor the substantive contributions of Southwest archaeology is presented exhaustively. Rather, we have chosen to use a light editorial hand and encourage our contributors, each of whom is an expert in the field, to explore topics from their own perspectives. In what follows in this introduction, we first, briefly, characterize the Southwest as a distinct region in North America. We then develop a general background and framework that introduces the major themes of the papers that are enlarged upon in each of the two sections of the book.

Defining the Southwest

To some extent, the American Southwest is the romantic construct of journalists (especially Charles F. Lummis), artists (from Ernest L. Blumenschein to Georgia O'Keeffe), and the tourist industry. Yet, it is also a geographic region that is characterized by aridity, comparatively low population densities, modest industrial development, and until after World War II, little in the way of Euro-American commercial development. In the Southwest, indigenous American Indian societies continue to occupy the same lands they inhabited for centuries prior to the arrival of Europeans. The region, before becoming part of the United States, was part of the Spanish Empire in the Americas, and later part of Mexico. The documentary history of the Southwest does not mention Pilgrim ancestors searching for religious freedom nor does it concern Dutch or English commerce. Documentary history in the Southwest began with the chronicles of the *entradas* of Fray Marcos de Niza to the Pueblo of Zuni in 1539, followed by the large, well-organized expedition under the direction of Francisco Vásquez de Coronado in 1540–1541, and the colonizing expedition of Juan de Oñate in 1598 (Cordell 1989a; Riley 1987). From the perspective of anthropologists from the eastern United States, the Southwest is an internal exotic location that serves as an appropriate crucible for development of anthropology as a discipline concerned with understanding cultural diversity.

The Southwest as a region offered twentieth-century anthropology a unique palette of diverse tribes of American Indians, strong, traditional Hispanic communities, and a history nearly devoid of Anglo Europeans. For cultural anthropologists, the Southwest was an accessible field area in which studies of various groups began as early as the 1880s (Fowler 2000:321–342). For archaeologists, the arid and relatively sparsely populated landscape provided excellent conditions of site preservation, while the living Native peoples served as analogues through which archaeological materials were interpreted (Fowler, this volume; Spielmann, this volume). While archaeological research in the Southwest followed the intellectual agendas of American archaeology generally, the abundance of well-preserved sites and artifacts and the immediate presence of American Indian descendants of ancient traditions influenced the ways in which those agendas were followed. Most generally, the large number of sites and the quality of the archaeological record made the Southwest a preferred locale for large scale excavation projects that could enhance museum collections and provide a training ground for students (Fowler, this volume; Mills, this volume). The presence of American Indians living traditionally, on their ancestral lands, promised opportunities for collaborative research among cultural anthropologists and archaeologists, although these opportunities were not necessarily fully developed (Fowler, this volume; Snead, this volume; Spielmann, this volume). The intellectual background of archaeologists trained in Europe or Latin America and working in that portion of the Southwest that lies in Mexico added a different set of questions (Kelley and MacWilliams, this volume).

ANTHROPOLOGICAL BEGINNINGS

In the mid-nineteenth century, undisciplined speculation that Adolph F. Bandelier would characterize as the "Romantic School" (Bandelier 1885) dominated ideas about American Indians, who were thought to represent, variously, polygenesis, descendants of denizens of Atlantis, or remnants of the lost tribes of Israel (Wauchope 1962). Joseph Henry, founding secretary of the Smithsonian; and later John Wesley Powell, of the Bureau of American Ethnology; and Frederic Ward Putnam, of Harvard, all of whom are justifiably considered among the founding fathers of American anthropology, attempted to distance themselves from the Romantic School. They "labored mightily to place anthropological investigations upon a strictly scientific basis" (White 1940[1]:1–2), which at the time meant working within the evolutionist framework developed by Lewis Henry Morgan. Morgan arranged to have Bandelier work in the Southwest and in Mexico, and it was Morgan's work that inspired Victor Mindeleff's studies of Pueblo architecture, Frank Hamilton Cushing's ethnographic work at Zuni, and the beginning of Jesse Walter Fewkes's career in archaeology (Cordell 1989a; Fowler 2000, this volume; Longacre 1970; Taylor 1954). Morgan was concerned with the development of institutions: the family, the state, private property, and law, as were many of his contemporaries. He developed a grand scheme of unilineal evolution outlining stages through which all societies passed and in which some human groups remained (Morgan 1870, 1877). It was the grand scheme itself, as well as certain transitions within it, to which Franz Boas and his students later, correctly, objected as "conjectural history" (cf. Boas 1932).

Given the saliency of characterizing political and social institutions in Morgan's evolutionist program, it may be difficult to understand why so much attention—or any at all—was paid to archaeology and material culture. Among the kinds of observations that could be made and documented objectively were descriptions and measurements of monuments and artifacts. These served to indicate the relative level of development achieved by ancient societies (Cordell 1989c; Fowler 2000; Taylor 1954). The observations went far beyond noting, for example, that American Indians lacked ironworking technology, and hence could fit an evolutionary pigeonhole in Morgan's grand scheme. Rather, archaeological remains did two things. First, they could be measured and evaluated to provide an aesthetic assessment of their quality which could also indicate the evolutionary level of the society (Hinsley 1981:89–90). Second, especially in the Southwest where there are living American Indians who use and understand objects much like those found archaeologically, the objects provided tangible evidence for continuity from the past to the present which was essential in order to refute the mythical Atlantian migrations of vanished races. Morgan was concerned with institutions among American Indians before they had been changed by contact with Europeans, and Morgan distrusted Spanish chronicle accounts. Archaeology therefore could provide the historical continuity that challenged the cataclysms that were essential to the conjectural history of the Romantic School. As Curtis Hinsley (1981:98–90) states so well, "methodologically, continuity was critical. Like geology, a scientific anthropology could not admit discontinuities and cataclysms in the record."

Archaeological remains were important to the evolutionist program. For the early evolutionists, the remains provided a substantive record of the degree of mental and therefore social development of various American Indian societies. The record consisted largely of things, objects that were amassed in enormous numbers by major and minor museums, at least in part because they "spoke for themselves" about the mental condition of their makers (Cordell 1989c:39; Fowler 2000:148–186, 261–274).

We begin the contributed chapters of the volume with Fowler's paper, which discusses and evaluates the research in Southwest archaeology conducted by individuals working within the evolutionist framework and the institutional contexts within which they worked. In addition to an extensive history of field research in the Southwest and the Great Basin, Fowler has devoted considerable time to the history of American archaeology and anthropology.

Culture History and the First New Archaeology

There are many reasons why American archaeology moved away from grand scheme evolutionist perspectives. Among the major difficulties for archaeology was the evolutionist presentation of American Indian society as homogeneous—over time—as well as throughout the Americas (Longacre 1970). This began to change with the advent of the first "New Archaeology" in the 1910s and 1920s (Snead, this volume). In the Southwest, practitioners of this New Archaeology included Nels Nelson, Alfred V. Kidder, Earl Morris, and Neil Judd, among others. The principal tasks of this New Archaeology were to construct firm frameworks within which to order remains in space and in time and to develop *archaeological* methods of establishing intercultural relationships that do not depend on ethnographic analogy (Snead 2001, this volume). The goal was to write accurate, not con-jectural, culture histories of Native American peoples. As Snead (this volume) relates, many of the key contributions to archaeology during this time were advances in method, particularly in ways of developing sound chronologies. While the goals were clearly anthropological, the focus on archaeological method had the ironic effect of distancing archaeology from ethnology. James Snead's paper herein focuses on the period of crucial change in southwestern archaeology during the years from 1910 to about 1930. Snead (2001, this volume) has a long-standing interest in the history of southwestern archaeology and has conducted innovative archaeological research for several years on the Pajarito Plateau and adjacent areas in New Mexico.

In the Southwest, because the continued presence of living American Indians made it a field area for both ethnologists and archaeologists, there continued to be a permeable boundary between the two subfields. Ethnologists made major contributions to archaeology and some archaeologists contributed to ethnology. For example, while he was doing ethnography at Zuni, A. L. Kroeber (1916) demonstrated that potsherds collected from the surface of archaeological sites could be used to develop a relative temporal ordering, a technique that provides the backbone of southwestern survey archaeology. Kroeber (1917) also, of course, described Zuni social organization in *Zuñi Kin and Clan*. Two decades later, Julian Steward (1937) proposed a model of the transition from lineage to clan and the formation of villages, using room to kiva ratios. This model laid the foundation for archaeological thinking that sense could be made of social organization from largely architectural material data. On the other hand, archaeologist Florence Hawley Ellis used both archaeological and ethnographic information to examine Pueblo social organization (1951) and conducted ethnographic research on the social organization of Jemez Pueblo (1964).

In American archaeology, in general, the culture-historical approach focused on chronology and the definition of culture areas, the latter promulgated principally by ethnographer Clark Wissler. Ethnologists interested in culture history emphasized the unique configurations of beliefs, ideas, social practices, and items of material culture making up noncomparable cultures. For American archaeology, however, "culture" was primarily a geographic taxonomic unit. Without making any attempt to operationalize the concept of culture prevailing at the time, archaeologists ignored it while absorbed in creating temporal and spatial frameworks for prehistory (Watson 1995:689). As Snead (this volume) points out, this approach is exemplified by Kidder's work at Pecos Pueblo (1924) and the creation of the Pecos Classification (Kidder 1927). The latter was the first developmental classification of the prehispanic southwestern "culture" conventionally referred to as the Anasazi cultural tradition. The Pecos Classification, defining seven sequential periods (Basketmaker II, III, and Pueblo I, II, III, IV, V) is still used by southwestern archaeologists working with Ancestral Pueblo remains. However, while it is a useful and convenient device to organize archaeological data, it references architecture and pottery, not ancient tribes or other social units (Cordell 1997:23). Ancestral Pueblo and Anasazi are not the same entity, and neither one represents a single tribe or cultural group. Archaeologists and Pueblo Indians recognize that today's Pueblo Indians represent combinations of more than one archaeological tradition. Modern Pueblo Indians are similar culturally; however, they vary in features of social organization and speak six different indigenous languages. And modern Pueblo Indians are adamant in pointing out that their ancestors did not speak "Anasazi."

One of the most elemental and enduring results of Wissler's culture area approach in the Southwest was dividing prehispanic southwestern peoples into discrete archaeological "cultures," which are now conventionally labeled Anasazi (or Ancestral Pueblo), Hohokam, and Mogollon. Many students today take these as given, although some archaeologists argue their utility (Speth 1988). If these categories are understood to be taxonomic units relating primarily to geographic areas within which there is similarity in house forms, settlement configurations, pottery styles, and synchronicity in change over time, then the act of defining these conceptual categories reflects tremendous knowledge of the archaeological record and the ability to synthesize vast quantities of data. In their chapter, J. Jefferson Reid and Stephanie Whittlesey, who have conducted major archaeological research programs in the Mogollon region for a number of years, use unpublished diaries of preeminent southwestern archaeologist Emil W. Haury to chronicle how the Hohokam and Mogollon cultures came to be defined. Their presentation illuminates the institutional and intellectual contexts in which Haury worked when, with Harold S. Gladwin, he defined the Hohokam culture and later went on to define the Mogollon. While the notion of Mogollon culture continues to be controversial, the fact that both constructs are useful more than half a century after their initial formulation is a tribute to Haury's command of southwestern data, the breadth and scope of his field experience, and his political skills. As Reid and Whittlesey (this volume) demonstrate, Haury was able to use the institution of the field school, as well as the resources of the American Anthropological Association and the Society for American Archaeology to advance the utility of his concepts.

Institutional Contexts and Research Agendas

In the Southwest, archaeological field schools have long been important institutions in the critical task of training the next generation of professionals. Despite a plethora of introductory college courses and textbooks, archaeology depends greatly on "apprenticeships" in field experience, and these are commonly gained initially through organized field schools. Fowler (2000) and Snead (this volume), particularly, write about an earlier tradition of southwestern field schools, organized largely by Edgar L. Hewett, which followed an eclectic path that served to create public support for archaeology. As Reid and Whittlesey (this volume) and Snead (this volume) discuss, field schools may also forward professional and academic agendas. Barbara Mills (this volume), who has directed the University of Arizona field school for much of the last decade, provides a thorough history of southwestern field schools from their informal beginnings as excursions to their academic maturity as settings for research and student training. The changes she notes in the museums and universities that have organized field schools and the kinds of questions these field schools have addressed add a layer of understanding to the intellectual trajectory of southwestern archaeology.

In terms of land area, about a third of the Greater American Southwest is today part of Mexico. Kelley and MacWilliams (this volume) focus on the archaeology of the north Mexican states of Chihuahua and Sonora, which has been investigated by scholars working from both the United States and Mexico. Kelley and MacWilliams are especially well qualified to present the international perspective. Kelley, born in the United States and with a Ph.D. from Harvard, has lived in Canada for many years, serving as professor of archaeology at the University of Calgary where Canadian-born MacWilliams earned his doctorate. Their review points out that while all archaeologists recognize that the roots of the prehispanic cultures of the Greater American Southwest lie in Central Mexico, U.S. and Mexican archaeology developed largely independently as scholarly pursuits. Hence there have been very different frameworks within which archaeologists understood and appreciated ancient cultures in the Greater American Southwest. Forty years ago one project, the Joint Casas Grandes Project led by Charles Di Peso, brought Mexican and U.S. archaeologists together to study cultural development in the Casas Grandes Valley and at the remarkable site of Paquimé. As Kelley and MacWilliams illustrate, the synergy of that project continues to bear fruit today in new research and new theoretical directions.

Most of the archaeological work conducted in the Southwest today is being done by archaeologists employed in the private sector. This institutional context was unimagined in 1900 and did not exist even in 1950. Beginning in the early 1950s, a series of increasingly comprehensive federal and state laws and regulations mandated that archaeological work be conducted to assess and, if needed, mitigate environmental impacts of federally funded or licensed land-altering projects. Over time, most of this work has come to be done by archaeologists working for, or with, private sector consulting firms. This publicly mandated archaeology has led to enormous changes in a very short period of time to archaeological practice in general and specifically to archaeology in the Southwest. William Doelle and David Phillips (this volume) have devoted their careers to private sector archaeology. Here they offer the insights gained from their own professional experiences and survey data from others who have made a commitment to private sector archaeology. Doelle and Phillips offer unique, insider perspectives on the motivations, rewards, and challenges for those who have created and continue to influence this crucial, and growing, aspect of archaeology.

Linda Cordell (this volume) concludes the first section of this volume with a retrospective and prospective look at the current status of southwestern archaeology and some of the challenges and opportunities she sees for the near future. Cordell, who as director of the University of Colorado Museum is concerned about archaeological collections, notes that as of late 2001 nearly 250,000 archaeological sites had been recorded and numbered in Arizona, New Mexico, and southwestern

Colorado, with an estimated 10 percent of the total land area having been surveyed. There are untold thousands more—recorded and unrecorded—in southeastern Utah, west Texas, and northern Mexico. The existence of known sites, collections, and their data currently pose a major "curation crisis." Repositories are overflowing; data management often lags behind. The crisis is nationwide, not just limited to the Southwest. Preservation of collections and their data and access to them are and will be major issues in the decades ahead.

Cordell also notes that the themes archaeologists address may be related to the larger social and political contexts in which they work. In the Southwest today, these involve national, state, and tribal governments as well as expanding intellectual frameworks. The Native American Graves Protection and Repatriation Act (NAGPRA) of 1990 is bringing Native Americans and archaeologists together, without ethnographer intermediaries. New dialogues are occurring among archaeologists, anthropologists, and indigenous peoples throughout the world. The character of those dialogues in the Southwest reflects the unique multicultural and diverse legal statuses of the groups involved (Cordell, this volume). Some themes that seem to be emerging for the future include building collaborative ethnohistoric archaeological research with tribes, developing multifaceted meanings of landscape, and providing anthropologically informed perspectives on the southwestern colonial experience.

CONTRIBUTIONS AND CONTINUING THEMES IN SOUTHWEST ARCHAEOLOGY

Having brought the institutional contexts in which southwestern archaeology developed and is practiced up to the present, the second section of this book includes papers that examine both new and persistent themes in southwestern archaeology, focusing particularly on those that are providing new insights and suggesting new avenues and directions for research. We begin the section with Stephen Nash and Jeffrey Dean's discussion of the development of paleoenvironmental reconstruction. Nash studied tree-ring dating and archaeological dating in general as part of his doctoral program at the University of Arizona, where Dean has long been professor both at the Laboratory of Tree-Ring Research and the Department of Anthropology.

While in many ways the development of archaeology in the Southwest mirrors the archaeology of other regions of America, some unique characteristics of the Southwest contribute to American archaeology in general. The arid and fragile environments of the Southwest have always generated questions about the influence of environmental factors on ancient cultural developments. For example, was the thirteenth-century depopulation of much of the Colorado Plateau the result of drought? The development of various methods of paleoenvironmental research allied southwestern archaeology not with other subfields of anthropology but with the natural sciences, especially geology. Within the field of paleoenvironmental studies in general, the Southwest provides an unparalleled laboratory that not only produces information that enhances understanding of the past but knowledge that is of crucial importance to the future of all of humanity.

The Southwest has been a focus of Paleoindian archaeology since the discovery, in 1927 at Folsom, New Mexico, of a stone spear point in association with an extinct form of bison. The Folsom site holds a deservedly important place in American archaeology because it provided the first incontrovertible evidence of humans in North America during the late Pleistocene (Cordell 1997:68). Bruce Huckell has conducted extensive research programs on Paleoindian and Archaic archaeology in the Southwest (11,500 to 1500 B.P.). His chapter explores archaeological research on this period during the twentieth century. Anthropological and archaeological understanding of this long period of time has depended considerably on the methods and techniques of paleoenvironmental investigations described by Nash and Dean. Huckell's approach emphasizes both the development of substantive information about this important and long period of time, as well as the novel methods and techniques used in its study. He appropriately situates this aspect of southwestern archaeology in regional context; however, the nature of the archaeological record he develops is tied to larger themes of national and international scope, especially the initial peopling of the Americas and the transition from hunting and gathering to agriculture in New World contexts.

Since about 1850, when the first extensive descriptions were published of spectacular ruins in Chaco Canyon, New Mexico, of the ruins and canal systems in the Salt and Gila River basins in Arizona, and of Paquimé, in Chihuahua, archaeologists and others have speculated about the sorts of sociopolitical systems that may have existed in those places (Fowler 2000:50–70). Suggestions that these remains reflect societies that were less egalitarian than modern American Indians of the Southwest reverberate with questions about appropriate use of ethnographic analogy, potential lack of continuity between the archaeological past and modern American Indians, and the credibility of archaeology that to some extent must depend upon both (Cordell 1989b). Since the 1970s, extensive archaeological work had been done in all three locales, but as yet there is no agreement among archaeologists on how to describe or characterize the kinds of political or social hierarchies that may have existed there. The lack of agreement reflects the seriousness of the question for archaeology. What methods are available to archaeology to describe social and political systems that may not have modern analogues? What methods are there to unravel the changes in social and political organization that set apart a descendant from their ancestors? Stephen Lekson has spent a good part of his archaeological career working in and studying the archaeology of Chaco Canyon, recently synthesizing the results of years of research there (Lekson 1999, 2005). From his perspective, sociopolitical complexity may be said to exist in any society, past or present, when "the few make decisions for the many." The forms of complexity, however, may be many and varied, ranging from hierarchical, centralized political structures, to managerial elites, to more subtle and diffuse forms of control and decision making. Lekson (this volume) reviews and critiques archaeological debates about the nature of sociopolitical complexity in Chaco, the Salt and Gila River areas, and at Paquimé. He concludes that the forms of complexity varied from locale to locale. For the Chacoan case he suggests that there was some form of oppressive hierarchy that Pueblo peoples in later times sought to ameliorate through various social and political institutions seen in historic pueblos and recorded ethnographically.

Lekson's paper forefronts questions about the appropriate use of ethnographic analogy. Katherine Spielmann (this volume) directs insightful comments on this issue by providing a thoughtful retrospective view. While she is critical of early twentieth-century archaeologists who either uncritically accepted or uncritically rejected ethnographic analogy, she finds that archaeologists have used ethnographic analogy more creatively since the 1970s with the shift away from interest in culture history to a focus on behavior. Spielmann has conducted extensive research on the formation of the first large Pueblo settlements in the Salinas area, on the eastern periphery of the Southwest. She proposes a more nuanced use of ethnographic analogy and of ethnohistory that is particularly important to new understandings of this period (from about A.D. 1280 to 1450) of aggregation in the American Southwest. Focus on this period also provides a venue for new collaborations among Native

Americans and archaeologists, and Spielmann is generally optimistic about future directions such collaborations may take.

Robert Preucel's paper exemplifies the kind of insights that may be provided by the collaborations Spielmann suggests. He is specifically concerned with how ethnicity developed among southwestern groups and how ethnicity might be detected archaeologically. As Fenton points out:

> ethnicity is about social classifications emerging within *relationships*.... These are not simply groups—a static category—but social relationships in which people distinguish themselves from others.... The enduring dimensions of social life around which ethnic identities are built are...ancestry, culture and language.... [B]ut for ethnicity to spring to life it is necessary that *real or perceived differences of ancestry, culture and language are mobilized in social transactions* [Fenton 1999:6, emphasis in original].

Preucel (this volume) reviews early twentieth-century and more modern approaches to questions of ethnic identification, showing how archaeologists' own theoretical orientations play out in the way ethnic groups have been defined. Preucel has actively been conducting collaborative research with Cochiti Pueblo for several years. Informed by the perspective this research has afforded, he argues that archaeology informed by practice theory may be particularly promising in exploring issues of identity.

As we have noted, the Southwest was a colony of the Spanish Empire long before the arrival of Anglo Americans. When Bandelier began his studies of the Southwest in 1880, he recorded Spanish mission ruins, including those of Pecos, Guisewe, Quarai, and Abó, among others. Yet, there was no systematic archaeological investigation of the mission ruins in the period 1910–1930. By and large, interpretations of missions in the twentieth century were derived from historical and architectural perspectives; they were not anthropologically informed. Ivey and Thomas, who have collaborated in Mission period archaeology in New Mexico, cogently review the status of Spanish Mission archaeology in the Southwest. They note that prior to the 1990s, only Hawikuh, at Zuni, and Awatovi, at Hopi, were studied systematically by archeologists. Both Ivey and Thomas have extensive experience with Mission period sites. Thomas has excavated mission sites on Saint Catherine's Island off the coast of Georgia; both have researched mission archaeology on the West Coast. Ivey and Thomas compare mission archaeology in the Southwest with the much more extensive programs in the southeastern United States, as well as to those in California. These comparisons provide suggestions for more methodologically and theoretically systematic approaches for mission research in the Southwest.

Finally, David Wilcox, who has conducted archaeological research in virtually all corners of the Southwest and provided innovative syntheses of many of the topics addressed in this volume, provides a concluding discussion that puts the history of the past 100 years of Southwest archaeology into the larger context of intellectual histories of scholarly disciplines in general. Within this framework he asks if there is anything here for others outside our field and suggests that there is if we examine how archaeological agendas of the past were set and how those of future research will be set. Wilcox admonishes us to see the setting of archaeological agendas—past and present—within the context of larger social forces. He asks who will set the course of future Southwest archaeology, what support they can muster, and what is the potential of the archaeological record. These fundamental questions should motivate further examination of the chapters in this book and ongoing intellectual inquiry into the workings of our field.

In sum, the papers in this volume are a tribute to the rich archaeology of the American Southwest, and to the determined and innovative scholars who teased knowledge about the past from the archaeological record. Southwestern archaeology was and continues to be a source of innovation in American anthropology and this stimulation seemingly will continue. We hope our readers will find this book informative and a useful guide to an extensive and worthwhile literature. We hope, too, that the chapters will be useful to others in thinking about their own research, be it in the Southwest, or elsewhere.

2

The Formative Years: Southwest Archaeology, 1890–1910

Don D. Fowler

Putnam, Pepper, and Chaco Canyon

Archaeological ruins were objects of fascination from the time of the U.S. invasion of Mexican territory in 1846. But it was the discovery of the "Cliff Dwellers" in 1875 that stimulated major interest in southwestern archaeology across the United States (Fowler 2000:50–70, 81–84). Public interest was intensified by the discovery of large ruins in the Mesa Verde by the Wetherill brothers in 1888 and the collections they and others made there, as well as in Grand Gulch, in Utah, and in the Tsegi country in northern Arizona in the subsequent decade (Blackburn and Williamson 1997). Richard Wetherill moved to Chaco Canyon, in New Mexico, in 1896. There, supported by funding from wealthy New Yorkers, the Hyde brothers, and officially sponsored by the American Museum of Natural History, he and his brothers dug in Pueblo Bonito and other ruins. The excavations were professionally legitimized by Frederic Ward Putnam, at the time concurrently the director of the Peabody Museum at Harvard University and the Anthropology Department of the American Museum. Putnam sent a young employee, George Pepper, to oversee the excavations. At the instigation of Edgar Lee Hewett (see below) and other prominent New Mexico citizens, the federal government ordered the excavations to cease in 1902.

George Pepper had never been west and had far less archaeological experience than the Wetherill boys. Despite his inexperience, he ultimately made useful contributions to southwestern archaeology and the understanding of the sociocultural complexity represented by Chacoan sites (Pepper 1920; see Reyman 1989; Lekson, this volume). Pepper also seems to have been the first in the Southwest to use datum points and grids to establish three-dimensional provenience of artifacts in his excavations of rooms in Pueblo Bonito (Pepper 1909, 1920:163–177). The collections from the excavations were deposited in the American Museum in New York and were studied by various archaeologists throughout the twentieth century.

Three archaeologists from the Smithsonian Institution were active in the Southwest during the 1890–1910 period, Walter Hough, of the U.S. National Museum, and Jesse Walter Fewkes and Frank Russell, of the Bureau of American Ethnology (BAE). Russell (1868–1903) received a Ph.D. in anthropology from Harvard under Frederic Ward Putnam and was employed by the BAE from 1900 to 1903. In 1900 and 1901 he made extensive archaeological surveys in the Gila–Salt River drainage of southern Arizona. He spent the winter of 1901–1902 studying the Pima, then returned to Washington to write his report. He came back to Arizona in early 1903 seeking to cure his tuberculosis but could not and he died later that year. His study of the Pima (Russell 1908) remains a standard work; therein he first used the Pima term "Hohokam" for the archaeological remains of the northern Sonoran Desert area, a term adopted by southwestern archaeologists in the 1930s (Reid and Whittlesey, this volume).

FEWKES AND HOUGH IN THE SOUTHWEST

Two marks of professionalism in a scholarly discipline are that individuals get paid to do research and that they do so in accordance with a plan, or research design, to answer questions of intellectual interest to adherents of that discipline. In this sense, the first professional archaeologist in the Southwest, as opposed to those paid by various institutions to simply dig in sites for museum specimens (Parezo 1986, 1987; Wade and McChesney 1980, 1981), was Frank Hamilton Cushing in 1886–1889. Cushing initiated a major interdisciplinary program, the Hemenway Southwestern Expedition, funded by philanthropist Mary Hemenway of Boston. But he never brought his program to fruition and he was fired in 1889. The only substantive product at the time was his research plan, published after he was let go (Cushing 1890; see Fowler 1992:52–56). Nonetheless, he had a major influence on those who followed him.[1]

Jesse Walter Fewkes (1850–1930), trained as an ichthyologist, succeeded Cushing as director of the Hemenway Southwestern Expedition (Adams and Zedeño 1999; Hinsley 1983). After a brief attempt at ethnography at Zuni, Fewkes moved to Hopi, primarily First Mesa. There, until 1894, he was closely tutored and assisted by Alexander McGregor Stephen. Stephen, who worked for Thomas Varker Keam (see below), had learned a great deal about the Hopi from his own observations, but even more from a physician, Jeremiah Sullivan, who lived in Sichomovi village on First Mesa from 1881 to 1888 (Hieb and Diggle 2004:412–413). Without Stephen's extensive knowledge of Hopi, Navajo, and the Southwest, Fewkes would have accomplished far less than he did (Fowler 2000:138–139, 164–166; A. Patterson 1994; Stephen 1936). In 1894 both Stephen and Mary Hemenway died. The latter's death effectively terminated the Hemenway Southwestern Expedition and Fewkes's position. Through Smithsonian connections, principally George Brown Goode, Fewkes was hired in 1895 by the BAE on a contract basis to do southwestern archaeology. In 1896 he was given a regular position, which continued until his death in 1930.

MYTHS AND MIGRATIONS

A major premise of the Hemenway Southwestern Expedition, as Cushing (1890) formulated it, was that Pueblo myths and legends about prehispanic migrations have a historical basis. Therefore, one job of the ethnologist was to link places mentioned in the myths and legends to archaeological sites on the ground. This was in accord with Lewis Henry Morgan's (1880, 1881) dictum of working backward from ethnology to archaeology. Victor and Cosmos Mindeleff, who worked for the BAE in the 1880s, followed Cushing's premise in their classic studies of Puebloan architecture and migration legends, guided by the detailed knowledge of Sullivan and Stephen (Mindeleff 1891; Mindeleff 1900).

Fewkes basically took up where the Mindeleffs left off. Just as they had done, he gathered, at first through Alexander Stephen, clan migration legends and stories from First Mesa Hopi elders about places various clans had lived prior to arriving at the Hopi mesas. He planned and conducted archaeological surveys and excavations to validate or verify the migration stories (Fewkes 1900). He also collected as many artifacts as possible for the U.S. National Museum in the process.

Fewkes (1898, 1900) was in the field in the summers of 1895–1897, assisted by Walter Hough. In 1895 he surveyed the Verde Valley, then dug at Sikyatki and Awatovi; in 1896 he dug at Homolovi and Chevelon Pass. In 1897 he dug at Kintiel (which he linked to Zuni), then conducted a reconnaissance into the Upper Gila Valley. Hough thus gained a good idea of the country he would focus on later. In 1898–1900 Fewkes was primarily doing laboratory work and writing. In 1901 he was again in the field working at Isleta del Sur near El Paso, Texas, at Senecú, in south-central New Mexico, and in the vicinity of Paquimé (Casas Grandes) in Chihuahua (Fewkes 1901b:794, 1902). But his attention was soon diverted elsewhere.

The brief Spanish-American War of 1898 had netted the United States Puerto Rico and the Philippines and afforded the Smithsonian new research opportunities in both places. Between April 1902 and June 1905, Fewkes spent many months in Puerto Rico, all across the Caribbean, and in Mexico (Fewkes 1907a, 1907b). With the completion of that work, he returned to the Southwest for excavation and stabilization work. In 1906 the federal Antiquities Act was passed (Thompson 2000a) which provided a legal basis for the Department of the Interior to fund efforts to conserve and protect sites designated as national monuments or contained within national parks. The Interior Department contracted with the Smithsonian to do the work, and Fewkes took up the task, starting with Casa Grande, from 1906 to 1908, then on to Spruce Tree House, Cliff Palace, and other ruins in Mesa Verde National Park.

THE MUSEUM-GATES EXPEDITIONS

Walter Hough (1859–1935) was the quintessential museum curator, fascinated by material culture and what it can be made to tell about human behavior; he never met an artifact he didn't like or ever forgot (Judd 1936). During the 1895 season, Fewkes got Hough started on ethnobotany, an interest he pursued at Hopi and later across the Southwest and into northern Mexico (Hough 1897, 1898, 1906).

In early 1901, Peter Goddard Gates, a wealthy resident of Pasadena, California, approached the U.S. National Museum with an offer to finance an archaeological and ethnographic expedition to the Southwest (Pavesic 1999:140). Gates was a friend of Adam Clark Vroman, owner of a popular Pasadena bookstore. The inimitable Charles Fletcher Lummis, cofounder of the Southwest Museum in Los Angeles, had led Vroman to the Southwest. He was an exceptionally gifted amateur photographer whose southwestern photographs, taken primarily between 1895 and 1904, are classics (Vroman 1961; Webb and Weinstein 1973).

The upshot was the Museum-Gates Expedition jointly funded by Gates and the U.S. National Museum. A second expedition in 1905 included excavations in Tularosa Cave, which yielded "a collection of several thousand artifacts, especially valuable because of its richness in perishable objects" (Hough 1914:1; see Martin et al. 1952). In between, Hough did further surveys in the Mogollon country in 1903, combining those data with his 1901 findings (Hough 1907).

The 1901 expedition included a week spent at Hopi visiting Hano, where Vroman (1961:87–89, 93) made his famous portraits of Nampeyo and her oldest daughter Annie Healing, and watching and photographing dances and people at Shipolovi, Sichimovi, Shungopavi, Mishongnovi, and Oraibi (Vroman 1961:74, 80–85, 90–92, 96–105). Hough's primary concern was to increase the collections of the U.S. National Museum. This is reflected in the last paragraph of his report. Between May 3 and September 23, 1901, he visited 55 ruins and excavated 18 in a region 200 miles north-south and 70 miles east-west. This involved 800 miles of wagon travel. "The work, however, was quite successful, 2,500 specimens having been collected" (Hough 1903:358).[2] Hough's reports were among the first to consider issues of settlement patterns, and his and some of Fewkes's work called attention to the archaeological region later termed "Mogollon" (Reid and Whittlesey, this volume).

FEWKES'S AND HOUGH'S CONTRIBUTIONS

In light of later concerns of southwestern archaeologists, several themes emerge from the work of Fewkes and Hough that remained important throughout the twentieth century. These include the related topics of museum collections, site protection, and looting; the waxing and waning of interest in migrations within the larger context of culture history studies; and the uses of ceramics in archaeological analyses.

By 1901–1902, Smithsonian collectors had been shipping railroad carloads of archaeological and ethnographic objects from the Southwest to Washington, D.C., for two decades. But museum curators and administrators felt that more—and yet more—objects were needed (Parezo 1986, 1987). They believed that "traditional" ethnographic, as well as archaeological, artifacts were fast disappearing. Better they be in *our* museum than someone else's, or be lost to the tourist or casual collector. Curators from newer museums felt they had to compete, to get the "good" collections for their institution before some other museum did. In 1900–1910, George A. Dorsey, for the Field Columbian Museum (founded 1893), and Stewart Culin, for the University of Pennsylvania Museum (founded 1889), acting in concert, were actively and aggressively buying both ethnographic and archaeological collections across the Southwest and elsewhere in North America, as were agents for several European museums (Fowler 2000:228).

Many collections were provided by the Indian trader and cultural broker Thomas Varker Keam (Graves 1998:139–170; Hieb and Diggle 2004:414–420), who had a wide network of Indian and Anglo collectors and looters providing him with archaeological and ethnographic artifacts. He then resold the materials to museum agents, or to the increasing numbers of tourists who found their way to his Keams Canyon, Arizona, trading post. He had actively been supplying Smithsonian collectors since 1879 and others soon thereafter. The best known example is the so-called Keam collection, which Fewkes purchased for $10,000 on behalf of the Hemenway Southwestern Expedition and subsequently deposited in the Harvard Peabody Museum (Wade and McChesney 1980, 1981). Fewkes (1919:220) later reported that Keam assembled and sold many collections, including a "rich collection of pottery" from Sikyatki and Awatovi to the Museum für Volkerkünde in Berlin. In 1901 Walter Hough put the topic of collections, protection, and looting into context:

One of the most depressing features connected with the work in the Pueblo region is the evidence of vandalism and unskilled exploration encountered on almost all of the prehistoric sites. The extent of this devastation can scarcely be realized. No ruin is so obscure or inaccessible that some sheep herder or prospector has not put in some of his tedious hours digging in it. [Early settlers usually just picked up surface artifacts.] Later the various governmental explorations called widespread attention to the ruined pueblos of the Southwest, and soon it was found that relics from these pueblos had commercial value. With this entering wedge, the collecting of "relics" became a business, and men traveled the region for the sole purpose of tearing up the ruins for their private gains. Almost every trader either employed Indians to dig or bought all the specimens that Indians brought in at a nominal price, and many were the men who had "collections" for sale. A few of these individuals, profiting by the scientific methods of governmental and institutional explorations, were careful to catalogue and localize the specimens as far as possible second hand, finding that such data increased the value [Hough 1903:357].

Despite his sense of righteous scientific umbrage, Hough bought a number of such looted collections for the U.S. National Museum, and, indeed, hired some of the diggers for his own excavations.[3]

REJECTING MIGRATION "MYTHS"

In 1917 Clark Wissler (1917a), chair of the Anthropology Department at the American Museum of Natural History, proclaimed a "New Archaeology" concerned with stratigraphy, seriation, and typology, based on the works of Nels Nelson, A. V. Kidder, and their peers (Fowler 2000:275–320; Snead 2001:97–123, this volume). Morgan's (1880, 1881) premise of working from ethnography back to archaeology, which implied unbroken cultural continuity, was rejected. Continuity in culture history was something to be demonstrated case-by-case, not assumed out of hand. Two years earlier, Wissler's colleague at the American Museum, Robert Lowie (1915), had flatly denied that indigenous oral accounts had any historical basis, thus, as Peter Whiteley (2002:406) so cogently puts it, "consigning them to a cognitive dump without explanatory value in relation to the past." The Young Turk New Archaeologists applied a double tar brush to Fewkes, Hough, and a few others, such as Edgar Lee Hewett (see below). The latter's "old fashioned" archaeology paid no attention to stratigraphy and seriation; they took migration myths and legends seriously and tried to use them to understand and interpret archaeological sites. With few exceptions, conjoining traditional indigenous accounts and archaeology was largely anathema in southwestern archaeology for the next six decades.

CERAMIC ANALYSIS

As Barbara Mills (1999a:243) notes, "ceramic ware and type designations have been both bane and blessing to Southwestern archaeologists." Certainly without the "ceramic bacillus," as A. V. Kidder (1957[2]:82, cited by Fowler 2000:285) once called it, southwestern archaeology would be very different. That pottery might be used as some form of cultural-historical marker was evident to John Russell Bartlett (1854) in 1852, who made and illustrated collections of sherds from around Casa Grande, in Arizona, and Paquimé, in Chihuahua. Adolph

Bandelier seems to have been the first to recognize that ceramics might serve both as cultural markers and relative time indicators (Fowler and Wilcox 1999:214; Wilcox and Fowler 2002:155–158).

Fewkes and Hough were keenly aware of the importance of pottery for archaeological analysis. "No remains of human art and industries are more important to the student of ethnology than pottery, since upon such remains (which invariably bear the impress of tribal individuality and environment) the origins, range, and state of culture of groups of men are indicated" (Hough 1907:25). They presented distributional and comparative data on wares, forms, and designs, thinking that all three data sets might serve as cultural or ethnic markers. For example, Fewkes (1904:Plate LXX) published a map showing percentage distributions of major pottery wares across the headwaters of the Gila and Little Colorado rivers and northward to the Hopi mesas. Hough (1903:288) defined subregions of the same territory in terms of predominance of certain pottery wares: 1) White Mountains, south of the Little Colorado and Puerco rivers: red and gray wares; 2) the Little Colorado River valley: gray wares; 3) Hopi Buttes, B Biddahoochee, and Jettyto [sic]: yellow wares. Although based on far more sophisticated analyses, and drawing on a century of additional work, the subregions proposed by Mills (1999a; Mills and Herr 1999) look similar to Hough's.

Fewkes took ceramic analysis to a new level with his studies of the "paleography of the pottery" as he called it. He recognized the importance of designs as expressions of myths, legends, and more general religious ideology, especially at Hopi where he drew on his own ethnographic work and what he had learned from Alexander Stephen (A. Patterson 1994). His classic studies of Sikyatki (Fewkes 1901a:631–728, 1919, 1973) and Mimbres pottery designs (Fewkes 1914, 1923, 1924) were baseline documents for the century of technical design analysis of Puebloan and Ancestral Puebloan pottery that was to follow. Some few of the many major examples include Brody (1977), Brody et al. (1983), Bunzel (1929), Chapman (1933–1936, 1936, 1970), Crown (1994), Mills and Crown (1995), Peckham (1990), and Washburn (1977).[4]

Both Fewkes and Hough had a general sense that some pottery wares and/or design styles were relatively older than others. But it was A. V. Kidder's (1915) study of Pajarito Plateau pottery and his demonstration that potsherds could be effectively used both as cultural and relative time markers that made possible the seriation studies and space-time constructs of the New Archaeology after 1914–1915 (Snead

2001:97–123, this volume). Ceramic analyses, and interpretations thereof in ways not envisioned by Fewkes or Hough, became of central concern in southwestern archaeology. Pots and potsherds, subjected to increasingly fine-grained seriational, stylistic, and chemical analyses, were grouped into ever more narrowly defined "types." Pottery types often then came to be reified as the basic, objective hard data of southwestern archaeology (Colton 1953). That, however, is another story (Fowler 2000:275–319; Snead 2001:97–123, this volume).

The full intellectual history of how ceramics analyses, and the data generated therefrom, have been used in support (or refutation) of numerous and varied social, cultural, and demographic processes in the Southwest remains to be written. Excellent recent contributions to such a history include Patricia Crown's (1994) analysis of how Salado polychrome has been used to tell stories about sociopolitical systems, economic alliances, migration, religious ideologies, or ethnicity, or all of the above, and the papers in Mills and Crown (1995) on ceramic production analyses and the kinds of stories that may be derived from them.

DEFINING "ETHNIC DISTRICTS"

As noted above, the federal order of 1902 that forced the Wetherills to cease excavations in Chaco Canyon was issued at the instigation of Edgar Lee Hewett, who was just making his move onto the archaeological scene in the Southwest (Fowler 2003; Snead, this volume). Seeking legitimacy within the new professionalism in American archaeology, Hewett (1908d) acquired a doctorate from the University of Geneva. In his dissertation, using materials from earlier government reports he had written, Hewett described the "Pueblo Region" as a distinctive "culture area" in the Southwest. The region contains portions of four river basins, the Rio Grande, San Juan, Little Colorado, and Gila, as well as the internally draining Chihuahua Basin. Each basin "represents a sub-area of culture and each has its own individuality." Each sub-area has "numerous districts...in which common cultural peculiarities are to be found, while special differences in construction, decoration, industrial techniques, mortuary customs, etc. display *ethnic variations. These sub-areas are called ethnic districts*" (Hewett 1993:10–11, emphasis added). Examples are Chaco Canyon and Mesa Verde in the San Juan Basin and Pajarito and Pecos in the Rio Grande. Hewett (1993:29) noted, however, that his scheme referred only to cultural items, "for there is no analogy whatever between cultural and linguistic areas."

The point here is that Hewett was seemingly the first to use the concept of ethnicity in the Southwest. Preucel (this volume) explores how ethnicity has been used in southwestern archaeology from Hewett's day to the present.

SUMMARY

As a long-time student of intellectual history, especially that of southwestern anthropology, it is apparent to me that many ideas, like clothing fashions, come, go, and return (Fowler 1992, 2000; Fowler and Wilcox 1999; Wilcox and Fowler 2002). The Young Turk New Archaeologists of 1917 derided Fewkes, Hough, and Hewett for their old-fashioned, "romantic" ideas. The Young Turk New Archaeologists of 1961 derided the by then aged (or deceased) Turks of 1917, and their successors, for the same reason. But by 1997, Fewkes, at least, was receiving some kudos for his archaeology and ethnography (Adams and Zedeño 1999). By 2001 prehispanic migrations in the Southwest were once again being discussed in polite company—for example, the Mogollon-Zuni Conference at the Museum of Northern Arizona (Gregory and Wilcox 2006). Such discussions require, if not acceptance, at least a reevaluation and rehearing of approaches to culture history taken by Frank Hamilton Cushing (1890) and Adolph Bandelier (1890–1892) and carried forward by Fewkes, Hough, and Hewett (Whiteley 2002). In between, throughout the twentieth century, there was an enormous amount of archaeological research and the accumulation of millions of specimens. While some ideas waxed, waned, and waxed again, others were advanced, tested, and rejected. The results of this ongoing effort are discussed and analyzed in the papers in the present volume.

NOTES

1. Only since the 1990s, as Curtis Hinsley and David Wilcox have resurrected and begun publishing materials on Cushing and the Hemenway Southwestern Expedition, has it become clear just how prescient Cushing was in his thinking about archaeological methods and problems (Hinsley and Wilcox 1995, 1996, 2002).

2. One of Hough's finds, and his interpretation thereof, resonate a century later with concerns relating to purported Ancestral Pueblo violence. In the cemetery of Ruin 2 of the Canyon Butte ruins,

> the workmen came upon a mass of broken human bones, which proved to be the remains of three individuals. Some of the bones bore traces of fire, and there was no evidence that with them had been interred any organic material; moreover, marks of the implement with which the bones had been fractured

were discernible. Undoubtedly here was evidence of cannibalism, but as the
find is unique so far in this region it probably only indicates anthropophagy
from necessity. Ceremonial cannibalism among the North American Indians
was not unknown, however, as references in the early writers bear witness
[Hough 1903:313].

A century later, Hough's "undoubtedly" would likely be greeted with the same
acceptance or rejection that end of the twentieth century "undoubtedlys" regarding the existence of Ancestral Puebloan anthropophagy have been (Bullock 1998;
Darling 1999; Haas and Creamer 1993; LeBlanc 1999; Turner and Turner 1999).

3. By 1902 joint American Association for the Advancement of Science
(AAAS) and American Anthropological Association committees on archaeological
protection legislation were in place and a campaign had begun that resulted in
passage of the 1906 Antiquities Act (Thompson 2000a). But the act did not stop
the looting, as Neil Judd (1924) complained in the 1920s; nor did additional
legislation (and all that came with it) in 1979 and thereafter (Hutt et al. 1992).

4. Although Fewkes's role in stimulating the work of the Hopi-Tewa potter
Nampeyo was overstated by the authors of one of his obituaries (Swanton and
Roberts 1931), thus becoming part of southwestern folklore for decades, certainly
he did note the fine quality of her work. The elegant ceramics of Nampeyo and
her descendants have, of course, been celebrated by many others throughout the
twentieth century, most recently by Blair and Blair (1999), Kramer (1996), and
Streuver (2001).

3

Paradigms, Professionals, and the Making of Southwest Archaeology, 1910–1920

James E. Snead

A contemporary perspective on the early history of Southwest archaeology comes down to us from 1917, delivered on the occasion of the opening of a new building intended to house the art collection of the Museum of New Mexico in Santa Fe.[1] The public festivities included a "congress of science, art, and education" to which notables from the state and from around the nation had been invited. The dedication itself was delivered by Frank Springer, a prominent New Mexican who was a patron of Southwest archaeology as well as a paleontologist in his own right (Schuchert 1928). Springer had supplied the funds for the new museum and took the opportunity of the dedicatory speech to reflect. "[I]t will be profitable," he noted,

> to take a brief retrospect of the activities in southwestern Archaeology leading up to the state of public interest which makes an event like this possible. These will fall readily into three epochs, almost comparable to the great periods of general intellectual history: First, Pioneer scientific investigation; Second, Vandalism, marked by indifference, neglect, and destruction; Third, the Renaissance—the rise of systematic research [Springer 1917:3].

In Springer's eyes the previous decade had been one of considerable achievement in Southwest archaeology. Surveys had been initiated, excavations conducted, and discoveries made. Of equal importance were the new museums and research institutions, which provided bases for scholarship and exhibits for the education of the populace. Although

Springer paid tribute to three men to whom the foundations of this renaissance could be attributed—Adolph Bandelier, W. H. Holmes, and Jesse Fewkes—his praise was directed specifically at Edgar Lee Hewett, the director of the Museum of New Mexico, whose name appeared in capital letters in the published text of Springer's speech.

Among the scholars and dignitaries attending Springer's speech was one who saw the advance of Southwest archaeology in considerably different terms. Clark Wissler, curator of anthropology at the American Museum of Natural History in New York, had spent the previous decade developing and overseeing his own program of Southwest research. In the process a series of new methods had been developed and applied to historical, anthropological problems in the region, an approach that Wissler was soon to call the "New Archaeology" (1917a). From Wissler's perspective, there were very few similarities between the program in which his institution was engaged and Hewett's enterprises.

In general, historians of anthropology have shared Wissler's views, and have seen developments in the Southwest during the 1910s as laying the foundations for the chronologically based archaeology that dominated the discipline for a generation, perhaps a "paradigm" in the Kuhnian sense (Kuhn 1962; e.g., Willey and Sabloff 1980:84). In the context of Southwest archaeology itself, however, the emergence of a common research tradition that occurred in the second decade of the twentieth century was a more intriguing process than the straightforward emergence of an intellectual perspective prefiguring modern agendas (cf. Lyman et al. 1997). In fact, the conceptual terrain of Southwest archaeology in the pre–World War I period was complex. The basic rationale for archaeological research differed from camp to camp: distinct and competitive rationales shaped scholarly interaction, the exchange of ideas, and the pursuit of patronage. As important as the various intellectual justifications for southwestern scholarship were the different practices adopted by the researchers themselves, within distinct institutional contexts (cf. Snead 2001).

The competitive conditions of Southwest archaeology in this critical period did indeed shape practices and ideas that underlie much of Southwest archaeology as it exists today. Among these, I will focus on three areas of concern: the coalescence of intellectual themes, which I call "a common goal"; the appearance of the first identifiable cadre of Southwest archaeologists, or "a community of inquiry"; and possibly the most critical element but also the most frequently overlooked, "the creation of an audience" for Southwest research.

A COMMON GOAL

The earliest periods of Southwest archaeology were characterized by diverse and eclectic ideas, both on the nature of southwestern antiquity and on its potential value for scholarship (cf. Fowler 1992, 2000, this volume). By the beginning of the twentieth century, however, increasing quantities of data and the formalization of anthropology as a professional discipline allowed for the emergence of a few shared ideas, central to which was that the close linkage between precolumbian and historic peoples in the Southwest meant that ethnography and archaeology provided complementary information on the ancient past. "The ruins of the prehistoric settlements abound in relics of the ancient tribesmen," wrote J. W. Powell, "and the relics are largely interpretable through researches in the modern pueblos" (1895–1896:lxxxii). Such sentiments motivated many of the first generation of anthropologists working in the Southwest, such as Frank Hamilton Cushing (cf. Hinsley 1983; Hinsley and Wilcox 1996, 2002). And yet even in 1910 such assumptions prompted considerably different responses from the scholarly community.

One of the new anthropological approaches to the ancient Southwest was that of Edgar Lee Hewett (Figure 3.1). An educator by training, Hewett conducted archaeological excursions in New Mexico beginning in the mid-1890s, and when appointed as president of the state normal school in Las Vegas in 1898 quickly established a support structure for a research program (for example, Bloom 1939; Chauvenet 1983; Fowler 1999, 2000; Snead 2001; Thomas 1999; Thompson 2000b). Working at first through the Santa Fe Archaeological Society and then the various southwestern branches of the Archaeological Institute of America, Hewett developed a network of patronage that provided sufficient funding for fieldwork (Snead 2002a). The leverage provided by such

Figure 3.1. Edgar Lee Hewett, 1909. Courtesy, Photo Archives, Fray Angélico Chávez Library Palace of the Governors. Neg. no. 7331.

a grassroots campaign contributed to an increasing national profile, culminating in the establishment of the School of American Archaeology in Santa Fe in 1908 under his direction (Hinsley 1986). By 1910 Hewett's standing was such that he was rumored to be seeking the presidency of the American Anthropological Association (P. E. Goddard to A. M. Tozzer, letter, 22 December 1910, AMT).

Hewett couched himself as the inheritor of the mantle of Adolph Bandelier (cf. Hewett 1908a; Lange and Riley 1996), and his fieldwork centered upon the ruins of the Pajarito Plateau that Bandelier had first described. From the beginning, Hewett was committed to an integrative approach to the study of the past, incorporating archaeology, ethnography, linguistics, and geography (1908b). This approach anticipated the multidisciplinary archaeological strategies of subsequent generations, and on the surface resembled the anthropological programs promoted by Franz Boas and his students. Hewett's excavations at the Rito de los Frijoles in 1910, for instance, were augmented by linguistic research conducted by John P. Harrington and Barbara Freire-Marreco (see Warrior 2003), while plant data were collected by the botanist Wilfred Robbins, and Junius Henderson studied the local geology. Frank Springer, who funded much of the Pajarito research, argued that the "ultimate aim of these correlated investigations [was] to find out how the mind of man has been influenced by his environment; how his beliefs and life have been created, modified, continued, or destroyed by his physical surroundings" (Springer 1910a:624). The new chief of the Bureau of American Ethnology, Frederick Webb Hodge, participated in the project and wrote that it would be "far-reaching in effect" (F. Hodge to W. Kelsey, letter, 15 October 1910, File 17.25, AIA).

Despite its holistic character, however, Hewett's "anthropology" differed considerably from that of the eastern institutions. His education in teacher's colleges and then at the University of Geneva had occurred entirely outside the intellectual environment of American anthropology then developing, and he was seen as a rogue element by some of the major figures of the movement, particularly Boas (cf. Fowler 1999:179). Among the characteristics of this approach was assigning priority to historical, rather than ethnographic, questions. From Hewett's perspective, archaeology was augmented by ethnology, not vice versa, and the word "anthropology" does not appear in his major programmatic statement (Hewett 1908b).

Hewett's base of operations within the Southwest itself, and his reliance on local sources of funding, also conditioned his approach. Local

Euro-American attitudes toward Native Americans were ambiguous at the turn of the twentieth century, shaped by economic concerns, Progressive-era morality, and identity politics. Study of the southwestern past could not be divorced from perceptions of the southwestern present. "The age of the Pueblo is buried deep in the dead past of this commonwealth," pronounced one editorial. "Efforts to revive it will meet with ridicule" (*Santa Fe New Mexican* [SFNM], 5 July 1910). Such attitudes were common in spite of the considerable public interest in archaeology, an incongruity made possible by decoupling the "history" represented by the ruins being excavated from the living Native American population. The vogue for "Cliff Dwellers," a mysterious ancient race who had vanished from the earth, reflected this process in a way analogous to popular ideas about "Mound Builders" in the Mississippi and Ohio valleys that had flourished generations earlier (Trigger 1989:105).

Hewett thus walked a fine line between those who saw his work as a scientific endeavor and those for whom archaeology was a source of regional pride and identity. On the one hand, he had close personal relationships with Pueblo people and repeatedly interceded on their behalf in the face of bureaucratic incursions (for example, S. Naranjo to E. L. Hewett, letter, 28 March 1916, ELH).[2] Excavations at sites such as Puyé and Tyuonyi were largely conducted by workers from the Pueblo of San Ildefonso. However, he approached the question of the relationship between Pueblo peoples and archaeological sites with a studied ambiguity. Despite considerable evidence to the contrary, for instance, he argued that there had been no connection between the ancient peoples of the Pajarito Plateau and the modern Tewa of nearby villages, instead using the term "Pajaritan culture" to describe the original inhabitants of the area (Hewett 1909). Such terminology, which appeared in the popular press as well as scholarly articles (cf. SFNM, 22 June 1910), did not explicitly deny the linkage between the ancient and modern, but nonetheless generated distance between the two and opened sufficient interpretive "space" for Hewett to pursue research without contravening the expectations of his local audience (see Snead 2002b).

In many ways Hewett's successful negotiation of the sociopolitics of Southwest archaeology was a result of his focus on the process, rather than results. His educational background led him to emphasize the value of experiential learning, an idea rooted in late nineteenth-century efforts to reform science education (see Benson 1988). Even Hewett's early work, such as an expedition to Chaco Canyon in 1902 (Snead 2001:56), emphasized student participation, and over subsequent years the training of archaeologists became a fundamental part of his program. Such an educational approach was central to his alliance with the Archaeological Institute of America, which turned to Hewett to establish the School for American Archaeology as a counterpart to the American Schools in Rome and Athens (Hinsley 1986; Snead 2002a).

Hewett thus constructed a Southwest archaeology that brought research and education together in a matrix controlled at the local level. The fact that this approach also furthered his own aims for power within American anthropology should not discount the fact that it represented a real model for how the discipline could be constructed. The opposition to Hewett expressed by Boas and others was not only rooted in personal dislike, but in their realization that his vision of the way things ought to be done was viable and in direct competition with their own.

* * *

If sociopolitical considerations and educational agendas shaped Hewett's approach to Southwest research, the southwestern ambitions of the museums and universities of the Midwest and eastern seaboard were heavily influenced by professional and institutional competition. In the case of the American Museum of Natural History, this process had begun the early 1890s, when Frederic Ward Putnam had been brought in to establish a new program to capitalize on the scholarly and public reputation of anthropology in the wake of the World's Columbian Exhibition. Putnam's need for high quality collections to exhibit and his cultivation of New York patron Talbot Hyde had led to a southwestern expedition in 1896.[3] Four years of excavation at Chaco Canyon established the American Museum in the field. Political entanglements on the ground in New Mexico and in New York, together with Putnam's 1903 resignation, sidelined the effort, circumstances that did not improve during the short, stormy tenure of Franz Boas as his replacement (Snead 1999). Thus during the period when Hewett was developing his Southwest research program, the American Museum was largely inactive in the region.

Clark Wissler was appointed to succeed Boas in 1906 (Figure 3.2). Despite a lack of seniority that was expected to be disadvantageous, he proved to be adept at museum politics and held the position for nearly 40 years. Resembling Hewett in his Midwestern roots and pedagogical training, Wissler had gone to Columbia University to pursue a graduate education and thus joined the growing anthropological circle surrounding Boas (Freed and Freed 1983, 1992; Reed 1980). The two men do not appear to have been particularly close, and it was only after the withdrawal of a more favored student that Wissler was put on the American Museum's payroll (F. Boas to H. C. Bumpus, letter, 16 May 1902, AMNH). Nonetheless his experience with Boas and position in the associated network of anthropologists left him well positioned to establish programs of fieldwork in light of evolving professional agendas.

Figure 3.2. Clark Wissler, 1918. Courtesy of Special Collections, American Museum of Natural History Library. Neg. no 36896.

In 1909 Wissler revived the Southwest program of the American Museum as an integrated anthropological research effort. One of his models was the Jesup North Pacific Expedition, launched a decade earlier and designed to reestablish the museum as a leader in the field (Cole and Long 1999). Funding was obtained from philanthropist Archer Huntington; Pliny Earle Goddard and Herbert J. Spinden were quickly dispatched to New Mexico to collect ethnographic and linguistic data as well as to obtain artifacts from Puebloan and Athapaskan communities. Archaeological research was intended to add a historical dimension to the emerging ethnological profile. "How can we study cultures," Wissler wrote one colleague, "without being able to trace one for an appreciable span?" (C. Wissler to H. C. Bumpus, letter, 24 December 1909, AMNH). From his perspective, new methods emphasizing chronology provided the means for archaeology to remain relevant in the culture-focused anthropology of the 1910s, and the Southwest was the appropriate place to develop such a strategy.

The complex, empirical archaeological research mandated by this program required a competent fieldworker, and when the opportunity came up Wissler hired University of California student Nels Nelson,

Figure 3.3. Nels C. Nelson, 1925. Courtesy of Special Collections, American Museum of Natural History Library. Neg. no. 36888.

whose study of shell mounds around San Francisco Bay was considered to have prepared him to develop new chronological methods (Figure 3.3) (Snead 2001:106; see also Browman 2002b; Browman and Givens 1996).[4] Over the subsequent six years Nelson excavated hundreds of rooms in archaeological sites across the northern Southwest. His use of arbitrary units in stratigraphic excavations at Pueblo San Cristobal in the Galisteo Basin in November 1914 provided the sought-after chronological breakthrough, and was rapidly publicized (Nelson 1916). Wissler informed the project's patron that the work had provided "a very definite chapter in the history of the Southwest" (C. Wissler to A. Huntington, letter, 28 January 1915, File 23, AMNH). He also moved swiftly to capitalize on the prestige conferred by Nelson's innovations (contra Browman and Givens 1996: 85), and the museum launched new projects at Chaco Canyon, Aztec Ruin, and at Zuni.

Most of this work took on a distinctly chronological character. Nelson's own efforts were soon eclipsed by the contribution of others, such as Alfred Kroeber, who was conducting a kinship study at Zuni in 1915 under the auspices of the American Museum. Kroeber spent his off-hours visiting local archaeological sites and almost casually developed a strategy of frequency seriation using surface distributions of potsherds (Fowler 2000:288; Kroeber 1916).[5] Wissler also began a correspondence with A. E. Douglass at the University of Arizona that was to lead to dendrochronological dating (Nash 1999). Within a 10-month period, the American Museum's chronological paradigm had become influential throughout the Southwest.

The success of the Wissler program, however, came at the expense of his original intentions for the Huntington Survey, which had promised an integrated anthropology of the American Southwest. Neither Goddard nor Spinden completed their work, and while some of the other research was published (Kroeber 1917), a brief discussion in

Wissler's *The American Indian* (1917b) was the only attempt to coordinate ethnography and archaeology in the Huntington Survey. Instead, Wissler diverted resources into archaeology, in part because of the promise of the chronological work but also because of the leverage it provided against the program's competitors, both within anthropology and within his own institution. Museum politics were increasingly hostile to Wissler's regime, conditions under which more spectacular "discoveries" with direct public appeal were required to stave off funding cuts. Excavations at Aztec Ruin, which began in 1916, generated headlines and maintained the American Museum's high profile but ironically made little contribution to the chronological program. Thus while the New Archaeology represented the first viable research paradigm in Southwest archaeology, the American Museum's ability to contribute to it faded fairly rapidly. Nelson himself was dismayed by the direction the program had taken, and found himself unable to follow up on his earlier efforts. A few years later he wrote a colleague that, "on inquiring casually whether our Southwest Survey had 'fizzled out', I was told 'No, it had been brought to a successful conclusion.'" (N. Nelson to A. Kidder, letter, 19 April 1921, NCN.).

* * *

The archaeological initatives of Edgar Lee Hewett and Clark Wissler shared, at the outset, broad anthropological goals and integrative approaches to the study of the southwestern past. As they evolved, however, these programs took markedly different directions. The failure to place the chronological findings of the Huntington Survey within a broader cultural context meant that its impact was greatest on archaeologists alone, and had little influence on other aspects of American anthropology.

It is ironic, given Hewett's archaeological bias, that his work had only a limited impact on archaeology itself. The publication of ethnographic reports based on the Rito de los Frijoles fieldwork (Harrington 1916; Robbins et al. 1914) was not followed by an archaeological report of equal weight. Instead, Hewett launched himself into a number of programmatic diversions that promoted his School of American Archaeology as a national center for research and education but were bereft of any meaningful scholarly production. These included fieldwork at Quirigua in Guatemala and the Panama-Pacific Exposition in San Diego. With the program in part beholden for its success to the southwestern public, it was in any event unlikely that a substantive contribution to an understanding of the precolumbian past could be made by Hewett's team.

By 1917 it was thus the chronological approach developed by Wissler, Nelson, and Kroeber that had seized the attention of archaeologists working in the Southwest. An interest in ethnography continued; A. V. Kidder, whose work at Pecos was to become the most influential research program of his generation, recruited Elsie Clews Parsons for a related ethnographic study. Parsons's efforts at Jemez Pueblo (1925), however, were largely parallel to, rather than integrated with, the Pecos excavations, and Kidder's 1924 summary of Southwest archaeology devotes far more attention to issues of chronology and the distribution of "traits" than it does to "cultural" aspects of the Puebloan past.[6]

This divergence of interests worked both ways. Wissler had been successful in developing a widely applicable theoretical perspective, but not in using it to build stronger connections between archaeology and the rest of anthropology. As chronological research grew in popularity, it became increasingly less relevant to ethnographers interested in kinship, linguistics, and social organization. The "New Archaeology," as Wissler had proudly named it, was just that: by 1917 a common goal existed for most archaeologists working in the Southwest, but in most cases it was anthropology in name only.

A COMMUNITY OF INQUIRY

Southwest archaeology at the turn of the century had been the domain of a remarkably small group of people. The slow pace of professionalization within American anthropology meant that the number of students was small and spread thinly across the country. Archaeological interest among residents of the Southwest was eclectic and typically secondary to other pursuits. And yet one of the most striking features of the subject by 1917 was the emergence of a cadre of archaeologists who worked closely together and who perceived the ancient Southwest and its peoples in similar ways. The development of this group, an example of what the historian of science Thomas Haskell calls a "community of inquiry" (1977:19), marked a critical stage in the history of Southwest archaeology, one that defined the maturity of the pursuit.

The cadre of Southwest archaeologists that emerged in the 1910s shared a number of characteristics that distinguished them from their mentors, who had universally entered archaeology from other careers and with eclectic educational preparation. Frederic Ward Putnam, who had overseen the American Museum's excavations at Pueblo Bonito in the 1890s, was trained in the natural sciences and had not visited the Southwest until he was in his late fifties (see, most recently, Browman 2002a; Hinsley 1999; Snead 2001). Jesse Fewkes was younger but came from an identical background, while W. H. Holmes had been an artist with the United States Geological Survey of the Territories when he first entered the region in 1872 (Fernlund 2000; Goetzmann 1966). Neither Hewett nor Byron Cummings, who developed archaeology programs first at the University of Utah and subsequently at the University of Arizona, obtained advanced degrees until relatively late stages in their careers. The first student in an American doctoral program to come to the Southwest to gain archaeological field experience was probably John Reed Swanton, who participated in the Bonito excavations in 1898 but was sufficiently discouraged by the episode to shift his interests to ethnology (MS 4651, NAA). It was not until the famous 1907 field school, in which Harvard undergraduates A. V. Kidder, Sylvanus Morley, and John Gould Fletcher worked with Hewett in Colorado and New Mexico (cf. Givens 1992), that the developing professional programs in eastern universities became integrated with Southwest research. These links were fragile, however, in large part due to the growing antipathy between Hewett and the anthropological establishment (Fowler 1999).

Perhaps more important than university backgrounds was shared field experience. In the course of their early Southwest work Kidder and Morley were joined by native southwesterners who had learned their archaeology "on the ground." These included Earl Morris, Jesse Nusbaum, and Neil Judd, all of whom were raised in the region. Judd was a nephew of Byron Cummings and worked both for his uncle and Hewett while still of high school age, while Morris's father was a Farmington-based relic hunter prior to his murder in 1904 (Lister and Lister 1968:10). Nels Nelson found this group more congenial than his colleagues in New York, perhaps because of his own unorthodox background as a Danish immigrant raised in the Upper Midwest.[7] Receiving less historical attention was Leslie Spier. A precocious high school student who had worked on the chronology of the Trenton Gravels of New Jersey for Wissler, Spier came west as a member of the American Museum's team. Much of his later career was spent in ethnology, however, obscuring important contributions to the chronological work.

In the five years between 1912 and 1917 this younger generation of archaeologists worked closely with each other. Ultimately all were employed by eastern or national institutions, insuring that Southwest archaeology became central within the discipline. Some intellectual ties were maintained to ethnologists, such as Wissler, Kroeber, and later Elsie Clews Parsons. In essence, however, this was a cadre of archaeologists, forged in the field and focused on tangible issues associated with empirical data.

As with all emerging cadres, the first wave of "new" archaeologists saw themselves very much in opposition to the established order. Jesse Fewkes, of the Bureau of American Ethnology, was in particular singled out for criticism (Fowler 1992:30). "In entire accord with your general attitude towards the Southwest archaeological problems and their solutions," Nelson wrote Kroeber in 1915. "All the younger men are of the same turn of mind I am sure. But meanwhile Dr. Fewkes and the like will continue to run around skimming the cream of the specimens" (N. C. Nelson to A. L. Kroeber, letter, 2 September 1915, ALK). The feeling, apparently, was mutual. "It seems Fewkes is considerably disturbed over the breaking up of his nearly completed archaeological work for the Southwest," a colleague wrote Nelson. "If we could have kept out Fewkes would have had it settled in a little while" (P. L. Goddard to N. C. Nelson, letter, 8 December 1916, File 404, AMNH). Nelson's response was direct: "The time is very near at hand when we shall be in position either to verify or disprove the opinions of all the traditionalists.... As a scientist he [Fewkes] has no right to expect his conclusions to stand without modification" (N. C. Nelson to P. L. Goddard, letter, 17 December 1916, File 404, AMNH).

Opposition to Fewkes, and also to Hewett, was based on their domination of large areas of the Southwest and on their resistance to research focused on chronology (cf. Schwartz 1981:262). Fieldwork in much of northeastern Arizona was sufficiently under the control of the Bureau of American Ethnology so that little outside scholarship was possible there, much to the dismay of the younger generation. The Galisteo Basin technically fell within Hewett's sphere of influence, and Nelson was careful both to obtain permission for his work there and to adopt a low profile (N. Nelson field journal, 17 July 1912, NCN). In Kidder's case, his longstanding relationship with Hewett was an asset in negotiations over the Pecos project (Givens 1992:42), as was his relationship with the Kelly family who owned the site (see Kelly 1972). This modest rapprochement between Hewett and the eastern institutions, however, was ruptured in 1916, when he attempted to launch new research at Chaco Canyon in the face of competing claims (Fowler 1999; Snead 2001:119). A period of competition between institutions and individuals ensued, concluding only when Neil Judd outmaneuvered all competitors and began work at Pueblo Bonito on behalf of the Bureau of American Ethnology and the National Geographic Society in 1921. Hewett, who understood the workings of alliances better than most of his associates, focused his efforts on his own network, built largely from students who had attended his field schools in the years after 1910. His dominant personality, however, meant that the archaeologists who remained with him had little independence, either physical or intellectual. It was not until the Chaco Canyon field schools of the late 1920s (cf. Fowler 2003:316), a time when large numbers of students and Hewett's gradual relaxation of authority allowed the conditions to change, that a cadre based in *southwestern* institutions emerged.

The solidarity among the chronological archaeologists was tangible, as was their commitment to the evolving intellectual program. Nelson's initial Galisteo Basin research had been conducted largely in isolation, but in later years he spent much of his time traveling the back roads of the Southwest, visiting the different projects of the Huntington Survey. Although decision-making authority rested with Wissler, these journeys allowed the archaeologists to compare notes and discuss strategy. Regular correspondence was also an important factor in developing shared frames of reference. "I think we should get the thing down to common terms & your method, it seems to me, is the better one," Kidder wrote Nelson in 1916 (A. V. Kidder to N. C. Nelson, letter, 19 August 1916, NCN). Some rivalry was also expressed; Spier and Morris chafed under Nelson's cautious empiricism, and Morley privately criticized his use of arbitrary stratigraphy (S. G. Morley to C. Wissler, letter, 19 September 1921, File 709, AMNH). This occasional tension did not, however, obscure the enthusiasm which the various fieldworkers brought to their work. "Feast your eyes on the accompanying chart," Spier wrote Wissler, "and then know that I can duplicate it with forty more sites from the Ojo Caliente region, or with others from any part of the valley. Here's history in curves for you" (L. Spier to C. Wissler, letter, 27 September 1916, File 145A, AMNH; Spier 1917).

For all their prominence, however, the cadre of chronological archaeologists remained fragile. None of them were based in a university, and thus few younger students were recruited. Kroeber, who worked closely with Spier in 1916 and described him as "enthusiastic, aggressive, tense, and ready to gnash his teeth" (A. L. Kroeber to C. Wissler, letter, 29 July 1916, File 145A, AMNH) played no direct role in fieldwork thereafter. This vulnerability was displayed when the funding for the Huntington Survey finally ran out: Earl Morris spent several years thereafter conducting archaeological pack trips for cotton broker Charles Bernheimer (Lister and Lister 1968:107), activity that fit more closely the patron/scholar relationships of the 1890s than the new intellectual agenda. Ironically, it was the emergence of a second southwestern cadre at the end of the 1920s, students based in the region but who took to heart the chronological innovations of their predecessors (cf. Nash 1999:70), which solidified the gains of their elders.

AN AUDIENCE

The making of Southwest archaeology was as much the creation of a constituency as it was establishing a new area of scientific interest. In the words of Hewett partisan Charles Lummis, what was required was "not so much more students, nor more scientific societies run by Latin professores nor even more devoted souls toiling and starving to investigate—but an audience" (quoted in Fiske and Lummis 1975:71). Funding, as well as the acknowledgment of authority that is essential to professionalism, relied on the recognition by the American public that an activity had value. Prior to the turn of the century a number of developments, including the display of southwestern antiquities at the World's Columbian Exposition and the resultant "Cliff Dweller" vogue, laid the groundwork for popular interest in the region (cf. Nash and Feinman 2003). It was not until the 1910s, however, that the relationship between Southwest archaeology and the public was fully institutionalized, providing the critical framework within which the emergent "community of inquiry" could pursue its common goals.

Support for Southwest archaeology during the 1910s was divided between museums, educational institutions, governmental agencies, and scholarly societies. For most of these organizations, funding was precarious. With the exception of the Bureau of American Ethnology, most of these endeavors relied on the interests of patrons and closely reflected their particular ambitions. Archer Huntington's steady but hands-off support made the long-range research of the American Museum possible, while the excavations conducted by Frederick W. Hodge at Hawikuh under the auspices of the Museum of the American Indian reflected the competitive instincts and thirst for collections of his patron George Heye (cf. Kidwell 1999; Snead 2001:158). The archaeological interests of local institutions and societies, such as the Museum of New Mexico and the Southwest Museum, were closely aligned with matters of identity and cultural nationalism, thus hinging on the construction of museums and educational outreach. Under these conditions it was difficult to sustain research initiatives, since interest waned rapidly once the galleries had opened. At times during the 1910s the activities of these different groups came into alignment, to impressive effect; excavations conducted in the summer of 1916, for instance, included Morris at Aztec, Lucy Wilson at the Pajarito Plateau site of Otowi, Kidder at Pecos, Spier at Zuni, and Nelson at Pueblo Bonito, while Jesse Fewkes worked at Mummy Lake and Far View House at Mesa Verde.

Despite continued instability in funding, sustained interest in Southwest archaeology during the 1910s was increasingly encoded into public policy. The initial wave of antiquities legislation, culminating in the Lacey Act of 1906 and the establishment of Mesa Verde National Park in the same year, was succeeded by initiatives to establish other parks and reserves (Lee 1970; Rothman 1989; Runte 1987; Thompson 2000a). National monument status sanctioned local aspirations, and was also expected to delimit authority over resources, archaeological and otherwise (Rothman 1992:11). The movement was thus characterized by alliances between scholars and boosters as well as by internecine struggles within the archaeological community, with eyes on future control of the archaeology. The creation of Navajo National Monument, for instance, was accompanied by considerable strife between federal and local interests (Jett 1992; Rothman 1989), while the establishment of Bandelier National Monument was delayed for years by conflict over such seemingly trivial matters as what the park was to be called (Rothman 1988). Similar issues of ownership and control were associated with the work at Aztec Ruin, with the American Museum first obtaining excavation rights, then purchasing the site, then arranging for it to become a national monument (cf. Lister and Lister 1990). The intensity of these debates reflected the perception that the stakes were high, and that southwestern antiquity represented a valuable resource to a variety of interests. Despite the vitriol, by the end of the decade several new national monuments had been inaugurated in the Southwest, further solidifying the place of archaeology in the public mind.

The creation of an audience for Southwest archaeology was also reflected in the development of new channels of communication with the public. Museums and exhibits remained the primary focus of outreach, visible in the opening of the Museum of New Mexico in 1910 (Snead 2001), the Southwest Museum the next year, and in Wissler's revision of the Southwest galleries at the American Museum during the same period (C. Wissler to H. J. Spinden, letter, 1 September 1909, File 224, AMNH). Another important strategy was the role of popular journals. This effort, which since the 1880s had produced the *American Antiquarian, American Archaeologist,* and *Records of the Past,* expanded dramatically with the launch of the Archaeological Institute of America's *Art and Archaeology* in 1914. Provided to the Institute's national membership, *Art and Archaeology* was an acknowledgment of the importance of public audience, which generated fierce arguments within the institute over appropriate subject matter and editorial control. Edgar Lee Hewett, for instance, worked ceaselessly to bring *Art and Archaeology* into his own domain (E. L. Hewett to P. Walter, letter, 3 March 1917, ELH), meanwhile producing a southwestern competitor in *El Palacio.* Blending archaeological news with notices of other cultural events, art, and poetry, popular journals played a critical role in establishing Southwest archaeology in the public mind (Snead 2006). The importance of this activity even penetrated the higher echelons of the profession; Clark Wissler's announcement of the New Archaeology appeared in the popular *American Museum Journal* (1917a) rather than a professional publication.

A final aspect of the creation of an audience for Southwest archaeology concerned the field school tradition. Although from the perspective of the archaeological profession field schools were intended as training grounds for students, the educational mission of these sessions from the beginning was more inclusive. For every A. V. Kidder and Sylvanus Morley there was a Maude Woy, who taught school in Denver, or a Nathan Goldschmidt, son of Santa Fe merchants, both of whom participated in the 1910 program on the Rito de los Frijoles (Snead 2001:140). Hewett was quite explicit regarding the value of such experience for members of the general public, and also emphasized the restoration of archaeological sites after excavation. These "field museums" (Hewett 1908c:51) were part of a loose system that included the Museum of New Mexico, all designed to further the educational goals of the community. Camp life and Native American lore were also part of the field experience. By 1920 large numbers of people with avocational interests had visited the Rito de los Frijoles and Puyé camps; they were followed by hundreds in the Jemez and Chaco field schools of the 1920s and 1930s (Gifford and Morris 1985; Joiner 1992; Mathien 1992; Mills, this volume).

Readers of *El Palacio,* visitors to Bandelier National Monument, and attendees of Hewett's campfires extended the archaeological experience into everyday life. As the Southwest became more integrated into the American mainstream, it retained some aspects of identity that were unique; archaeology played a role in this process, which also served to maintain archaeological work as a priority.

It is more difficult to evaluate the impact of Wissler's exhibits at the American Museum or similar efforts at other eastern institutions, since the audience they addressed was much larger and more complex. Isolated examples, however, such as visions of the ancient Southwest that appeared in film (Ellis 1997:22) and architecture (cf. Breeze 1990),[8] indicate that imagery of the region's past had indeed come to occupy a small corner of the American mind.

CONCLUSION

As Frank Springer gazed out over the audience gathered at the opening of the new museum in 1917, he saw many of those whose work had provided the substance of his narrative. Not all took joy in the occasion, nor were the speeches of Springer, Hewett, and classical archaeologist Francis Kelsey (another Hewett ally) the only sentiments expressed publicly on that day. Wissler, who prior to the conference had suggested to Nelson that they attend despite "some of our personal antipathies to Hewett," also addressed the gathering (C. Wissler to N. C. Nelson, letter, 2 September 1917, NCN.)

In Wissler's presentation the museum received its share of compliments, but praise was not his primary intent. "I know that no one likes to hear a moral sermon," he acknowledged, before going on to present a detailed argument for the inseparability of archaeology and anthropology in the Americas. "[H]e who turns his back upon the living peoples and seeks to solve unaided the mysteries of the ruins," Wissler announced, "will soon be overwhelmed in the vapory midst of his own theories." He went on to suggest that Hewett be replaced as director by "a scholar whose voice shall command the respect of the learned wherever he chooses to speak," an open jab that indicates why the speech was not reproduced in the museum's official publications and has been buried in Wissler's papers ever since (Misc. 7, Folder 6, BSU). What is most notable, however, is how Wissler's vision of an integrated, anthropological archaeology had already diverged from the reality on the ground in the Southwest as his own teams were putting it into practice.

Official commemoration of Wissler's New Archaeology took place four years later, when Neil Judd held a postseason gathering at his

Pueblo Bonito field camp, bringing together members of the cadre to discuss the progress of their work and its prospects. On that occasion Wissler, in a letter read to the attendees, adopted a more congratulatory and retrospective tone; "strange to say," he wrote, speaking of conditions a decade earlier, "there was considerable indifference and even hostility to the chronological idea" (C. Wissler to S. G. Morley, letter, n.d., Neil Merton Judd Papers, NAA). Against the backdrop of the new excavations of Pueblo Bonito and other Chaco sites, the ascendance of the chronological approach must have seemed assured, and any dissonance between the concept and its application muted. Galvanized by a common idea, Kidder, Judd, and their colleagues looked forward to future successes.

In many ways the agenda of Southwest archaeology over the next decades did reflect these hopes. The value of the 1927 Pecos Conference was both that it instituted a common periodization for different parts of the region and that it established (in the shape of future conferences) a setting for the discussion of other common problems (cf. Woodbury 1993). A community of inquiry was by this point well established. New centers for Southwest research sprang up, such as the Museum of Northern Arizona, Gila Pueblo, and the Laboratory of Anthropology, and many of the ideas promoted by Wissler, Nelson, and the rest were fundamental to the archaeological strategies adopted by these institutions. It is notable that many of these new efforts were opposed by Hewett and other members of the older generation, who correctly saw them as a threat to their own legacies.

Yet it is the *divergent* trends evident at the Santa Fe congress, in which archaeologists from different backgrounds were joined by educators, which provides an accurate illustration of Southwest archaeology in the 1910s. A decade of new data, collected in many cases with care and planning, had limited the conceptual space for undisciplined speculation that had been commonplace only a few years before. Legislation and institutions likewise increasingly structured what was possible, and a stable audience existed both to support archaeology and to follow its progress.

It was in particular to the wider audience that Springer addressed his final inaugural comments on the goals and prospects of Southwest archaeology. Trained in an earlier, less specialized age, he intuitively understood the importance of linking scholarly initiatives to public ambitions (Figure 3.4). "For the achievement of these purposes, as a laudable and thoroughly appropriate national object, upon a plane of

Figure 3.4. Frank Springer (left) and sculptor Cartianno Scarpatti, 1921. Courtesy, Photo Archives, Fray Angélico Chávez Library Palace of the Governors. Neg. no. 139070.

intellectual endeavor above the ordinary, and in which a prosperous nation may well take a patriotic pride," he concluded, "we invite the support of the American people" (Springer 1917:17).

NOTES

1. Currently known as the Museum of Fine Arts. The design of this building is also considered to represent a critical threshold in the development of "Santa Fe style" (see Wilson 1997).

2. He was also not averse to taking advantage of these relationships, as when he persuaded a delegation from the Pueblo of Santa Clara not to oppose his excavations at the ruin of Puyé (see Snead 2001:88–89).

3. Several recent studies have examined the role of Hyde patronage on Southwest archaeology in the 1890s (see Atkins 1993; Blackburn and Williamson 1997; Mathien 2001).

4. Despite claims to the contrary (cf. Praetzellis 1993:73), Nelson's research on shell mound stratigraphy was not directly influenced by Max Uhle (cf. Rowe 1954), who had departed California prior to Nelson's arrival. The two men did not actually meet until 1928 (N. C. Nelson to A. L. Kroeber, letter, 4 December 1954, ALK). More critical, perhaps, was the influence on both men of John Campbell Merriam, a prominent geologist on the University of California faculty who was the principal sponsor of the shell mound program, and who used Nelson to

check Uhle's results (J. C. Merriam to A. L. Kroeber, letter, 28 November 1904, Outgoing Correspondence, JCM; N. C. Nelson to J. C. Merriam, letter, 1 July 1907, Incoming Correspondence, JCM. See Browman and Givens 1996; Stock 1938).

5. Nelson had been in Berkeley the previous spring, writing up old reports (N. C. Nelson to C. Wissler, letter, 23 April 1915, File 404, AMNH), and undoubtedly briefed Kroeber on the chronological innovations while there. It is not difficult to imagine Kroeber perceiving new angles to this research and taking the opportunity provided by his stay at Zuni to put them into practice.

6. When, late in life, Kidder reevaluated his Pecos work, he acknowledged that a preoccupation with chronology may have resulted in missed opportunities (Kidder 1958:307).

7. Among other things, circumstances at the American Museum effectively prevented Nelson from continuing the graduate studies he had begun under Kroeber, which left him increasingly embittered.

8. The 1916 Cliff Dwelling, an apartment building at Riverside Drive and 96th Street in Manhattan, is one of the more remarkable examples of an "Anasazi chic."

4

Seven Years That Reshaped Southwest Prehistory

J. Jefferson Reid and Stephanie M. Whittlesey

In 1933, when I first encountered Southwestern archaeology in the field, though I was little aware of it then, the images of the Hohokam, the Mogollon, the Cochise, were being sketched on Haury's canvas, but it took some years for me and others to realize what was going on: that a world was being put together by a master craftsman out of scattered nuclei. Emil Haury is probably the only recorded person who has worked with such thoroughness in the areas inhabited by all of them, in addition to the lands of the Anasazi, and who has, thereby, accumulated a sweeping perception of the cultural panorama as a whole.

— WATSON SMITH (1987:108)

Emil W. Haury is recognized as one of the founders of modern southwestern archaeology. His name is linked most closely with the Hohokam and the monumental site of Snaketown in south-central Arizona (Reid and Whittlesey 1997:80–81). It is less well known that, during seven critical years in southwestern prehistory between 1930 and 1937, Haury and his colleagues at Gila Pueblo Archaeological Foundation defined the Hohokam, Mogollon, and Salado cultures and laid the groundwork for the later definition of the Cochise culture, the preceramic culture of southeastern Arizona. Before then, much of Arizona and New Mexico was prehistoric terra incognita. After that time, Southwest prehistory was fleshed out in a form that would endure, though not without definitional revision, relabeling, and tremendous controversy, to the present time.

Some background gives context to the significance—indeed, the groundbreaking nature—of these seven years and Haury's achievements. From the perspective of more than 60 years' development of Southwest archaeology, it is difficult to comprehend how poorly known the region was when Gila Pueblo Archaeological Foundation was established in 1928. Archaeologists initially assumed that the Southwest had little time depth and little variability in ancient human cultures (see Fowler 2000). Most archaeology until that time had focused on the Basketmaker and Pueblo ruins left by the Anasazi (Ancestral Pueblo) who lived on the Colorado Plateau. Other archaeological cultures were unknown or only glimpsed, however. Such ephemera were usually uncharitably classified as "backwater" or variant Anasazi (Reid and Whittlesey 1997:81).

This was also a time when culture classification was paramount. Long before archaeologists became concerned with processes of change and human adaptation, the focus of Southwest archaeology was placing cultures in time and space—the culture history approach. Its goal was to document variability in material culture according to these dimensions (Reid and Whittlesey 1997:15). By the 1920s, the Pecos Classification had established the outlines of Basketmaker-Pueblo cultural development through time. Almost nothing was known of the southern Arizona deserts or the mountain transition zone of Arizona and New Mexico. It was largely Haury's work that changed this monolithic understanding of Southwest prehistory.

We use the separate journal entries of Haury and his wife Hulda for the period between 1930 and 1937 as the structural outline to introduce the seven years that reshaped Southwest prehistory. Haury's synoptic chronology quoted here was written in 1988, and the seven-year period that is the subject of this paper was condensed from earlier journal entries. Hulda Haury's journal, titled "Calendar of Emil W. Haury's Activities," covers the period July 1927 to July 1, 1937. We quote from each and provide annotations and commentary relevant to our story (Emil Haury Journals, 1930–1937, Arizona State Museum Archive, University of Arizona, Tucson).

In 1928 Harold S. Gladwin and Winifred Jones MacCurdy established Gila Pueblo Archaeological Foundation in the mining town of Globe, Arizona (Haury 1988). The foundation's purpose was to support archaeological research on a scale that appears vast from a contemporary perspective. Gladwin's initial experiences at Casa Grande National Monument near Phoenix and his friendship with the great southwestern archaeologist A. V. Kidder led him to focus Gila Pueblo's efforts largely on the Hohokam, or the "Red-on-buff culture" as it was then known after the characteristic pottery (Reid and Whittlesey 1997:79). Haury joined Gila Pueblo Archaeological Foundation as assistant director in 1930 and spent seven years exploring, excavating, and writing about the cultures of the Southwest.[1] We turn now to these years.

SEVEN YEARS THAT RESHAPED SOUTHWEST PREHISTORY

Writing in the third person singular, Haury began the story told here in 1930: "June, joins Gila Pueblo Archaeological Foundation, Globe, Arizona, as Assistant Director. Works on Tusayan Ruin, Grand Canyon and carries out ruin surveys on South and North Rims and in the Canyon. October, tree-ring specimen trip to Sierra Ancha cliff dwellings, first visit to Canyon Creek Ruin."

Mrs. Haury's more detailed account amplifies the activities of the fall: "Sept. 1–10, 1930—Emil and George Dennis do survey of White Mt. region," and between "Oct. 10–25—[they] survey Sierra Ancha different ruins to collect tree-ring material, two weeks on horse back with Dewey Peterson." She also noted the short-lived Rye Creek excavation in the upper Tonto Basin: "Oct. 27, 1930—establish camp at Rye Creek." Just a few days later, on November 3, "Mr. Gladwin and Mrs. MacCurdy visit camp and decide that a week's more work should be enough. View camp as too elaborate."

The first six months at Gila Pueblo were significant in that 26-year-old Haury, already field savvy and youthfully energetic, expanded his grasp of variability in Pueblo archaeology. His knowledge extended from the Grand Canyon (Tusayan Ruin) to the Mogollon Rim region and farther south (the White Mountains), including the well-preserved masonry cliff ruins of the Sierra Ancha and the still enigmatic pueblos of the Tonto Basin (Rye Creek Ruin). The following year Haury drew heavily upon this broad knowledge of variability in context and landscape.

Haury wrote: "1931—January, excavations at Roosevelt 9:6 begun. April, Gila Pueblo Conference focusing on taxonomic problems. August, attends 3rd Pecos Conference in Santa Fe, New Mexico. September, enrolls in Harvard University for graduate work." Mrs. Haury recorded that "Work [at Roosevelt 9:6] winds up late January and Emil starts Roosevelt 9:6 report," but she did not mention the conference. Unlike her husband, she did record his absence during the two-month summer survey: "June 12, 1931—start of summer's survey of sites in

Ft. Apache, Whiteriver, Showlow, Reserve, Glenwood, Mimbres areas, finishing Aug. 12."

Mrs. Haury wrote of the remainder of 1931:

Aug. 31, 1931—off for Santa Fe for Pecos Conference, held Sept. 2, 3, and 4. Continue east for visits of family in Kansas and Oklahoma before going on to Cambridge.

Sept. 26, 1931—arrive Cambridge for Emil's study at Harvard. Have apt. at Holden Green. Hemenway collection will be his dissertation project.

Dec. 27, 1931—Emil proofreads manuscript of Roosevelt 9:6.

These cursory observations give no indication that 1931 was the pivotal year in the construction of the Hohokam and Mogollon culture concepts. Gladwin had been hot on the trail of the Red-on-buff culture, and most of Gila Pueblo's forays into the hinterlands were to define that culture's temporal and geographical limits. Roosevelt 9:6, which was located on the south side of the Salt River in the Tonto Basin, was a settlement on the northeastern boundary of this culture. Haury's excavation there defined the Colonial period. His report used the label "Hohokam" for Gladwin's Red-on-buff culture, contrasted the Hohokam with Pueblo culture to the north, and suggested the rather astounding possibility that the Hohokam had influenced the development of the latter group.

The Gila Pueblo Conference of 1931 that Haury mentioned was also a critical event. Gladwin convened it to address problems raised by the inability of the Pecos Classification to structure the archaeological variability of the desert Southwest, particularly southern Arizona. In his 1935 survey of southwestern archaeology, Frank H. H. Roberts (1935a:6–7) would equate the importance of the now forgotten Gila Pueblo Conference of 1931 with the always remembered Pecos Conference of 1927 that established the Pecos Classification.

By the beginning of summer 1931, Haury had grasped the archaeological variability of the plateau, the mountains, and the desert. He could define Hohokam and distinguish it from Basketmaker-Pueblo, both of which he had experienced firsthand. He knew that Hohokam was scarcely a backwater variant of Anasazi. He also knew that the Pecos Classification was incomplete and could not be extended to include the entire Southwest. With this background established at the tender age of 27, Haury began the mountain survey of 1931 with

Russell Hastings. This survey of east-central Arizona and west-central New Mexico revealed a consistent and repeated association of brown, plain ware pottery and deep pithouses that did not fit the Hohokam or Basketmaker-Pueblo pattern. Haury would return in 1933 and 1934 to excavate two sites located during this survey—Mogollon Village and the Harris site—to establish the time depth necessary to recognize a new culture. This task would be accomplished in 1936 with publication of Haury's *The Mogollon Culture of Southwestern New Mexico*.

Mrs. Haury began the following new year with a terse note: "1932—continue study, lab work, analysis of Hemenway material." Haury quickly summarized the entire year: "1932—Summer, excavates Canyon Creek Ruin and writes report. September, returns to Harvard for second year graduate studies. Works on Frank Hamilton Cushing's Hemenway Expedition collection made at Los Muertos and other ruins in the Salt River valley, Arizona, as basis for dissertation."[2]

Haury also reduced the following year to bare essentials: "1933—Early summer in Cambridge preparing photographs for dissertation, interrupted by visit to Dr. A. M. Tozzer's summer home in Tamworth, New Hampshire. At Dr. Roland B. Dixon's request inspects dolmen on Martha's Vineyard. August, starts work on Mogollon 1:15 in New Mexico." We must turn again to Mrs. Haury to give us a sense of timing. "July 12, 1933—finish packing; start trip west. Thesis (rough draft) done." The dissertation to which Mrs. Haury referred, on the site of Los Muertos south of Phoenix, provided Haury with a substantial argument for a model of Classic period Hohokam shared with Gladwin—that the Classic period was a product of a migration of and co-residence with the Salado people (Haury 1945). Concepts of Hohokam and Salado cultures were assuming a sharp image even before the first excavation of a Mogollon site.

Back to the Haury's journey west. Mrs. Haury wrote:

July 26, 1933—make stop at Silver City and Mogollon 1:15 to pick a camp site for on-coming "dig." On to Globe.

Aug. 1, 1933—to Mogollon 1:15. Emil, Hulda, Edith Sangster, Jim Simmons, Russ Hastings, Felix Manuel and Elihu Blackwater. Gladwin, MacCurdy at Red Mesa camp.

Sept. 16, 1933—break camp and return to Globe.

1934—preparation of Mogollon report.

May 20, 1934—Emil to Cambridge (goes via New Orleans for defense of thesis. May 28, get message that his exam was successful.

We continue with Haury:

1934—June, awarded Doctor of Philosophy degree by Harvard University. Summer, with Laboratory of Anthropology (Santa Fe) scholarship holders, excavates Harris Site, Mimbres Valley, New Mexico. Canyon Creek Ruin and Cliff Dwellings of the Sierra Ancha report published as Medallion Paper No. XIV. September 3, birth of first son. October, start first Snaketown excavations.

1935—Mother dies. Explore, with E. B. Sayles, the Willcox Playa and Whitewater Draw for Early Man buried sites, later to become known as the Cochise culture.[3]

1936—Summer, with E. B. Sayles, excavates White Mound Site near Allantown, Arizona. November, Cummings visits at Gila Pueblo to inquire about replacing him at the University of Arizona with his retirement imminent. Medallion Paper No. XX published, suggesting recognition of the Mogollon culture.

1937—June, terminates employment at Gila Pueblo. July, assumes new position at the University as Head, Department of Archaeology and as Associate Professor, succeeding Byron Cummings. First volume on Snaketown published (with others) as Medallion Paper No. XXV. Elected a Fellow, American Association for the Advancement of Science.

Thus comes to an end the seven-year period during which, working for the Gila Pueblo Archaeological Foundation, Haury excavated the first Hohokam site, assisted Gladwin in defining the Hohokam, excavated the first Mogollon site, discovered and defined the Mogollon culture, sketched the major characteristics of the Salado, and with E. B. Sayles recognized the existence of the Archaic period Cochise culture. Strikingly, all of this fieldwork and reporting took place during a time of nationwide economic depression and while Haury was pursuing his doctorate. By the end of this seven-year period, the Hohokam, Mogollon, Salado, and Archaic Cochise had been defined or recognized. Moreover, Haury had established the personal and professional habits, achieved the academic and professional credentials, and developed the philosophy of archaeology that would enable him to continue studying these cultures and, it would turn out, also to defend one of them against a cadre of critics.

To follow the subsequent intellectual history of these cultural constructs would certainly be intriguing, for all have provoked controversies that fill the literature still, but this task would require a book. We have chosen instead to follow the Mogollon, because they were most controversial when first proposed and seem most endangered today. In the following section, we seek to illustrate how Haury's pivotal years at Gila Pueblo Archaeological Foundation influenced the subsequent course of the Mogollon as an archaeological construct.

EMIL HAURY, THE MOUNTAINS, AND THE MOGOLLON

The Mogollon Culture of Southwestern New Mexico (Haury 1936) may be one of the most provocative publications in the history of southwestern archaeology (Reid 1986). It generated a polarization of southwestern archaeologists lasting for more than 20 years. Haury argued that the Mogollon should be recognized as a third culture distinct from Anasazi and Hohokam. He further maintained that the Mogollon culture was at least as old as Basketmaker, had pottery earlier, and late in its development was submerged by the Anasazi. Haury's Mogollon sequence ended with the shift from pithouses to pueblos around A.D. 1000.

Paul Sidney Martin (1937:233) reviewed the book as "so astonishing, so far-reaching, and so unorthodox that the worth of this report and of the new data contained therein probably will not be understood or esteemed for some years." Prophetically, he anticipated that "the hypothesis set forth in this excellent report will doubtless be scoffed at by many competent people." Martin's own research would place him beside Haury firmly in the midst of the ensuing controversy.

It took little time for a critical tone to enter the literature. In 1938, Paul Nesbitt reported his work on the Starkweather Ruin in the Mimbres Valley. The patriarch of southwestern archaeology, A. V. Kidder, reviewed the report in the following year. To Nesbitt (1938), the Mogollon did not represent a new cultural division; its elements were similar and in many cases identical to Anasazi, with some ideas borrowed from the Hohokam. He also saw Mogollon as no older than Pueblo I (A.D. 700–900) in the Pecos Classification. Nesbitt appears to have been influenced by Kidder, who viewed the material remains that Haury labeled Mogollon as the result of mixing of Anasazi and Hohokam traits. Kidder (1939:315–316) thought that the Mogollon mountain folk were "receptive rather than radiating"; they lacked individuality and had all the earmarks of a peripheral, borrowing culture. Only the early pottery was distinctive, and Kidder dispensed with this by seeing it as originating from another source, presumably Mexico. "If this be true," Kidder

(1939:316) wrote, then "Mogollon loses its sole significant claim to individuality."

In Nesbitt's and Kidder's arguments we can clearly see the influence of the Anasazi bias and the widespread perception that cultural manifestations differing from Anasazi were nothing more than variants of that culture or largely influenced by it. Both scholars appear to have underplayed the significant point of Haury's intimate involvement with Anasazi, Hohokam, and Mogollon. He was familiar with these cultures from survey and excavation. With such experience under his belt—experience that his colleagues lacked—Haury alone was capable of making the provocative assessments of the 1936 report.

Two questions marked the initial phases of the Mogollon controversy. First, were the mountain people so distinct from the Anasazi as to require a new label, and second, if they were distinct, were the Mogollon to be viewed as a culture equivalent to the Anasazi and Hohokam? The antiquity of Mogollon ceramics was also under fire. Pottery was the hallmark of southwestern culture and the principal ingredient of archaeological reconstruction. Anasazi archaeologists did not warm to the prospect of a backward mountain people making pottery before their Anasazi.

By 1939 it had become apparent that more fieldwork was required if the Mogollon concept was to be accepted. Haury, who was steeped in an empiricist archaeological tradition and conditioned by his years at Gila Pueblo to argue points with the shovel, was also ready to begin a field school program. For years Haury had hoped that Earl Morris, a highly respected Anasazi expert, would tackle the Mogollon problem with excavations in the Forestdale Valley (Haury 1985:139). Haury had faith that Morris would arrive at conclusions similar to his own, and, as an independent observer, would provide strong testimony for Mogollon distinctiveness. Because Morris was occupied with his own early sites near Durango, however, Haury tackled the problem himself. He began his first field school in the Forestdale Valley in 1939. Also in that year, Martin began his long-term investigations of the Mogollon in the Pine Lawn region of west-central New Mexico, a locale selected after reviewing the Gila Pueblo records of Haury's 1931 survey.

In 1942 J. O. Brew entered the fray with a harsh critique of John McGregor's (1941) *Southwestern Archaeology*, which was the first textbook synthesis to appear since Kidder's 1924 work. Brew opposed McGregor's attempt to establish Mogollon as a basic culture in the absence of what Brew considered as sufficient evidence and rejected the assertion that the Mogollon influenced other cultures. To Brew, the distinctiveness and antiquity of Mogollon were still unproven, as was its purported relationship to the Cochise culture—Mogollon as an outgrowth from local Cochise roots. The only statement McGregor had made concerning the Mogollon that was acceptable to Brew was that it was poorly known. Haury, however, had seen Cochise and Mogollon in the flesh, as it were, and was able to recognize numerous parallels between the ceramic culture and its preceramic antecedent. Brew chose to ignore this point.

The controversy took on a new dimension at that time. To countervailing interpretations of the archaeological evidence and to arguments based on faith and convention, Brew added an academically reasonable concern for rigorous definition and use of terms. Evidence, definition, and clarity of argument would be the themes of papers that appeared throughout the 1940s by Erik Reed, who had worked with Haury at the Mogollon Harris site and at Snaketown. Drawn principally from his two rejected Harvard dissertations, Reed's arguments resulted by the end of the 1940s in an expanded conception of Mogollon culture.

In 1950 Reed, who had long argued in support of the Mogollon concept, completed his summary of the traits that set it apart from the Anasazi. Although he recognized that similarities between the Anasazi and Mogollon after A.D. 1000 constituted a general Pueblo pattern contrasting with the Hohokam, to Reed the differences that existed between the former two groups required separate labels. Mindful of the general similarities and specific differences, he suggested the term "Western Pueblo" for the Mogollon culture.

New evidence was systematically added to the old through the methodical excavation and reporting by Martin and John Rinaldo of their work in New Mexico. They went beyond demonstrating Mogollon separateness to grapple with problems at the early and late ends of the sequence (Martin and Rinaldo 1950a, 1950b; Martin et al. 1949, 1952). At Tularosa Cave, where one of the longest Mogollon sequences was discovered, they claimed to have extended the Pine Lawn phase back to 150 B.C. through radiocarbon dating. Martin and Rinaldo gave the impression that the controversy was remote and the contentious issues were resolved in their minds, so that they could attend more interesting areas of cultural reconstruction such as social organization (Martin and Rinaldo 1950b). After the 1954 summer season, Martin and Rinaldo packed up their camp for good and left west-central New Mexico to investigate the Mogollon elsewhere.

By that time, Haury had shifted the University of Arizona Archaeological Field School to Point of Pines in east-central Arizona. There, the Mogollon controversy would loom large, and Haury would marshal his students to collect additional evidence that eventually resolved the controversy and solidified the connections between Mogollon and Cochise. He would also organize a series of conferences to debate the finer points of culture classification. The 1948 and 1951 Pecos conferences were held at Point of Pines to discuss the issues and to examine evidence in the field (Woodbury 1993). The synthetic document resolving the 20-year debate would emanate from Point of Pines. This was Joe Ben Wheat's (1955) *Mogollon Culture Prior to A.D. 1000*. According to Wheat, the dissertation's purpose was to synthesize all that was known about the Mogollon. In the process, although he did not avow it, the Mogollon concept was also validated. Although the book "does not purport to be a final 'answer to the Mogollon problem'" (Wheat 1955:vi), in retrospect we can see that it was the answer to the problem as it was then posed.

Wheat addressed all of the contentious issues surrounding Mogollon—antiquity and chronology; relation to the Cochise, Anasazi, and Hohokam; and the priority of Mogollon pottery over Anasazi pottery. The persuasiveness of the presentation stemmed from three facets of the book: 1) a branch map showing geographic distribution of Mogollon; 2) a period-phase chart insinuating time depth and phase contiguity; and 3) a thorough comparison of pottery, architecture, and village plan. Wheat's work was a model of archaeological argument in the culture history school. The impact of this prodigious synthetic statement was enhanced by its unparalleled distribution as a site report and a memoir of two major scholarly societies. It is impossible not to see Haury's hand in orchestrating this work and his academic stature in its publication.

In December 1953 the American Anthropological Association held its annual meeting in Tucson. At the Southwest symposium, the newly minted Ph.D. Wheat presented a paper in defense of the Mogollon; J. O. Brew, Watson Smith, and Gordon Willey were discussants. The paper, which was essentially a condensed version of the concluding statements in his dissertation, was published with the other symposium papers in the August 1954 issue of *American Anthropologist* (Wheat 1954a).

The section of Wheat's dissertation reporting excavations at Crooked Ridge Village at Point of Pines was published in 1954 as a University of Arizona Bulletin (Wheat 1954b). In 1955 the Mogollon synthesis was published jointly as a Memoir of the Society for American Archaeology and an American Anthropological Association Memoir. This dual format made it possible for every member of the Society for American Archaeology and every member of the American Anthropological Association who had already received the August 1954 issue of *American Anthropologist* containing Wheat's condensed presentation to receive at least one copy of Wheat's validation of the Mogollon concept (some got two). No other piece of American archaeological scholarship received such treatment.

With this one-two knockout punch, the Mogollon controversy was annihilated by a thorough compilation of extensive excavation data distributed free of charge to every anthropologist and archaeologist in North America. The Mogollon problem had effectively ceased as a public topic of intellectual debate. Persistent disbelievers could do little more than whimper.

Martin and Rinaldo, having ceased work in New Mexico in 1954, began anew in 1957 with a field camp at Vernon, Arizona, from which to pursue their hypothesis that the Pine Lawn Valley Mogollon had eventually moved to Zuni. They continued to excavate and quickly report their work. By the beginning of the 1960s, the Mogollon concept had become so accepted in Vernon that it had become passé, and the fuss associated with it a quaint relic, like survey on horseback, of a bygone era in southwestern archaeology. In the coming decade, use of any cultural labels would be abandoned in favor of examining anthropologically relevant questions according to rigorous procedures of scientific investigation. Vernon was becoming a training camp for the "New Archaeologists."

Yet those who were convinced of the reality of the Mogollon culture remained a house divided. Alfred Johnson's (1965) dissertation submitted to the University of Arizona examined the development of Western Pueblo culture. Although seemingly an affirmation of Reed's synonym for Mogollon Pueblo, Johnson's work redefined Western Pueblo as a syncretism of Mogollon, Anasazi, and Hohokam features that transformed the old Mogollon into a new cultural entity. Reed's original concept thus changed meaning in the hands of those who saw Mogollon swamped by Anasazi after A.D. 1000. Haury staunchly maintained an Anasazi-swamping position during his entire professional career.

Because of the redirection in American archaeology and perhaps also because of the exhaustion engendered by the protracted controversy surrounding the Mogollon, the interesting questions raised during the debate and the distinguishing features of Mogollon culture and behavior remain essentially unresolved. Despite a biennial Mogollon Conference that ratifies broad acceptance of the concept, a commonly shared definition of Mogollon is unavailable. Increasingly, another redefinition and use of Western Pueblo is creeping into the literature along with assertions that there is no such thing as Mogollon (e.g., Elson et al. 1992:284; Mills 1999b:3–4; Speth 1988:201; Wilcox 1988a:207). Tainter and Plog (1994:179) write that "the notion of Anasazi and Mogollon as cultural traditions has outlived its usefulness and indeed, never was correct."

Beginning in 1963, fieldwork continued for 30 years at the University of Arizona Archaeological Field School at Grasshopper Pueblo in the mountains of east-central Arizona. Analysis extended another 10 years and is ongoing today. This work continued the tradition of empirical argument and fieldwork that Haury learned at Gila Pueblo Archaeological Foundation and translated to the pueblos and pithouses of the Forestdale Valley and Point of Pines. The research provides strong arguments in support of the Mogollon culture defined by Haury, elaborated by Martin and Rinaldo, and extended into the post–A.D. 1000 pueblo-building era by Reid (1989, 1999; Reid and Whittlesey 1997, 1999).

In summary, the seven years Emil W. Haury spent at Gila Pueblo Archaeological Foundation between 1930 and 1937 did far more than reshape Southwest prehistory as it was then understood. The lessons learned there were taken up by new generations of archaeologists trained in Haury's punctilious scholarship and at Haury's field schools. Their ideas continued to mold Southwest prehistory for a half century, and the legacy endures to this day (Reid and Doyel 1986). The events of these years shaped the outlines of the Mogollon, Hohokam, Salado, and Cochise cultures (the latter now known variously as the Late Archaic or Early Agricultural period culture of southeastern Arizona). They established the structure of the empirical argument that would be used to validate the Mogollon and defend it against a host of critical scholars. We hope that we have inculcated Haury's teachings and that his hand can be seen in our own work, too.

NOTES

1. Haury studied, worked, traveled, and taught with Byron Cummings at the University of Arizona. He received his bachelor's degree in 1927 and his master's degree in 1928, the year he married Hulda Penner. Although Haury

accepted Cummings's offer to teach in the Department of Archaeology at Arizona during the 1928–1929 academic year, he quit not long after because of mounting uneasiness at suddenly becoming faculty to his peers. He worked the following year with A. E. Douglass after participating in the signal event of "bridging the gap" in the tree-ring chronology. Douglass exposed Haury to the rigors of scientific investigation and while Douglass's teaching assistant he met Gladwin.

2. For a thorough history of the Hemenway Southwestern Expedition of 1886–1889, see Hinsley and Wilcox (1995, 1996, 2002).

3. Cochise is the Archaic (preceramic) hunting-gathering culture of the southern Southwest from the early Holocene until the appearance of pottery. Recognized by Haury and Sayles in the 1930s, it was defined in 1941 by Sayles and the geologist Ernst Antevs on the basis of buried sites in the Whitewater Draw region of southeastern Arizona. The Cochise developmental sequence is divided into three stratigraphically distinct stages: Sulphur Spring (10,000–8,000 radiocarbon years B.P.), Chiricahua (? to 3,500 B.P.), and San Pedro (3,500–2,000 B.P.). The relation to Clovis remains unclear, though chronometric evidence does not support contemporaneity. Sayles's Cazador Stage, considered transitional between Sulphur Spring and Chiricahua, has been seriously questioned by the reexamination of deposits at the type site. Reinvestigation of Bat Cave reliably dates the introduction of maize and squash to around 1200 B.C. Cochise has long been thought to be ancestral to Mogollon.

5

Curricular Matters:
The Impact of Field Schools
on Southwest Archaeology

Barbara J. Mills

More than any other geographic area, the American Southwest is associated with the training of archaeological students. Each year dozens of
colleges and universities offer credit for participation in southwestern
fieldwork. Over the past century, these field schools have accounted for
hundreds of field seasons and the training of thousands of students. The
Southwest is truly a laboratory for anthropology (Fowler 2000), and
this laboratory has been populated by field school students and staff
members who have changed the course of southwestern anthropology.

The role and impact of field schools in southwestern archaeology
have changed along with the goals of general archaeology, the economic and political milieus in which they were conducted, and the personalities and intellectual orientations of those involved. In this chapter
I sketch a history of archaeological field training in the Southwest and
place this history in its social, political, and intellectual context. I emphasize the contributions of field schools to knowledge about the past
in terms of changing archaeological goals. Because of the large number of field schools in the Southwest, I have not attempted to provide
a comprehensive inventory, nor do I discuss all of the many and important substantive research contributions archaeological field schools
have made in each region.

My definition of a field school is that it offers archaeological training, usually for college or university credit, through participation in an
archaeological research project in the field. There are also less structured opportunities for field training, such as those offered by private
foundations. Examples of large research projects in which students

have received valuable training, albeit without university credit, are the Rainbow Bridge–Monument Valley Expedition in the 1930s (Woodbury 1990:9), the Awatovi Expedition of Harvard's Peabody Museum in the same period (Smith 1971:xx–xxii), and more recently, the Glen Canyon Project (Jennings 1966).

I subdivide this chapter into four parts. First, I discuss the earliest field schools of Edgar Lee Hewett and Byron Cummings. Both individuals were bridges between the explorer/antiquarians of the late nineteenth century and the scientific archaeology of the twentieth century. Both men were educators first, latecomers to the field of archaeology, and founders of the two oldest field programs in the Southwest. Second, I discuss field schools of the historical particularist period of Americanist archaeology. The dual goals of chronology and reconstructionist archaeology channeled fieldwork—and field schools—of the 1930s through the early 1960s. Third, I review the role of southwestern field schools in the formation of the "New Archaeology" in the 1960s. Lastly, I comment on field schools during the last two decades of the twentieth century, including diversification in research goals and pedagogy.

The Earliest Southwest Field Schools: 1907–1920

Two major forces controlled archaeology at the turn of the century: 1) private collectors and patrons, and 2) eastern museums. Educational opportunities in western states were fewer than in the east, and those that existed emphasized teacher training. The founders of the two earliest southwestern field schools, Edgar Lee Hewett and Byron Cummings, were college educated, but neither of them had formal training in archaeology. They viewed field schools as important for training future archaeologists while using archaeology to promote their own institutions. They were able to combine these purposes by building on two general trends of the period: regionalism and romanticism. Each did so in remarkably different ways.

Hewett had a hand in most of the major cultural and educational institutions in New Mexico during the early twentieth century (Elliott 1987; Fowler 1999, 2000; Hinsley 1986; Snead 1999, 2001). Besides conducting the first archaeological field courses in the Southwest, he helped establish the Museum of New Mexico, the School of American Archaeology of the Archaeological Institute of America (now the School of American Research [SAR]), the Department of Archaeology and Anthropology at the University of New Mexico (now the Department of Anthropology), and the Santa Fe Archaeological Society. His entry into New Mexico archaeology was, however, not through formal class-room training or fieldwork. This lack of university certification kept his work from being respected by the eastern archaeological establishment and by many other archaeologists in future years. Instead, he was an organizer and a visionary who aggressively used archaeology to further his own agenda by drawing on the support of prominent southwestern civic and social leaders and by actively opposing the eastern archaeological establishment.

Hewett started out in the Southwest as a schoolteacher in Florence, Colorado, in 1890. His friendship with Frank Springer, a wealthy Republican attorney and distinguished paleontologist, led to Hewett's appointment as the first president of New Mexico Normal School in Las Vegas (now New Mexico Highlands University). Here he began his archaeological lecturing through the university extension program (Snead 2001:52; Snead, this volume).

With the support of Frank Springer, Hewett moved his attention to Santa Fe. He became active in the Santa Fe Chamber of Commerce and promoted Santa Fe as "The City Different." He also helped to establish preservation codes that would maintain the city's architectural homogeneity (Wilson 1997). Hewett's agenda combined romanticized notions about the past, whether ancient or historic, with the promotion of regional interests (Snead 2001). These interests extended to archaeological site preservation through his support of the Antiquities Act of 1906 (Thompson 2000a), an intense battle with eastern archaeologists over control of archaeological sites, and the establishment of the first archaeological field training program in the Southwest.

Charles Pickering Bowditch reluctantly recruited Hewett for a fellowship in Central America with the Boston-based Archaeological Institute of America (AIA). The AIA wanted to expand their fellowship and field programs in New World studies, but had difficulty in finding a suitable candidate. The AIA committee, made up of Bowditch, Frederic Ward Putnam, and Franz Boas, settled on Hewett for the fellowship in 1905, even though he had ideas that ran counter to what the committee supported. Hewett wanted to involve avocational archaeologists in archaeology because he knew that they controlled much of the financial support and power base at the time. He also stressed the importance of conservation and preservation of archaeological sites. Hewett's ideas formed a different model for archaeology than that promulgated by the eastern institutions of the time with their emphases on formal training, exclusive access to archaeological sites, and a relative lack of concern over how archaeological objects were acquired for museums. Hewett's model was supported by Francis Willey Kelsey of the University of Michigan, who, along with Jesse Walter Fewkes, supported Hewett's appointment. When Kelsey assumed the AIA presidency in 1906, Hewett had the support he needed. Hewett lobbied for the Antiquities Act of 1906 and returned to Santa Fe as director of the newly established School of American Archaeology (Hinsley 1986:220–226).

In 1907 Hewett began field training in the Southwest by recruiting three students from Harvard through Alfred Tozzer: Alfred V. Kidder, Sylvanus Morley, and John Fletcher. They were taken to southeastern Utah and, after a morning's worth of instruction, were told to survey for the next three weeks (Kidder 1960). Hewett returned to pick them up and then took them to New Mexico where they conducted excavations at Puyé. Fletcher hated his experience and left archaeology to become a poet, receiving the Pulitzer Prize in 1939 (Fowler 2000:266). The other two made many contributions in the Southwest and Mesoamerica, though arguably not because of the training they received from Hewett, whose sink-or-swim pedagogical style (Hewett 1943:149–154) became renowned (Chauvenet 1983:80; Fowler 1999:176, 2000:265–266).

Hewett continued field training through another AIA-sponsored field school on the Pajarito Plateau in 1908. Later that year, the AIA committee met to support the establishment of a School of American Archaeology facility in Santa Fe. In 1909 it was announced that the school would be based in the Palace of the Governors. A few months later, the Museum of New Mexico was established by the New Mexico State Legislature, also based in the Palace of the Governors. Hewett's field school of 1909 was again on the Pajarito Plateau, working in both Frijoles Canyon and again at Puyé (Fowler 2000:268).

As discussed by Snead (2001:125–127), the early 1900s was a period of cultural nationalism and the establishment of the museum fit well with this new national agenda. Politicians and other community leaders in New Mexico sought legitimacy for that territory by establishing ties to the landscape that would both attract tourists and buoy the state's image in a country still controlled by wealthier eastern states. Within the new milieu, ruins in the Southwest were not viewed as the product of the tribes living in the Southwest, but rather as romanticized vestiges of a "vanished race." Hewett's field school was conducted with the support of politicians and donors whose goals were to elevate the resources of the Southwest in the popular imagination by separating the past from present-day Pueblo societies (Snead 2001:131).

The field course of 1910 was even more ambitious. It was offered jointly by the School of American Archaeology and the Bureau of American Ethnology (Fowler 2000:269). Interdisciplinary in focus, it incorporated archaeologists, ethnologists, linguists, geologists, and botanists. Students were recruited, not from universities and colleges, but from the general public. Through his battles over control of the School, Hewett had alienated himself from the very academic institutions that would have sent him students (Snead 2001:140). Nonetheless, Hewett's populist and integrative approach proved to be highly successful and attracted a large number of participants, especially from western states. They excavated at Tyuonyi, attended evening lectures, visited archaeological sites, and attended dances at local pueblos (Springer 1910a, 1910b).

Public participation in the school's field program was a major part of Hewett's vision. In 1911 and 1912 fieldwork was conducted at Tyuonyi, but the length of the field sessions and the actual amount of participation by students in the excavations were much less than in previous years. Students listened to lectures in Santa Fe and then largely watched excavations by the staff. This popularization of archaeology did not sit well with many professional archaeologists and Hewett was widely criticized. By 1914 there was no field component, only public lectures. Fieldwork was reinstated during the 1916 summer field program, which focused on excavations at Puyé. The students were again more heavily drawn from the local community (Snead 2001:146–152).

The School of American Archaeology was renamed the School of American Research in 1917. Although field programs continued to be offered by the new school and the Museum of New Mexico, they were "little more than outings" (Snead 2001:164). Nonetheless, Hewett's early field schools had made several important contributions. They provided more advanced training for the staff who supervised excavations. In addition, they provided a way for the local community to become engaged in archaeology, which often led to financial support for cultural institutions and heritage preservation in the Southwest. And finally, Hewett's field schools established a tradition of field education in the Southwest that continues to the present day (Snead 2001:165).

Like Hewett, Byron Cummings was not initially trained as an archaeologist. He was a professor of Classics at the University of Utah and headed that department from 1895 to 1915. During his last 10 years as head he was also the dean of the School of Arts and Sciences.

In 1906 he was influenced by Hewett, who visited the university on one of his lecture trips, to form a regional AIA chapter (Wilcox 2001). Soon afterward Cummings led expeditions to Utah and Arizona, including Rainbow Bridge, Navajo Mountain, and Tsegi Canyon. Neil Judd (Cummings's nephew) was a student at the University of Utah at the time and served as Cummings's field assistant from 1907 to 1909 (Judd 1968:3). Alfred Kidder was codirector of the 1908 excavations on Alkali Ridge. Each summer for the next six years, Cummings explored the canyons and mesas of the Four Corners region and conducted excavations at several pueblos (Tanner 1954:4–6).

In 1915, along with 16 other faculty members, Cummings resigned from the University of Utah in a protest over academic freedom (Fowler 2000:260; Thompson 2006). Cummings offered his services to the president of the University of Arizona, Rufus Bernhard von KleinSmid, who hired him to be a professor of archaeology and to organize the university museum. Arizona had achieved statehood in 1912 and the University of Arizona was in an expansion phase when Cummings arrived. He proved to be a team player and was given much latitude to establish a community base and to build the collections (Wilcox 2001).

Like Hewett, Cummings inspired community interest in archaeology through public lectures, which drew on his knowledge of Greek and Roman history and southwestern archaeology. The classicism of ancient societies around the world as linked through an appreciation of the antiquities of the Southwest. Regionalism and romanticism were again being used in the institutionalization of southwestern archaeology. Cummings raised money for the museum, began to acquire new collections, and worked closely with avocational archaeologists to form regional societies including the founding of the Arizona Archaeological and Historical Society in 1916. What began as a small mineral and ornithology collection with a few artifacts that all fit into one room quickly became the major state repository for archaeological and ethnological collections, many of which were donations from local community members (Tanner 1954; Wilcox 2001).

Also like Hewett, Cummings used summer field programs to help build institutions. Because Cummings was based at a university, his field schools more directly related to the training of students drawn from academic settings. The field school became part of the professionalization of archaeology students. Cummings's first field school in 1919 included 15 students: 8 men and 7 women. The "Summer Course among the Cliff Dwellers" would "consist of mapping sections of the country, drawing plans of pueblos, studying excavations, and identifying and classifying materials uncovered, to be embodied in reports on different phases of the summer's work" (from Cummings's flier, reproduced in Gifford and Morris 1985:399).

Excavations were conducted at Kin Clit So (Yellow House, NA 2652) and Kin Clit Chi (Red House, NA 2655) in the Navajo Mountain area, but only the men were allowed to excavate (Brace 1986:195). The course was offered again in 1920 with three men and six women accompanying Cummings to northern Arizona (Gifford and Morris 1985:398). From 1921 through 1930, Cummings worked at the site of Cuicuilco near Mexico City (1924–1925) and at sites in the Tucson area. Institutional demands, including the presidency of the University of Arizona from 1927 to 1928, required his attention in Tucson. Although he took students with him into the field during this period, he offered no formal field school again until 1934. By then the field school would follow a slightly different model, one appropriate to a new era in the history of field schools in the Southwest.

Culture Areas and Chronologies: Southwest Field Schools 1927–1965

The field schools of the late 1920s through the mid-1960s shared a concern for the delineation of culture areas on increasingly smaller scales, and the establishment and refinement of chronologies. The 1927 Pecos Conference suggested a sequence of development for the Southwest that was untested in many areas. Even with the maturation of dendrochronology as an archaeological tool in 1929 (Bannister and Robinson 1986), sites needed to be sampled and those without suitable wood required dating with other techniques. These concerns were not exclusively those of southwestern archaeologists, but the Southwest became exemplary in the development of chronologies and the classification of variation thought to reflect different cultures. No better place than field schools could be found to train students in the new historical particularism that prevailed at the time.

As Gifford and Morris (1985:398) observed, field schools of the late 1920s marked the beginning of a new trend. While some students accompanied professors in excavations that followed the older expeditionary model of a field school, more permanently based field camps were established to which the project returned each season. These included Hewett's next phase of field schools in the Jemez and Chaco areas, Cummings's work at Kinishba, Emil Haury's projects in the

Forestdale Valley and at Point of Pines, and the establishment of the Grasshopper Field School by Haury and Raymond Thompson. After the Chaco Canyon field schools, the University of New Mexico conducted multiyear field schools at several sites in the Middle Rio Grande area, including Pottery Mound, Yunque, and Sapawe.

The field schools of this period shared a focus on large sites, especially those dating to the Pueblo IV period (Spielmann 1998:12–13). Multiyear excavations could be conducted that engaged graduate student staff members and enrolled students alike. Staff members returned to the field in multiple summers and learned how to run large excavation projects while collecting material for their theses and dissertations (Mathien 1992; Reid 1999). For many of these field schools, archaeological results were poorly reported, except for the work of graduate student staff. These long-term field schools also became the breeding ground for institutional rivalries.

Chaco Canyon was one of the earliest locations for the new model of a field school during this period. In 1927 Edgar Hewett was appointed head of the new Department of Archaeology and Anthropology at the University of New Mexico (UNM). Hewett's hire resulted from his alliance with the university's president, James F. Zimmerman, who recognized how archaeology and anthropology could fit with the emergence of UNM as the premier academic institution in the state (Joiner 1992:50–51). Bloom (1939:22) describes visiting Hewett in his Santa Fe office the same year he was hired at UNM, while he was trying to prune the list of 50 organizations to which he belonged in some capacity. Hewett maintained his affiliation with the School of American Research, however, along with his headship of the department at UNM. Thus, when he began his excavations at Chaco, it was a multi-institutional endeavor that allowed Hewett to continue his public agenda along with a new university-based educational program. This association lasted from 1929 through the 1936 field season.

The joint UNM/SAR field school at Chaco proved to be both administratively complicated and subject to legal problems stemming from "a crazy quilt of ownership" (Joiner 1992:51). Although the federal Antiquities Act of 1906 provided federal protection for many of the sites in Chaco Canyon, other sites were on private land and the university owned still others. Because the region was poorly surveyed, and apparently poorly marked, the National Park Service erected structures on university land. For similar reasons, Hewett conducted excavations on federal land without a permit, thinking that he was working on private land. The stage was set for "an archaeological range war" (Lister and Lister 1981:111). In addition to these problems, Hewett did not get along with Donald Brand, who replaced him as head of the UNM Department of Anthropology in 1936 and who had a very different administrative style. In 1938 an anonymous entry in the *New Mexico Anthropologist* appeared announcing the severing of ties between the School of American Research and the University of New Mexico. Since Brand was the editor of the publication, he probably wrote it. Although Hewett continued as a professor in the Department of Anthropology, it was clearly in name only (Anonymous 1938a:62).

The next entry in the *New Mexico Anthropologist* described the field sessions that the University of New Mexico now offered at both Chaco and Jemez. The Jemez Field School was a more general one, "open to any individual interested in Anthropology who can meet the University matriculation requirements" (Anonymous 1938b:62). By contrast, "The Chaco Field Session (housed in the newly completed Research Station) will be open to qualified upper division and graduate students" (Anonymous 1938b:63). This continued the tradition of two levels of field training that Hewett had established.

During the pre- and post-Hewett years, hundreds of students participated in the research at Chaco (Joiner 1992; Mathien 1992). The UNM Field Headquarters established on the south side of the canyon, just west of Casa Rinconada, included facilities to house a large number of students, staff, and visitors. In 1936 there were 47 students and 26 staff (Brand et al. 1937:9). During the 1929–1931 and 1933–1935 seasons, extensive excavations were conducted at Chetro Ketl (Hawley 1934). The field school also conducted excavations of great kivas at Casa Rinconada, Kin Nahasbas, and Chetro Ketl (Vivian and Reiter 1965). Tseh So (Bc50) was the first small site to be excavated in Chaco Canyon (Brand et al. 1937). The only other small site to be reported was Leyit Kin (Dutton 1938). The UNM Chaco field sessions ended in 1947 with many of the excavations still unpublished (Vivian and Mathews 1965:27).

As with many other field schools of the period, the importance of the Chaco Canyon field schools was their impact on the training of staff and students. Staff members who worked at the UNM Chaco field schools included Wesley Bliss, Donald Brand, Bertha Dutton, Florence Hawley (Ellis), Frank Hibben, Clyde Kluckhohn, Marjorie Ferguson Lambert, Robert Lister, Paul Reiter, Anna O. Shepard, James Spuhler, and R. Gordon Vivian. Many of them were at the beginning of their careers. Shepard was 26 in 1929 when she helped excavate the trash mound at Chetro Ketl, although her first southwestern fieldwork was in 1923 when, at the age of 20, she was a student at the SAR Field School at Gran Quivira (Cordell 1991:133). Other participants, such as Dorothy Keur, were students at the field school and then went on to direct their own projects in the Southwest (Babcock and Parezo 1988:143).

Another impact of the Chaco field school was to bring about recognition of the variability in regional sequences in the Ancestral Pueblo area. The chronological refinements at Chaco made possible by architectural sequences, ceramic change, and dendrochronology brought out nuances in the dating of sites that demonstrated how much earlier the great houses were than the aggregated sites of the "Great Pueblo" era in other parts of the Southwest. Although the contemporaneity of small and great houses begged further interpretation, little attention was paid to social or political interpretations. One exception was the work of Clyde Kluckhohn (1939), but he ultimately turned to cultural anthropology. His disillusionment with the narrow goals of many archaeologists of the time (Kluckhohn 1940) stimulated his student at Harvard, Walter W. Taylor, to write a scathing critique of archaeologists of the historical particularist period in the Southwest and Mesoamerica (Taylor 1948).

Great Pueblos were also part of the particularistic goals of Cummings's new field school at Kinishba on the Fort Apache Indian Reservation (Cummings 1940). He began excavations at the site in 1931, officially establishing a field school in 1934 that continued through the 1937 season. By this time Cummings was 77 years old, the oldest archaeologist to direct a field school in the Southwest. This field school included not only training in how to excavate, but also involved the reconstruction of a major section of the pueblo. An on-site museum was built to house the artifacts, which was part of his plan to establish regional museums throughout the state (Wilcox 2001). At this time, Cummings was head of the Department of Archaeology and director of the Arizona State Museum at the University of Arizona as well as director of the Kinishba Museum (Tanner 1954:12).

In 1937 Emil W. Haury replaced Cummings as head of the Department of Archaeology at Arizona. Haury had his first excavation experience with Cummings at Cuicuilco in Mexico and had earned his B.A. (1927) and M.A. (1928) under Cummings's direction. From 1930 to 1937 Haury worked for Harold S. Gladwin as assistant director at the Gila Pueblo Archaeological Foundation, surveying throughout Arizona and New Mexico and conducting excavations at several sites that re-sulted in the definition of several culture areas (see Reid and Whit-tlesey, this volume). In 1937, when the 77-year-old Byron Cummings retired as head of the Department of Archaeology, he contacted Haury, who had completed a Ph.D. at Harvard earlier that year, and offered him the job. Haury became head of the Department of Archaeology in 1937 at the age of 33 and the following year renamed it the Department of Anthropology. Cummings retained the directorship of the Arizona State Museum for one more year and Haury was appointed director of the museum in 1938 (Thompson 1995; Wilcox 2001). The following year, Haury offered his first field school in the Forestdale Valley on the Fort Apache Indian Reservation.

The goals of the Forestdale Valley Field School were twofold. First, because of his own experience with Gila Pueblo, Haury believed strongly in the importance of training students in fieldwork. The sec-ond goal was to test the viability of the Mogollon concept at the edge of what was considered to be the Mogollon area. Paul Martin was exca-vating at the SU Site in the Pine Lawn Valley, so Haury looked farther west. Based on his 1931 survey of the Forestdale Valley for Gila Pueblo, Haury had identified the Bear Ruin as the earliest site in the area. Exca-vations were conducted at this site in 1939 and 1940 and they produced tree-ring samples dating in the seventh and eighth centuries. From ex-cavations at Tla Kii during the 1940 and 1941 seasons came tree-ring dates in the eleventh and twelfth centuries (Haury 1985). The Bluff Site, excavated in 1941, turned out to be earliest of all. The small suite of tree-ring dates from the Bluff Site placed it in the third and fourth centuries, making it at that time the earliest dated site with ceramics in the Southwest. The Bluff Site provided Haury with the evidence for what he thought was long-term Mogollon presence in the Forestdale Valley. Thus, in three seasons, Haury launched his field school and ac-quired the data to help counter criticisms of his Mogollon concept, an idea that was repudiated by many archaeologists such as Earl Morris, A. V. Kidder, and J. O. Brew (Reid 1986; Whittlesey 1999).

Following World War II, Haury continued to pursue definition of the Mogollon with the establishment of the University of Arizona's Ar-chaeological Field School at Point of Pines on the San Carlos Apache Indian Reservation. The Forestdale facility had been a tent camp, but Point of Pines involved construction of a permanent base of 12 buildings, an investment in facilities that would be used for 15 years, from 1946 through 1960. Edward (Ned) Danson and Raymond Thompson were assistant directors for some of these years, with Thompson the resident acting director for the final years (Gifford and Morris 1985:402; Haury 1989:127, 130). Haury's (1989) monograph on the Point of Pines Field School describes the events of each summer—visitors, students, brushes with forest fires, and the difficulties of getting supplies and people into what was a particularly isolated area of Arizona—but only touches on the social and political contexts in which he worked.

One of the most important political factors was that the Point of Pines Field School was part of Haury's goal to establish a doctoral degree program in anthropology at the University of Arizona, a goal he began pursuing the very first year of his tenure at Arizona. The Ph.D. had become recognized as the necessary graduate degree in anthropology and by establishing a doctoral program at the University of Arizona, Haury ratcheted up the visibility of the University of Arizona in the eyes of local administrators as well as within the national anthropological community. As a Harvard graduate, Haury was able to co-opt the eastern establishment's criticisms of archaeologists such as Hewett and Cummings for his own purposes (Thompson 1995:651). The Ph.D. program at the University of Arizona was established in 1948 and the first two graduates were Charles C. Di Peso and Joe Ben Wheat. Wheat's (1953, 1954b, 1955) dissertation and subsequent monographs were based on field school excavations at Point of Pines. His work validated Haury's concept of the Mogollon, quelling criticisms that had largely come from archaeologists in eastern institutions.

A major success of the Point of Pines Field School was the intensive training that it provided for staff and students. Haury placed great value on research opportunities for students and Point of Pines was the best realization of that dream. A high proportion of students went on to become professional archaeologists, many returning as staff in future years. The staff was largely selected from the graduate student ranks of the growing Department of Anthropology at the University of Arizona. They were also selected from previous participants at the field school. For example, Raymond H. Thompson had been an undergraduate participant at the Point of Pines Field School in 1947 (Thompson 1991:12). In a career trajectory similar to Haury's, he completed his graduate work at Harvard University and then became field school director, head of the Department of Anthropology, and director of the Arizona State Museum.

Even with the many dissertations and master's theses that were published using Point of Pines Field School data, like the UNM/Chaco field schools, publication of the results did not keep pace with the large amount of excavated material (Haury 1989:125). By the time the field camp closed, 33 sites had been tested or more fully excavated (Haury 1989:Table 6.1). Many of these were the basis of published theses and dissertations, but most did not receive more widespread circulation. Major exceptions include Cienega Site (Haury 1957), Crooked Ridge Village (Wheat 1954b), Nantack Village (Breternitz 1959), AZ W:10:51 (Wendorf 1950), several cave sites (Gifford 1980), and Turkey Creek Pueblo (Lowell 1991). To a great degree, the lag in publication was because Haury's and Thompson's energies were spent during the academic year maintaining and expanding the many anthropological programs at the University of Arizona. Field directors during the summer, they were both consummate administrators during the academic year. Haury's decision to return to Snaketown in the 1964–1965 academic year and his subsequent write-up of that material permanently diverted his attention away from the Point of Pines material.

The last three years of the Point of Pines Field School marked a change in the funding structure for archaeology in the Southwest. In previous years, Haury had received support from the university, private donors, and private foundations such as the Wenner-Gren Foundation for Anthropological Research. But in 1958, National Science Foundation (NSF) funding was acquired. Haury was part of a NSF advisory group that had lobbied for archaeology to be funded within the social sciences. Point of Pines was one of the first projects to be supported by the NSF in the Southwest and it marked a transition in the epistemology and funding of many future field schools.

ARCHAEOLOGICAL FIELD SCHOOLS AND THE "NEW ARCHAEOLOGY": 1965–1980

Archaeology turned a significant corner in the mid-1960s with the advent of the "New Archaeology." Jobs in colleges and universities were plentiful and freshly minted Ph.D.s in archaeology, many of whom trained in the new theoretical approach, quickly populated university departments across the country. During the 1960s, the amount of funding for archaeology also increased. Within the NSF, archaeology as a proportion of anthropology awards increased rapidly from 1960 to 1968 (Yellen and Green 1985). A large number of these awards were for southwestern projects and many had a field school component.

Field schools figured prominently in the promulgation of the New Archaeology of the 1960s and early 1970s. Although neither Carter

Ranch nor Broken K Pueblo was excavated as part of field schools, they grew out of the collaboration of University of Chicago students and Field Museum anthropology researcher Paul S. Martin. Inspired by Lewis Binford, the Chicago students who worked with Martin included William Longacre and James Hill. These and other students would become the first wave of the New Archaeologists to be hired. Field schools became the means by which large excavation programs could be funded and the Southwest became a testing ground for the New Archaeology.

Longacre was hired as an assistant professor at the University of Arizona in 1964, the year after he completed his dissertation on Carter Ranch, specifically to take over the directorship of Arizona's Archaeological Field School as Thompson took over leadership of the Department of Anthropology and the Arizona State Museum. In 1962 Raymond Thompson had spent one season with the field school at the Ringo Site in southeastern Arizona (Johnson and Thompson 1963), which was followed the next year by the establishment of a field camp at Grasshopper that would remain in use for 30 years. Longacre took the reins during the 1965 season and he encouraged students and staff to apply the principles of the New Archaeology, including the use of an explicit research design, sampling, and hypothesis testing within a multidisciplinary framework. This interdisciplinary approach continued throughout Longacre's directorship of the field school (Longacre and Reid 1974:10; Longacre et al. 1982). In addition to its interdisciplinary focus, the field school's research goals were to understand climate change, social organization, economic organization, and stylistic interaction. These research issues were all explored in tandem with the pedagogical goals of field and laboratory training, interpretation, and "exposure to archaeological theory within its anthropological context" (Thompson and Longacre 1966:257).

Student participation from 1965 through 1971 at Grasshopper was bolstered by the NSF's Advanced Science Seminar Program, which funded travel, tuition, and fees for the enrolled students and made it one of the most competitive field schools in the country. The core of the field school was a student training program that continued Haury's formula of an intensive series of lectures and student research projects, a tradition continued under J. Jefferson Reid's directorship (1979–1992) and one that remains a part of the University of Arizona Archaeological Field School pedagogy today. Student projects conducted throughout the 30 years of the program became the germ for dozens of theses and dissertations on the Grasshopper material (Reid 1999).

The New Archaeology also significantly altered the way that Paul Martin approached his field projects. He explicitly changed the form of the questions that he asked and the structure of his summer program. He lost one long-time staff member, John Rinaldo, but gained several others, including many students and staff eager to bring the methods of the New Archaeology to the field. In 1965 Martin won a grant from the NSF's Undergraduate Research Participation Program (Martin 1974, 1975a:6). This support continued through 1971 (Martin 1975b:1). The field school was based out of Vernon, in east-central Arizona, just above the Mogollon Rim from the Fort Apache Indian Reservation not far from the Grasshopper Field School. There was, in fact, a good deal of interaction between these two field schools.

The flier advertising the Vernon field program had the header "New Perspectives in Archaeology," a direct acknowledgement of Binford's influence. This announcement clearly laid out the tenets of the New Archaeology, including the explanation of variability in human behavior, hypothesis testing, and the discovery of regularities that would allow prediction (Anonymous 1968; Martin and Plog 1969). Undergraduates attending the Vernon Field School were expected to read one work on the philosophy of science before they reached the field and once there, were expected to pursue an independent research problem (Anonymous 1968). Among the philosophers of science referenced were such authors as Carl Hempel, Thomas Kuhn, and Ernst Nagel. In 1968 Thomas Kuhn was one of the guest lecturers at the Vernon Field School (Figure 5.1). The staff that year, including Mark Leone, Fred Plog, and Ezra Zubrow, were convinced that they were part of a scientific revolution. They had invited Kuhn to help legitimize the New Archaeology. Michael Schiffer (personal communication 2002) was an undergraduate student that year and describes Kuhn's visit as exhilarating, but a distinct letdown for the staff. Kuhn did not think that the New Archaeology constituted a "true" scientific revolution.

Even if it was not part of a Kuhnian scientific revolution, the Vernon Field School encouraged a generation of undergraduates in southwestern archaeology, many of whom went on to graduate school and became professional archaeologists (including Norman Yoffee and Timothy Earle). Martin's approach was to create an intellectual climate in which students were encouraged to challenge past generalizations and graduate students participated in actually designing the research. Martin adhered to a scientific model, but he also recognized that science must be relevant, "bear social responsibility," and that "a value-free

Figure 5.1. The philosopher of science, Thomas Kuhn (far left) with the Vernon Field School, 1968. Courtesy of Michael Schiffer.

anthropology is a myth" (Martin 1975a:11). The social relevance of the Vietnam War era had been merged with processual archaeology.

One of the most important changes in archaeological field schools occurred in the late 1960s with the regular incorporation of survey techniques in the curricula. Survey data were compatible with the New Archaeology's focus on the relationship between environmental variability and settlement patterns. Fred Plog, in particular, advocated the use of archaeological survey to balance archaeologists' attention to large sites (Hantman and Schiffer 1995). He was able to convince a large number of southwestern archaeologists to cooperate in the investigation of hypotheses relating to settlement distributions. This group, known as the Southwestern Anthropological Research Group or SARG, brought together researchers to address the central question: Why are population aggregates located where they are? (Euler and Gumerman 1978; Gumerman 1971). Field schools directed by James Hill and Fred Plog in the Chevelon area; Watson, LeBlanc, and Redman in the El

Morro Valley; and R. G. Matson and William Lipe in the Cedar Mesa area were among the projects that contributed to the SARG database.

Another innovation in field school curricula was more directly related to cultural resources management (CRM). One of the first CRM projects in the Southwest, the Glen Canyon Project, actively incorporated students. The major contracts were split between the University of Utah and the Museum of Northern Arizona. Both institutions incorporated students as field assistants. Students from the University of Colorado also volunteered for the project during the summer months (Jennings 1966:4–5). The Glen Canyon Project ran from 1957 through 1963 and resulted in the training of many students in the archaeology of the Colorado Plateau and the exigencies of archaeology under contract.

In 1960 the Fort Burgwin Research Center and the Museum of New Mexico collaborated in the first field school explicitly designed to train students in "salvage archaeological techniques" (Eddy 1966:7). Students attended preliminary lectures, participated in archaeological excavations being conducted by the Museum of New Mexico in the Navajo Reservoir district, and then returned to Fort Burgwin for artifact analyses. Although short-lived, the expansion of the field school curriculum under Fred Wendorf was a harbinger of future training needs.

DIVERSIFICATION: FIELD SCHOOLS IN THE LATE TWENTIETH CENTURY

In the latter part of the twentieth century, field schools functioned as much for training students for jobs in cultural resources management as for potential academic positions. The shift from academic to applied contexts was reflected in where students obtained employment after their attendance at field schools as well as a small number of field schools that were part of CRM projects.

With a growing segment of students going into applied work, a number of CRM projects incorporated field schools in an innovative way, including the Black Mesa Archaeological Project (originally based out of Prescott College) and the Dolores Archaeological Project (DAP), conducted by the University of Colorado at Boulder with Washington State University as a principal subcontractor. Both universities incorporated field schools as a small part of their efforts on this very large project. The Washington State University field schools of 1979, 1980, and 1982 were codirected by William Lipe and Timothy Kohler. The curriculum was designed to meet the standards of the Society of Professional Archeologists (SOPA). Students worked in the field alongside experienced paid crew members during the first two years. Although this was successful, most students seemed to learn more in the third year when they worked on their own site at their own pace. Overall, this large project provided many opportunities for positive interactions between students and professionals in various fields of archaeology and environmental studies. This contributed to preparing students for later work in CRM or academic research (William D. Lipe, personal communication 2002).

The growing importance of public archaeology also led to non-university-based field schools. The most enduring of these in the Southwest is the Crow Canyon Archaeological Center. High school, college, and the out-of-school public alike all participate in these programs. Undergraduate and graduate students are more likely to be hired as interns, but the curriculum and structure of the program is based on a traditional field school model. The Crow Canyon program demonstrates how public outreach and education, research, and fund-raising can be balanced to achieve multiple goals.

Most field schools in the late twentieth century focused on incorporating students into research-based projects that were determined by the interests of their project directors. Research problems were, and still are, commonly generated by broader issues in archaeology, such as exchange, migration, identity, colonialism, household and community organization, and sociopolitical organization. In most cases, it would be impossible to differentiate the research design of a field school–based excavation project from any other. Fostering this synergy was the Society for American Archaeology's ruling as unethical field schools that did not have explicit research goals.

The funding for field schools has significantly changed during the past two decades. As university funding for field schools has dwindled, competition for external support has increased. Indeed, I would argue that the need for a combination of university and external support has significantly fueled the development of method and theory in southwestern field schools. Important sources of funding throughout the end of the twentieth century include the NSF, the National Geographic Society, and the Wenner-Gren Foundation for Anthropological Research. All of these require that research conducted in the context of field schools be problematized and explicitly tied to broader anthropological and archaeological issues.

Concluding Thoughts

In concluding this chapter, I offer the following observations on the impact of field schools on southwestern archaeology. First, as Gifford and Morris (1985) pointed out, most southwestern field schools have been located on the Colorado Plateau or the cool, highland transition zone between the plateau and basin and range country. The southern deserts were not seen as practical for training students, whose main time for fieldwork was during the summer. The contribution of field schools to Hohokam archaeology, therefore, has been minimal. This situation has been rectified more recently by a spring semester field school offered by Paul and Suzanne Fish through the University of Arizona in the Tucson Basin. A similar situation prevails for northern Mexico, but for other reasons. Excavation permits are not granted for training non-Mexican students on Mexican archaeological resources. This has limited the exposure of students, unless they are incorporated into standard research projects (Kelly and MacWilliams, this volume), to this important area of the American Southwest and the Mexican Northwest.

Second, although women were excluded from excavations at Cummings's first field school in the Four Corners, women's participation in field schools throughout the last 100 years has been high. One could argue that this is an area in which gender equity in archaeology has been fully achieved. Many field schools throughout the twentieth century included a large number of female staff, including the UNM Chaco Canyon Field School. Hewett was known for his support of female students such as Bertha Dutton, Florence Hawley (Ellis), and Marjorie Ferguson Lambert (Joiner 1992:56). Under Brand, a majority of the students were female in 12 out of 15 of the Chaco Canyon Field School seasons (Joiner 1992:58; Mathien 1992). Even if other projects showed a bias toward male students in the hiring of staff members, they tended to show gender equity in student participation. Toward the end of the twentieth century, female students have tended to outnumber male students and a large number of southwestern field school directors have been women. Recent examples include field schools of Arizona State University (Michelle Hegmon, Margaret Nelson, Katherine Spielmann), Grinnell College (Katherine Kamp), Michigan State University (Allison Rautman), Northern Illinois University (Winifred Creamer), Portland State University (Barbara Roth), Southern Methodist University (Patricia Crown), University of Arizona (Suzanne Fish, Barbara Mills, Lisa Young), University of Calgary (Jane Kelley), University of California–Santa Cruz (Judith Habicht-Mauche), University of Colorado (Catherine Cameron), University of New Mexico (Linda Cordell, Margaret Nelson, Ann Ramenofsky), and Western New Mexico University (Cynthia Bettison). Earlier examples include Cynthia Irwin-Williams (Eastern New Mexico Univeristy), Florence Hawley Ellis (University of New Mexico), and Frederica de Laguna (Bryn Mawr College).

Third, field schools in the Southwest over the past 100 years show a shift in the interaction between Native Americans and archaeologists. Early field schools employed tribal members as laborers, rather than as participants, more in line with the colonial model for archaeology practiced throughout the world. At the UNM/Chaco field school Native Americans dug while the students took notes, exposed and excavated burials, and conducted survey and mapping (Joiner 1992:52). Native American students were rarely incorporated, and usually not actively recruited, into most field schools until the end of the twentieth century. Even today, the number of Native American students who have attended archaeological field schools is very low. Several factors have precluded more widespread participation, including: 1) the cost of attending; 2) an image of archaeologists as "grave diggers"; and 3) the fact that those students who are interested in archaeology and heritage issues often find employment and learn archaeological techniques on the job (Mills 2000a).

Fourth, southwestern field schools demonstrate that pedagogy and research can be successfully combined (Cordell 1989b; Woodbury 1989). Field schools have played an important part in the development of archaeological method and theory, while at the same time demonstrating through practice how archaeology is done in the field. Most field schools in the Southwest are part of larger research projects, defined by the research interests of the project directors. Early field schools tended to focus on more particularistic goals, such as the development of sequences in different areas of the Southwest. This significantly changed in the 1960s with NSF support for archaeology. If field school directors were to compete for this funding, they needed to do more than simply offer a summer course. The scientific paradigm for archaeology significantly expanded in the New Archaeology, which, more than in any other area of the world, tested its ideas in the Southwest.

Fifth, field schools have been as much about training advanced student staff members as they have student participants. Graduate students learn new skills as staff members that prepare them to conduct their own field schools. In addition, they actively participate in the overall research program and have been responsible for bringing large amounts of field school excavation programs to publication.

Today, students who enroll in archaeological field schools in the
Southwest have a wide range of field opportunities to select from and
are using their skills from field schools in a number of different contexts.
The many possibilities for employment in cultural resources archaeology make field schools an important training ground. This is especially
true as CRM reaches maturity in the discipline and the demand for
trained field archaeologists continues. Opportunities to engage with
Native American communities are also increasing. As ethical, political,
and legal mandates for archaeological field schools converge, heritage
preservation and training of Native American archaeologists I hope
will become more common.

ACKNOWLEDGMENTS

My thanks to many colleagues who provided stories of and references
to field schools, including William Lipe, Art Jelenik, and R. Gwinn
Vivian. I couldn't include them all, but they were certainly fun to hear
about. Carol Gifford, William Longacre, J. Jefferson Reid, Michael
Schiffer, and Raymond Thompson are to be especially thanked for their
excellent comments. Finally, I thank Don Fowler and Linda Cordell for
their kind invitation to write this chapter.

6

The Development of Archaeology in Northwest Mexico

Jane H. Kelley and A. C. MacWilliams

Erik Reed created the much-quoted definition of the Greater Southwest as extending roughly from "Durango (Mexico) to Durango (Colorado), and from Las Vegas (New Mexico) to Las Vegas (Nevada)" (1951:428). Here we consider the archaeology of the two Mexican states of Chihuahua and Sonora (Figure 6.1). This area lies to the north of the conventional northern boundary of Mesoamerica, drawn through the Mexican states of Durango and Sinaloa, and to the south of the international border.

During the twentieth century, northwest Mexico was a region where archaeological research proceeded in fits and starts. Researchers quickly realized that Mexican cultivars and pottery-making knowledge bridged the distance between Mesoamerica and the Southwest, and that both areas bore important relationships to the Northwest. Given its proximity to the Southwest, archaeology in the Northwest has been profoundly affected by North American intellectual traditions in terms of research problems, methods, and individuals working on both sides of the international border. Mexican archaeologists, however, approach the region from a different perspective than foreigners. The Joint Casas Grandes Project that brought Mexican and Southwest archaeologists together four decades ago in the Casas Grandes Valley provides a model of transborder cooperation. During the past dozen years, growing ranks of investigators from Mexico and elsewhere have created a rapidly changing picture of archaeology in both Chihuahua and Sonora. Ongoing debates about how northwest Mexico sits between the complex societies of the south and middle level Ceramic period societies to the north is enriched by the Northwest being a meeting point of Mexican and North American intellectual traditions.

MEXICAN ARCHAEOLOGY

Mexican archaeology developed somewhat independently from archaeology elsewhere in North America (Benavides 2001; Bernal 1980; McGuire 2002; Oyuela-Caycedo et al. 1997; T. Patterson 1994; Politis 1995, 2003; Trigger 1989; Vasquez León 1994). After the 1910 Revolu-

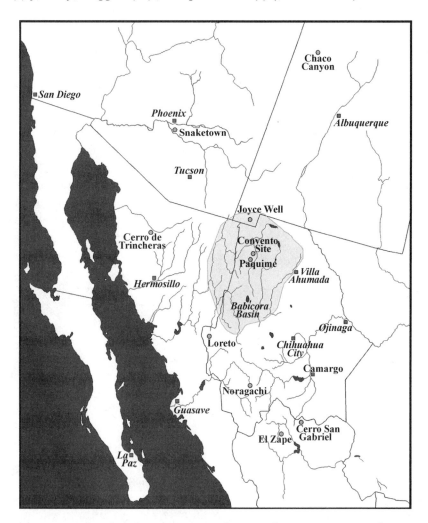

Figure 6.1. Map of northwest Mexico and surrounding regions. Drawn by A. C. MacWilliams.

tion, the Mexican government became interested in incorporating precolonial history into the national story. Indians and mestizos emerged from the revolutions as a prominent, participating segment of central and southern Mexican society (Lorenzo 1981:199) in a way never achieved in the United States or Canada. This inclusion fuelled the *indigenismo* movement of the 1920s and was given additional impetus under the administration of President Lazaro Cardenas in the 1930s (Politis 1995:204). Archaeology played a key role in linking the modern state of Mexico to precolonial history through the indigenismo movement (Fowler 1987:234).

Important philosophical and organizational structures developed during the early decades of the twentieth century—structures that continue to define Mexican archaeology. In spite of recurrent relationships between North American and Mexican archaeologists, such as the founding of the short-lived International School of Archaeology and Ethnology (Bernal 1980), Mexican archaeology always had important dimensions that set it apart from its northern neighbor. While being quite familiar with American views, intellectual stimulation for many Mexican scholars came from Europe, and especially from France, Spain, and Germany.

A strong historicist tradition developed early in the century in which sites appropriate for tourism and interpretive museums became a central focus (Trigger 1989:181). Vasquez León (1994:72) argues that this is something Mexico shares with south European countries and former colonies. The more than 150 sites with interpretive museums open to tourism are overwhelmingly located in central and southern Mexican monumental sites.

There is a long-standing evolutionary perspective in Mexican archaeology (Lorenzo 1981:201). T. Patterson (1994) wrote "An Appreciation" of social archaeology in Latin America in which he argues that this evolutionary perspective is modeled on various streams of intellectual Marxist thought beginning before the Russian Revolution. A stronger Marxist perspective emerged in a number of Latin American countries during the 1970s. This process was aided in Mexico by the earlier arrival of left-leaning academic refugees from the Spanish Civil War such as Angel Palerm, Pedro Armillas, and Pedro Carrasco (Benavides 2001:357; Politis 1995:220). A group of Latin American scholars met at the 1970 meeting of the International Congress of Americanists in Lima, followed by the Teotihuacán Reunion in 1975, and continued with the regular meetings of the Oaxtepec group through the 1980s. The Teotihuacán group, dominated by prominent Mexican archaeologists, lashed out at American New Archaeology as debasing Latin America under the rubric of *"culturas* folk*"* and as scientism that was incongruent with popular interests (Lorenzo et al. 1976:28, 32). The American New Archaeology of the 1960s and 1970s represented "politically neutral science which did not fit well with the socially and politically conscious archaeology" and which was flavored by North American imperialism (McGuire 1992:66; see also Benavides 2000).

Archaeology in Mexico has been strongly centralized for decades both at the educational and administrative levels. The Instituto Nacional de Antropología e Historia (INAH) was created by presidential decree late in 1938 and established in 1939. Within that body, the Consejo de Arqueología is the ultimate arbitrator of all archaeological work done in the country. Internal and foreign archaeological projects must be approved by the INAH and the *consejo* and must report their findings to the consejo. INAH-sponsored archaeology continues to be dominated by the

> maintenance, preservation, recordation of the archaeological patrimony... an enormous workload for these archaeologists, leaving very little time for "independent research." In this context most of the research budget goes to monumental archaeology projects, which will reinforce national identity and at the same time generate revenue through tourism [Oyuela-Caycedo et al. 1997:370].

INAH is not just peopled by anthropologists, archaeologists, and historians. Architects outnumber archaeologists.

The Escuela Nacional de Antropología e Historia (ENAH) is separate from the INAH. Originally headquartered on the upper floor of the old Museum of Anthropology on Moneda Street in Mexico City, it moved with that museum to the new quarters in Chapultepec Park. Branch schools of ENAH have been established outside of Mexico City. In addition to ENAH, the Universidad Nacional Autónimo de México (UNAM) and other colleges and universities offer anthropological and archaeological training with a wide range of perspectives being represented. The impact of such schools of thought on the *practice* of archaeology appears to be minimal because of INAH's mandates. Students who champion social archaeology and Marxism, for example, are likely to go to work for INAH, join projects approved by INAH, or leave the profession (Oyuela-Caycedo et al. 1997:370). ENAH and the universities such as UNAM are the main places where some forms of processualism as well as Marxism took root in the 1970s, and where French poststructuralism took root in the 1990s.

The legacy of this complex history is fully operative in the Northwest today through the permitting requirements of INAH and the consejo. Most Mexican archaeologists are trained in UNAM and ENAH in Mexico City, or in the regional ENAH schools. They are still strongly oriented to monumental sites, with little preparation for the kinds of sites found outside the boundaries of Mesoamerica. Archaeologists who come north often have to do on-the-job preparation for the different kinds of archaeology that they encounter. For students trained on monumental sites, artifact scatters and non-monumental architecture can be acquired skills. Fortunately, these skills are now being learned by Mexican students on a number of projects in Chihuahua and Sonora. McGuire (2002:181) contrasts the training of Mexican and American students working on the Cerro de Trincheras project in terms of conventions of excavation, definition of kinds of data to be collected, and stratigraphic interpretations.

Mexican Archaeology in Northwest Mexico

A common view of the vast area beyond the northern Mesoamerican boundary is exemplified in the closing chapter of Ignacio Bernal's *A History of Mexican Archaeology*:

> The north and the whole central area of the Republic of México, which lie outside of the frontiers of Mesoamerica, were a good deal neglected, owing in large part to the very peculiar nature of the archaeology of those regions. A few permanent centers excepted, the area contains no clearly defined sites to be explored. Researchers had therefore to investigate caves, woods and valleys for the scarcely visible traces of the wandering peoples who had once lived there, while primitive settlers had been few [Bernal 1980:180].

Mexican archaeologists often describe this region and the adjacent southwest United States as "Oasis America," "Aridoamerica," or the "Gran Chichimeca." Compared to tropical Mexico, this is a reasonable assessment.

Early contributions by Mexican scholars reflect the wider context of Mexican archaeology. What may have been the first professional Mexican archaeological foray into the Northwest occurred in 1911 during the Mexican Revolution when Carmen Alessio-Robles, among others, visited Paquimé (Brand 1933), establishing the practice of expeditionary viewing of the north from the center of the country. Almost from the outset, Mexican archaeologists integrated environmental considerations and geography into their interpretations. Alessio-Robles (1929) described the geography of northwest Chihuahua as integral to the archaeology, providing a foundation for explaining how numerous pueblo sites of irrigation farmers could thrive in arid land. This early environmental approach was seen as relatively passive in that climate provided some opportunities and not others. Eduardo Noguera (1930:5) offered a comparable view, suggesting that Casas Grandes sites coincided with an interval of wetter climate. Pedro Armillas (1969) linked the location of a shifting northern Mesoamerican frontier to climatic change. In 1943 the Third Mesa Redonda, entitled El Norte de México y el Sur de los Estados Unidos, had a session focused on the geography of the north.

INAH extended its network of regional centers into the north during the 1970s and 1980s. Until then, Mexican archaeologists were working from a homebase in central Mexico more distant than the starting points for many researchers coming from the adjacent United States. The establishment of the Sonora and Chihuahua centers, with the creation of full-time investigator positions allowed nonexpeditionary Mexican research programs to be established and sustained. However, regional INAH archaeologists are undertaking their projects in the face of rapid development and destruction of resources.

Recent Mexican research emphasizes multidisciplinary sources of information. For example, Polaco and Fabiola Guzmán (1997) identify fossil voles near the Medio period site of Galeana that they suggest may reflect a marshy habitat in the area at about A.D. 1300–1450 when the site was inhabited. Pearson and Sánchez Martínez (1990) summarize dendrochronological work at Cuarenta Casas in the Sierra Madre Occidental—a region with few absolute dates from archaeological sites. Macrobotanical analyses of samples from Olla Cave, located farther north in the sierra, is used by Montúfar López and Reyes Landa (1995) to make inferences about subsistence, with the conclusion that there are many similarities between the prehistoric occupants of Olla Cave and the modern Tarahumara diet. Within Mexican archaeology, multidisciplinary research is certainly not unique to the Northwest, but has its own importance because of perceptions about the harshness of northern deserts and absence of grand Mesoamerican-scale archaeology.

Research in or involving the Northwest has become increasingly varied intellectually as the region's archaeological resources are seen as a worthy research specialty, and as that research matures with increasing numbers of researchers. Among these interests, the important link between tourism and archaeological priorities is seen in Guevara Sánchez's work (1985) in providing detailed information about prominent site locations now identified as archaeological sites on tourist maps, continuing the tradition of integrating research with economic and ideological factors of the state. González Arratia (1985) provides an example of Marxist archaeology in the southwest corner of Chihuahua and adjoining Coahuila as she seeks theory for understanding social dynamics of production. Basic goals of archaeology such as detailed project reporting (Braniff 1985), chronology, and synthetic discussions of the region (e.g., Cabrero G. 1993; Márquez-Alameda 1990) are no less important to Mexican scholars than to those from elsewhere. Economic ties between regions continue to be of great interest, as is illustrated by Villalpando's (1988) study of shell networks.

Recent government-sponsored PROCEDE *ejido* surveys demonstrate the utility of having resident Mexican archaeologists in the north. The ejidos, or communally held lands, can now be sold—something that was prohibited until recent years. This radical change in government policy provided the impetus for the extensive surveys that have taken INAH archaeologists into every corner of both states.

FOREIGN ARCHAEOLOGY IN NORTHWEST MEXICO

Each period of foreign investigations in northwest Mexico reflects the dominant interests and attitudes of that time and the place of origin of the investigators. Carl Lumholtz and Adolph Bandelier were the first visitors to the Northwest with some anthropological background. Both belonged to a generation of scholarly explorers with interests in origins and evolutionary stages, in gathering extensive information on living peoples, and in describing prominent archaeological sites (Fowler 2000:97ff, 237). Bandelier (1892) drew attention to the rich Spanish language documentation that exists for areas previously held by Spain and Mexico. He also introduced some important methods to northwest Mexican archaeology such as skillful mapping of *cerros de trincheras* and submitting shell from Paquimé to a specialist to determine if it was from the Sea of Cortés. Lumholtz's (1902) account of his extensive travels through parts of Chihuahua and Sonora describes excavations, particularly in Cave Valley, and includes a rudimentary breakdown of Casas Grandes pottery.

Evolutionism gave way to grouping together geographically re-stricted groups of people or artifacts in the late nineteenth century (Trigger 1989:162). Northwest Mexico was usually, if vaguely, included in definitions of the Southwest culture area. This perception has distant roots in travelers such as Hardy (1829:466) and Bartlett (first published in 1854) who offered comparisons between Paquimé and ruins on the Gila River in Arizona and continued with reiterations from Bandelier (1892) and Kidder (1916:267). Holmes's (1914) culture area map sep-arates northwest Mexico from the southwest United States, but goes against what was becoming the prevailing view that the Casas Grandes area was part of the Southwest (Hewett 1908d), although not without differences (Kidder 1924). On the other side of the Sierra Madre Oc-cidental, Sauer and Brand (1931) suggested that Trincheras culture sites were at least Pueblo IV in age, and numerous investigators perceived important relationships between Sonoran cultures and the Hohokam in Arizona (Figures 6.2 and 6.3). Kirchhoff's (1954) definition of the Greater Southwest is, even today, widely used (see McGuire 2002).

With foreign investigators prone to seeing northwest Mexico as a continuation of familiar patterns from north of the border, the impe-tus for research often was pursuit of interests that were formulated in the Southwest, although Monroe Amsden (1928), who "merely set out to see what archaeological remains were to be found in northeastern Sonora," provides a refreshing contrast. As basic chronology and clas-sification were worked out for the Southwest, it was inevitable that such interests would draw archaeologists south.

Figure 6.2. View across the massive adobe Medio period walls of Paqui-mé, Chihuahua. Photo by A. C. MacWilliams.

Figure 6.3. Cerro de Trincheras, Sonora, looking south. Photo by A. C. MacWilliams.

Figure 6.4. E. B. "Ted" Sayles on survey in northwestern Chihuahua during the spring of 1933. Photo courtesy of the Arizona State Museum Photographic Archives.

During the late 1920s and the early 1930s several American archaeologists and geographers did extensive surveys in Chihuahua and Sonora, providing descriptions that provided regional coverage beyond the most impressive sites (Amsden 1928; Brand 1933; Ekholm 1939; Sauer and Brand 1931; Sayles 1936) (Figure 6.4). Sustained research in the Northwest failed to emerge from this promising flurry of research. Carey and Lister were unusual in returning to Chihuahua in the 1950s to follow up on their 1930s work. The enigmatic aura of large sites such as Paquimé and Cerro de Trincheras, created by a paucity of regional, contextual information, was somewhat subdued by these surveys and occasional excavations. Paquimé was no longer seen as the Vale of Aztlán, as Hewett (1923) had argued.

In keeping with the times, foreign archaeologists involved in northwest Mexico around the 1930s often found migration to be a useful explanation for what they did and did not observe. They were attracted to the areas within Chihuahua and Sonora having abundant, conspicuous late Ceramic period sites. Earlier sites were not sought with comparable diligence, leaving the apparent puzzle of where inhabitants of later sites originated. Migration was repeatedly invoked to explain the presence of later sites, especially where the argument seemed to dovetail with the disappearance of people elsewhere (Brand 1935; Gladwin 1936).

Figure 6.5. Donald D. Brand in 1969, some 40 years after his pioneering Chihuahua survey. Photo courtesy of the Department of Geography, University of Texas, Austin.

Over the next two decades, projects were intermittent in the Northwest, although important work in Cave Valley by Lister (1958) included the suggestion that Casas Grandes had Mogollon roots, and that the sierra may have served as a corridor of diffusion. Some notable applications of meticulous methods occurred during this interval. Carey (1931) graphed and compared pottery types by frequency from excavation levels. Brand (1935) used systematic collections to determine the distributions of pottery types in northwest Chihuahua. Brand (1938) used speciation of marine shell from the Sea of Cortés to discuss regional trade (Figure 6.5).

The course of archaeology in Chihuahua was redefined abruptly and profoundly with the start of the Joint Casas Grandes Project in 1958. This project represents a major landmark of cooperation between INAH and a foreign institution. Within a year, Charles C. Di Peso, director of the Amerind Foundation in Dragoon, Arizona, was using results of excavations in the Casas Grandes Valley to suggest at the Society for American Archaeology meetings that Toltec traders had shaped the course of events at Paquimé and throughout the region (Figure 6.6). Di Peso's 1968 chronology for northwest Chihuahua temporarily threatened to redefine the ceramic periods for the Southwest. These interpretations and others, such as the suggested origin of Gila Polychrome pottery in Chihuahua (Di Peso 1976), have been critiqued extensively in the ensuing years (Kelley and Villalpando 1996). His contributions to archaeology in Chihuahua greatly outweigh the controversial interpretations. The wealth of data published by Di Peso (1974) and colleagues includes many achievements with few precedents in Chihuahua archaeology, including extensive tree-ring dating (later revised by Dean and Ravesloot [1993]), the first radiocarbon dates from the entire state, provenience studies, the most systematic treatment of Chihuahuan pottery to date, excavation data from pre-Puebloan open sites, and the first solid sequence for the region.

Eduardo Contreras, the INAH representative on the project, supervised major restoration work at Paquimé, very much in keeping with the Mexican practice of making archaeological sites accessible to the

*Figure 6.6. Charles Di Peso, codirector of the Joint Casas
Grandes Project from 1959 to 1961. Photo courtesy of the
Arizona State Museum Photographic Archives.*

populace (Contreras 1970). The 1995 opening of the Museo de las Culturas del Norte at the site of Paquimé, subsequently named a World
Heritage Site, reflects the growing importance of the north within Mexico. The site itself is open for public touring; it is presently under the
care of Eduardo Gamboa, an INAH archaeologist trained in Italy in
architectural reconstruction. The legacy of this project serves both foreign and Mexican approaches to archaeology.

Research in the interior of Sonora during the 1970s became a
proving ground for then current theories, with some thought provok-
ing results. In his 1980 paper, Pailes endorsed logical-positivism, general systems theory, and world systems theory in reporting a major
survey along the Río Sonora. He suggested that eastern Sonora was
once a frontier of Paquimé. Pailes and Reff (1985) describe Paquimé
as an urban trading center that ultimately collapsed because of difficulties in importing goods from Mesoamerica. Interestingly they conclude that residents of Paquimé could not gain control of surrounding
local economies, and even stimulated their independent development.
Di Peso (1983), influenced by this work in Sonora (see McGuire 1993),
also applied a world systems theory position to explain what he considered to be guiding Mesoamerica relations with the north. Subsequent

assertions that world systems theory provides a basis for understanding Mesoamerican-Northwest relations (e.g., Braniff 1995) have drawn minimal interest from archaeologists active in northwest Mexico.

Riley (1985) suggests that at the time of contact in the mid-1500s there was probably a series of political units (he shows nine "statelets" on a map), each confined to a river valley, centred around primate towns. He believed that these statelets were a response to the breakup of Casas Grandes. Doolittle (1988:60), who also supports the idea of statelets, favors local development. McGuire and Villalpando (1989) have doubts about the existence of the Sonoran statelets, believing that the population estimates central to this argument are inaccurate.

More recently, a widening range of theory has been applied to understanding archaeology in the Northwest. Peer-polity interaction has been used to explain the working of midlevel societies in Chihuahua (Minnis 1989) and Sonora in the Cerro de Trincheras area (McGuire et al. 1994), as has prestige exchange (Bradley 1999; Pailes 1990; Vargas 1995). In the latter framework, elite individuals gain or maintain power through access to rare resources. This is an intriguing concept given the abundance of marine shell found by Di Peso and colleagues at Paquimé. González Arratia (1991) focuses on archaeological evidence of the activities of women in the Bolson de Mapimi. Douglas and Quijada López (2000) are providing new information from eastern Sonora, including evidence of the presence of Viejo period remains of the Chihuahua or Casas Grandes culture in that area. Within Chihuahua, recent stylistic analyses have produced insightful results referring to both pottery (VanPool 2002), and rock art (Mendiola Galván 1997; Schaafsma 1997). Ethnography and archaeology have never been easily separated in northwest Mexico due to the rich colonial records and ethnographies of surviving indigenous groups. Ethnoarchaeological work continues (e.g., Graham 1993; Lewenstein and Sánchez B. 1991).

Sustained survey and excavations around Paquimé have enabled Whalen and Minnis (2001) to provide substantial contributions to an understanding of the region. This work has introduced many important approaches for investigating midlevel societies into northwest Mexico's archaeology. Approaching the Medio period of northwest Chihuahua as a regional system, with an underpinning of substantial settlement distribution data, places Paquimé into a context that does not require intervention from afar (Whalen and Minnis 2001:205). Other projects involving the Museum of New Mexico, and the University of New

Mexico, INAH, and UNAM are investigating other parts of the regional system (see Cruz et al. 2004).

Projects are spreading out into previously uninvestigated, or barely investigated, areas such as west-central Chihuahua where the Proyecto Arqueológico Chihuahua has documented both Viejo and Medio period sites on the southern edge of the Chihuahua or Casas Grandes culture (Kelley et al. 1999) (Figure 6.7), as well as documenting a culture characterized by small agricultural hamlets located to the south of the Chihuahua culture (MacWilliams 2001).

However, it should be remembered that large parts of northwest Mexico may lack the prehistoric social organizations centered around pueblos such as those so central to definitions of the Southwest (see McGuire 2002). These areas, particularly in the south approaching Mesoamerican territory, may precipitate questions that Southwest archaeology does not anticipate.

Several topics have retained dominating interest throughout the development of archaeology in northwest Mexico, because of their wide-reaching anthropological interest. The northward spread of agriculture, particularly involving maize, from southern Mexico is one of these topics. Chihuahua and Sonora are between the area of origin and the southwest United States, where corn agriculture predates 3000 B.P. Recent results from Cerro Juanaqueña, near Janos, Chihuahua, reveal the presence of maize, at large cerro de trincheras sites, by approximately 3,100 years ago (Hard and Roney 1998). Carpenter

Figure 6.7. Pit house at the Calderon site (Ch-254) in the Upper Santa Maria Valley, 1999. The first Viejo period site investigated since Charles Di Peso's work at the Convento Site. Photo courtesy of Proyecto Arqueológico Chihuahua.

and coauthors (1999:10) have dated maize from La Playa in Sonora to about 2200 B.P. Routes and processes by which agriculture using Mexican cultivars spread into the southwest United States continue to be debated. At various times in the past the Sonoran coastal plain (Beals 1943:249) and the Sierra Madre Occidental (Haury 1962:113; Lister 1958:115) have been suggested as routes for this process. These alternatives all involve northwest Mexico in an event of importance over a much larger area.

A second, overlapping research theme that is as old as archaeological research in northwest Mexico concerns defining the relationships which existed between Mesoamerica and the Northwest and the adjacent United States. Interest in this topic is predominantly within a narrow time frame of the final centuries before Spaniards arrived, and in reference to the identified midlevel societies of the region. Consequently, the southern halves of both states are not really considered in the numerous discussions of the topic.

Unquestionably there are objects and representations that point to origins and/or relationships to West Mexico and Mesoamerica. These occur not only in northwest Mexico, but in the Southwest. These manifestations of Mesoamerican "influence" contribute to recognizing the Northwest and Southwest as parts of a larger region. What they mean about development, social organization, and beliefs in the north remains unresolved. Southwestern archaeologists have been faced with reasons to consider this issue any number of times (cf. Ferdon 1955; Mathien and McGuire 1965), but this was particularly the case during the years that Di Peso argued that the north was part of Mesoamerica. David Wilcox (1986) and David Phillips (2002) analyze variant models of relationships between the two areas. Phillips defines the "Gap," the "Corridor," the "Migration," the "Pochteca," and the "World Systems" models. He regards the Gap and Corridor models as products of extremely incomplete information. Wilcox and Phillips both argue for multiple modes of cultural exchange. Similarly, McGuire (2002) views the Northwest as a web of relationships.

An intriguing sidelight is the division between who is currently most actively interested in Mesoamerican-Southwestern contacts and who is not. Those working actively in the Northwest focus more on local and regional understanding, while those who are most interested in long distance relationships tend to work outside Chihuahua and Sonora (see, for example, Carot 2000; Foster and Gorenstein 2000; Kelley 1980, 2000; Reyman 1995; Weigand and Weigand 2000). Few archaeologists have enough background in both areas to make in-depth studies about the two ends of the continuum. Ben Nelson, who has worked in both Mesoamerica and the Southwest, compares complexity, hierarchy, and scale between La Quemada in Zacatecas and Chaco Canyon, New Mexico (Nelson 1995). He concludes that although Chaco Canyon appears to have been organized on a larger geographical scale than La Quemada, the latter system was more hierarchically organized.

INTERNATIONAL COOPERATION AND RELATIONSHIPS

Important relationships between Mexicans and Americans existed throughout the twentieth century. A long history of international cooperation has often involved Mexican archaeologists providing foreign scholars with extensive, practical help. For example, Sayles (1933) depended on Eduardo Noguera to arrange export of sherd collections. A fair number of Mexicans have been trained in the United States (and more recently, in Canada). Eduardo Noguera went to Harvard and Manuel Gamio attended Columbia. The Tercera Reunión de Mesa Redonda of the Sociedad Mexicana de Antropología, held in Mexico City during 1943, brought together many people from both sides of the border to focus on the state of knowledge about northwest Mexico, the southern United States, and Mesoamerica in the context of relationships between regions. With the recent surge of research in the Northwest, other cross-border meetings such as the 1991 Pecos Conference held in Casa Grande and the 1998 Southwest Symposium held in Hermosillo focus on the region and follow the Mesa Redonda precedent of including participants from within and outside of Mexico. The increasing number of joint projects and the mobility of both foreign and Mexican students between projects results in improved access to the theories, methods, and goals of the archaeologies from both sides of the border.

SUMMARY

More than a century after archaeological work began in northwest Mexico, large sections of Chihuahua and Sonora remain practically untouched. Investigations have occurred predominantly in northwestern Chihuahua and a few regions within Sonora. This situation is changing rapidly through the widespread ejido surveys and as new projects expand into less studied corners of the area. Important archaeological similarities between northwest Mexico and the southwest United States are not in question. Although the relationships between these regions and Mesoamerica are unlikely to be accepted as J. Charles Kelley and Di Peso wanted (Figure 6.7), any such inferences will be increasingly well grounded in improved knowledge of the Northwest. The Northwest is becoming a place with its own range of priorities and questions. Increasingly, developments in the Northwest will inform directions in the Southwest.

ACKNOWLEDGMENTS

David Kelley, David Phillips, Andrea Freeman, Alice Kehoe, and Joe Stewart read drafts of this paper and offered useful comments. INAH, the Consejo de Arqueología, and the INAH regional centers in Chihuahua and Sonora permitted our work and extended many courtesies and kindnesses. We have had seminal discussions with the coterie of archaeologists now working in the Northwest. The Proyecto Arqueológico Chihuahua, with which we were both associated, was funded by the Social Sciences and Humanities Research Council of Canada. Linda Cordell and Don Fowler invited us to participate in the celebration of a century of southwestern archaeology at the 2001 meetings of the American Anthropological Association. Our thanks to all.

7

From the Academy to the Private Sector: CRM's Rapid Transformation within the Archaeological Profession

William H. Doelle and David A. Phillips Jr.

Archaeology had its origins in museums, universities, and government agencies. Over the first two-thirds of the twentieth century, these institutions were sufficiently dynamic to manage labor-absorbing projects for the Works Progress Administration (WPA), carry out the River Basin Surveys, and develop reservoir salvage and highway salvage programs. A tremendous amount of archaeology was accomplished through creative programs that involved government partnerships with museums and universities. Then, in two decades, there was a dramatic shift to private sector dominance of compliance-driven and contract-funded research. There are no authoritative figures on the scale of private sector archaeology, but it seems likely that it is a quarter-billion-dollar per year enterprise. This is based on some very rough calculations. First, there are nearly 25 firms that are members of the American Cultural Resource Association (ACRA) as "large firms" that do $3 million or more worth of business per year. Second, because not all large firms are members of ACRA and there are a myriad of smaller private firms, it seems likely that the more than $75 million in annual business of the large ACRA member firms is less than one-third of the national total. Multiplying these fuzzy numbers and assumptions yields a figure of roughly $250 million per year. Even though the scale of private sector archaeology is not precisely defined, the magnitude is clearly large, and it has become large within a relatively short time frame.

To better understand this transformation, we apply three different but complementary perspectives. First, we discuss changes in legal, institutional, and financial frameworks that helped plant the seeds for the rapid emergence of private sector CRM. Second, we examine statistical data that help define the transformation in objective terms. Third, we look at this transformation through the eyes of individuals who made it happen. These include the authors but also about two dozen other individuals who pioneered private sector archaeology in the American Southwest.

LEGAL, INSTITUTIONAL, AND FINANCIAL CHANGES

In the second half of the 1900s, the National Historic Preservation Act of 1966, the National Environmental Policy Act of 1969, and the Archaeological and Historical Preservation Act of 1974 (the Moss-Bennett Act) touched off a massive expansion of archaeology in this country. Archaeology was increasingly funded by contracts issued to achieve compliance with one or more of these laws. In the Southwest, though, there were already strong institutional frameworks for contract archaeology, due to the Highway Salvage programs started under the authority of the Antiquities Act of 1906 (Wasley 1957). New Mexico had the first program of this kind; since 1954 the state highway department has continuously funded research by the Museum of New Mexico. In 1955 a similar program was started in Arizona, where work assignments were based on the traditional research areas of the Museum of Northern Arizona and the Arizona State Museum. The program was later consolidated at the Arizona State Museum.

King et al. (1977) provide an overview of historic preservation legislation and changes in the archaeological discipline during the 1960s and 1970s. They argue that the "salvage archaeology" philosophy, which originated in the 1930s, emphasized rapid gathering of data prior to major construction projects, with little subsequent attention to analysis and reporting. Sooner or later this approach was bound to collide with the "New Archaeology" that developed in the 1960s, given the latter's emphasis on written research designs, broad analytical approaches, and interpreting past human behavior in ecological terms. Such approaches required larger budgets than those fueling the salvage mentality developed in the 1930s.

King et al. (1977) further note that the New Archaeology developed largely through funding from the National Science Foundation (NSF). The NSF began its support for archaeology in 1954 (Casteel 1980), and by the 1960s it had become a major source of archaeological research dollars. By 1980, however, an *American Antiquity* article by Richard Casteel (1980:170) concluded that the "NSF may soon cease to be a viable source of funds for scientific research in the area of domestic archaeology if recent trends continue." Just five years later, in the same journal, Yellen and Greene (1985:333) found that "in 1983 the level of funding [from NSF] had fallen to only one third of a high reach[ed] in 1968." Meanwhile, MacDonald (1976:vii) stated that "the employment situation in archaeology has steadily deteriorated in the past few years. As recently as five years ago the job prospects of a bright young doctoral student were quite good; a similar situation is unlikely to recur in the future." There is good reason to believe that beginning in the late 1970s, graduate students were not hearing optimistic stories about the opportunities that they would find upon graduation.

Even as funding and jobs for academic archaeology began to ebb, the situation in contract-based archaeology grew more hopeful. In Arizona the original Highway Salvage Program had received only minimal funding for conducting analyses and preparation of reports but in 1972, the Arizona State Museum was able to start a new and better funded program, the Cultural Resource Management Section. In the early 1970s, Arizona State University and the Museum of Northern Arizona began to take on similar contract-based archaeology projects. The Office of Contract Archeology was established at the University of New Mexico by 1973, and the Cultural Resource Management Division was in place at New Mexico State University by 1974. This institutional reflex was an old one: for decades, institutions had responded to new funding opportunities by creating special programs. Two things were different about the new programs, however. First, they were staffed by current or recent students who used the programs as a lab for the New Archaeology they had just learned. Second, the programs functioned like small businesses within the larger institutional setting. For example, the Cultural Resource Management Section (later called a division) at the Arizona State Museum had its own overhead rate to support bookkeeping and other administrative functions that it could not count on the university to provide. The university's standard overhead rate was figured on top of this internal overhead. These small business units grew over time, and the overhead money that they brought into their parent institutions was viewed positively by university administrators. However, only a small fraction of the money trickled back down to the units that produced it.

There were also legal accommodations that were essential to the transformation. In Arizona, for example, the State Antiquities Act did not allow for issuing of permits to private, for-profit organizations. While Raymond Thompson (then director of the Arizona State Museum) might have used this situation to exclude for-profit firms from state lands, in 1983 he asked a friendly legislator to sponsor a bill that would "modernize the language" of the State Antiquities Act. A significant barrier to private sector archaeology was thereby eliminated.

Another hurdle for contract-based archaeology was the requirement for curation of notes, maps, photographs, and artifacts "in perpetuity." The fledgling private firms could not be trusted to carry out that obligation, yet they were beginning to generate large volumes of collections and notes. Curation could have been a fatal conundrum for private firms. The Arizona State Museum and the Museum of New Mexico both took lead roles in providing curatorial services to private firms. The way for this was smoothed by museums' long-standing experience in accepting collections and archives from private donors, so the biggest institutional change was to begin charging for curatorial services. Fortunately, museums were also good at soliciting and accepting other people's money.

Another important addition was the use of competitive bidding in the archaeological procurement process, especially by federal agencies such as the National Park Service. At least through the 1960s, federal CRM funds were typically disbursed through intergovernmental agreements or through sole-source contracts with nonprofit institutions. Given the limited number of providers of archaeological research services, factors such as location and previous research history were used to determine recipients of funds. For private researchers to gain access to this funding, it became necessary to apply existing competitive procurement processes to archaeology. Universities and museums unwittingly helped trigger the change, because by the early 1970s the amounts of money involved led to the breakdown of old unwritten agreements under which institutions carved out exclusive research "turfs." Once these institutions began to compete with each other for lucrative research contracts, the way was opened for the private sector to join the chase.

STATISTICAL TRENDS

Having defined some of the structural changes behind the emergence of private sector archaeology, we turn to data that document when and how the transformation occurred. The data for our analysis come from the New Mexico Cultural Resources Information System (NMCRIS, pronounced "Nim-Kriss") online database of more than 70,000 archaeological activities in the state of New Mexico, maintained by the Archaeological Records Management Section (ARMS) of the New Mexico Historic Preservation Division. The data reflect all forms of archaeology, CRM derived or not. Also, for the period being studied, NMCRIS is heavily biased towards survey projects over other forms of archaeological activity. Thus, while this database has its limits, NMCRIS allowed us to examine trends across an entire state, using highly structured and easily retrieved data.

We have divided the practitioners of archaeology into five categories: 1) for-profit enterprises; 2) nonprofit enterprises whose primary purpose is to do CRM; 3) governments; 4) institutions (mostly universities and museums); and 5) archaeological societies/miscellaneous. From Figure 7.1 it is clear that for most types of organizations, the number of entities involved in archaeology has been more or less static. The exception is for-profit enterprises, which from 1971 to 1995 went from almost nonexistent to numerically dominant. Admittedly, Figure 7.1 conceals an important fact: while the number of governments doing archaeology is almost unchanged, many governments have more branches doing archaeology than they once did.

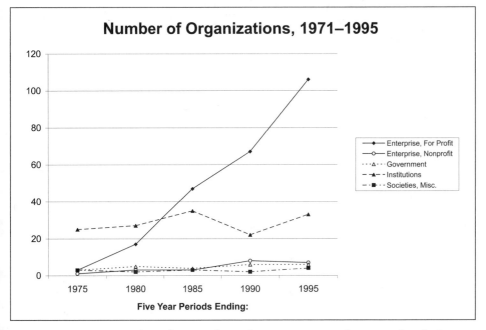

Figure 7.1. Temporal trends in numbers of organizations conducting archaeological projects in New Mexico between 1971 and 1995.

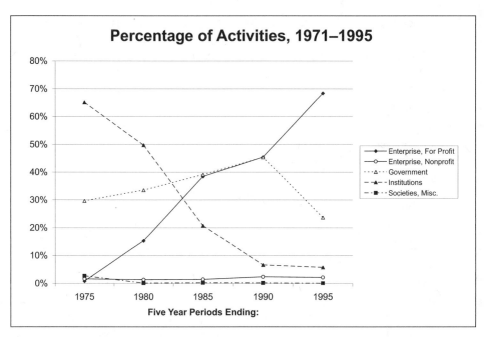

Figure 7.2. Temporal trends in percentages of activities performed by different types of archaeological organizations in New Mexico.

Tracking the number of organizations working in New Mexico does not provide a sufficient measure of how work was distributed across the different organizational types. Fortunately, the NMCRIS data indicate how many registered activities were underway at a particular moment (though some activities may have lasted through more than one analytical period), which allows a comparison of activity levels by type of organization (Figure 7.2). It is clear from Figure 7.2 that as of the early 1970s, universities and museums conducted the lion's share of archaeological activities in New Mexico; governments had a smaller but still sizeable piece of the action; and no one else was a contender. A decade later the for-profit sector had displaced the universities and museums but government was more than holding its own. A decade after that, universities and museums were only minor players, government was conducting fewer activities, and the for-profit entities had taken over the dominant position once held by universities and museums.

Figures 7.1 and 7.2 show *what* happened; now we consider *why* it happened. Figure 7.3 shows the phenomenal rise in number of registered activities from the early 1970s through the early 1990s; during this period the number of activities increased over 3,000 percent! We believe that this explosion in archaeological work, fostered by new laws, is the primary factor behind the transformation of the for-profit sector from a curiosity to the most active part of the profession. Examination of Figure 7.4 shows that this rapid growth had a differential effect on the various organization types involved in archaeology. As late as 1980, everyone but

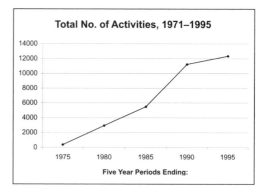

Figure 7.3. The steady increase in the total number of archaeological activities in New Mexico.

the archaeological societies responded to the growing need for CRM by taking on more projects. Then, in the early 1980s, universities and museums went the other way, actually doing fewer projects. Given the institutional goals and organizational constraints of universities and museums, endless growth was neither necessary nor desirable; indeed, cutting back on CRM efforts probably freed up space, administrative support staff, and other resources for the core purposes of the institu-

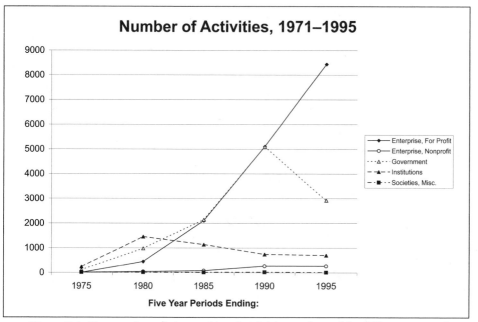

Figure 7.4. Temporal trends in number of activities performed by different types of archaeological projects in New Mexico.

tions. In contrast, governments continued to increase their activity for another decade as they tried to match the growth in need. In the early 1990s this trend was also reversed, as governments apparently decided that it was easier to push off some of the work on others. It is noteworthy, though, that government is the only not-for-profit organization type that continues to have a substantial piece of the pie. Finally, there is the for-profit sector, which shows continuous strong growth. Faced with a rapid and sustained growth in the need for a specific service, universities and museums and even governments were responsive to a point, but only the private sector kept expanding to meet the need.

Still, it might not have turned out this way. The rapid expansion of the private sector was based on more than the simple growth indicated by Figure 7.3; the specific requirements for complying with Section 106 of the National Historic Preservation Act and other laws fostered a kind of archaeology for which small businesses were especially suited. We examined a sample of 204 registered activities between 1971 and 1995, and we found that 188 of the cases in our sample were archaeological surveys. Because the early NMCRIS data are biased towards surveys, it is possible that the frequency of surveys was not quite as high as the 92 percent rate that our sample suggests, but it seems safe to say that at least 80 percent of CRM projects during this period were, in fact, surveys. Thus, the new historic preservation laws generated a heavy

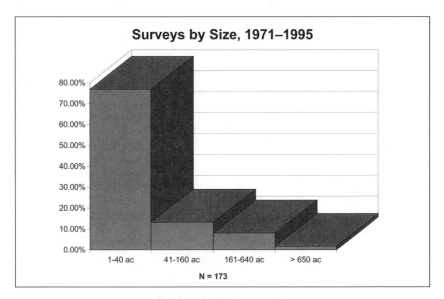

Figure 7.5. Frequencies of archaeological surveys by size in acres.

emphasis on projects that could be done with a minimum of equipment and special expertise. Moreover, as Figure 7.5 shows, most of those surveys were small enough to be done by a single person. Figure 7.5 is based on a sample of 173 registered surveys with known acreage; the mean is 71 acres but the median is only 8 acres! If CRM in the 1970s and 1980s was mostly small surveys, we can see how small private enterprises could compete with big institutions—and why many universities and museums might not even be interested in competing for such work. CRM companies also did large, elaborate projects, of course, but a steady diet of small surveys probably nurtured the private sector until it could compete for any project.

In summary, the NMCRIS data objectively document the emergence of for-profit enterprises as the dominant organizational type in CRM. They also indicate the factors that helped ensure the survival of archaeologists who chose that route. The data we used are from New Mexico, but similar circumstances prevailed across the Southwest. For a fuller picture of what happened, we consider what founders of private sector firms have to say about their motivations and experiences.

The Inside Story

In 2001 we sent a questionnaire to 28 individuals who established firms in Arizona or New Mexico between 1970 and 1990 (Figure 7.6). We summarize the responses received from 15 persons. Of these 15 individuals, 14 are still heads of firms or CRM divisions within larger multidisciplinary firms. At first glance a survey of 15 persons may seem trivial. However, consider the following: First, most of these firms were started in the decade from 1975 to 1985. Second, total employment of all 15 firms at startup was only 30 persons. Third, the remaining 14 individuals today employ over 275 full-time personnel in their archaeological enterprises. The magnitude of that accomplishment helps this small sample to carry real weight.

The respondents to our survey include 2.5 times as many men as women, but there is an even balance between M.A.s and Ph.D.s. In numbers, that is two female Ph.D.s and two female M.A.s; six male Ph.D.s and five male M.A.s.

It is interesting to see when people started their firms relative to when they received their highest professional degree. There appear to be two groups, one early and one late. Members of the "early" group established their firm within four years of getting their degree, while those in the "late" group started their business an average of 12 years

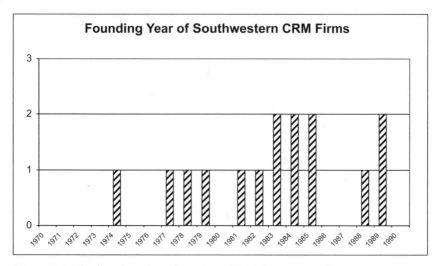

Figure 7.6. The founding dates for private CRM firms responding to our survey.

after receiving an advanced degree. One firm was actually started by several graduate students who found that their university teaching assistantships were running out. In the short run they were able to achieve a higher income than the $200 per month their teaching assistant jobs earned them. This case is the sole example of fairly inexperienced persons starting up a firm. In every other case, those who started a firm had multiple years of work in other CRM settings. A common theme was that the negative experience that an individual had working in another CRM or related job led them to feel that they could do it better on their own.

The average age of the early group was 32 years, while the late group averaged 43 years of age when they founded their company. The average age of the company for these groups is almost the same—19 for the early group and 17 for the late group—but the current size of the firms in these two groups is dramatically different. The early group has an average of 29 employees, whereas only one firm in the late group currently has more than three employees. The early group is dominated by Ph.D.s (75 percent), while the late group is predominantly M.A.s (83 percent). From this information it seems reasonable to generalize that the so-called early group represents young Ph.D.s who used the opportunities of a growing CRM market to build sizable firms, whereas the late group represents older M.A.s who took the opportunity to use their education and previous experience to gain security and independence by establishing a small firm and keeping it manageable.

So, what do these people say motivated them to go into private sector consulting? The questionnaire asked them to rank five potential motivations—each on a scale of 1 to 5, where 1 is low and 5 is high. The highest-ranking reason given was a desire for independence, which scored 4.2 out of 5. Next was the ability to pursue personal research interests, at 3.8, followed by a desire to innovate, at 3.6. Control over where one lived averaged 3.0, and financial expectations were the weakest motivator at 2.4.

In general these folks appear pretty idealistic. They value their independence highly, want to pursue research, and are not all that motivated by money. A large number also expressed how naïve they were—freely admitting that they had no idea ahead of time how hard running their own business would be.

Given the risks involved in starting a new business, it is interesting that nearly 50 percent of the founders reported that they achieved a confidence that their firms would succeed after only a single year of being in business. For others in our sample their early years in business were much more stressful, and overall our respondents took an average of almost three years to feel comfortable that they would succeed.

It is also striking that there is not evidence of large numbers of failed firms on the brief historical landscape that we are considering. Our best guess is that small, private firms had a strong competitive advantage within a growing market. The first competitive advantage was structural. Universities are bureaucratic structures geared to hiring permanent staff or filling positions that fit into the academic year. Lawyers, multiple layers of approval, and high overhead rates all contribute to institutional inefficiency. The new small firms that emerged were near opposites. They could move rapidly, usually having only one decision maker. Furthermore, for some private sector clients, such as oil and gas companies, small, private firms were an attractive option because they were more comfortable with other for-profit concerns than with "ivory tower" institutions.

The second competitive advantage may have been motivational. Directors of university and museum CRM programs often had tenure or other "hard-funded" positions within state or other institutional budgets. Firm owners not only lacked tenure, they could not put a meal on their tables if they failed to do their job. Furthermore, as owners, their personal reputation and integrity were on the line over everything they and their company did. The power of such motivations may not be obvious to those who have not been there, but we can underscore that they are huge.

To conclude, we have shown that the rapid emergence of private sector archaeology would not have happened without changes in the laws, institutional frameworks, and funding for archaeological studies. At the same time, it was necessary for individuals to recognize the opportunities inherent in those changes, and to parlay those opportunities into successful enterprises. If, at the outset, the difficulties and dangers had been more obvious, we suspect that fewer individuals would have pursued careers in the private sector. Still, the choices were made, the careers were pursued, and archaeology is different than it was a few decades ago. When we observe the rapid emergence of private sector archaeology, we are really talking about a change that took place among a single generation of archaeologists. Understanding why they made that change requires that we appreciate that generation's subjective outlook and experience even as we consider the objective changes in the broader context in which they acted.

THE FUTURE?

In closing, it is important to look toward a major event that is looming on the near horizon—the retirement of the pioneers who established private firms about two decades ago. The transition that we have discussed was relatively rapid, given the historical trajectory of the discipline of archaeology. The entrepreneurs who were willing to take on the risks of moving into a new institutional setting to conduct archaeology have almost always had a strong personal role in the success of their company. Many learned on the job and grew their firms "a little bit bigger" or "a lot bigger." These firm owners are now beginning to wonder how they are going to deal with the succession process as their company moves from their ownership to someone else's. In the two years since the first draft of this paper was prepared, we have noted an increased pace of discussion of this topic among our colleagues, and at least one firm represented in our survey has been sold. Making the transition from a founder to a new owner is a tremendous challenge, and it is not at all clear how well the existing firms will fare. What this does portend is that the next decade will be one of continuing change. For those looking to a career in CRM, there are still significant opportunities for those with an entrepreneurial spirit, because it is a near certainty that a number of firms will not meet the challenges that are about to face them. It is also a safe bet that the private sector will respond rapidly to change, so we feel comfortable in predicting that the private sector will continue to be the dominant player in the archaeological arena for at least several more decades.

8

Southwest Archaeology Today with an Eye to the Future

Linda S. Cordell

Compared to other parts of North America, the Southwest is unique for its combination of culturally diverse, vibrant indigenous peoples, visible and accessible archaeological resources, and abundant publicly owned land. These provide the context and texture of the archaeology that is accomplished there today. The reasons for its archaeological uniqueness are rooted in the physical environment of the region which has implications for the way research is envisioned and carried out.

The Southwest is a land of contrasts and diversity united by an arid climate. The Southwest encompasses portions of several different physiographic provinces, climate zones, and vegetation provinces. Its ancestral Native American inhabitants were not united by a single language or political system. They were united by their ability to cultivate indigenous American crops in an environment that was and is barely suitable for horticulture. Most of the Southwest is an inhospitable land for farming with Euro-American technology. As Josiah Gregg, assessing the commercial potential of New Mexico in 1844, noted, it "possesses but a few of those natural advantages which are necessary to anything like a rapid progress in civilization" (Gregg 1954:98).

Commenting on the environment of Chaco Canyon, today a World Heritage Site, A. V. Kidder wrote, "the district is little better than a desert: many parts of it, indeed, are absolutely barren wastes of sand and rock" (1924:179). The archaeology of this desolate land, described as being "so far from Heaven and so close to Texas" (Armijo in Bradford 1973:5), is fixed by its dry and barren essence. The benefit to archaeology, of course, is that with consistent aridity, preservation of normally perishable materials is excellent. With the land unsuited to Euro-American agricultural practices and lacking a coastline or navigable rivers important to the development of modern commerce, human population growth has been kept to a minimum, and the relentless encroachment of Euro-American industry has been relatively slight compared to much of the rest of the continent. Descendants of the initial American Indian inhabitants of the Southwest, while deprived of much of their original land and access to key resources, persist in the land of their ancestors, many living in villages that have existed for centuries. So, too, have the descendants of other peoples in sequential layers of relative newcomers, Hispanic descendants of Spanish and Mexican colonists and Euro-Americans. Each human layer experienced a past that differed from those of other cultural traditions. Today, within the culturally heterogeneous Southwest, many pasts are understood and valued in diverse ways. Each human layer, each culturally distinct, living tradition, has a stake in the tangible evidence of the past.

Preservation Responsibilities

Passage of the Lacey (Antiquities) Act of 1906, and the establishment of Mesa Verde National Park as the first national park created to preserve archaeological resources, codified the legal authority to preserve archaeological sites and collections for the American people. The Antiquities Act and the National Historic Preservation Act (NHPA) of 1966 and its amendments institutionalized the foundations of the thousands of pages of policy, orders, rules, regulations, and guidelines that all archaeologists whose research is in the United States follow today.

The impact of these laws is arguably felt most strongly in those regions where there is a great deal of federal land and a great many antiquities. It should be no surprise that 92.7 percent of all federal land is in the west and that more than half the land area in the western states is federal acreage. The southwestern states of Utah, Arizona, Colorado, and New Mexico rank fifth, fourth, ninth, and eleventh nationally in federal acreage. There are states with more federal land and higher percentages of their total lands federally owned and managed. Those states (Alaska, Nevada, California) either have climates that do not preserve visible archaeological remains or were inhabited by relatively mobile populations over the most of their human occupations and hence have fewer archaeological resources than the southwestern states.

Archaeological Resources

The southwestern states maintain site file records that give us an idea of the magnitude of archaeological resources on and in the ground. As of fall 2001, New Mexico had assigned about 138,000 numbers to individual archaeological sites with less than an estimated 10 percent of the state having been systematically surveyed (Timothy Seaman, personal communication 2001). The Colorado Historical Society site records for the Colorado River basin portion of southwestern Colorado only lists 13,423 sites with 4.1 percent of that area surveyed (Lipe 1999:79). A similar figure is probably appropriate for southeastern Utah. Arizona's site file system (AZSITE) records 71,117 sites (Rick Karl, personal communication 2001). For the portion of the Southwest in the United States, then, there are about 235,963 documented and numbered sites with less than 10 percent of the land base having been surveyed. These numbers do not include sites in that portion of the Southwest in northern Mexico or known sites that are not recorded in state databases. I suspect record managers in the region would agree that there are slightly more than 2.5 million visible archaeological sites in the region and that this is a conservative estimate. New Mexico alone has been adding about 4,000 sites to its Archaeological Records Management Section (ARMS) site files each year (Timothy Seaman, personal communication 2001), and AZSITE has added about 1,000 sites a year, employing three graduate research assistants for fewer hours than are needed to keep up with the job (Rick Karl, personal communication 2001).

The enormity of these numbers has a variety of consequences. As citizens we are concerned about protecting more than 2 million archaeological resources from vandalism, looting, and accidental disturbance. It is obviously important to know what kinds of sites and the locations of sites we must protect. As anthropologists and archaeologists, in addition to caring about protecting cultural resources, we want to glean the most accurate information from these sites about the past that we can. We currently have at least basic distributional information on about a quarter of a million sites. Analysis of this information allows for the development of regional syntheses, state plans, and context statements (e.g., Cordell 1979; Lipe et al. 1999; Stuart and Gauthier 1981) that summarize much of what we know and provide direction for future research. The basic distributional information and subsidiary analyses are virtual data laboratories for preliminary exploration of a variety of archaeological hypotheses and for interpretive regional studies that explore the dynamics behind the numbers. Joseph A. Tainter's (1988) examination of societal collapse is an example, as are the papers about the post-Chaco era (e.g., Adler 1996), and the various studies of paleoclimate and its influence on human settlement patterns (Kohler and Van West 1996; McIntosh et al. 2000; Van West 1996). David

Stuart's (2000) *Anasazi America* uses data about Chaco Canyon to explore the consequences for our own times of rapid economic growth in an unpredictable environment.

The numbers of recorded sites in the context of the more than 100 years over which southwestern archaeology has been an active endeavor have several implications. For one, it is unlikely that the region will enjoy the celebrity of discovering something truly new such as a previously unknown preceramic city. Southwestern archaeologists are also painfully aware that the number of recorded sites represents uneven coverage and hence caution against making statements that might reflect potential sampling biases. We expend a great deal of effort, justifiably, trying to reconcile data from different databases. The enormity of the databases and the rapidity with which they are expanded are probably among the reasons why regional context statements are not regularly revised and updated and perhaps also why the databases themselves are underutilized for general archaeological research.

Given the numbers and our rightful concern about guarding against statements based on potentially biased samples, I suggest that we will need to invest in institutions (people, salaries) that provide data/information management. These cannot be drawn from the few resources currently allocated to recording information. We need information managers who will continually assess the reliability, precision, and accuracy of what we know and who will assist in developing regional syntheses. Ideally, the information management systems should be Geographic Information System (GIS)-based with the capability to link with nonarchaeological GIS systems maintained by other disciplines. This is a model that is currently being implemented in New Mexico and in Colorado, with New Mexico Cultural Resources Information System (NMCRIS) and Colorado Compass, respectively.

CURATION CRISIS

With about one quarter of a million known sites and 100 years of excavation, the Southwest is also in the midst of what is known nationally as "the curation crisis." While it is true that most early ethnographic and archaeological exploration in the Southwest was instigated in order to amass collections for East Coast museums (Fowler 2000:220–233, 248), the roots of the current crisis go back to the same antiquities legislation that mandates protection of archaeological sites and to insuring that collections from federal lands and their associated data are properly cared for in perpetuity (Thompson 2000c:4). Until about the

1960s, the numbers of archaeological collections from public lands were small enough that they could be managed by state and university museums. In 2005 this is no longer true for university and state museums in the Southwest, corresponding to the growth of public archaeology and federally mandated cultural resources management (Doelle and Phillips, this volume).

The curation crisis was anticipated. Museums have been warning private sector cultural resource management firms and federal agencies of it for decades (Novick 1980). The crisis goes far beyond a lack of shelf space. It touches the core of archaeological ethics (Childs 1999, 2004). Archaeological resources are nonrenewable. We have adopted a conservation ethic that requires that collections be maintained intact (not dispersed) and in good condition for future research that is expected to include new analytical methods and techniques (Childs 1999:40, 2004). We rue the years before radiocarbon dating when archaeologists tossed charcoal onto the back dirt pile. We know that residue analysis and pollen washes will help us answer important questions about past food preparation, diet, and nutrition. In recognition of the poor state of curation facilities, inadequate record keeping, and a lack of accountability for federal collections, minimum standards were set by uniform regulations published in the Code of Federal Regulations in 1990 (CFR 36, Part 79). In the same year, the publication of the Native American Graves Protection and Repatriation Act (NAGPRA) also required identification of certain types of materials, a task that obviously necessitates good record keeping (Ferguson and Giesen 1999). Many museums do not meet the minimum physical standards as established by CFR 36, Part 79. The idea of deaccessioning collections is anathema to our conservation ethic but we cannot in good conscience keep deteriorating collections or inaccessible data that support them.

Museums and federal agencies are still assessing the extent and implications of the curation crises on a national level (Bustard 2000; Childs 2004). Archaeologists in the Southwest, who have just acknowledged reaching a curation Rubicon, suggest some directions for solutions. Museum directors and statewide organizations of archaeologists are trying to develop consortia of federal, state, and private sector entities to pool resources to construct curation facilities. The Anasazi Cultural Heritage Center in Dolores, Colorado, a tribute to the foresight of William Lipe and David Breternitz, could serve as a model for such consortia. The Bureau of Reclamation (BOR) and the Bureau of Land Management (BLM) developed the center to house collections from sites inundated through the Dolores River Project. The center is managed by the BLM. To my knowledge it is the only federal curation facility that was provided for before a major reclamation project was undertaken. It suggests that collaboration among agencies is possible and benefits archaeologists, the agencies, and the public.

In addition to providing safe physical facilities for collections, future use of collections will require upgrading information about existing collections and developing shared databases and priorities for collection use. NAGPRA requires that databases and policies for some types of collections (human remains, associated funerary objects, and objects of cultural patrimony) be developed and implemented. It is time for archaeologists to require and develop funding for databases and policies for all archaeological collections. Archaeologists are in the best position to assure that databases are constructed which link collections that were split among institutions in the early twentieth century when this was a common practice (see Lister and Lister [1968] for the Bernheimer expedition and Lister and Lister [1981] for work in Chaco Canyon). Archaeologists also can assess and maintain priorities for use of existing materials. For example, many of our museums hold unprocessed tree-ring and/or radiocarbon samples that if submitted for analysis would resolve issues of regional importance. Existing museum collections provide venues for exciting research that would enrich our understanding of the past. Making information about those collections accessible to researchers would encourage research to go forward.

Trends in Archaeological Work Settings and Research

The ways in which archaeological materials, including sites, artifacts, and records, are used today and will be used in the future depend on the kinds of research questions archaeologists and their constituents ask. As Don Fowler, James Snead, and J. Jefferson Reid and Stephanie Whittlesey in their contributions to this volume point out, the questions are conditioned by the different institutional contexts within which archaeologists work, or as Melinda Zeder concludes, "by far the most important factor shaping archaeological research interests is one's work setting" (Zeder 1997:121). Building on Zeder's (1997) study, I have looked at the distribution of our numbers among different work settings and tried to determine those sectors of archaeological endeavor in the Southwest that are currently experiencing growth, perhaps shifting the direction of future research. The categories of southwestern archaeologists I use differ from Zeder's, yet the overall pattern of our results is much the same. I estimate percentages as follows: academic and museum (12 percent), private sector (CRM) (20 percent), government (32 percent), tribes (22 percent), and other (14 percent).

Among Zeder's (1997:59) conclusions are that the majority of archaeologists working in government settings are in western states, and that more than half of the private sector archaeologists responding to her census work in the West and Southwest. It is not surprising that the work settings for archaeologists in the Southwest are predominantly in the government and private sectors (see Doelle and Phillips, this volume), and this has important implications for research. In general, government and private sector archaeologists share a stronger interest in historic archaeology than do their academic and museum colleagues. This interest is expected, but as I note below, has an additional twist in the Southwest because of the participation of federally recognized tribes. Also, as might be expected, government and private sector archaeologists express more interest in cultural ecology and culture-historical approaches to archaeology than do academic and museum professionals who indicate higher levels of interest in processual and postprocessual frames of reference. Both groups of archaeologists express about equal interest in theory building and the development of archaeological method (Zeder 1997:131, 138).

Although I do not have precise figures (and I suspect that my efforts toward precision could become a lifetime job), I estimate that there are nearly 600 employed professional southwestern archaeologists and perhaps half that number of avocational archaeologists who have joined state and local archaeological societies. One important trend is that the number of avocational archaeologists is growing as active retirees move to the Southwest, and the community of avocational archaeologists in the Southwest is tremendously important to the development of professional archaeology in the region. Avocational societies conduct a variety of field schools and encourage their members to obtain certification. These provide professional training and are not in any sense like the Hewett-led field school tours described by Barbara Mills (this volume). Over the past decade, avocational societies have undertaken enormous tasks in documenting rock art, maintaining site protection programs, and generating funds to support research. Also growing are programs that work to enlist volunteers through education and participation in archaeological work. These include the U.S. Forest Service's "Passports in Time," the programs of Crow Canyon Archaeological Center, and university and museum projects that include Earthwatch or university-based alumni volunteers, among others. Among the research fields most obviously enhanced by volunteer effort, the avocational initiative in recording rock art augments studies that use rock art to illuminate general questions such as those about cultural boundaries (Young 1988) and warfare (Schaafsma 2000).

RELATIONSHIPS WITH TRIBES

It should not, but may, come as a surprise that in the Southwest, there are almost as many archaeologists working for federally recognized tribes as there are archaeologists working for federal and state agencies combined. Although it has recently downsized, in 1999 the Navajo Nation's program was the largest historic preservation office in the United States (Ferguson 1999:34). The Hualapai, Camp Verde Apache, Mescalero Apache, White Mountain Apache, Salt River Pima–Maricopa Indian Community, Gila River Indian Community, Hopi Tribe, and Zuni and Jemez pueblos are also actively engaged in archaeology with considerable political, social, and economic impact on archaeology in the Southwest.

There are social and intellectual differences in the kind and level of American Indian involvement in archaeology with large-scale consequences in the Southwest because of the great number and diversity of tribes. Under the 1992 NHPA amendments that officially recognize that traditional cultural properties and religious sites are eligible for inclusion on the National Register of Historic Places, all of the tribes enumerated above have historic preservation programs that conduct archaeology on their lands. Archaeology also brings revenue to the tribes. Many traditional cultural properties and religious sites are also archaeological sites while others are not, and as T. J. Ferguson (1999:34) explains, the expanded NHPA definitions allow for and encourage linking ethnographic and archaeological components of historic preservation. As noted above(Zeder 1997:135), nationally, government and private sector archaeologists are more interested in historic archaeology than are archaeologists who work in academic settings. In the Southwest, this interest in the historic period includes ethnographic and ethnohistorical research domains largely because of responsibilities to and participation of the tribes. These enrich our understanding of the past. We are beginning to see the results of collaborative research with tribes, for example in Desert Archaeology's recently reported research (Ferguson and Lomaomvaya 2001) on Highway 89, which highlights the Native American ethnohistoric perspective. Outside of the NHPA mandates, but also in the spirit of collaborative research that expands the direction of ethnographic archaeology, is Robert Preucel's (1997) work with Cochiti Pueblo at Old Kotyiti.

Tribal participation in the implementation of the NHPA is not uniform. Most southwestern tribes take responsibility for conducting archaeological and ethnographic research on their lands. Others also regulate archaeological and ethnographic research on their lands by assuming functions formerly fulfilled by state historic preservation offices. In the Southwest, the White Mountain Apache, the Hualapai, and the Navajo Nation have assumed these regulatory functions as matters of tribal sovereignty (Ferguson 1999:34). In the common parlance of southwestern archaeology today, one speaks of state historic preservation officers (SHPOs) and tribal historic preservation officers (THPOs). On perhaps a trivial level this means that information about archaeological sites on Navajo lands (more than 44,000 km^2) is not recorded in state archives. These sites do not get Laboratory of Anthropology (LA) or AZSITE numbers, and data about them are buried deeply in gray literature. It also means that tribes have the authority to establish agendas for archaeological research on their lands. While this injects a note of concern about intellectual freedom in the hearts of some archaeologists, most archaeologists who work in the Southwest appreciate that while American Indians do not view their past the way archaeologists do, they often incorporate culturally relativistic approaches that include collecting archaeological data scientifically without precluding alternative interpretations (Ferguson 1999:36).

What is unprecedented is that American Indians have and are using the legal authority to conduct archaeological research on their lands according to their own agendas and values. Furthermore, the Navajo Nation Archaeology Department (NNAD) at Northern Arizona University (NAU) is unique nationally in providing student training to Navajo and other Native American NAU students in the fields of archaeology and anthropology. These developments provide an opportunity to achieve understanding of a variety of alternative histories and readings of the past.

While tribal participation in the NHPA has a number of implications for archaeological research, the direction that is most advanced to date concerns multifaceted meanings of landscape as construct, history, place, and source of knowledge for living traditions (Anschuetz 2000; Anschuetz et al. 2000; Feld and Basso 1996; Ferguson 1999:37; Naranjo 1995). We should not expect that there will be an archaeology of landscape as a unified research paradigm. Rather, the discussions of landscape reference a field of knowledge that is valued in different cultural traditions currently understood in a spirit of cultural relativism. I can only express my personal hope that these discussions do not lead to an ethnoscience of landscape but dynamic and encourage productive avenues of multivocalic inquiry.

The formal discussions and collaborations among southwestern tribes and archaeologists may allow us all to develop new models and ways of thinking about the past. For example, archaeologists (McGuire and Saitta 1996) have argued that exploring social hierarchy in the prehispanic Southwest has been hampered by the "tyranny" (Upham 1987) of standard ethnographic models of egalitarian Western Pueblo society. The issues of social hierarchy and political complexity that Stephen Lekson addresses in this volume may be more easily explored directly by the tribes themselves. Perhaps, as appears to be occurring in discussions of landscape, all of our academic anthropological notions of social hierarchy may be at once too simplistic and too Western. The tribes may offer perspectives that will force us to rethink these received wisdoms.

RESEARCH IN NORTHERN MEXICO

During most of the twentieth century, southwestern archaeologists confined their work to the U.S. side of the U.S.-Mexican border, although there were always a few whose pursuit of specific problems drew them south. That changed as a result of Charles Di Peso's work with the Joint Casas Grandes Expedition focused on the enormous site of Casas Grandes (Paquimé). Within the past 10 to 15 years, the pace of archaeology in northern Chihuahua, Sonora, and Sinaloa has increased dramatically as a cadre of archaeologists sought to place Paquimé in its cultural context and pursue other research issues (Kelley and MacWilliams, this volume).

Work in Mexico with Mexican archaeologists provides another perspective on research agendas and interpretations of the past. The value of archaeology its very different in the context of Mexican national interests than it is in the United States. Mexican nationalism is rooted in *mestizaje*. In Mexico, mestizo culture is national identity and archaeological information is useful mestizo history. This situation establishes a tense dynamic between Mexican professional archaeologists and the Mexican government that involves authority over interpretation of antiquities and the uses of archaeological information (McClung de Tapia 1999). In this context, it is relevant that the name "Mexico" derives from "Mexica," the name of the dominant cultural tradition of the Valley of Mexico. Much of El Norte (Chihuahua, Sonora, and Sinaloa) is considered Chichimec territory, although Chichimecs never existed as a cultural group. In fact, Braniff and others (2001) in a spectacular regional synthesis specifically use the phrase "Gran Chichimeca" to rescue both the Mexican Northwest and the U.S. Southwest from being "directions from" rather than regions. In the United States, as Fowler (2000:viii–ix) reminds us, the Southwest is southwest of New York, Boston, and Washington, D.C. El Norte de México is north of Mexico City. The Gran Chichimeca, or El Norte, is not often a high priority for Mexico City. It is difficult to establish the grandeur of Paquimé alongside Teotihuacán. I think the Mexico of Teotihuacán, Monte Albán, and Chichén Itzá is where U.S. southwestern archaeologists learn humility.

Currently, the resurgence of interest and research in northern Mexico is expanding southwestern theoretical horizons to begin to encompass newer variants and modifications of world systems (e.g., Peregrine and Feinman 1996) approaches that are used elsewhere in Mexico. We might also look to Mexico as a potential model for the missing anthropological archaeology of the Mission period that Ivey and Thomas (this volume) lament. The U.S. Southwest was long a Spanish colony. Native Americans on both sides of the international border shared the colonial and mission experience, as, from quite different perspectives, did Spanish colonists and their mestizo descendants. These offer comparative databases that could be used to evaluate the diverse cultural implications of missionization. These also provide a variety of contexts in which to explore issues of ethnogenesis and ethnic identity (Preucel, this volume). Among Mexicans, Hispanic southwesterners, and Native Americans, the frames of reference for the archaeological past are not always "other." They are cultural continuity and often identity.

CONCLUSIONS

As we move into the twenty-first century, there is an opportunity to comment on the larger themes that will engage us as anthropological archaeologists. I have mentioned some of these in context above including more fully exploiting geo-referenced databases, building collaborative ethnohistoric archaeological research with tribes, developing multifaceted meanings of landscape, exploring the contexts and meanings of social hierarchies, adding to modified versions of world systems approaches, and developing and sharing with other cultures southwestern perspectives on colonial experiences. In addition, because of superb paleoclimatic records of the Southwest (Nash and Dean, this volume) developed largely through the Laboratory of Tree-ring Research at the University of Arizona, southwestern archaeologists will continue to participate in national and international discussions of human response to global climate change (McIntosh et al. 2000). With the well-documented antiquity of human use of the fragile environments of the Southwest and close interdisciplinary relationships with other natural scientists (Huckell, this volume), southwestern archaeology should contribute to understanding anthropogenic change, threats to biodiversity, and long-term adaptations to environmental variability. The long and data-rich Archaic record (Huckell, this volume) allows continued comparison with "stable" hunter-gatherer traditions worldwide.

We are beginning to use the superb archaeological data of the Southwest to address questions of general anthropological interest. Patricia Crown's (2000) edited volume does this as contributing authors elaborate on the diverse and changing paths of gender relations and the development of gendered hierarchies. Those of us who consider ourselves culture historians will continue to fill in the gaps in the chronologies and culture histories of southwestern traditions. We will also try to describe the "events" we infer from the archaeology in terms that are meaningful to the anthropological archaeology we espouse, recognizing that this is a time in the history of archaeology when there is little consensus about worthy research efforts (Cordell 1994b). We may cast our descriptions in terms of modified world systems approaches, ideology, ethnogenesis, alternative power relations, selectionism, or optimum foraging models.

Native Americans surely and perhaps also Mexican archaeologists will write alternative culture histories depending on indigenous frames of reference, philosophies, and diverse historiographic criteria (i.e., Lomatuway'ma et al. 1993). It will be interesting to see if there are any shared criteria for validation among alternative approaches. Perhaps we will learn how alternative histories may serve to enhance mutual understanding among archaeological audiences. At the outset of this paper, I noted that each of the culturally distinct, living traditions of the Southwest has a stake in the tangible evidence of the past. I believe that anthropological archaeology will flourish if all stakeholder perspectives are respected. Perhaps the diversity will foster synergistic vision and energy.

The contexts in which our pasts are explored today are increasingly tied to federal and state law, to public policy, and to global economics. Archaeology is increasingly a commercial enterprise operating through legislative mandates but with academic, scientific, and humanistic goals. These present us with enormous challenges. As southwestern archaeologists, we must try to develop means of overcoming the alienation expressed by Simon Ortiz (1992:235) when, in his poem about Montezuma Castle, he wrote: "This morning I have to buy a ticket to get back home." While this will certainly be difficult, we might find a way through the kinds of consultative processes begun with NAGPRA. In the context of questions and dialogue among stakeholders regarding specific archaeological sites, we could make progress. I do not minimize the difficulties involved in just getting the players to the table, but in the long run I believe it will have been worth the effort.

II. The Contributions of Southwest Archaeology

9

Paleoenvironmental Reconstructions and Archaeology: Uniting the Social and Natural Sciences in the American Southwest and Beyond

Stephen E. Nash and Jeffrey S. Dean

In this paper, we selectively and idiosyncratically review the development and application of several paleoenvironmental reconstruction techniques in southwestern archaeology. An exhaustive review has never been attempted; it would fill volumes and take years to complete but is sorely needed. Because of our interests and experience, as well as the various techniques' comparative analytical value to the archaeology of the Southwest, we focus on significant contributions in alluvial chronology, palynology, pack rat midden studies, and tree-ring reconstructions. (Though we do not ignore contributions by archaeozoologists [see Klein and Cruz-Uribe 1984] and archaeobotanists [see Ford 1979], these receive less attention in this paper because such studies are most often directed at reconstructing prehistoric subsistence practices, the study of which is only tangential to paleoenvironmental reconstruction.) Before addressing these historical contributions, it is important to examine a number of underlying characteristics of paleoenvironmental research that become apparent in a detailed reading of the literature. These variables, which should be critically evaluated for all paleoenvironmental research, include change through time, diversity across space, and the fragmentary nature of the record.

THE UBIQUITY OF CHANGE

If there is one underlying characteristic indicated in the record of global Quaternary environments, it is change (Dincauze 2000; Wright and Frey 1965). Scholars recognized in Europe at least four Quaternary glaciation episodes by 1900. They also recognized that glaciation brought attendant changes in sea level, streamflow regimes, soil formation processes, and plant and animal community composition and placement (Péwé 1954). Changes in plant and animal communities were postulated to move in stepwise fashion, such that the North American ecozones first described by Clinton Hart Merriam (Merriam and Stejneger 1890), simply moved along predictable elevational and latitudinal gradients. If this model had been accurate, it would then have been a relatively straightforward procedure to reconstruct botanical and faunal sequences in any location and to correlate these with known glacial advances and retreats. Such was not, however, the case. It is now recognized that the complex changes wrought by repeated glaciation led to complicated and difficult to reconstruct gene flows, extinctions, disjunctions, and other biogeographic processes (Wright and Frey 1965). Reconstruction of these processes is made all the more difficult by the highly diverse nature of the environment in the Southwest. In some cases, the rapidity, frequency, and ubiquity of change preclude the discussion of equilibrium conditions at all (Betancourt et al. 1990).

The European Pleistocene glaciation record nevertheless became, and remained, the baseline against which early southwestern paleoenvironmental reconstructions were compared. Geologists and geomorphologists therefore invested a great deal of time trying to tie southwestern paleoclimate to the European record in the early part of the last century. In the end, it turned out that only the last glaciation, during the Pleistocene, is relevant to the human occupation of the New World. Scholars eventually realized that this glaciation is poorly recorded in terrestrial records of the semiarid Southwest, and therefore they had to develop or adopt new techniques, such as tree-ring, pollen, gastropod, faunal, midden, varve, and botanical analyses, in order to reconstruct prehistoric southwestern environments. In this, they proved amazingly creative and resourceful.

THE DEMON OF DIVERSITY

A second underlying characteristic of the Southwest and its paleoenvironmental record is diversity. The American Southwest contains portions of three major ecozones. It is a key junction of Quaternary deposits and geomorphic surfaces of the semiarid basin and range province to the west, the glaciated Rocky Mountains on the northeast, and the plateau country to the north (Kottlowski et al. 1965). It is characterized by a wide range of climatic and biotic zones, stemming from the vast differences in elevation, temperature, precipitation, albedo, and other variables found in the region (Martin and Mehringer 1965). Though paleoenvironmental scholars are presented with a diverse number of potentially reconstructable variables, the comparability of one data set with another is never guaranteed. Indeed, most paleoenvironmentalists recognize that they are dealing with highly complex systems and therefore must remain cognizant of, if not directly address, issues of space, scale, interaction, and stability versus equilibrium (Butzer 1982; Dincauze 2000; Gladfelter 1977). Archaeologists, on the other hand, are interested in events, which have finite durations and occur in sequences, and processes, which operate at different frequencies and with different amplitudes, not all of which may be discernible to human senses (Dean et al. 1985) or recognizable in the archaeological record (Schiffer 1987). Commensurability of these various data sets is always an issue.

THE FRAGMENTARY RECORD

Paleoenvironmental records in the Southwest are fragmentary because each manifestation, whether tree-rings, alluvial sequences, or pollen records, is not preserved evenly across space and through time. To complicate matters, in any given analysis the environmental specialist can only sample the fragmentary record, and assumptions and biases are therefore introduced to the dataset being analyzed. These issues are familiar to archaeologists, but as Dincauze (2000:28) recently pointed out, "not even the best sampling can overcome the fact that all sediments and materials available from the remote past have been subject to non-random selection." To complicate matters further, recent analyses from a variety of datasets have made it clear that environments have existed in the past for which we have no modern analogues, and that initial conditions, which may be unknowable, affect current situations (see Dincauze 2000:34).

Another aspect of the fragmentary nature of the paleoenvironmental record is the differential sensitivity of various paleoenvironmental techniques to environmental variability. Obviously each technique captures only a limited number of the many environmental factors that exist

(Dean 1988b). For example, alluvial chronostratigraphy records the accumulation and erosion of floodplain sediments and the rise and fall of alluvial groundwater levels; palynology reflects changes in plant pollen production and in the spatial distribution of vegetation communities; and dendroclimatology reveals variations in several climatic variables. These deficiencies are compounded by the fact that each technique is sensitive to only a limited portion of the total range of variability spanned by the factor(s) it controls. Alluvial chronostratigraphy "sees" only low frequency variations and is blind to rapid fluctuations in floodplain conditions; palynology detects middle to low frequency variability in vegetation elements; and traditional dendroclimatology is most sensitive to high frequency rather than long-term climatic variability.

Keeping in mind the problems just noted we turn to significant contributions to paleoenvironmental reconstruction and their effects on our understanding of southwestern prehistory.

PALEOENVIRONMENTAL RECONSTRUCTION AND THE CULTURE HISTORY PARADIGM

Culture Areas

The first published synthesis of southwestern archaeology, Alfred Vincent Kidder's (1924) *An Introduction to the Study of Southwestern Archaeology,* contains descriptive, geographically organized summaries of known archaeological sites. It includes a basic discussion of then current environmental and topographic conditions, but it otherwise ignores the environment as a data source with which to better understand the archaeological record. Kidder and his peers cannot, of course, be faulted for this emphasis, for they were trying to understand and describe, often for the first time, the material remains of prehistoric cultures in the region, not the adaptive strategies of the prehistoric cultures or variability in paleoenvironmental parameters. Some anthropologists, particularly Alfred Kroeber (1939) and Clark Wissler (1926), were beginning to recognize the importance of environment as a causal variable, and did so using a commonsensical conflation of cultural and natural areas that is implicit in Kidder's analysis. As Kroeber (1939:205) wrote: "No culture is wholly intelligible without reference to the noncultural or so-called environmental factors.... [However] in each situation or area different natural factors are likely to be impinging on culture with different intensity."

Human Antiquity

Two discoveries in 1926 changed North American archaeology forever (see Fernlund 2000; Meltzer 1983). The discovery of spear points in undeniable association with bones of an extinct megafauna (*Bison taylori*) at Folsom, New Mexico (Figgins 1927; see Haynes 1986; Rapp and Hill 1998), and the discovery by Emil Haury and Byron Cummings of nondiagnostic ground stone artifacts (subsequently identified as Cochise culture objects) underlying the skull of an extinct mammoth (Haury 1953; see Haynes 1986), opened two new dimensions of archaeological research in the Southwest—one temporal, the other ecological. On the temporal front, it became clear that humans had been present in the New World and the Southwest in the late Pleistocene. This was far earlier than most archaeologists had been willing to accept in the 1920s. On the ecological front, it was clear that humans had hunted extinct faunas for which there were no existing analogues in the New World. As a result, the question of the antiquity of humans in the New World came to the fore once again, and geologists began to use alluvial geochronology to estimate the age of such sites by extrapolating from known rates of erosion and deposition (Antevs 1935; Bryan 1941a). One might presume that questions about human subsistence would have come to the fore as well, and that zooarchaeological methods (Brewer 1992) would have been developed, but the index-fossil approach to extinct species was apparently enough for archaeologists working within a culture history paradigm.

Despite the zooarchaeological and geological potential of these sites, very little work was done on them (Huckleberry 2000; Rapp and Hill 1998). After Folsom, and subsequent discoveries at Clovis, New Mexico, Lindenmeier, Colorado, and other sites, the primary objective amongst archaeologists was a culture history of the various projectile point styles being discovered (Holliday 2000). Nevertheless, certain archaeologists, like Paul Sidney Martin (Martin et al. 1949; see also Antevs 1955a, 1955b), recognized the archaeological importance of alluvial stratigraphy and the geologic-climatic method of dating such sites.

Alluvial Stratigraphy and Geologic-Climatic Dating

Perhaps because of their sensitivity to the massive environmental changes associated with the advance and retreat of Pleistocene glaciers, geologists were among the first to concern themselves with environmental change and its effects on the inhabitants of the Southwest. As early as the 1870s, Edward Drinker Cope (1875:173) noted the erosion of alluvial sediments since the abandonment of sites in the Gallina area of New Mexico. The systematic study of alluvial deposits and their possible relevance to human occupation of the region began in the 1920s with the work of Kirk Bryan in both the Colorado Plateau and desert provinces (Bryan 1922, 1940). In developing alluvial sequences, Bryan worked closely with archaeologists and anthropologists and developed a keen understanding of how the documented environmental changes might have affected human subsistence (Bryan 1941b). This research culminated in his classic investigation of the potential effects of alluvial deposition and erosion on the prehistoric populations of Chaco Canyon, New Mexico (Bryan 1954).

Bryan's work and personal contacts began a research tradition on the plateau that was sustained by his students and colleagues at Harvard University and the United States Geological Survey (USGS). Primary among these individuals was John Tilton Hack, whose 1930s work with the Rainbow Bridge–Monument Valley Expedition in Tsegi Canyon and with the Peabody Museum's Awatovi Expedition resulted in *The Changing Physical Environment of the Hopi Indians of Arizona* (Hack 1942). This work set the standard for relating human behavior to changing floodplain conditions and established the foundation for subsequent geomorphic studies of floodplain alluvium on the plateau. Hack's model of the interaction between Puebloan agriculture and alluvial aggradation, degradation, and hydrology still guides archaeological attempts to understand southwestern human ecology (Adams 1951; Dean 1969, 1988a).

Hack's work inspired several of his USGS colleagues whose research often was conducted in conjunction with archaeological projects. Working with the Glen Canyon Project, Maurice E. Cooley (1962) expanded the geographic scope of Hack's research to the Colorado River and strengthened the model of floodplain processes developed by Bryan and Hack. In connection with the Black Mesa Archaeological Project, geologists from the USGS Astrogeology Program in Flagstaff, led by Thor N. V. Karlstrom, expanded Hack's and Cooley's work to cover most of northeastern Arizona (Karlstrom et al. 1976), further refined the geomorphic model (Karlstrom 1988; Karlstrom and Karlstrom 1986), and explored the impact of alluvial variability on human societies (Dean et al. 1985; Euler et al. 1979; Plog et al. 1988). Several other geomorphic investigations illuminate the relationships between human groups and deposition-erosion sequences in Chaco Canyon (Force et al. 2002; Hall

1977; Love 1980), McElmo Canyon (Force and Howell 1997), and the *bajada* of Sleeping Ute Mountain (Huckleberry and Billman 2000).

The southwestern deserts saw the development of a separate tradition of archaeologically related geomorphic research, sparked by the work of Ernst Antevs. After working on glacial varves in Europe and North America, Antevs (1955b) shifted his attention to arid western North America and developed his late Quaternary sequence of alternating warm and cool periods: Pluvial, Anathermal, Altithermal, and Medithermal. As part of the Gila Pueblo Archaeological Foundation's study of the Cochise culture, Antevs combined this framework with detailed studies of alluvial sediments along Whitewater Draw in southeastern Arizona to illuminate the physical environment of these Archaic period people (Sayles and Antevs 1941). Subsequent work in the southern Southwest built on the foundation established by Antevs. Research by C. Vance Haynes (1981) was focused on illuminating the stratigraphic relationships of Paleoindian mammoth kill sites in southern Arizona. Michael R. Waters reexamined the classic Whitewater Draw stratigraphic sequence (Waters 1986) and documented the alluvial stratigraphy of the Tucson (Waters 1988), Tonto (Waters 1998), and Gila River basins (Waters and Ravesloot 2000) in order to relate human behavior to changing alluvial and hydrologic conditions.

PALEOENVIRONMENTAL RECONSTRUCTION AND CULTURAL ECOLOGY: MERGING THE SOCIAL AND NATURAL SCIENCES

The repertoire of paleoenvironmental reconstruction techniques available to archaeologists and culture historians in the 1930s was limited essentially to geoclimatic studies and tree-ring studies (see below), though tentative progress was being made in palynology, zooarchaeology, archaeobotany, and other studies. Julian Steward's (1937) "Ecological Aspects of Southwestern Society" provided a new conceptual framework, cultural ecology, with which archaeologists could begin making more sophisticated use of paleoenvironmental data.

Steward (1937; see also Steward 1955) focused on the origins of Pueblo and Yuman clans and attempted to identify ecological variables that might have had an impact thereon. In so doing, he sought to downplay, though not disregard, diffusionist explanations that did not have an environmental component: "[My] analysis of Southwestern society assumes that cultural process, and therefore sound historical reconstruction, can be understood only if due attention is paid to the economic or ecological factors that shape society" (Steward 1937:88).

Further, "the theory developed here cannot admit of rigid proof. Its merit lies in providing an explanation in terms of cultural dynamics [e.g., processes] and raising a series of problems [e.g., hypotheses] of economic determinism that are subject to scrutiny in other areas" (Steward 1937:101). Steward examined archaeological remains from across the Four Corners area to conclude that descent is determined according to the relative economic importance of men and women in a given society, that increases in food supply led to larger populations and therefore larger bands, and that it is "inevitable" that these bands will become clans in the long run. Steward did not attempt to identify the mechanisms by which such changes might occur.

Steward was also an archaeologist. He published this seminal contribution at a time when archaeologists were still engaged in culture history and therefore did not have the baseline data with which to consider culture process. Environmental summaries, if present in archaeological site reports at all during this period, typically included descriptions of local flora, fauna, and topography. Because Steward's work focused on the relationship between community, technology, and adaptation, it is uniquely suited for adoption by archaeologists. Though many archaeologists did not directly cite Steward, it is clear that in the coming decades cultural ecology formed a strong theoretical foundation on which much archaeological knowledge was built (e.g., Martin et al. 1949).

PALEOENVIRONMENTAL RECONSTRUCTION AT THE MILLENNIUM: A PLETHORA OF POSSIBILITIES

The vocabulary of paleoenvironmental reconstruction in the Southwest at the millennium is complex. The particular concepts, methods, and techniques applied in any given situation will be determined by site characteristics, research questions, budgets, and the knowledge, biases, skills, and abilities of the archaeologist. In this section, we review the developmental history of but a sample of remarkable techniques that are currently used by southwestern archaeologists.

Dendroclimatology

Dendroclimatology is the highly specialized science of reconstructing climate parameters from precisely dated growth rings in trees (Fritts 1976). Dendroclimatology achieved its modern configuration in the 1960s, when computers made quantitative analysis easier, but paleoenvironmental inferences were possible quite early in the development of tree-ring dating (Douglass 1914). Therefore, this method warrants attention.

In December 1928 Andrew Ellicott Douglass of the University of Arizona noted that he had recently united many of his prehistoric tree-ring specimens into a 590-year-long chronology that was separated from the dated chronology by a gap of unknown duration. His comments on the nature of that gap are telling because they suggest that Douglass, who was an astronomer, recognized the paleoenvironmental implications of his data. He wrote to Neil Merton Judd of the United States National Museum, "there is evidence...that the gap represents some great crisis in the history of the Pueblo people" (A. E. Douglass to N. M. Judd, letter, 5 December 1928, Laboratory of Tree-Ring Research, University of Arizona, Tucson). Six months later, in June of 1929, Douglass wrote "the gap period was due to a great drought in the late 1200s" (A. E. Douglass to G. Grosvenor, president of National Geographic Society, letter, 29 June 1929, Douglass Papers, University of Arizona Library Special Collections, Tucson; see Nash 1998, 1999, 2000). In the nearly 70 years since Douglass coined the phrase, the "Great Drought" has become one of the most common, if not the most common, extracultural agents invoked to explain the massive changes evident in the late thirteenth-century archaeological record across the Southwest.

An abundance of empirical data suggests that a major climatic anomaly affected much of the Southwest between 1276 and 1299. From a climatological standpoint, the Great Drought was not the longest dry spell to affect the Southwest, nor was it the most severe, though it was geographically widespread. From an archaeological standpoint, however, the Great Drought is significant because of the many and varied changes that are apparent in the prehistoric record at about that time.

Harry Thomas Getty, an anthropologist and dendrochronologist at the University of Arizona, provided a typical treatment in his report on tree-ring dates from Balcony House at Mesa Verde. He wrote:

It is quite noticeable that none of the [tree-ring] dates go beyond the beginning of the Great Drought.... This lends decided weight to the theory that the great drought caused the final abandonment of Mesa Verde [Getty 1935:23].

Getty's archaeological colleagues used the Great Drought in similar fashion to explain the appearance of populations in areas such as east-central Arizona or the northern Rio Grande. Many of these early researchers realized that droughts would have serious and negative effects on food production, health, and interpersonal relations, and they were willing to see the Great Drought as a sufficient cause for the abandonment of large regions such as the Four Corners area. Given the prevailing culture-historical and migrationist paradigms in American archaeology, the analytical task became one of identifying sources or destinations for prehistoric migrations.

Quantitative studies of the relationship between tree-rings and climate came to the fore in the 1950s with the work of Edmund Schulman at the Laboratory of Tree-Ring Research. His 1956 book *Dendroclimatic Changes in Semi-Arid America* remains a classic if underappreciated contribution to the field. On the basis of nearly 15 years of fieldwork along the lower forest border zones of the western United States, Schulman developed numerous local ring chronologies, and by incorporating increasingly sensitive and long-lived trees into these sequences, he refined his reconstructions of rainfall and streamflow. By firmly establishing the quantitative relationship between tree-rings and climate across the Southwest, Schulman set the stage for the dendroclimatic boom that originated in the 1960s.

Physiological ecologist Harold C. Fritts arrived at the Laboratory of Tree-Ring Research at the University of Arizona in 1960 and initiated a revolutionary approach to dendroclimatology that emphasized tree physiology and the use of multivariate statistics (Fritts 1976). Fritts's approach spawned archaeology-related qualitative (relative) dendroclimatic reconstructions for the Wetherill Mesa Project (Fritts et al. 1965), the Grasshopper area (Dean and Robinson 1982), and the northern Southwest (Dean and Robinson 1977). The last of these presented statistical departures from long-term mean tree-growth indices (and therefore precipitation) in the form of contour maps that archaeologists could compare to settlement pattern data and population reconstructions in an attempt to infer causal relationships.

Subsequently, archaeological tree-ring data were used to produce quantitative dendroclimatic reconstructions expressed in standard units of measurement such as inches of precipitation, degrees of temperature, and Palmer Drought Severity Indices (PDSI). Rose et al. (1981, 1982) reconstructed precipitation and other climatic variables for Arroyo Hondo Pueblo and the Four Corners area, respectively. Burns's (1983) innovative reconstruction of annual maize crop yields and simulation of Anasazi storage marks the first quantitative study of relationships among tree-ring data, agricultural production, and human coping (storage) behavior. This allowed Burns (1983) to conclude that the Great Drought represented the worst interval of maize storage shortfalls to have plagued southwestern Colorado's Anasazi.

Van West (1990, 1994a) refined Burns's analysis by converting PDSI values for different soil types into annual maize yields within a Geographic Information System representation of southwestern Colorado. Her analysis indicated that there was always enough productive land to produce sufficient maize to support a large population, even during dry periods such as the Great Drought at the end of the thirteenth century. That Burns and Van West could arrive at such divergent conclusions on the basis of related data sets is partly a function of methodological differences and partly of Burns's estimates being mitigated by simulated storage behavior. More recently, quantitative dendroclimatic reconstructions have infused archaeological studies of the Dolores River valley (Van West 1994a), the central Mesa Verde areas (Dean and Robinson 2002; Van West and Dean 2000), and Chaco Canyon (Dean 1992; Force et al. 2002; Powers et al. 1983; Sebastian 1992). Moreover, dendrohydrologic reconstructions of streamflow have been integrated into the archaeology of the Little Colorado River drainage on the Colorado Plateau (Van West 1994b) and of the Salt and Verde River valleys in the Sonoran Desert (Graybill et al. 1989).

Dendroenvironmental reconstructions have grown from common-sense evaluations of impressionistic and qualitative hypotheses regarding environmental causes and behavioral effects to sophisticated and quantitative studies of tree-rings, climate, and human behavior. Progress has been tempered by the fact that highly technical paleoenvironmental reconstructions are often beyond the analytical grasp of archaeologists, and because such studies require a number of exceedingly stringent data sets that limit the arenas in which they can be performed. Archaeologists working in the Southwest have nevertheless benefited from significant advances in dendroclimatic reconstructions over the past seven decades.

Pack Rat Midden Analysis

Since its initial development by Phil V. Wells in about 1960, archaeologists have benefited from the results of analyses of one of the most remarkable sources of paleoenvironmental data yet discovered—pack rat middens (Betancourt et al., eds. 1990). Pack rats (*Neotoma* sp.) generally forage for food and raw materials within about 30 m of their dens. These voracious collectors thus return samples of local fauna to their dens, and each sample is then cemented in place by rat urine. Because generations of pack rats can reside in the same locations for thousands of years, these seemingly amorphous entities include well-preserved records of floral and faunal change through time.

On the basis of pack rat midden analysis, Julio Betancourt and Thomas R. Van Devender (1981) found that pines were once present in Chaco Canyon. Arthur M. Phillips (1984) studied pack rat middens, which included dung from extinct ground sloth, to conclude that the sloths were eating essentially modern vegetation prior to becoming extinct about 11,000 years ago. He used this inference to rule out climate change as a cause for their extinction.

The crowning publication in pack rat midden studies is *Packrat Middens: The Last 40,000 Years of Biotic Change*, edited by Betancourt, Van Devender, and Paul Schultz Martin (1990), which includes contributions from both the Old and New Worlds, but tends to focus on the American West.

Pack rat midden studies have illuminated, at the macrofossil level and in the absence of the influence of culture, aspects of southwestern paleoenvironments that otherwise were not available to archaeologists. There are clearly sources of bias in the midden record, but when these paleoenvironmental reconstructions are juxtaposed against zooarchaeological and archaeobotanical studies, pollen, and tree-ring records, the environmental picture can come into surprisingly robust focus.

Palynology

Pollen studies were first developed in Europe and were slow to take hold in North America in general and the Southwest in particular (Eiseley 1939). After Paul B. Sears (1932) first used fossil pollen data to reconstruct the paleoenvironment of late Holocene climates in eastern North America (see Bryant and Hall 1993), researchers in the Southwest began to take note. However, just as investigators initially and erroneously assumed that tree-ring dating would not work in more temperate environments, archaeologists and geoscientists assumed that pollen analysis would not work where peat bogs did not exist, and therefore would not work in the Southwest. As Loren Eiseley (1939:135) wrote: "It is difficult to believe that these [arid] soil zones are ever likely to supply pollen in amounts sufficient to eliminate the probability of error to the same degree as peat bogs, or to obtain such unbroken sequences upward." Eiseley (1939) did acknowledge that pollen had been found preserved in ground sloth dung (Laudermilk and Munz 1934), and in dry lakebeds (Sears 1937), but the general feeling was that pollen analysis would not work in the Southwest.

By the mid-1950s, palynologists (Clisby and Sears 1956; Sears and Clisby 1952) had used fossil pollen from nonarchaeological sediments to develop a climatic sequence for the Southwest. Roger Anderson (1955) had found a statistically sufficient number of pollen grains in a sample collected by Charles Di Peso at Ramanote Cave in southern Arizona. In the late 1950s, Paul Schultz Martin of the Geochronology Laboratory at the University of Arizona spearheaded initial pollen studies and trained Peter Mehringer, Richard Hevly, and James Schoenwetter, all of whom would go on to make significant contributions of their own right. Martin (1963a) used palynology to comment on the environmental contexts for the early human occupation of Arizona. The seminal contribution in southwestern pollen analysis was Martin's (1963b) *The Last 10,000 Years: A Fossil Pollen Record of the American Southwest.*

James Schoenwetter (1961) analyzed pollen samples from 18 archaeological sites excavated by Paul Sidney Martin in Arizona and New Mexico to demonstrate that a useful pollen chronology could be developed from archaeological samples. As a result of his analysis, he inferred four periods in which different environmental conditions obtained during the last 3,500 years.

In 1964 Schoenwetter and Frank Eddy attempted to apply alluvial and palynological data to the solution of archaeological problems in the Navajo Reservoir district of New Mexico. They postulated that the repeated occupation and abandonment of the Navajo Reservoir district is, in most cases, explainable with reference to effective moisture, and that population growth was related to agricultural potential (Schoenwetter and Eddy 1964:127; see also Hill and Hevly 1968).

In the mid-1960s, analyses began to focus on differential pollen distributions within sites (both profiles and features) in an effort to identify differential economic uses of plants or changes in plant use through time. Human coprolites (Reinhard and Bryant 1992) were used as sources of pollen data to reconstruct environmental data in southern Utah (Callen and Martin 1969; Martin 1964). These studies found great variability in the fecal pollen spectra analyzed. Given that southern Utah is characterized by a relatively stable baseline pollen spectrum, their tentative conclusion was that the coprolites indicated dietary variation. Martin and Byers (1965) used pollen analysis to determine whether terraces were in fact used for agriculture and whether climate change had caused the final abandonment of Wetherill Mesa.

Schoenwetter (1970) made a strong case that palynology should be considered in all phases of archaeological research design. In an analysis of some 56,000 pollen grains from 18 samples and the Cienega Creek site, he used correlations between samples and ceramics to refine the level of resolution of the pollen sequence to 25- or 50-year intervals. James N. Hill (1970) recognized that the pollen data indicated that the Great Drought could not have caused the abandonment of Broken K Pueblo, that a shift from winter to summer dominant rainfall pattern may have had something to do with it, and that the generalized tree-ring and pollen curves for the Southwest indicated the same trends. Similarly, William A. Longacre (1964) incorporated the new pollen analyses in a synthesis of occupations in the Hay Hollow Valley.

Stephen A. Hall (1985) has published a bibliography of all known fossil pollen studies in the Southwest, including those from archaeological sites, though an update of this compilation would be welcome.

Integrative Studies

Inevitably, environmental scientists and archaeologists came to realize that, because the various paleoenvironmental techniques are sensitive to different environmental processes and to different aspects of those processes' variability, reconstructions based on these techniques differ qualitatively and quantitatively from one another. Around 1980 efforts began to combine different reconstructions into more complete pictures of the total range of environmental variability that confronted the human occupants of the Southwest. One academic program and two large contract projects led the way in this effort: the University of Arizona Archaeological Field School at Grasshopper in central Arizona, the Dolores Archaeological Project (DAP) in southwestern Colorado, and the Black Mesa Archaeological Project (BMAP) in northeastern Arizona.

The Grasshopper field school invited a number of natural scientists to undertake a wide variety of studies of the local environment. Though these studies were not integrated into a single model of past environmental conditions, the results (Longacre et al. 1982) illustrated the astonishing range of paleoenvironmental data pertinent to the human occupation of an area that could be accumulated.

Kenneth Lee Petersen (1988) of DAP combined pollen analysis of cores from lakes in the La Plata Mountains of southwestern Colorado with an upper tree line bristlecone tree-ring chronology from Almagre Mountain in the Colorado Front Range to reconstruct elevational changes in the upper (temperature controlled) and lower (precipitation controlled) limits of the agricultural zone in southwestern Colorado. These fluctuations in the width of the farmable zone have been integrated into numerous interpretations of the prehistory of this area.

BMAP assembled a group of outside scientists to investigate the past environment of the region surrounding Black Mesa (Gumerman 1988; Karlstrom et al. 1976). This effort included geomorphic studies of alluvial and colluvial sediments (Karlstrom and Karlstrom 1986), hydrology, palynology (Hevly 1988), radiocarbon and tree-ring chronometry, bioarchaeology, and dendroclimatology (Dean 1988b). Because of the variety of specialists involved, it soon became apparent that different techniques produced different kinds of environmental information that were not always comparable. The effort to resolve this predicament led to the identification of three types of environmental variation based on the periodicity of the controlling natural processes (Dean 1988a, 1996). Stable factors do not vary appreciably over the span of the analysis and need not be reconstructed because present conditions are adequate indicators of past conditions. Low frequency process (LFP) variables are controlled by natural processes with periodicities greater than 25 years, an arbitrary cutoff equated with one human generation. High frequency process (HFP) variables exhibit periodicities less than or equal to 25 years. These distinctions allow different kinds of reconstruction to be related to one another, have informed many subsequent archaeological efforts to relate human behavior to environmental stability, variation, and change (Cordell 1998; Dean 1992; Dean and Van West 2002; Kaldahl and Dean 1999; Orcutt 1991; Van West and Dean 2000), and have been incorporated into research designs of several large projects. Finally, integrated paleoenvironmental reconstructions have been used to create production landscapes for agent-based computer models of Anasazi settlement and subsistence dynamics in northeastern Arizona (Dean et al. 2000) and southwestern Colorado (Kohler et al. 2000).

Increasingly sophisticated environmental reconstructions have led to increasingly sophisticated models of prehistoric behavior in response to environmental change (Dean 1988a; Dean et al. 1985, 1994). These efforts seek to move beyond the "sterile exercise[s] in pattern matching" of old and attempt to develop a "coherent theoretical approach to adaptive culture change" (Ahlstrom et al. 1995:125–126). The annually resolved reconstructions allowed by tree-ring dating have opened doors of archaeological inference that are unattainable in time periods and regions in which dendrochronology cannot be applied.

CONCLUSION

By the late 1950s, the seeds for extensive and detailed paleoenvironmental reconstructions in the Southwest had been sown, but archaeologists had not yet reaped the harvest. As Haury (1958a:69) noted, "coordinated studies of paleoecology in the Southwest, leading to a clear appreciation of the problems and conditions, have yet to be made."

In celebrations of the twenty-fifth anniversary of the Society for American Archaeology, neither of two published summaries, one national (Johnson 1961), the other regional (Lister 1961), mention paleoenvironmental reconstructions as significant contributions, though Lister (1961:41) notes that "archaeologists now take more advantage of the researches of physiographers, ecologists, and ethnobotanists." Later overviews (e.g., Longacre 1973) do not mention progress on the paleoenvironmental front either.

By the late 1960s and early 1970s, contributions in paleoenvironmental reconstruction had nevertheless come to fruition as ancillary or corollary projects at excavations conducted by Paul Sidney Martin and other southwestern archaeologists (Martin et al. 1962, 1964, 1967). By the end of the 1970s, paleoenvironmental reconstruction techniques were being tested in archaeological settings by scholars who were formally trained in the various techniques.

By the early 1980s, problem-oriented paleoenvironmental research began to take a more centralized role in archaeological research. *Multidisciplinary Research at Grasshopper Pueblo, Arizona* (Longacre et al. 1982) took such a perspective to its logical extreme in an attempt to delimit the economic basis of prehistoric Mogollon society, to test the hypothesis that a slight climatic shift occurred at about A.D. 1300 (see Schoenwetter and Dittert 1968), and to determine the cause of abandonment of the region about A.D. 1400. Contributions to this volume span the analytical spectrum from the study of modern environments (Holbrook and Graves 1982) to archaeological sediments (Whittlesey et al. 1982), geology (Agenbroad 1982), dendrochronology (Dean and Robinson 1982), aquatic fauna (S. Olsen 1982), terrestrial fauna (J. Olsen 1982), microfauna (Holbrook 1982), avifauna (McKusick

1982), floral remains (Bohrer 1982), and pollen (Kelso 1982). These contributions illustrate the degree to which myriad paleoenvironmental analyses can be integrated into long-term archaeological research projects.

Archaeologists working in the Southwest and interested in paleoenvironmental reconstruction are blessed by spectacular preservation, a diverse array of potential datasets, and a vast body of method and theory with which to attack their problems of choice. Though we cannot know everything we would like about paleoenvironments, southwestern archaeologists have long been at the forefront of critical evaluations of new techniques and tests of the veracity thereof. From sediments to tree-rings, pack rats to pollen, the American Southwest has yielded a paleoenvironmental record that is nothing short of remarkable. Unfortunately, the very nature of these sciences requires that students become, in effect, highly specialized apprentices, with no guarantee that employment opportunities will arise in the long run (see Eighmy 2000). The literature is rife with publications by scholars who made significant contributions in paleoenvironmental studies and then moved on to other positions or topics. This lack of continuity may pose problems for the long-term production of paleoenvironmental data. We hope that archaeologists will continue to approach the integration of the paleoenvironmental and archaeological records with vigilance, creativity, and dedication.

10

The First 10,000 Years in the Southwest

Bruce B. Huckell

I would like to begin with a lament I have sounded in the past: there is probably less known about any millennium between 11,500 and 1500 B.P. than about any 200-year period after 1500 B.P. Since the late nineteenth century, scholarly attention has tended to focus on the last 1,500 years of this long record. It is easy to understand the reasons for this disparity. With few exceptions, hunter-gatherers had vanished, been pushed to the margins of the Southwest, or had their traditional settlement-subsistence systems compromised by the time that archaeologists began to visit. The subtle traces of their passing on the landscape excited no particular interest among nineteenth-century archaeologists. For the most part, few twentieth-century archaeologists actually focused their research on what came to be recognized as the preceramic period; many of the most important sites were discovered by chance rather than design. It is somewhat ironic, then, that the proportionately little effort focused by twentieth-century archaeologists on the southwestern preceramic has produced results so important at the national level.

For the purposes of this presentation, I have taken a "greatest hits" approach. There is no space to recapitulate the geographic, temporal particulars of the preceramic record; the reader should consult recent overviews for such information (Hofman and Graham 1998; Huckell 1996; Matson 1991; Simmons 1989a, 1989b). I begin with a few words about the development of the record. Following this I present what I perceive to be the standout contributions by the archaeologists who have developed this record, and then offer some ideas about goals for the new century.

Employment of the terms "Paleoindian" and "Archaic" in this paper reflects contemporary usage, which, as most archaeologists recognize, conflates periods of time with subsistence adaptations (Cordell 1997:102–106). "Paleoindian" serves to designate those cultures in the Southwest from about 11,500 to 8,500 or 8,000 radiocarbon years ago whose economies seem to have included a greater focus on hunting. Archaic economies, which featured increased exploitation of plant seeds (marked by the appearance of ground stone milling equipment) and the pit roasting and/or boiling of plant and other foodstuffs (reflected by heated rock cooking technology), appear by at least 8,500 or 8,000 radiocarbon years ago and in some areas of the Southwest last until the arrival of ceramic vessels in the early centuries A.D. Some 3,000 or more years ago, however, Archaic groups in many parts of the Southwest incorporated cultivation of maize and other crops into a hunting-gathering subsistence base. Whether or not "Archaic" is still an appropriate term to describe this farming-foraging economic pattern remains the subject of debate; "Early Agricultural period" has been proposed as an alternative (Huckell 1995, 1996). This problem underscores the implications of using temporal, rather than economic, grounds for defining these culture-historical terms.

Discussion of this 10,000-year time period requires some adjustments in both the geographic scale and environmental conditions that most archaeologists use in considering the Southwest. With respect to the former, use of boundaries that define the Southwest at A.D. 1000 are less meaningful at any earlier time. Thus, a more flexible sense of geographic limits will be employed. It should go without saying that preceramic prehistory prior to about 3,000–4,000 years ago played out under environmental conditions unlike those of the present. Reconstructions of paleoenvironmental conditions in the region have provided a broad outline of the dynamics of the last 12,000 years (Betancourt et al., eds. 1990; Thompson et al. 1993). Climate, biotic community composition and location, and geomorphic process type and intensity have all varied considerably, creating opportunities and constraints to which preceramic societies had to adapt.

DEVELOPING A RECORD

As we begin the twenty-first century, we cannot claim to have complete understanding of the preceramic culture history for the region. It is important to bear in mind that the archaeological creation of this 10,000-year-long record over the last century was largely the product of historical circumstance and biases produced by the sampling of a lengthy, complex history of occupation over a vast geographic space. The discovery of the Basketmakers in the late nineteenth century was the first hint of the existence of a pre-Puebloan, prepottery culture in the region, and was followed by focused professional investigation of Basketmaker caves in the first two decades of the twentieth century (Matson 1991). By the time of his 1924 synthesis of southwestern archaeology, A. V. Kidder was able to characterize the Basketmakers as lacking pottery and the bow and arrow, hunting with the atlatl and dart, growing corn and beans, gathering wild plants, and using caves for storage and disposal of the dead. He speculated that their simple, ephemeral dwellings would be found in open sites near arable land, and that a date of 1500–2000 B.C. for the beginnings of Basketmaker culture was probable. While thus characterizing the known record, he also postulated the existence of an earlier,

> more or less nomadic people, thinly scattered over the country, ignorant of agriculture and pottery-making. Their life must have closely resembled that of the modern Digger tribes of the Plateau; that is to say, they dwelt in more or less makeshift houses, and subsisted principally on small game: rabbits, prairie dogs and doves; and on such wild vegetable products as grass-seeds, berries and roots [Kidder 1924:118].

Kidder's predictions about the existence, if not the variety, of the pre-Basketmaker archaeological record were remarkably prescient. When the first Pecos cultural classification was presented (Kidder 1927), Basketmaker II was applied to the known cave record of farmer-foragers and Basketmaker I was reserved for their hypothesized preagricultural ancestors. However, the discovery of the Folsom culture in that same year (Figgins 1927)—accepted as perhaps late Pleistocene but certainly no younger than the early Holocene—revealed that a huge span of time (some 6,000 or more years) separated Basketmaker II and Folsom. Clearly, a single phase such as Basketmaker I could not fill this gap (Kidder 1936b).

What rapidly followed was the recognition of other cultural complexes that seemed to be of potentially similar age to Folsom but which have proven to actually fill the gap. The earliest examples include Gypsum, Pinto, and Lake Mohave all defined at the western or northwestern margins of the Southwest and first thought to be of late Pleistocene age. However, beginning in 1935, E. B. Sayles, Ernst Antevs, and Emil

Haury began building the record of the Cochise culture from sites buried in riverine alluvium in southeastern Arizona (Sayles and Antevs 1941). The Cochise culture was proposed as an unbroken, three-stage sequence spanning the period from be-yond 8000 B.C. through 500 B.C. The presence of ground stone milling equipment in the earliest (Sulphur Spring) stage and its lack of projectile points clearly differentiated it from Folsom. Haury's (1950) excavation of Ventana Cave in 1941–1942 gave further substance to the preceramic record, and was the first instance of a single site with an extensive preceramic record beneath a ceramic (Hohokam) occupation (Figure 10.1). Thus, what has come to be called the Archaic period was recognized shortly after the Folsom discovery, and for the first time the length of time covered by the preceramic period was populated with

Figure 10.1. Two of the archaeologists most responsible for shedding light on southwestern preceramic prehistory. E. B. "Ted" Sayles (left) and Emil Haury (right) visiting Ventana Cave, 1947. Photo courtesy of Arizona State Museum, University of Arizona (ASM negative 2202).

archaeological cultures that fit Kidder's predictions. From the 1940s through the 1980s, an amazing array of Archaic "complexes," "cultures," and "traditions" was identified (Huckell 1996:Table 1); most were of limited geographic extent, poorly placed in time, and of uncertain relationship to one another. The development of radiocarbon dating after 1950 permitted some, but not all, of them to be placed in time. The first attempt to integrate them into a larger, more encompassing frame of reference was Jennings's (1957) Desert Culture concept, which was a more explicitly materialist and ecological treatment of the problem. In fact, Jennings's idea was based in discussions among archaeologists across North America concerning an Archaic stage of cultural development (Willey and Phillips 1958). Later efforts to create a regional framework included the Picosa (Irwin-Williams 1967) and Southwestern Archaic (Berry and Berry 1986; Huckell 1984; Irwin-Williams 1968, 1973).

Not so easily accommodated under Kidder's vision of pre–Basketmaker II were the so-called big game hunting cultures that were discovered at about the same period, including Folsom and what would later come to be known as Clovis and other Paleoindian cultures (Howard 1935). The separation of Paleoindian and Archaic was problematic because the basis for their separation—time or subsistence ecology—was unresolved. In fact, "Paleo-Indian" was first used by Roberts (1940) for all potentially ancient archaeological manifestations, but was not formally defined; "Early Man" was another term used commonly and with similar meaning (Sellards 1940). Wormington (1957:3) ultimately suggested use of "Paleoindian" (or "Paleo-Indian") to describe cultures that hunted now-extinct animals, presumably predating 6000 B.P. In the 1940s and 1950s fieldwork was conducted at sites that became pivotal in constructing a more detailed culture-historical record and for sorting out differences in the age and paleoecology of preceramic groups. The Naco (Haury 1953) and Lehner (Haury et al. 1959) Clovis sites were dug in southeastern Arizona; Sellards (1952) and others continued research at Blackwater Draw and documented the stratigraphic separation of Clovis, Folsom, and later Paleoindian complexes such as Portales. Relationships between Paleoindian cultures and what have come to be viewed as Archaic cultures also became clearer, although the relationships between Sulphur Spring stage Cochise and Clovis were the subject of debate as late as the 1960s (Haury et al. 1959: 26–27) and beyond.

The 1960s and early 1970s was a time when explanatory goals were ascendant in American archaeology. In southwestern preceramic studies, culture history remained a focus of study, but theories about cultural ecology and processes of culture change began to have an impact as well. The rise of contract archaeology (CRM) was perhaps the most significant boon to the study of southwestern preceramic prehistory, promoting rapid gains in knowledge after about 1970, and it is within this realm that most preceramic—especially Archaic—archaeology is done today. This closely coincided with the development of more sophisticated anthropological investigation of contemporary hunter-gatherers, and as well with a tremendous increase in the numbers of archaeologists in the region. The concomitant shift from descriptive to explanatory research in archaeology opened new, productive avenues for research. Southwestern preceramic studies shifted accordingly to investigate subsistence, settlement organization, and mobility, which remain the principal topics for investigation today.

SUBSTANTIVE CONTRIBUTIONS

Out of many, there are two substantive contributions of twentieth-century southwestern preceramic research to American prehistory that stand out: one is the proof of a late Pleistocene human presence in the New World and the second is the discovery of the antiquity and impact of maize agriculture in the region.

Human Antiquity in North America

It was a site at the Southwest–Southern Plains boundary that was pivotal in the establishment of human antiquity in North America. An extended debate in the late nineteenth and early twentieth centuries centered on the age of human arrival in the New World. Meltzer (1994) has discussed this debate over the "American Paleolithic" in detail; suffice it to say that as of 1925, general consensus held that humans had reached North America in the last few thousand years. Discovery of a distinctive grooved spear point among the bones of a species of bison believed to have been extinct by the end of the Pleistocene (both in undisputedly ancient, primary geological deposits) provided compelling proof of human presence in New Mexico more than 10,000 years ago (Cordell 1997; Figgins 1927; Meltzer 1994). Particularly critical in the acceptance of the evidence was the visit by A. V. Kidder to the site in 1927 to view the evidence in situ, and his subsequent endorsement of the association (Kidder 1936b). If any doubts lingered about the Folsom site, they were quickly dispelled by rapid confirmatory discoveries of Folsom sites in Colorado, Wyoming, and New Mexico's Llano Estacado (Renaud 1931). E. B. Howard's investigations at Blackwater Draw in 1933–1937 (Boldurian and Cotter 1999; Howard 1935) yielded additional evidence of Folsom points, and, more importantly, revealed the existence of other point types now recognized as Paleoindian. Folsom points, in clear association with bones of extinct bison, were also recovered by Roberts (1935b, 1936; Wilmsen and Roberts 1978) at Lindenmeier, Colorado.

While Folsom ended the debate about *the presence* of humans in the Southwest and North America during the late Pleistocene, it did not resolve the question of *when* humans had first reached the New World. Howard's research at Blackwater Draw ultimately helped to establish Clovis as earlier than Folsom, and a postulated ancestor-descendant relationship between Clovis and Folsom was clear by the 1940s (Sellards 1952). Two of the best known Clovis sites in North

America—Naco (Haury 1953) and Lehner (Haury et al. 1959)—lie in southeastern Arizona; they provided important examples of Clovis hunting of mammoths. These sites were important in the genesis of Martin's (1967) overkill hypothesis, which continues to fuel debate about late Pleistocene megafauna extinction in North America and the rest of the globe to this day. Archaeologists also disagree about the importance of mammoths and other large mammals in the Clovis diet (Meltzer 1993). Finally, southwestern Clovis sites continue to be important touchstones in the debate over whether Clovis hunters were the "first" to colonize the New World (Feidel 2000). Putative pre-Clovis cultures have been identified in the Southwest, including Sandia (Hibben 1941), simple core-flake-chopper industries known as San Dieguito–Malpais (Hayden 1976) and New River (Peru 1984), and the material from pre-Clovis levels of Pendejo Cave (Chrisman et al. 1996). It is likely that the Southwest will continue to play a role in this debate over the initial colonization of the New World.

Agriculture

A second substantive contribution of southwestern archaeological research that has nationwide significance is the story of the development of maize agriculture. The Southwest is at the northern end of the pathway by which maize and other cultigens came north from Mexico and ultimately spread across much of what is today the United States. Herbert Dick's (1965) serendipitous choice of a west-central New Mexico rockshelter known as Bat Cave for excavation in 1947 provided the first definitive evidence that prehistoric southwestern cultures had grown crops long before Basketmaker II. Dick, in collaboration with botanist Paul Mangelsdorf, reported uncarbonized maize cobs from preceramic levels that were morphologically more "primitive" than those from Basketmaker II sites on the Colorado Plateau. The earliest maize was linked to Chiricahua stage (Middle Archaic) artifacts, and the first radiocarbon dates suggested that it dated to the third or fourth millennium B.C. Squash was recovered from these same levels, and the overlying San Pedro stage levels produced beans. Confirmation of the presence of early cultigens in preceramic contexts was quick in coming from Paul Martin's work at Tularosa and Cordova caves (Martin et al. 1952) as well as O Block Cave (Martin et al. 1954) and the open Cienega Creek site in the Point of Pines area of east-central Arizona (Haury 1957).

By 1960 Emil Haury recognized a pattern in the occurrence of maize and other cultigens that he organized into an explanatory model for early southwestern agriculture (Haury 1962). He proposed that the concentration of maize in preceramic sites positioned in the Mogollon Highlands above 1,850 m reflected the greater moisture requirements of early maize, thus explaining its corresponding absence from sites of similar age in the arid river valleys of the region. Further, the arrival of maize had little impact on southwestern cultures for nearly 2,000 years, as shown by the apparent absence of any change in preceramic material culture (particularly food-grinding implements) subsequent to the arrival of cultigens and the fact that villages and pottery did not appear until the early centuries A.D.

In its essential form, Haury's model endured for 20 years with refinements contributed in the 1980s by Ford (1981) and Minnis (1985). Ford (1981) suggested that early crops could not be dietary staples due to their low productivity and the inherent conflict between farming at one locale and the mobility demands associated with hunting and gathering. The value of agriculture was twofold: it provided maize and other cultivated resources localized in time and space, and ground disturbance associated with cultivation promoted concentrated stands of wild annuals that had long been important resources for hunter-gatherers. Minnis (1985) proposed that low-level agriculture could be easily incorporated into hunter-gatherer economies as long as the goal was simply to supplement hunting and gathering. Minor labor investment in planting and little or no cultivation of the developing crops would not interfere with mobility associated with foraging. Wills (1988) agreed that crops served to increase spatial and temporal resource predictability, and suggested that this played out against uncertainty about access to wild resources brought about by increased human population density and competition.

Beginning in 1981 with the reinvestigation of Bat Cave (Wills 1988) and the critical reanalysis of radiocarbon dating of early agriculture by Berry (1982), adjustments to the age and cultural context of agriculture were possible. Wills showed that the earlier excavation methodology employed at Bat Cave had erroneously suggested association of maize with Middle Archaic deposits; a Late Archaic association was more probable. Both Wills and Berry were able to demonstrate that the use of wood charcoal to date maize, rather than directly dating maize itself, had resulted in inflated ages for early maize. Berry concluded that there was little support for maize predating about 500–750 B.C. Wills, employing the new atomic mass spectrometry (AMS) technique, was able to directly radiocarbon date Bat Cave maize and squash to between 3200 and 2100 B.P. Both Wills and Berry suggested that it was the San Pedro occupation (Late Archaic) rather Chiricahua (Middle Archaic) with which agriculture was associated.

Also in the 1980s and 1990s, investigation of late preceramic sites in the lower elevation, more arid river basins of southeastern Arizona produced evidence of mixed farming-foraging economies of similar antiquity to those in the classic Mogollon Highland sites. These sites were open residential localities containing small, circular pit structures, burials, storage pits, processing pits, and thick accumulations of artifacts, fire-cracked rocks, and ash and charcoal (Huckell 1995; Mabry 1998; Sayles and Antevs 1941). Indications of large special-purpose structures and canal irrigation were also forthcoming (Mabry 1998, 2002). Flotation of sediment samples from the features at these sites produced carbonized maize that was directly dated to the period between 2500 and 3000 B.P., showing that early maize could be grown just as well at 2,500 ft as 6,000 ft. Such sites suggested that the basic tenets of the Haury model—little or no impact of agriculture, mesic-adapted cultigens, and movement of agriculture into the Southwest via the highland corridor—were in need of revision. An alternative view—that maize cultivation was a key component of a mixed economy and that it promoted development of sedentary villages adjacent to arable river floodplains—was proposed (see Matson [1991] and Wills and Huckell [1994] for a summary). The unusual site of Cerro Juanaquena (Hard and Roney 1998) in northwestern Chihuahua revealed another type of areally extensive, substantial residential site founded at least in part on maize farming, and discovery of open pithouse sites on the Colorado Plateau (Gilpin 1994) showed that this pattern of mixed farming-foraging was widespread across the late preceramic Southwest.

METHODOLOGICAL CONTRIBUTIONS

Southwestern preceramic archaeology has contributed to archaeological methodology most substantially in the pioneering of interdisciplinary, collaborative research. This has involved Quaternary geologists, paleoecologists, paleontologists, and botanists, but only one aspect of interdisciplinary collaboration—geoarchaeology—is treated here due to space limitations. The principal reason for this choice lies in the realm of context—a disproportionately large number of preceramic southwestern sites lie buried within alluvial, eolian, and rockshelter depositional environments. Discovery of the initial evidence of the antiquity of human occupation at Folsom was due to a widespread geologic phenomenon—arroyo cutting—that began in the late nineteenth and early twentieth centuries. Geologists were among the first to be interested in the phenomenon of arroyo cutting, and in understanding the age and climatic implications of buried deposits revealed by arroyos. The archaeological record offered them a chance to better understand the ages of buried deposits representing repeated cycles of ancient arroyo cutting and filling. Conversely, archaeologists quickly understood that geologists could help them understand past environmental conditions under which human cultures developed; a natural mutualism thus developed in the Southwest.

Certainly the earliest and probably the most prominent component of southwestern interdisciplinary research is the collaboration of archaeologists with Quaternary geologists. Beginning in the mid-1920s and extending to about 1960, two such figures stand out prominently: Kirk Bryan and Ernst Antevs (Haynes 1990). Both were interested in glacial and postglacial environmental change, Antevs principally from the perspective of climate and Bryan more from the study of alluvial processes. The central role played by these two men is perhaps a bit harder for us to appreciate today. Prior to the development of radiocarbon dating they were the only scientists in a position to help archaeologists construct a temporally anchored record of preceramic culture history. Both Antevs and Bryan used complex techniques of stratigraphic description and correlation to both understand the climatic conditions that had created the deposits in which archaeological sites occurred as well as to plug those deposits into what was known of Quaternary glacial and postglacial chronology. By the mid-1930s, both men were actively collaborating with archaeologists at Paleoindian sites such as Folsom, Blackwater Draw, Sandia Cave, Naco, and Lehner, as well as at Archaic sites such as Ventana Cave, the Cochise sites, and the San Jose sites (see references in Haynes 1990). Antevs (1948, 1955b) created an enduring, three-phase model of postglacial variations in temperature and moisture that was used by archaeologists for decades for dating, environmental reconstruction, and explanation of human behavior. Bryan (1941b) provided archaeologists with the so-called Alluvial Chronology (later refined by Haynes [1981]). This model was based on correlations of deposits of known age from across the western United States and Bryan's recognition that temporally and stratigraphically consistent patterns in deposition and erosion occurred widely.

Armed with new tools, Quaternary geologists have continued to collaborate with southwestern archaeologists in the post-^{14}C revolution portion of the twentieth century. Most prominent among them is Vance Haynes, whose work with late Pleistocene and Holocene alluvial geochronology and climate has significantly refined understanding of paleoenvironments and the responses of geologic processes to climate change (see Haynes [1995] for an example). Haynes has refined Bryan's alluvial chronology, and has been instrumental in deciphering the complex alluvial records at Paleoindian sites such as Blackwater Draw, Sandia Cave, Folsom, Murray Springs, Lehner, and Naco as well as dozens of lesser known Archaic sites. Haynes has shown that by approximately 11,000 B.P., megafaunal extinction was complete, and that this was at least in part linked to the "Clovis drought" that preceded the Younger Dryas climatic cooling (Haynes 1991). Several geoarchaeologists have contributed significantly to southwestern preceramic studies, including Michael Waters's (1986) reinvestigation of Sulphur Spring sites along Whitewater Draw that finally demonstrated that these sites postdated Clovis.

THEORETICAL CONTRIBUTIONS

In 1994 extended discussions by Lewis Binford and Cynthia Irwin-Williams were presented as the concluding chapters in a volume of collected papers discussing Archaic period research in the Southwest (Vierra, ed. 1994). Binford's assessment was that Archaic research, particularly as it concerned settlement patterns, remained mired in traditional approaches that emphasized essentialist treatments of artifacts, sites, and phases/cultures as units of study, and that any attempts to study process within such a framework were doomed to failure. Until the focus of research shifted to "many independently justified dimensions of formal variability and the explanation of patterning on those dimensions at different observational scales," studies of the Archaic would not meaningfully contribute to theory building (Binford 1994:528). Irwin-Williams (1994), reviewing the development of studies in the southwestern Archaic after ca. 1965, expressed satisfaction and optimism with the developing use of scientific hypothesis generation and testing over the 1970s and 1980s. In essence, Irwin-Williams celebrated what Binford found disquieting. I suggest that the analyses by both Binford and Irwin-Williams are valuable but that neither by itself provides a full picture. The field of southwestern preceramic prehistory is neither devoid of good research that contributes to theory building, nor are hypothesis generation and testing sufficient in the absence of valid theoretical frames of reference. A look at one area of research concern—social and ecological aspects of land use—may be illustrative.

The last quarter of the twentieth century in the Southwest saw researchers interested in issues of human paleoecology begin to apply both models of the empirical generalization kind as well as more theoretically driven propositions about hunter-gatherer organization to the preceramic record. Some of these were exactly the sort that Binford found useless. They employed unwarranted assumptions about the nature of a site—that attributes such as site size, artifact density, and diversity can be directly correlated with occupation by a particular type and size of social unit—and classified sites into preestablished categories. Studies of these sorts are properly criticized as simply reifying and imposing preconceived typologies, often loosely based on ethnological studies, on the archeological record with no attempt to understand the variety of cultural and environmental forces that create and structure the archaeological record.

On the other hand, there have been genuine attempts to apply theory to the study of preceramic southwestern land use. These have usually been in the realm of testing models or propositions about how past patterns of land use can be perceived, and disproportionately they are based on the work of Binford and his students. Most often thought of as processual and "Middle Range" theory, work on hunter-gatherer organization (Binford 1980, 1982), mobility (Kelly 1983, 1995), and technological organization (Nelson 1991) all share a focus on the broader issue of hunter-gatherer land use and ecology. These propositions about the organization of past hunter-gatherer societies rely heavily on understanding past biotic environments and how recent hunter-gatherers have exploited such environments. The goals are ultimately to understand the underlying bases that result in broad patterns of hunter-gatherer behavior. Since the mid-1980s, archaeologists working in the Southwest have found such models convenient for structuring inquiries, and studies rooted in them increasingly have appeared over the past two decades. As noted above, in some cases they have been misapplied in an essentialist manner, where the goal seems to be classification of sites, assemblages, or human paleoecology. However, in many cases, archaeologists have attempted to determine the archaeological correlates that might be associated with particular behaviors, and how changes in ecology or behavior might be manifested and perceived in the material record.

One positive example is the study of technological organization and patterns of land use. From the mid-1980s on, preceramic archaeologists were concerned with issues of hunter-gatherer mobility including the scale of group movements, the pattern of movements across a landscape, and the organization of technology to facilitate such movement. One of the first such efforts was Steve Shackley's use of obsidian geochemistry to track the movement of Archaic groups in the Southwest (Shackley 1988, 1996). Recognizing that some of Binford's ideas concerning mobility organization and range could be explored by use of X-ray fluorescence to document obsidian source and artifact geochemical variation, he examined variation in obsidian projectile points and other artifacts as a means of tracking Middle Archaic mobility ranges. His work demonstrated that Middle Archaic points were routinely found hundreds of kilometers from known sources, thereby providing a measure of mobility range. Further, the presence of obsidian from montane sources at sites in the intermontane basins supported ethnographically based theoretical expectations concerning use of lowland and upland environments. Similar efforts in the San Juan Basin of New Mexico (Vierra 1994), involving nonlocal obsidian and other raw materials, led to the inference that Early and Middle Archaic groups there used high residential mobility to cover large territories. Both Shackley and Vierra also found lessened use of obsidian during the Late Archaic/Early Agricultural period, and proposed that this reflected reduced mobility as a concomitant of subsistence change. In New Mexico and on the Southern Plains, Dan Amick (1994, 1996) and Phil LeTourneau (2000) have conducted similar studies, applying visual lithic artifact sourcing of cherts to examine Folsom raw material selection and use as a means of reconstructing regional patterns of technological organization, mobility, and land use.

Also noteworthy are the more recent attempts to examine the archaeological record from a landscape, rather than site-based, perspective. In the mid-1980s, several southwestern archaeologists began to establish the concept of viewing the archaeological record as a sampling problem needing more appropriate responses than the often simple notions of "site." Doleman (1994) has discussed the complexities and challenges of this approach based on his attempts to apply it in south-central New Mexico, and Irwin-Williams and her colleagues also experimented with it in north-central New Mexico. While it is clear that prehistoric foragers exploited the landscape in ways that are far more complex than traditional site-based characterizations of subsistence and settlement are able to recognize, attempting to develop sufficiently sophisticated theoretical models and methodological tools to move towards a broader perspective is challenging. Among these challenges are issues concerning geomorphic processes of burial and exposure of artifacts and features; distortion of the archaeological record caused by repeated use of a landscape over millennia; development of ways of dating what are now "nondiagnostic" artifacts (debitage and unretouched tools for example); and establishing paleoenvironmental records of sufficient detail to understand local conditions at specific times in the past.

THOUGHTS FOR THE FUTURE OF SOUTHWESTERN PRECERAMIC ARCHAEOLOGY

I would like to close by looking ahead to ways in which the study of preceramic sites in the Southwest can or should progress to ensure further significant contributions to North American archaeology. First, despite all that we have learned about the preceramic period during the twentieth century, we still have high quality culture-historical data for only a small part of the record. It is noteworthy that we are still trying to identify and delimit in time projectile points that are common in many regions of the Southwest, including ones that long have been targets of Archaic period research. While some may disagree with the importance of this endeavor, it is difficult to quarrel with the fact that unless one knows the broad outline of the culture-historical record, the study of more interesting issues is well nigh impossible. Projectile points remain our most basic, best tools for identifying time and tracing regional interaction. The comparatively recent recognition of the Cortaro point (Roth and Huckell 1988) has proven of critical importance, because it now appears to be a key marker for the arrival of agriculture in the southern Southwest some 3,500 or more years ago. Continued additions to and refinement of the basic culture-historical record are fundamental to progress in other areas of knowledge.

Second, it is clear that in the future CRM investigations will provide the bulk of new information on preceramic, particularly Archaic, occupations. The last quarter of the twentieth century witnessed a radical change in the way in which southwestern archaeology was conducted. The national commitment to preserve, protect, and recover the human past as it was threatened by development resulted in a quantum leap in data acquisition. To single out one example, the Arizona Department of Transportation has expended millions of dollars on highway projects that have brought to light the impressive Early Agricultural period villages near Tucson (Gregory 2000; Mabry 1998). Well-funded projects such as these have revolutionized knowledge of the late preceramic period over the past decade, and have particularly increased understanding of the spread and incorporation of agriculture into hunter-gatherer economies. Also, it is important to recognize that few academic departments in the Southwest today are actively pursuing long-term research focused on the Archaic. This is nothing new; students and faculty with long-term research commitments to preceramic prehistory have generally been few throughout the twentieth century. However, one positive trend that developed over the last two decades was the development of partnerships between academic departments and CRM firms to encourage students to use CRM projects for dissertations. Such partnerships are, I believe, a vital part of the future of the continuing development of southwestern archaeology and for repaying in as many ways as possible the national commitment to historic preservation. Interestingly, Paleoindian sites are rarely encountered or investigated as part of CRM projects; research of this type remains rare and is usually pursued by academic or museum archaeologists.

Finally, the rapid developments in hunter-gatherer theory over the past two decades have provided us with tremendous resources to employ in learning about ancient hunter-gatherers. We have barely scratched the potential of this new world. For understandable reasons, processual theoretical constructs have dominated work in the Southwest and will likely continue to do so for the foreseeable future. However, evolutionary theory—be it selectionist or evolutionary ecology—offers other ways to frame investigations of past hunter-gatherers. Its application should be encouraged. In particular, human evolutionary ecology has been shown to be very useful for the study of early agriculture (Winterhalder and Goland 1997), and is only now beginning to see use by southwestern archaeologists.

In closing, I must say that I am very optimistic about the future of preceramic archaeology in the Southwest. As we close the books on the twentieth century and look back at the important contributions to anthropological knowledge that were highlighted here, we should look forward to the opportunities to build on this foundation. The southwestern United States is a tremendous laboratory for the study of the first 10,000 years of human history, and we have barely scratched the surface of its potential. Hopefully, the contributions made by southwestern preceramic research over the course of the twenty-first century will at least equal if not exceed those made by the twentieth-century pioneers in this field.

11

Complexity

Stephen H. Lekson

SIMPLIFYING COMPLEXITY

What is complexity? The term did not exist (in its current usage) in the early days of southwestern archaeology. When "complexity" frothed to the top of the southwestern stew in the 1970s, it meant hierarchical, centralized political structures. (I exclude here "complexity" of the Santa Fe Institute variety—an intriguing and useful concept, but an entirely different use of the word; see Kantner [2002].) And by "hierarchical, centralized structures" we meant institutionalized leadership: chief, king, queen, cacique, council, *tlatoani*. Hierarchical leadership need not be male, nor solitary, nor despotic. Hierarchical leaders can be elected, appointed, or anointed. They can indeed be several, as in a council or "managerial elites" (of which, more below). They can be obeyed or ignored. But when few begin to make decisions affecting many, an interesting threshold is crossed. Centralization of decision-making is one solution to collective action problems that has important political and evolutionary consequences.

The variable ability of leaders to enforce (or of the led to defy) decisions is a key dimension of complexity, as used here. There exists a straw man of complexity in southwestern archaeology, and elsewhere, that supposes centralized hierarchies must control, in despotic detail, the lives of the led. Our expectations for southwestern hierarchies might impress the Sun King or Joe Stalin. Centralized hierarchies in the ancient Southwest (if any) could hardly have been totalitarian states, with tight control over subjects and regions.

Complex political formations were largely absent from southwestern archaeological thinking prior to the 1970s, due to the foundational premises of our field. "Most studies conducted prior to the late

1970s simply ignored the topic (particularly in the Pueblo area)" (Plog 1995:189). So even nontotalitarian complexity was, when it was finally proposed, a hot topic. It was new and challenging. Debates over the presence or absence of hierarchical, centralized political structures in the Southwest all but dominated conferences and journals. The arguments grew rancorous in the mid-1980s, particularly in the debates over Grasshopper–Chavez Pass data sets. Heated exchanges sometimes slipped into unpleasant ad hominem rhetorics. The argument itself seemed unending and unendable.

By the late 1980s, complexity was a place where angels and archaeologists feared to tread. Many reached this conclusion, or something like it: If the Grasshopper–Chavez Pass debate could not be resolved, then we lack tools of resolution. Barbara Mills, in her introduction to *Alternative Leadership Strategies in the Prehispanic Southwest*, summed it up: "debates became unproductive largely because they concerned an unsolvable problem" (Mills 2000b:5). By "alternative leadership strategies" Mills meant, of course, alternatives to hierarchical, centralized political complexity.

It is no coincidence that the 1990s was a decade of agency, households, and cults in southwestern archaeology—anything but hierarchies. Hierarchical complexity was branded a methodological dead end, and the term "complexity" itself was redefined and complicated to encompass a remarkably wide range of concepts. These newly complicated complexities sit above, beyond, beside, beneath but largely in place of hierarchical, centralized structures. Ben Nelson's conclusions of his comparison of Chaco and La Quemada sound the charge: "Given current paradigms, our inclination when comparing two polities is to ask 'How complex were they relative to each other?'—instead we should be asking 'How were they complex?'" (Nelson 1995:614). Ask not if they were complex, but how they were complex: the mantra of New Complexity in the Greater Southwest.

The Southwest is indeed home to societies, past and present, that offer remarkable textbook examples of alternative leadership. Pueblos are famous for their social and political leveling devices, flattening tumescent hierarchies. I will argue that those remarkable systems cannot be understood except in the context of and in reaction to complex hierarchical episodes in the past, and in particular Chaco Canyon. Chaco, I will argue, gave Pueblos an example of complexity—hierarchical, centralized political structures—which they endured and then rejected, developing leveling mechanisms to ensure Chaco would not happen again.

This was a process that can only be understood by looking at very large areas and very long periods of time. By seeing alternative leadership at individual sites or districts, and thereby rejecting hierarchy at larger scales of southwestern prehistory, we not only risk disservice to that history but also miss a key factor in the creation of those remarkable alternatives. Understanding the role of complexity in the development of alternative leadership strategies requires large temporal and spatial scales.

Hierarchical, centralized political structures have been a tough sell for the ancient Southwest. I see three major reasons for this: 1) foundational premises, 2) data sets, and 3) scale. Conclusions reached by the earliest archaeologists and ethnologists have become our bedrock, foundational premises, but they were (for this issue) wrong. The data sets over which the most heated debates raged in the 1970s and 1980s were simply inappropriate for the question of complexity. And the geographic and temporal scales on which the inquiry has been framed have been far too small. Happily, these themes represent a roughly chronological narrative of complexity in the Southwest.

FOUNDATIONAL PREMISES

Our founding fathers and mothers "just said no" to complexity in the Southwest, and particularly in the Pueblo Southwest. Those bedrock concepts represent the mingled works of early scholars and pioneer thinkers—the teachers of our teachers' teachers. They are so distant that we do not even study them: they have become the culture of southwestern archaeology. That culture defines what is proper to the field: the glass ceiling, the lines inside which we stay.

Ever since Europeans first encountered the Southwest, there has been controversy about complexity. Coronado traveled north in 1540 hoping to reach Cíbola—reputedly, a very rich and very complex place. The Southwest had that reputation, and not just from overheated friars' tales: Native informants confirmed the Southwest's complexity. But Coronado was sadly disappointed by the farming villages and towns he encountered. The earliest Spanish accounts report, emphatically, that the Southwest was not a new Mexico—that is, southwestern Pueblos were not complex, a bitter disappointment for them, and a harbinger for us.

In 1848 the United States effected a change of regime. The spectacular ruins in New Mexico, Arizona, and Colorado were discovered (again) by Anglo America. The popular press attributed these structures to a

"Lost Race," undoubtedly of Old World origin. With the publication of Prescott's *Conquest of Mexico* in 1843, an enormously influential book at the time, the Lost Race gave way to the Aztecs. According to Prescott, the mythological homeland of the Aztecs was to the north, so southwestern ruins were considered by many intelligent people to be Aztec. The (Aztec) Southwest was long ago complex, even if Pueblos today are not.

The connection of southwestern ruins to the higher civilizations of Mexico has been a constant theme in arguments about southwestern complexity since at least the 1840s, and it continues today. Even though early scholars, such as Gallatin (1848, cited in Fowler 2000:68) rejected the idea, southwestern ruins continued to be associated with the Aztecs or various lost races until late in the nineteenth century—much like the Mound Builders in the eastern states. Those who attributed southwestern ruins to Aztecs were scorned by serious scholars as romantic. Indeed, the Aztec angle was dismissed by Charles Lummis as "the romantic view," an error needing correction.

What, then, was truth? What was the ancient Southwest really like? I offer here four examples from early scholars: Bandelier, Morgan, Kidder, and Hewett. These are the foundational figures who shaped our field.

Adolph Bandelier went to the Southwest in the late nineteenth century specifically to investigate the connections between the Southwest and ancient Mexico. He saw little to connect the two, and indeed he was unimpressed with what he found in New Mexico:

> The picture which can be dimly traced into this past is a very modest and unpretending one. No great cataclysms of nature, no waves of destruction on a large scale, either natural or human, appear to have interrupted the slow and tedious development of the people before the Spaniards came [Bandelier 1892:592].

This cheerless view of southwestern prehistory, plodding doggedly along to Pueblo-hood, was subsequently codified in the Pecos Classification.

Bandelier's Southwest was far less interesting than the older, "romantic" Southwest, but it was anthropologically relevant, and even important. Lewis Henry Morgan argued that the remarkable communal "village life" of the Americas actually *began* at Chaco Canyon and adjacent areas of the San Juan drainage (Morgan 1881). Chaco was the ur-commune from whence came the communes of all other New World societies. Morgan included the Aztecs in his communal category, so he had no trouble normalizing Chaco's architecture:

It is evident that they were the work of the people, constructed for their own enjoyment and protection. Enforced labor never created them...they were raised by the Indians for their own use, with willing hands, and occupied by them on terms of entire equality. Liberty, equality, and fraternity are emphatically the three great principles of the gens [clans], and this architecture responds to these sentiments [Morgan 1965:310].

Alfred V. Kidder, a true foundational figure in southwestern archaeology, agreed with Bandelier and Morgan. Pueblos were simple—magnificently and democratically simple:

Few races have gone as far toward civilization as did the Pueblos while still retaining the essential democracy of primitive life. Most other peoples, as they advanced from savagery, have first set up for themselves, and later fallen under the domination of, rulers temporal or religious; aristocracies or theocracies have sprung up; and the gap between the masses and the classes has become wider and wider. But among the Pueblos no such tendency ever made headway; there were neither very rich nor very poor, every family lived in the same sort of quarters, and ate the same sort of food, as every other family [Kidder 1924[1962]:343–344].

My final example comes from Edgar Hewett. Hewett was no match for Bandelier, Morgan, or Kidder as a scholar, but he trained many southwestern archaeologists—far more than any other individual in the early days of our field. Hewett was a founding father, indeed, and one of the most effective popularizers of southwestern archaeology. His opinions on matters such as Chaco Canyon and its monumental buildings shaped subsequent thinking. Hewett (1936:13) likened the enormous Chaco ruins to monuments of Egypt, Mesopotamia, Asia Minor, and Middle America, but he believed that their construction

was no unwilling work under the lash of priestly or kingly task masters; the American Indians were never so ruled. It was the spontaneous impulse of a virile people, comparable to the heaping up of great mounds far in excess of actual needs, by insect communities [Hewitt 1936:23].

Pueblos, by these accounts were now and always had been politically simple, notable not complex.

The continued presence of Pueblos in the Southwest led to an especially close relationship between ethnology and archaeology. This, too, is a foundational principle. Bandelier's 1890 novel *The Delight Makers* set the tone, using ethnography to reconstruct prehistoric Pueblo lifeways, albeit in fiction. Appeal to Pueblos became the standard operating procedure for archaeology: dig all summer and then ask Pueblo people to help interpret the findings. Neil Judd turned to Santiago Naranjo of Santa Clara (among others); Edgar Hewett had a very wide circle of "Pueblo friends." Early archaeologists routinely appealed to the Pueblo people and Pueblo ethnology for interpretive models. Kidder agreed:

> These fascinating communities preserve the ancient culture of the Southwest in almost its aboriginal purity; even the most sophisticated of them are little more than veneered by European civilization, and we can still, as Lummis has so aptly phrased it, "catch our archaeology alive" [Kidder 1924[1962]:144].

Faith in the direct comparability of modern and ancient Pueblos underwrote early archaeology; it, too, is a foundational premise. Indeed, the apparent political simplicity of modern Pueblos was important in the foundational premise of ancient simplicity. And how did the founding fathers and mothers picture the Pueblos? During the final decades of the frontier, southwestern peoples were portrayed in exhibitions and newsprint as simple and peaceful (Pueblos) or simple and savage (Apaches). A chorus of ethnographers and popularizers of the Southwest throughout the early twentieth century emphasized the simple (i.e., noncomplex) nature of the contemporary Pueblo people. I will not attempt a full review here, but offer instead a single, extremely influential example from (at last!) a founding mother.

Ruth Benedict's *Patterns of Culture*, published in 1934, presented a view of Pueblo people that appealed strongly to an intellectual community recovering from the horrors of World War I. Zuni was idealized as an egalitarian, peaceful society: a model of what could be. Although its vision of Zuni has not survived later scholarship, *Patterns of Culture* remains one of the most influential American anthropological books ever published. Benedict cemented the egalitarian view of Pueblos, ancient and modern, by describing the emphasis on equality and active suppression of expressions of power. Of the Zuni, she says:

Personal authority is perhaps the most vigorously disparaged trait in Zuni. A man who thirsts for power or knowledge, who wishes to be as they scornfully phrase it "a leader of his people," receives nothing but censure and will likely be persecuted for sorcery [Benedict 1934:98–99].

Modern Pueblos were egalitarian and decidedly noncomplex. And they had elaborate leveling mechanisms—such as sorcery charges for untoward ambition—for suppressing hierarchy. Pueblo leveling mechanisms are a wonder to the world, examples of how societies might operate without "the social inequality so many consider the bane of modern life" (Johnson 1989:387).

Modern ethnology questions the stereotype of egalitarian Pueblos (e.g., Brandt 1994; Plog 1995:190–192). Perhaps things are not quite so simple in the Pueblos as they seemed to Ruth Benedict. Archaeology acknowledges that the Pueblo present is more complicated (if not to say complex) than the communal democracies proposed by Bandelier, Morgan, Kidder, and Hewett, but appears to maintain a prior simplicity: that is, even if modern Pueblos were slightly complicated, they must have developed from simpler roots. This belief is codified in the Pecos Classification—much reviled but used. The Pecos Classification posited a steady, unilinear, specific evolution of the modern Pueblos (after the recognition that Basketmakers and Pueblos were indeed of one stock) from simple hunter-gatherers, to simple agriculturalists, to pueblo-dwelling ancestors of the modern Pueblos. Its systematics were artlessly additive—first corn, then pottery, then small pueblos, then kivas, then large pueblos—to cumulatively create the modern Pueblos. Bandelier was right: a tedious progression, indeed.

The steady progress presented by the Pecos Classification was challenged from time to time. Frank Roberts (1935a) suggested that Pueblo III represented a climax of sorts ("Great Pueblo") and the following Pueblo IV represented a diminution or decline ("Regressive Pueblo"). Roberts dared to suggest that the past was not simply a long prologue for the present but it was instead different: more elaborate, more complex. His proposal met with no enthusiasm and indeed considerable hostility, in part because Regressive Pueblo appeared to belittle modern Pueblos. The term "Regressive Pueblo" is never used today, and the Pecos Classification confirms a steady development from simple to simple.

These examples map the bedrock, foundational premises underlying southwestern archaeology. Those early premises form long-buried strata supporting layers of later scholarship. The contours of southwestern archaeology conformed to these foundational premises, until they were challenged in the 1970s. Unfortunately, the challenge focused on inappropriate data.

Data Sets

It is fair to conclude that, in general, egalitarian models of ancient southwestern societies were accepted in southwestern archaeology from the turn of the nineteenth century to at least 1970. In major synthetic studies of the culture history era neither the term nor the idea of complexity appear at all (e.g., McGregor 1941, 1965; Taylor 1948, 1954). Complexity did not exist; it was not even a topic for discussion. That changed in the 1970s.

Complexity rose from nonissue to central matter in the 1970s and 1980s, over (in retrospect) rather unlikely sets of data: the Grasshopper–Chavez Pass debates. In brief, the debate pitted an egalitarian, nonranked interpretation of Grasshopper (a very large pueblo in the Mogollon uplands of central Arizona; see Reid and Whittlesey [1999]) against perceived "managerial elites"—that is, hierarchical complexity—at Chavez Pass (a very large pueblo, about 85 km northwest of Grasshopper; see Upham [1982] and Upham and Plog [1986]). Grasshopper–Chavez Pass was an important chapter in southwestern archaeology. It had long-reaching effects, not the least of which was situating subsequent arguments about complexity geographically, in the Western Pueblo area of Arizona. Most arguments for or against complexity were evaluated using Hopi, Zuni, and other Western Pueblo data (e.g., recently, in continuations of the debate by Feinman et al. 2000; McGuire and Saitta 1996). In my opinion (see also Ware 2001), the geographic emphasis on Western Pueblos seems misplaced, and blunts the effectiveness and diminishes the utility of the methodological and conceptual contributions of the debate (which were real, on both sides). For recent treatments asking the same questions of Eastern Pueblos see Creamer (2001), Creamer and Haas (1998), and Ware (2001).

Grasshopper and Chavez Pass, I think, were odd places to debate complexity. If we are looking for complexity in the Southwest, why not go right to the recognized Pretenders? Why quibble about complexity among Western Pueblos when there are Chaco Canyon, Paquimé, and

Hohokam? I turn to the usual suspects of southwestern complexity: our strongest data sets for complexity in the Southwest.

Claims of complexity for Chaco went far beyond the "managerial elites" of the Grasshopper–Chavez Pass debates. Many of us thought Chaco was politically complex (e.g., Judge 1979; Schelberg 1984; Sebastian 1992); some of us thought that Chaco was a state (Wilcox 1996). These claims had their day, and then suffered a serious reverse in Gregory Johnson's concluding remarks in *Dynamics of Southwest Prehistory* (Cordell and Gummerman 1989). Johnson was invited to "bring some additional measure of objectivity to the proceedings" (Johnson 1989:371) of a multiauthored review of the Southwest. Absent tools to resolve the Grasshopper–Chavez Pass debate and to "diagnose" complexity in the Southwest, we sought the wisdom of outside counsel. Johnson concluded that Chaco was a pueblo, and—from foundational premises—pueblos were egalitarian:

> The reader will have discerned that I harbor grave doubts about the ontological status of Anasazi chiefdoms [i.e., complexity]. Residential mobility, potential surplus availability, diet, patterns of labor investment, and variability in mortuary ritual simply seem very different from those I would expect in a hierarchical world of high borns and common folk.... The Chaco data can support a basically egalitarian interpretation [Johnson 1989:378, 386].

Alas, the data Johnson was given were not all that we could wish: new and old Chaco data for each category seem, to me and others, to speak strongly for highborns and commoners. But it is hardly fair to dispute in detail the decade-old, good-spirited comments of a conference discussant. And, in any event, it is Johnson's conclusion (not the details of his argument) that have reached the status of a near-foundation premise (DeBoer 2001; Feinman et al. 2000:451): no complexity at Chaco, no complexity in the Pueblo past.

Ben Nelson's (1995) "Complexity, Hierarchy, and Scale: A Controlled Comparison Between Chaco Canyon, New Mexico and La Quemada, Zacatecas" reaches a similar conclusion about Chaco and complexity (as hierarchical, centralized political structure), and is an article frequently cited by contemporary opponents of complexity. Chaco scores higher than La Quemada on a number of dimensions often considered relevant for complexity. But Nelson concludes that Chaco was not complex, in the sense of centralized hierarchy, while La Quemada was: "Comparison of these two particular cases demonstrates that the Chacoan entity was organized at larger scales, but La Quemada was more hierarchically structured" (Nelson 1995:599). This conclusion, while consistent with Nelson's assumptions and suppositions, seems at least partially predicated on the foundational premises of Pueblo archaeology: no complexity here. Because Chaco is where it is, and is historically linked to modern Pueblo peoples, it is more properly assumed to have been Pueblo-like: prayerful, consultive, collaborative, and not centralized and hierarchical. Nelson, like Johnson, saw no hierarchy at Chaco. Chaco is our strongest data set for Puebloan complexity. So, for many archaeologists, if not Chaco, then nowhere.

One of the boldest assertions of complexity in the ancient Southwest came with Charles Di Peso's (1974) multivolume study *Casas Grandes, a Fallen Trading Center of the Gran Chichimeca*, reporting his excavations at Paquimé in the early 1960s. Paquimé (also known as Casas Grandes) is not on the Colorado Plateau; indeed, it is not in the Pueblo region, as that region was defined in the 1960s. Consequently, Paquimé was free to be complex.

There was no doubt in Di Peso's mind that Paquimé was politically hierarchical and strongly centralized. *Casas Grandes* was a tour de force of culture history, but it expanded the culture history vocabulary to encompass terms and ideas inappropriate north of the border. Di Peso spoke of Paquimé as though it were part of Mesoamerica, with Mesoamerican political systems: pretty darn complex. Di Peso's (1974) report, alas, arrived too late. In the early 1970s, southwestern archaeology was repudiating culture history and turning to a range of "new" archaeologies. For that reason and others, *Casas Grandes* was seldom offered as evidence in the debates over complexity.

While some aspects of Di Peso's interpretation have not survived subsequent analysis, his reading of Paquimé as politically complex was ultimately convincing. By the early 1980s, Linda Cordell's *Prehistory of the Southwest* presented Paquimé as one of three "regionally integrated systems" (Chaco, Casas Grandes, and Hohokam; see Cordell [1984:246–283]). Moreover, Cordell notes that Paquimé offers a "stronger case for a regional system based on trade" than Chaco. Even Gregory Johnson, dour on Chaco, admitted that "Casas [Grandes] looks elite—even to me" (Johnson 1989:386).

Subsequent research supports Di Peso's contention that Casas Grandes was complex, although the sources, scales, and implications of that complexity have been revised, mostly downward and inward. Paquimé is no longer considered a Mesoamerican outpost. Rather, it is seen as a locally evolved complex society with strong (but post-facto) ties to Mexico (Whalen and Minnis 2001). Many archaeologists regard Paquimé as part of the Pueblo world (e.g., Cordell 1994a), but most Pueblo archaeologists think on Casas Grandes little, if at all. They should. If the Pueblo region includes Paquimé, complexity reenters Pueblo prehistory, by the back door. Paquimé was a pueblo; Paquimé was complex; therefore, Pueblo prehistory included episodes of complexity. This is not simply a curious syllogism; it is a point of some importance to which we will return.

Hohokam in southern Arizona, the third example of appropriate data, should have been beyond the reach of Pueblo archaeology's foundational premises. Hohokam presents a strong set of data for complexity by virtue of the remarkable canal systems of the Salt-Gila Basin. We must look as far south as the Andes for comparable systems (Doolittle 1990). At one time in anthropology's long history, canal irrigation on this scale bespoke complexity, and there persists, with good reason, an aura of complexity about massive public works such as Hohokam canals.

Cushing had described the Classic period Hohokam as complex as early as 1890, but Gladwin and Haury's work in the 1930s suggested that the seemingly complex developments of the Classic period were the result of a migration of Salado people into the region. In retrospect, this seems a curious argument, since Salado was Puebloan, and Pueblos were notoriously simple. Haury eventually concluded that Hohokam was not merely non-Puebloan, but in fact a Mesoamerican people who migrated into southern Arizona (Haury 1976). This, by itself, does not entail complexity. There were noncomplex societies in ancient Mexico.

Paul and Suzanne Fish, in a review of "Hohokam Political and Social Organization," note "a lack of consensus in Hohokam archaeology concerning basic aspects of sociopolitical organization. Simultaneous usage of contrastive terms for organizational character such as hierarchical and egalitarian or tribe and chiefdom, can be found among different scholars" (Fish and Fish 1991:168). Mainstream interpretation has Hohokam organized noncomplexly, like modern Pima (e.g., Wilcox 1991; Wilcox and Sternberg 1983). McGuire concludes that "an egalitarian ethos governed the everyday lives of the Hohokam" (McGuire 2001:39). Doyel, in contrast, speaks of "emerging complexity" in the Colonial and Sedentary periods (Doyel 1991:246). The disagreements seem to parallel those surrounding ancient Pueblo societies, but there is a striking difference. Hohokam has some remarkable evidence of or conditions for complexity that the Pueblo region lacked. Let us appeal to authority: Johnson rejected Puebloan complexity on the basis of high residential mobility, low potential surplus, relatively low levels of labor coordination, poor diets of proposed elites, and unremarkable mortuary differentiation of proposed elites (Johnson 1989:378). Hohokam had most of these things, and in spades: high residential stability in extremely long-lived sites; high potential surplus with large-scale irrigation of the Sonoran desert; and high degrees of labor coordination to build and maintain the remarkable canal systems. Canals and the attendant possibility of large surpluses make Hohokam a far more appropriate data set for investigating complexity than Grasshopper and Chavez Pass. Yet one gets the impression that Arizona archaeologists, having witnessed the debates of the 1970s and 1980s at much closer range than the rest of us, are content with ambiguity, happy with the "enigmatic Hohokam" (Fish and Fish 1991:168).

SCALE

To introduce themes of geographic and temporal scale, Chaco is my example because we know a lot about Chacoan time and space. For Hohokam and Paquimé, time and space are less certain. The chronology of Chaco is well understood and its geography well recognized. In this section, I introduce themes of time and space and argue for their fundamental importance to complexity.

Space first: I will not rehearse here the "Chacoan regional system"—between 150 and 200 great houses (many with associated great kivas, "roads," and residential communities) found over an area from 107° to 110° longitude, and 34° to 37° 30' latitude (Lekson 1991, 1999; Fowler and Stein 2001). For the questions posed here, we can usefully compress the range of opinions about great houses into two positions, comparable to constitutional debates two centuries past: "federalists" (like myself) who interpret the Chacoan region as integrated by central political authority at Chaco Canyon (that is, complex); and "antifederalists" who favor local autonomy (and relative simplicity) over much or most of the Chacoan region (see papers in Kantner and Mahoney 2000). For antifederalists, Chaco was either geographically limited in its political influence, or an apolitical regional center of ritual and pilgrimage, or simply a local aberration with only limited power or interest beyond its canyon.

The key features for delimiting the Chacoan region are great houses: massively built, formally designed structures defined most easily in contrast to expediently built, informal houses that constitute 95 percent of Anasazi architecture. A particularly clear example of an "outlier" great house is Chimney Rock, 150 km northeast of Chaco. The architectural contrast between the Chimney Rock great house and the domestic structures of its surrounding community is remarkable. The great house looks very much like structures in Chaco Canyon, and few (if any) archaeologists would argue that it represents a local development. Most outlier great houses are less certain than Chimney Rock; their variabilities and ambiguities foster doubts.

Historically, there were two waves of antifederalism towards great houses. First, when the idea of a Chacoan region was first mooted in the 1970s and early 1980s, antifederalists denied the reality of the great house pattern, particularly in their individual areas; this NIMBY-ism eventually fell before the press of data. The empirical pattern of great houses has been generally (but not entirely!) accepted for over a decade. Long enough for a change of academic generations and another swing of the pendulum: a second wave of more serious antifederalism, which recognizes the empirical pattern but, because of variability within great houses, denies the regional integration of federalist models. Great houses, like any artifact, display a range of variability (displayed graphically in Lekson 1991:Figures 3.3–3.5; see also Kantner and Mahoney 2000). Antifederalists find that variability damning to claims of regional integration and favor instead scenarios of local evolution or development. Federalists find demands for cookie-cutter uniformity unreasonable: the architectural signatures of ancient empires were quite variable (think of Rome), and nothing so authoritarian as empire is being proposed for Chaco. Moreover, the variability of architecture at Chaco Canyon itself parallels and probably exceeds the range of variability within the regional great houses. The geographic scale of Chaco continues to play a key role in assertions and denials of ancient complexity.

Let us shift focus from geographic to temporal scale and invite back to the table, briefly, Hohokam and Paquimé. Time requires historical rather than spatial thinking. Ask not how big was Chaco, but how long was Chaco? Conventionally, Chaco is dated from A.D. 900 to 1150, but well-dated events within that span show that the canyon's real florescence began as late as 1020, while its demise commenced as early as the 1080s and concluded by 1135. Sixty years, perhaps: a short run for a capital. I have argued that the political experiment begun at Chaco did not end there, but continued at Aztec Ruins until the final abandonment of the region in the final decades of the thirteenth century (Lekson 1999, 2002). Chaco and Aztec together total a more respectable two centuries. Was Chaco a flash in the pan or a dynasty? A momentary aberration or a strong pattern? Our reading of Chacoan and post-Chacoan chronology has profound implications for its complexity or its simplicity. To illustrate the importance of time, and the need for new ways of dealing with time, I return briefly to Hohokam and Paquimé. The interpretation of each is profoundly influenced by differing magnitudes of time.

Hohokam is remarkable for the depth of its prehistory, especially given startling new data on large, late Archaic pithouse villages in the Sonoran desert. Hohokam persists in place, remarkably. Its canal infrastructure changed and developed through time, but compared to the rainfall farming tactics of Chacoan populations, Hohokam irrigation tied towns to places for centuries. Hohokam was remarkable for its deep sedentism, for its depth in place. Paquimé, in contrast, may have appeared out of thin air and burned, cometlike, a short brilliant course through southwestern prehistory. Paquimé is, in a sense, all about time. Di Peso (1974) thought it sprang up out of nothing, imported from Mexico. If so, Paquimé raises the level of complexity beyond anything suggested for the Southwest: Di Peso's Paquimé was an outpost of civilization. Whalen and Minnis (2001) derive Paquimé from local sources: homegrown complexity that they compare to Chaco's. While most archaeologists dismiss Di Peso's claims, the jury still is out on Paquimé's precedents. As Whalen and Minnis note, it is difficult to identify a large population prior to that of Paquimé (Whalen and Minnis 2001). Time plays as much a role as space in the interpretation of complexity at Paquimé.

Southwestern complexity is presented to us in curiously short bits: a presence/absence condition in particular times and places. There are parallels here with our treatment of space. New Archaeology treated each site as a case, each valley as a "natural laboratory." With the recognition of "regional systems" in the 1970s and 1980s, we realized that larger spatial frameworks might reveal rather different political organizations than those evident at smaller scales. With the revival of historicity in postprocessual approaches of the 1990s, southwestern archaeology may begin to consider longer time-spans—not of *longue durée* or *mentalité* or habitus—but of *history*, dynamic and causal, in our evaluation of ancient social formations. Complexity leaves tracks through time, as well as structures on space.

COMPLICATING COMPLEXITY

Recall Johnson's (1989) pronouncement, "Chaco data can support a basically egalitarian interpretation." Johnson's was not the last authoritative deflation of Chacoan and southwestern hierarchy. Essays reaching similar conclusions include those by respected arbiters such as Norman Yoffee (2001; Yoffee et al. 1999) and Colin Renfrew (2001). In the face of such formidable opposition, it would seem prudent for procomplexity southwesternists to strike their tents; but something in the data, or in the water, keeps the notion alive. Warren DeBoer, a trenchant essayist, mocked southwestern pretensions:

> Are Southwestern archaeologists still recovering from Johnson's devastating critique, trying to reinvent their own brand of home-grown complexity? Why does a regional archaeology wish to find complexity? Is complexity a positively valued polarity? Does it get grants? [DeBoer 2001:24].

Complexity (as I have used it here) is unfashionable, out of step with southwestern times. Recent thinking favors alternative reconstructions of Chaco (and other candidates for complexity) which are nonhierarchical, decentralized, uncomplex. In an important volume *Alternative Leadership Strategies in the Prehispanic Southwest* (Mills, ed. 2000), the first essay is a new reading of Chaco by W. H. Wills. He concludes that while Chaco "involved leaders," its glory days were shaped and driven by "communitas, or anti-structure" (Wills 2000:41, 43). Wills's "anti-structure" joins other communal or alternative formations recently suggested for Chaco (e.g., Saitta 1997). Have we come full circle, back to Hewett's ants, "heaping up great mounds far in excess of actual needs"? No: all these authors allow that leaders directed the insectlike heaping. It is the nature of leadership that is at issue: something like a chiefdom, or something more corporate and Pueblo-like? Johnson's elaborate sequential hierarchy, for example.

Surely there were social formations in the past which are not represented in the (ethnographic) present, but it would be comforting to find parallels (if not analogues) for the corporate, sequential, nonhierarchies somewhere other than the ethnographic Pueblos. In arguments for alternative formations, the ancient Pueblos themselves seem to be the most frequently cited example (e.g., Feinman 2000:Figure 12.2). Are the alternate leadership strategies posited for Pueblos so unusual that they can only be internally referenced? Johnson (1989:386) recognized this problem, in obiter dictum to his verdict on Chaco: "We have garden variety 'chiefdoms' and 'early states' stacked ten deep under the lab table, but elaborate sequential hierarchies may have been rare phenomena." Yoffee agrees:

> Chaco, however singular it is, should not be considered an "essence", and it isn't something we can easily "type" by reading the literature closely enough to find a correspondence somewhere in the ethnographic present. I don't know if the Chaco "rituality" is unique in the world, but I do wish to keep open the possibility that it might be quite rare [Yoffee 2001:73].

Rarity should raise eyebrows, and doubts. How rare *are* elaborate sequential hierarchies and corporate chiefdoms and communal antistructures and ritualities? And, if we can muster a handful of those rarities, how many of them built things, produced things, did things like Chaco—not to mention Hohokam and Paquimé, where alternative leadership begins to rear its corporate head(s) (Mills, ed. 2000)? I think the answer to that question is: few, if any.

Corporate chiefdoms, communal hierarchies, and sequential hierarchies are rare, and this should make us cautious. The Southwest is unparalleled and exceptional; this, too, should raise flags of warning. Granted that Pueblo and other southwestern societies developed remarkable social and political systems that discourage centralized hierarchy, the question one may ask is: why? Perhaps *in reaction to* more familiar forms of complexity: oppressive centralized hierarchy at Chaco (Lekson 1999, 2002) or to class war in the Hohokam (Teague 1993). These topics are beyond the space and purpose of this essay, but it seems entirely possible that, in the Southwest, complexity bred simplicity. Feinman et al. (2000) suggest this possibility in their analysis of the pithouse-pueblo transition. They see a mix of "corporate" and "network" (that is, complex) structures characterizing pithouse villages, and "the pithouse-to-pueblo transition marked a significant organizational shift to more corporate forms of political action that also characterize historic and modern Pueblos" (Feinman et al. 2000:449; see also Feinman 2000). I argue that the shift from the *complexity* of centralized hierarchies to the *simplicity* of "alternative leadership strategies" occurred with different data sets, on different temporal and spatial scales, in the shift from Chaco and Paquimé to protohistory. But I agree that the corporate, communal, ritual structures that discouraged hierarchy in historic and ethnographic pueblos, and which framed the foundational premises of our field, came late, in response to ancient hierarchies in Pueblo prehistory. Unfashionable, unregarded, and unwanted, complexity—centralized, hierarchical political structures—had and has an important role to play in southwestern archaeology.

12

Ethnicity and Southwestern Archaeology

Robert W. Preucel

Ethnicity is currently enjoying a revival of sorts in the social sciences. It is often identified, along with race, class, and gender, as a major axis of cultural variability and change. Although it has proven difficult to define, most scholars regard ethnicity as a key social organizing principle minimally associated with a sense of collective identity and historical consciousness (Barth 2000; Vermeulen and Grovers 1994). It is closely related to the concept of kinship, but broader in scope since it unites larger social groups (Comaroff 1987). It is sometimes associated with race especially in those cases where biological characteristics are given a cultural inflection (Alba 1985; Rex 1986). And it is often linked to nationalism as new political economies emerge and transcend ethnic identities (Eriksen 1993; Gellner 1983).

Any consideration of ethnicity in archaeology must begin by acknowledging its controversial history in European prehistory. The first use of the term has been attributed to the latter half of the nineteenth century and nationalist interests in the common origins of Indian and European languages and the migrations of specific social groups (Malina and Vasícek 1990). Rudolf Virchow used ceramics to distinguish between Slavic and Germanic occupation layers at hillforts in Lusatia. Oscar Montelius used the direct historical approach to trace the roots of Germanic people in Northern Europe to the Mesolithic period. Gustav Kossina equated culture and ethnos and held that the Germanic people were derived from a single origin in northern Germany and southern Scandinavia. Despite connections with unpalatable forms of nationalism, ethnicity remains to this day an important interpretive concept in European archaeology (see Dietler 1994; Jones 1997; Shennan 1989).

Although it is true that ethnicity has not been a central focus of southwestern archaeology, it has nonetheless played a significant role in the shaping of the discipline. It is a pervasive undercurrent in studies of cultural identity, particularly those emphasizing culture area, style, alliance formation, and social boundaries. In addition, there have been several studies of ethnic migrations, ethnic coresidence, and ethnogenesis. Most of these studies make use of aspects of primordealist, instrumentalist, and practice-based approaches to ethnicity as defined in anthropology, sociology, and political science (Bentley 1987; Eriksen 1991; Jones 1997). In what follows, I use this tripartite classification to sketch a brief review of the history of the concept and to make some suggestions for future directions.

PRIMORDEALIST APPROACHES

Primordealist approaches regard ethnicity as an innate aspect of human identity inherited by birth and persisting through all social formations (Bromley 1974; Isaacs 1974). Such approaches were an implicit part of the theoretical frameworks of early southwestern archaeology and are historically linked to the culture area approach especially as it was developed in European thought. More recently, these approaches have been implemented by cultural historians and processual archaeologists in discussions of population migrations and ethnic coresidence. In general, there has been a basic assumption of a close correspondence between ethnic identity and specific cultural traits.

CULTURE AND ETHNICITY

In its formative years, southwestern archaeology drew from rival idealist and materialist theories of culture and ethnicity. Frank Hamilton Cushing, for example, was particularly influenced by the German ethnologist Adolf Bastian, best known for his doctrine of the psychic unity of mankind. This thesis holds that that there are certain elementary ideas (*Elementargedanken*) common to all humanity (Koepping 1983). These ideas are innate, but never actually realized. What are realized are the collective representations of a culture that he terms folk ideas (*Völkergedanken*). Folk ideas are, in turn, associated with the particular environmental characteristics and evolve through historical contact between peoples living within different ethnic communities. The relationships between folk ideas, ethnic groups, and environment were given spatial form in his notion of the "geographical province," a direct precursor to the culture area hypothesis.

Bastian's influence is clearly evident in Cushing's essay "Preliminary Notes on the Origin, Working Hypothesis and Primary Researches of the Hemenway Southwestern Archaeological Expedition" delivered at the Seventh International Conference of Americanists in Berlin in 1888. Cushing writes,

> a people carry through all succeeding environments,—relatively unmodified—the impress or the *Idea* of the earliest environment which affected their culture. From this, the history of any special culture, as such may be said to begin with the general conceptions or acquisition of and conformity to some special *Idea*. Embarking on the study of any one of these Special Cultures then, the Ethnologist has for his task the ascertainment of, first, what Idea possessed, so to speak, the primitive group of peoples he would study; second, how and through what influences that Idea originated and became fixed; and third, how, ever after, it modified or induced from the least to the greatest—not merely all lesser ideas,—but also, all the autochthonous Institutions specially characteristic of that culture [Cushing 1890:151, emphasis in original].

Adolph F. Bandelier, in contrast, was sharply critical of Bastian's work. In a review of his publication *Die Culturlander des Alten Amerika*, he characterized it as "two ponderous tomes filled with an uncouth conglomerate of ethnological ideas, historical facts, personal views, and quotations and purporting to be American archaeology and ancient history" and "of no value whatsoever" (Bandelier 1879:357, 358).

Bandelier found his inspiration in the writings of Lewis Henry Morgan, who viewed control over food production as the basis of human supremacy over nature (Lange and Riley 1996). For Morgan, human progress was associated with the "enlargement of the sources of subsistence" across each "ethnical period" (Morgan 1877:13). This latter term combines ethnicity with evolutionary stage, since each ethnical period was held to have a distinct culture and a particular mode of life according to its degree of relative advancement. Morgan considered village life to be a marker of the Middle Status of Barbarism and identified Zuni as an example.

Following Morgan's lead, Bandelier defined southwestern culture as a general type based upon a common sedentary lifestyle. He wrote, the vestiges of sedentary aboriginal life are scattered over a large portion of the area embraced in what is commonly termed the Southwest of the United States. With the exception of the great plains and vast arid plateaux, wherever permanent water could be secured we find traces of tribes accustomed to sedentary life and familiar with its characteristic arts. In many regions these evidences are slight, and show that the occupation has not been of long duration, or that it has not produced any high culture; in some localities civilization attained a development superior in degree as well as in form. Such differences, however, are only varieties of one general type. The ancient culture represented in the ruins of the Southwest appears therefore to have been nearly uniform in every section [Bandelier 1892:577].

This unitary view of southwestern culture was widely shared during the late nineteenth century. Cushing, for example, regarded "the sedentary cultures of at least Western America, both North, and South-American, ancient and Modern, as being really and simply representative of different periods, phases or branches of One Culture, the ARIDIAN" (Cushing 1890:194). This unitary view did not, of course, deny the obvious fact of local variability. There was a broad recognition of subregional differences which were attributed to specific environmental causes. Bandelier (1892), for example, identified 14 different provinces based upon a combination of geographical features and the locations of modern groups.

The earliest explicit use of the term "ethnicity" in southwestern archaeology was by Edgar Lee Hewett. Like Cushing and Bandelier before him, he regarded the entire Southwest as a single Puebloan culture region, "a territory where a dominant type of civilization is found" (Hewett 1937:8). He described five geographical subdivisions and within each recognized specific "ethnic districts" such as Chaco Canyon, Mesa Verde, Pajarito Park, and the Pecos Valley. These districts were defined on the basis of local variation in architecture, decorative style, technology, and mortuary practices, all of which he considered as evidence for ethnic divergence. Hewett's ethnic districts, however, were not widely adopted by his colleagues and A. V. Kidder's (1924) classic synthesis replaces them with the less controversial labels, "culture areas" and "areas of specialization."

By the 1940s, this unitary view of Puebloan culture broke down and four major culture areas—Anasazi, Hohokam, Mogollon, and

Patayan—were recognized, only one of which, the Anasazi, was considered to be, properly speaking, Ancestral Pueblo (Cordell 1984). This new classification system was a direct result of the increasing prominence placed upon some of Kidder's areas of specialization. In addition, scholars began to define minor culture areas, like the Sinagua and Salado, that lie in between and tend to share traits with one or more of the major culture areas.

Migration and Ethnicity

Migration was one of the central research topics in the nascent field of southwestern archaeology. Early scholars used oral history to trace specific modern groups back in time, thus providing a site-based history. Another influential approach characteristic of the initial culture-historical period has been to reconstruct the histories of different language groups on the basis of material culture traits. With the rise of processual archaeology in the 1960s and its dual critique of history and ethnographic analogy, migration fell out of favor and local adaptation was emphasized. In the last 10 years or so, migration has been revived as a legitimate research topic, and there have been major new interpretations (see Lekson, ed. 1995). Most of these studies rely less upon ethnographic analogy and more upon identifying continuities between spatially dispersed archaeological cultures.

The classic example of the use of oral history in archaeological studies of migration is Jesse Walter Fewkes's work at Hopi (Fowler, this volume). In his interviews with Hopi elders, Fewkes gathered numerous accounts of clan migrations. For example, he learned that Walpi was originally settled by the Snake and Bear clans and later augmented by Horn clan members who came from Tokonavi (Fewkes 1900). These Horn clan people were themselves intermixed with Flute clan people from the Little Colorado. His ultimate goal was nothing less than to verify all known clan legends by associating each with specific archaeological sites (Fewkes 1898). Although oral histories were rejected as nonempirical by most archaeologists in the 1920s, there are signs of a growing interest in integrating migration narratives with archaeology for academic research, land claims, and the Native American Graves Protection and Repatriation Act (NAGPRA) purposes (Bernardini 2002; Dongoske et al. 1993, 1997; Ellis 1967; Ferguson et al. 1995; Whiteley 2002).

The first archaeologist to investigate systematically the origins of modern Puebloan language groups was H. P. Mera. Focusing on the

Rio Grande Valley, he identified two waves of immigration following the collapse of Chaco (Mera 1935). The first wave was from the Gallina district around A.D. 1260. The second was from Mesa Verde about A.D. 1300 and linked with the transition from Santa Fe Black-on-white ceramics to Jemez and Galisteo types. He observed that the region in which eastern Keres is spoken lies in the center of the region where pottery shows the greatest degree of Mesa Verde influence, while the western Keres shows clear links to the western part of the southern Mesa Verde extension. This caused him to pose the provocative question: "Can the Keres language and Mesa Verde pottery be considered as parts of the same culture?" (Mera 1935:5).

This question prompted a series of trial reconstructions by Erik Reed and Fred Wendorf that associated pottery types with specific language groups. Reed (1949) posited the Chacoans as Towa speakers whose migration to the Rio Grande split the indigenous Tiwa people into northern and southern divisions. He also held that the Tewa migrated from Mesa Verde in A.D. 1300 followed by a Keresan migration from the west prior to A.D. 1350. Wendorf (1954) was critical of Reed's scenario and argued that the Towa could represent the Gallina–Mesa Verde intrusion and the Keres might be linked to the Puerco-Acoma migration around A.D. 900. Wendorf and Reed (1955) then collaborated in a classic synthesis of Rio Grande archaeology in which they linked Mesa Verde with the modern Keres and suggested that Tanoan dialects were native to the Rio Grande. They also argued that Cibola and Salado were ancestral to Zuni.

Perhaps the most influential study of this sort was offered by Richard Ford, Stewart Peckham, and Albert Schroeder (Figure 12.1). The authors all concurred on Jemez prehistory being linked to the Gallina, Rosa, and Los Pinos phases as well as on the movement of peoples from northern Arizona and southern Utah to form the ancestral basis of the Hopi. They also agreed that the Tiwa were an indigenous population in the Rio Grande Valley, but differed on the causes of their northern and southern division. They disagreed over the origins of the Tewa, with Ford and Schroeder identifying an Upper San Juan homeland and Peckham advocating an indigenous Rio Grande development. Finally, they each offered contrasting views on the origins of the Tano. In all these scenarios, they emphasized their provisional nature due to the untested assumption that pottery styles can be correlated with particular linguistic groups (Ford et al. 1972:37). Current studies in this vein have proposed that Tewa and Jemez ethnic groups can be distinguished on the basis of distinctive ceramics (e.g., Futrell 1999; Graves and Eckert 1999).

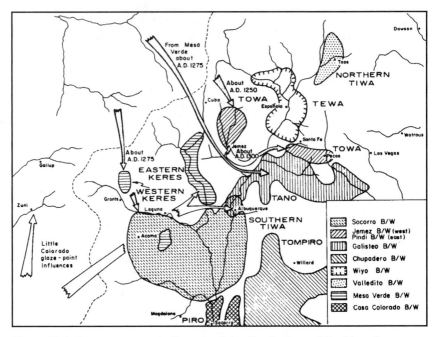

Figure 12.1. Pottery types as indicators of the distributions of Puebloan language groups, A.D. 1300 (from Ford et al. 1970:Map 5).

Whole archaeological cultures have been interpreted as multiethnic groups and the product of diverse immigration events (see also "Ethnic Coresidence" below). Two classic examples are the Sinagua and Salado. The Sinagua, originally defined by Harold S. Colton (1939), refers to the archaeological culture located in the Flagstaff area. Between A.D. 1046 and 1070 Sunset Crater erupted and precipitated a crisis for the local population, driving them out of their homeland (Colton 1946). After the eruption, the original inhabitants returned and were quickly joined by Anasazi, Hohokam, and Mogollon peoples, resulting in a mixture of cultures that stabilized within a generation to create a uniform Sinagua culture. Contemporary scholars, while accepting a degree of ethnic migration, have tended to stress local developments (Pilles 1996).

The term "Salado" was introduced by Winifred and Harold S. Gladwin (1930) to describe the archaeological culture centered in the Upper Salt River drainage and the region adjacent to Roosevelt Lake. There has been considerable debate as to its origins and ethnic makeup (see Lincoln 2000; Rice 1990). One influential view identifies two immigrations into the Tonto Basin (Clark 2001; Wood 2000). The first took place during the Preclassic period and was probably composed of both indigenous people and actual Hohokam people. The second occurred during the Classic period and involved an influx of western Anasazi people from the Tusayan or Kayenta areas. This immigration has been identified on the basis of architectural features such as kivas and Anasazi-derived ceramics (Crown 1994). Rice et al. (1992), however, have stressed the need for a biocultural approach in order to address ethnicity, and their genetic distance studies suggest that the Salado population was composed of a combination of Hohokam and Mogollon peoples.

ETHNIC CORESIDENCE

Ethnic coresidence refers to the presence of multiple ethnic groups residing in the same village or to multiple ethnic groups in different villages but living within the same community. Both of these situations are known historically. Some examples of the first case are the Tano people from the Galisteo Basin living at Santo Domingo (White 1935), Laguna people at Isleta (Parsons 1932), *genízaros* at various pueblos (Horvath 1979), and Spanish families living at Cochiti (Lange 1959). Examples of the second are the Hopi-Tewa residing in Tewa Village on First Mesa (Dozier 1966) and the Sandia at Payupki on Second Mesa (Hodge 1910).

A. V. Kidder (1920) adopted the ethnic coresidence thesis to account for the co-occurrence of Pueblo-style masonry rooms and collapsed log structures closely resembling modern Navajo hogans at *pueblito* sites in the Gobernador district. These sites also exhibit Spanish-style corner fireplaces, wood cut with metal axes, cow and sheep bones, and historic Puebloan ceramics. From these data, he concluded that the sites were built during the historic period and proposed that their inhabitants were Jemez refugees who joined the Navajo at the time of the revolt of 1696. New dendrochronological studies demonstrate that the majority of these sites were built in the first half of the eighteenth century and not immediately after the 1696 revolt (Towner and Dean 1996), but they do not, by themselves, disconfirm the coresidence thesis, since they could have been constructed by a later influx of Pueblo refugees joining with the Navajo.

Another example of ethnic coresidence is Clyde Kluckhohn's interpretation of the Chaco Canyon settlement system. Kluckhohn (1939:159) speculated that the Hosta Butte phase village dwellers and the inhabitants of the Bonito phase great towns may have possessed different cultural traditions. He drew an analogy with the Laguna group at Isleta, the Tewa on First Mesa, and the Keres in the Jeddito Valley to suggest that the inhabitants of Bc51 (a village site) possibly spoke a different language from that of the people of Pueblo Bonito (Kluckhohn 1939:159). He then speculated that the village inhabitants were migrants who had been attracted to the canyon due to the economic prosperity and ritual power of the towns and/or for protection. This view was modified by Gordon Vivian and Tom Mathews (1965), who argued that the Bonito and Hosta Butte phase sites were in situ cultural traditions that enjoyed a symbiotic relationship.

Several studies have interpreted Chaco–San Juan architecture in terms of ethnic coresidence. For example, Stuart Baldwin (1985) has used room size data to demonstrate the existence of ethnically mixed populations at Chaco outlier sites such as Lowry, Escalante, and Ida Jean. He proposes that since room size is partly deter-

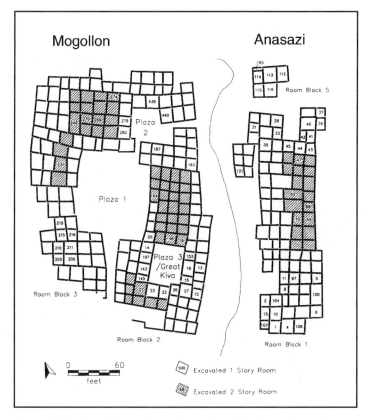

Figure 12.2. Mogollon and Anasazi residential units at Grasshopper Pueblo, (from Reid and Whittlesey 1999:113).

mined by a culture's proxemic system it cannot be borrowed and that the co-occurrence of the McElmo and Bonito architectural styles at these sites must therefore actually represent a native McElmo people augmented by Bonito phase Chacoans. Similarly, Gwinn Vivian (1990) has suggested that during the second half of the eleventh century Chaco–San Juan groups from the Chaco core area colonized territories previously occupied by Cibola or northern San Juan peoples. As evidence, he cites the presence of Chacoan-style outlier sites with great houses and great kivas placed immediately adjacent to previously established local villages.

Ethnic coresidence has also been offered to explain numerous sites in the Mogollon Highlands. These sites include Bear Ruin (Haury 1940), Walnut Creek Village (Morris 1970), Point of Pines (Haury 1958b), and the Shoofly Ruin (Redman 1993). The area with the strongest evidence, however, is the Grasshopper region. At Grasshopper Pueblo, Reid and Whittlesey (1997) have proposed that an enclave of Anasazi people occupied their own roomblock east of the plaza pueblo inhabited by the indigenous Mogollon population (Figure 12.2). This thesis is based upon ceramics and distinctive physical anthropological indicators. A similar conclusion is offered by Zedeño (1994) for Chodistaas Pueblo where ceramic studies indicate that the northern and southern roomblocks were occupied by two different groups.

INSTRUMENTALIST APPROACHES

Instrumentalist approaches regard ethnicity as a means of establishing social relations and negotiating access to economic and political resources (Cohen 1969; Glazer and Moynihan 1975). These approaches are closely associated with the emergence of processual archaeology. They are implicated in studies of style as a social variable, social boundaries, alliance formation, and ethnogenesis. Basically, there is a recognition that ethnicity is not a stable quality and that it varies over time and space in accordance with local conditions and characteristics. Specific cultural traits may thus signal ethnic differences in some cases, but not in others.

STYLE AND ETHNICITY

The social significance of style is a major research topic in southwestern archaeology (Hegmon 1992; S. Plog 1983). Particularly influential has been Martin Wobst's "information theory approach" to material culture. According to Wobst (1977:321), style is that component of formal variability that can be associated with the process of information exchange and which contributes materially to human survival. Style is thus an integral part of human adaptations and consistent with the functional systems theory orientation of processual archaeology (Binford 1962). Also influential have been the "style debates" between James Sackett (1985) and Polly Wiessner (1985) that have led to a consideration of isochrestic, iconographic, and symbolic variation in material culture.

An early example of the use of the information theory approach is Dorothy Washburn's (1977) symmetry analysis of Salado pottery. Beginning from the assumption that pottery production is an inherently social act, she argued that potters working within the same tradition should create pottery designs with similar symmetries. She then proposed that population migration and acculturation should be reflected in similarities and differences in design structure. In her studies of Salado polychromes, she found a high degree of similarity of design structures, which she interpreted as the product of an interacting community of potters. She also differentiated between local and nonlocal production, holding that designs based on a one-dimensional axis were likely locally produced and the more complicated two-dimensional and finite designs were probably nonlocal products.

Another example is Stephen Plog's (1980) study of changing ceramic styles in the Chevelon drainage. He suggests that the single, broad style zone from A.D. 400 to 900 is predictable given the infrequent contact between socially distant individuals since, as Wobst points out, the smaller the number of people the less efficient style becomes relative to other communication modes. During later periods, style zones become smaller in size and there is stylistic homogeneity within them. This, too, is consistent with Wobst's views since as the size of the social network increases so, too, should the amount of interaction between socially distant individuals. He then argues that the exchange of ceramics between groups increased the probability that they participated in processes of boundary maintenance.

In another study, Plog (1990) has refocused the style debate by suggesting that rather than choosing between Sackett's and Wiessner's approaches, it is more useful to consider how different kinds of style operate in specific contexts. For his study, he conducts an attribute analysis of four different decorative styles of Black Mesa ceramics dating from A.D. 750 to 1150. His results show that prior to A.D 1000 attribute frequencies are stable and exhibit isochrestic style while after that date they show considerable variability. He suggests that some decorative styles, like Dogoszhi Black-on-white, may have increasingly symbolized alliances across broad areas of the Southwest and may possibly be associated with the Chaco regional system. Because stylistic variation is complex, he concludes that similar studies should consider the full range of stylistic theories suggested by Sackett and Wiessner.

Michelle Hegmon (1995) has recently expanded upon Plog's work and considered style in terms of structure and difference. She finds a higher degree of diversity and structural variability in design style in the ceramics from Dolores region and across Mesa Verde than from Black Mesa and in the Kayenta region. For her, the high stylistic diversity of the Mesa Verde region may be an expression of small-scale social units such as household groups and/or sodalities, age-grades, or religious societies. The lower diversity of Black Mesa is more likely an expression of social solidarity and a means of maintaining a broad trade network. When this is placed within a diachronic framework, she identifies an increase in diversity in the Black Mesa context suggesting that social groups' differences may have become more important over time. Like Plog, she notes that style is multifaceted and there is no single theory sufficient to explain all aspects of style.

ALLIANCES

Alliances refer to social and political networks that are based upon specialized production, trade and exchange, and sometimes political stratification. The term was first introduced by Steadman Upham and Fred Plog. Upham (1982) used the term to describe patterns of ceramic exchange for the Western Pueblo district which he broke down into the Jeddito alliance and the Salado alliance. Fred Plog (1983) employed the concept in the context of differentiating large, distinctive sites with evidence of trade items, agricultural intensification, and social complexity (what he called "strong patterns") from small, heterogeneous sites with limited evidence of these characteristics (what he called "weak patterns").

An influential attempt to link ethnicity to alliance formation is David Wilcox's (1984, 1991) study of the emergence of polities during the protohistoric period. He suggests that after the decline of Paquimé, the Piro expanded southwards and settled evenly spaced villages along both sides of the southern Rio Grande. By the time of contact, the Piro district was a politically integrated, ethnic polity and possibly interacted as a socioeconomic system. He identifies a similar ethnic polity for the Tewa of the northern Rio Grande, the perimeter of which was marked by sites in defensive locations. In both cases, he places great emphasis upon a distinct uninhabited zone which he interprets as a marked boundary between the polities and their neighbors.

A more skeptical view of ethnicity and alliances is offered by Steadman Upham, Patricia Crown, and Stephen Plog (1994). They note that among the Acholi in East Africa it is the sociopolitical order that determines ethnicity, language, and other social practices, rather than the other way around. This causes them to question the possibility of identifying ethnicity in the prehistoric Southwest and to propose that homogeneity in material culture signifies only the existence of interaction and the sharing of information and perhaps people. When these patterns persist over time they are best understood as alliances. For them, ethnicity and cultural identity emerge only after previously unaffiliated groups become incorporated into the social, political, or economic organization represented by alliances.

SOCIAL AND ETHNIC BOUNDARIES

The study of social boundaries is a direct outgrowth of the study of the interrelations of style and cultural identity. Especially influential is Frederik Barth's (1969) classic work on ethnic groups and boundaries. Among his major contributions are his insights that ethnic groups are socially constructed within environmental constraints and ethnic markers, such as clothing, language, and food, and are best approached from a consideration of social boundaries. These boundaries emerge because social groups cannot exist in isolation and are only distinguished with respect to other groups.

Judith Habicht-Mauche (1993) has proposed that immigration of large numbers of people into the northern Rio Grande in the late thirteenth and early fourteenth centuries precipitated major changes in ethnicity and the formation of new social boundaries. The immigration led to increasing differentiation of local ethnic groups and the proliferation of regional ceramic styles. She suggests, citing Barth (1969), that interethnic competition is inherently unstable and eventually one group displaces the other. By the mid-fourteenth century, a new economic and social system developed to stabilize interethnic relations and reduce competition by mitigating the effects of reduced mobility and increasing territoriality. This is indicated by the emergence of new centers of craft specialization and the commodification of ceramics, particularly the famous Rio Grande glazewares. She defines this system as a "complex tribe" and the processes that led to the development of ethnic and interethnic alliances as "tribalization."

Similarly, Henry Wallace and William Doelle (2001) see social boundaries in the San Pedro Valley emerging as the result of multiple immigrations during the thirteenth and fourteenth centuries. They identify a social boundary dividing two ethnic groups on the basis of a spatially discrete distribution of copies of Middle Gila pottery and San Simon pottery. These pottery types exhibit distinctive design elements and make use of different technologies that are socially learned. Significantly, this boundary was not impermeable and ball courts are found at sites on both sides of the divide. They interpret this to mean that a common ritual system was adopted to minimize social tensions.

The relationships of major and minor culture areas have also been interpreted in terms of ethnic boundaries. An example is the Fremont-Pueblo frontier. Several scholars now identify an ethnic boundary at the Fremont-Pueblo frontier which developed at A.D. 500 and is defined by distinctive material culture traits. James Adovasio (1986), for example, has demonstrated clear technical differences in Anasazi and Fremont basketry technologies. Similarly, Phil Geib (1996) has noted consistent differences in coil forming techniques for Anasazi and Fremont pottery

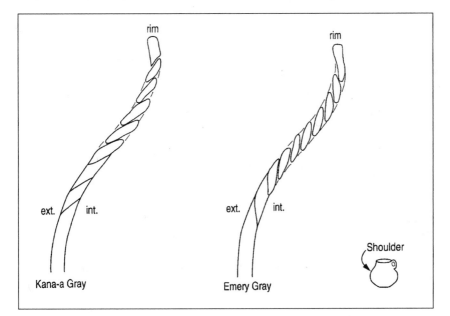

Figure 12.3. Anasazi and Fremont vessel wall forming techniques (from Geib 1996:Figure 36).

(Figure 12.3). As with Wilcox, Geib notes the existence of a broad buf-
fer zone with an absence of settlement as the clearest indicator of an
ethnic boundary. And as with Habicht-Mauche, he views this boundary as a result of competition over agricultural land which in turn led
to increased territoriality and defense.

ETHNOGENESIS

Ethnogenesis is a relatively new research topic and there have been, as
yet, very few systematic investigations. An influential example is Linda
Cordell's and Vincent Yannie's (1991) study of genízaro communities
in northern New Mexico. Of special concern to them are the limits of
inference in addressing ethnicity archaeologically. In an evaluation of
the material culture of three genízaro communities at Albuquerque,
Belen, and Abiquiu, they concluded that the archaeological identification of genízaro identity would be difficult and, in some cases, impossible. They suggest that the cases of residential segregation (Belen
and Abiquiu) held the greatest potential and genízaro identity might
be marked by pottery, the manufacture of stone tools, and possibly
techniques of food preparation. They conclude that we need to develop
methods of identifying emblematic style while simultaneously recognizing that the emblems that come to differentiate one ethnic group from
another will vary across social context.

PRACTICE-ORIENTED APPROACHES

Practice-based approaches are critical of both primordealism and in-
strumentalism and hold that material culture does not passively reflect
social and ethnic identities, but rather actively constitutes them through
the strategies and intentions of interacting groups in relation to culturally specific symbolic orders (Bentley 1987). These approaches have
their origins in anthropology and sociology and especially in the work
of Pierre Bourdieu (1977, 1990) and Anthony Giddens (1979, 1984).
They have been introduced to archaeology in the 1980s and 1990s by
postprocessual archaeologists (Hodder 1982; Jones 1997; but see Dietler and Herbich 1998) and have recently been introduced in southwestern archaeology.

A good example of a practice-based approach is Andrew Duff's
recent study of Western Pueblo identities. Although Duff (2002:20–21)
generally prefers the term "group identity" as opposed to "ethnicity"
because of the controversy over its use in prehistoric contexts (see Stark

et al. 1995), he argues that ethnicity can be viewed as a role that actors consciously adopt depending upon their self-interest and specific structural constraints. Those conditions that foster the selection of ethnic roles tend to perpetuate group solidarity. Those that de-emphasize it can result in the transformation of self and group identities. There is thus a recursive relationship between individual agency and structure with each having the potential to transform the other.

Duff's case study involves an analysis of social interaction and identity in the Upper Little Colorado and Zuni regions during the Pueblo IV period. Using evidence for ceramic manufacture and exchange as well as population density and settlement, he identifies two distinct patterns. The Zuni region is characterized by material culture that is internally consistent, and social interaction that is inwardly focused. He interprets this pattern to mean that group identity was fairly rigid and less susceptible to influence by individual agency. The Upper Little Colorado region, by contrast, is characterized by a series of nested interaction networks of variable material culture. This suggests that social boundaries are only loosely defined and that interaction with and incorporation of people from many different communities is ongoing. In this case, agency and structure existed in a more dynamic relation, a condition that fostered the introduction of katcina ceremonialism in the mid-1300s. The social dynamics of these two social systems drew members of both regions and eventually resulted in the ethnically distinct Hopi and Zuni settlements encountered by the Spaniards.

Another example is Robert Preucel, Loa Traxler, and Michael Wilcox's (2002) study of Pueblo ethnogenesis during the Spanish colonial period. We suggest ethnic categories were introduced by the Spaniards in the context of legitimizing their political economic system. The ascription of a "Pueblo" ethnicity to linguistically and culturally diverse Native peoples allowed asymmetric social and economic relations to appear both natural and broadly applicable. However, during this period of shared subjugation, Native leaders appropriated the ethnic category of Pueblo-ness and quite literally turned it against their oppressors to forge political unity and permit collective resistance. This can be seen in a series of revolt attempts, the most successful of which was the Pueblo Revolt of 1680. The new Pueblo ethnic identity was fragile and, after the revolt, it began to lose its salience as individual village leaders began to reassert their own authority and village-based identities once again became the defining social and political structures.

The local negotiation of these social distinctions can be seen at Kotyiti Pueblo, an ancestral Cochiti community consisting of a plaza pueblo and an adjacent *ranchería*. Traxler, Wilcox, and I suggest that Kotyiti leaders used plaza pueblo architecture to index the cultural revitalization movement and mediate social and political tensions between peoples from different home-villages (Preucel et al. 2002). In addition, Patricia Capone and I have argued that Pueblo women, including the women of Kotyiti, actively participated in the nativist aspects of this movement by reviving certain traditional design elements on their ceramics such as the double-headed key motif (Figure 12.4) (Capone and Preucel 2002). From this point of view, ethnicity is neither an essential quality, nor simply an adaptation to a local situation, but rather a mode of cultural production, one that is linked to the creation of new forms of historical consciousness.

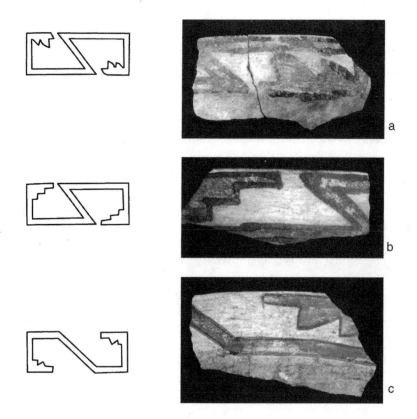

Figure 12.4. Design elements used on Pueblo Revolt period pottery as part of a pan-Pueblo ethnic discourse (from Capone and Preucel 2002:Figure 7.6).

ETHNICITY AND POLITICS

Concomitant with the renewed interest in ethnicity is a shifting political climate in which Native Americans are taking an active role in the writing of their own histories and in the disposition of their ancestral human remains and material culture in federally funded museums and other institutions (Echo-Hawk 2000; Watkins 2000). Perhaps the most important development in this area is the passage of NAGPRA in 1990. While ethnicity is not mentioned by name in the legislation, it is clearly incorporated in the term "cultural affiliation." Cultural affiliation is defined as "a relationship of shared group identity which can reasonably be traced historically or prehistorically between members of a present-day Indian tribe or Native Hawaiian organization and an identifiable earlier group" (43 CFR 10, 10.2[e]).

Some of the ambiguities regarding ethnicity and cultural affiliation are highlighted in the current dispute between the Hopi Tribe and the National Park Service regarding the cultural affiliation of human remains from prehistoric archaeological sites in Chaco Canyon National Historical Park and Aztec National Monument. Basically, the Hopi Tribe asserts that the National Park Service's compliance procedures assume that all southwestern tribes, including the Navajo, are culturally affiliated with the two parks (Hamilton 1999). The Hopi Tribe argues that this homogenization of Pueblo people as a collective ignores the diversity, uniqueness, and independence of their separate cultural traditions and is a political expediency that does not meet the minimum standard of the law.

The National Park Service, for its part, holds that it has complied with its NAGPRA obligations and appropriately determined that as many as 20 tribes may be affiliated. They claim that ethnic identities, such as Hopi, only emerged after the period of the aggregation of clans on the Hopi mesas (Wilson 1999). This argument means that multiple tribes, not only the Hopi, are affiliated with the archaeological cultures known as the Anasazi, Mogollon, Hohokam, Salado, Mimbres, Fremont, etc. Moreover, the National Park Service asserts that the Navajo have a cultural affiliation to Chaco Canyon. This analysis is based upon a consideration of oral tradition, historical data, biological evidence, anthropological research, and geographical information.

This dispute raises numerous questions. For example, the legal requirement to establish cultural affiliation through arguments for cultural continuity implies a theoretical commitment to a stable (primordealist) as opposed to a fluid (instrumentalist) approach to identity or ethnicity. Not surprisingly, the Hopi and the National Park Service express their perspectives on cultural affiliation in rather different ways. The Hopi argue that they are composed of multiple clans whose traditions and historical migrations are distinctive and go back into deep time. The National Park Service argues that the Hopi only became Hopi when their clans settled on Black Mesa. Here the debate has shifted from cultural affiliation to ethnic identity, since the very substance of what it means to be Hopi is in contention. The resolution of this dispute, and many others like it, will require a greater appreciation of the intersections of different standpoints and the structures of power than has heretofore been evidenced.

CONCLUSIONS

In general, southwestern archaeologists have adopted a cautious stance towards ethnicity. Most have approached it indirectly through considerations of culture areas, population migrations, style, alliances, social boundaries, and cultural identity. And in those cases where it has been explicitly addressed, it is rarely adequately theorized. This broad reluctance to engage with ethnicity may be due in part to the negative associations with its political uses in the rise of European nation-states in the nineteenth century (Trigger 1989) and, later on, with the abuses of the term by Nazi Germany (Arnold 1990; Veit 1989). Another reason may be the relegation of identity politics to historical archaeology (e.g., Delle et al. 2000; Ferguson 1992) and the intellectual legacy of race in America, which has tended to overshadow other forms of identity and difference. It may be significant that a similar restraint is also evidenced in borderlands history (see Anderson 1999; Radding 1998).

Each of the major approaches to ethnicity in the social sciences have been or are being used in studies of cultural identity and ethnicity in southwestern archaeology. A primordealist approach has played a significant, if underappreciated, role in the establishment of the field and is intimately linked to studies of migration and ethnic coresidence. An instrumentalist view was introduced by processual archaeology largely as a way of understanding stylistic variation, social boundaries, and alliance formation. A practice-oriented approach has recently been proposed to explore group identity and ethnogenesis and is, to some extent, an outcome of postprocessual archaeology. Of these approaches, the practice-based studies offer considerable promise because they acknowledge the strategic and positional nature of identity formation.

Two questions are commonly raised regarding ethnicity in archaeology. The first is its theoretical applicability. Numerous ethnographic studies have shown that ethnic groups are, in fact, products of colonialism, sometimes quite literally created by colonial administrators (Ranger 1991). Some scholars take this fact to mean that the term cannot be applied to precolonial contexts and well-bounded ethnic groups may not be characteristic of any nonstate society (Cameron 1995:118). But this reaction is too strong. There is no compelling reason to exclude ethnicity a priori, and it may be especially relevant in those contexts in which ideological movements and/or asymmetric forms of political economy come into contact. So, for example, in reconsidering the Hohokam as a multiethnic culture (Shaul and Hill 1998), we might pay special attention to their economic and political relations with communities on their margins, like Salado, where ethnic identities appear to be in flux.

A second question is methodological. After over a century of research, archaeologists have been unsuccessful in establishing any agreed upon material culture correlates of ethnicity (Shennan 1989). The problem here, however, is not faulty methodology, but rather the desire to identify an "ethnicity signature" applicable to all cultures at all times and places. This desire is in fact a vestige of our historical engagement with primordealist approaches. Moreover, the significance of ethnicity varies across social contexts in relation to other kinds of affiliations and social identities (David 1992; Hodder 1982, 1985; Meskell 1999). Future studies should abandon the search for universal correlates and focus instead upon specifying the local conditions and contexts in which specific social practices and forms of material culture are thought to signify ethnic identity.

ACKNOWLEDGMENTS

I am grateful to Linda Cordell, T. J. Ferguson, Don Fowler, Ian Hodder, Igor Kopytoff, Matt Liebmann, Lynn Meskell, and James Snead for their comments and advice on this chapter.

13

Ethnographic Analogy and Ancestral Pueblo Archaeology

Katherine A. Spielmann

The utility of southwestern ethnographic information for interpreting archaeological data has been an issue of debate among southwestern archaeologists since the beginning of the twentieth century. As I discuss in this chapter, in reality the problem has not been with ethnographic analogy per se, but with the stark, coarsely drawn, either-or approach taken to ethnographic analogy: *either* we can use Pueblo ethnography and ethnohistory to understand the archaeological record *or* we cannot, period. A more nuanced approach to ethnographic analogy—what behaviors, what contexts, which Pueblo peoples for which contexts and behaviors—has developed only recently and draws particular strength from direct involvement of Pueblo people themselves.

The acceptability of ethnographic analogy has been of special concern to those working with the aggregated pueblos that become characteristic of the Southwest from the late thirteenth century onward. On the one hand, Pueblo populations live where we work, in the kinds of structures that we have been excavating for more than a century, and there is a well-developed body of ethnographic information about modern Pueblo peoples. Moreover, many of these sites are ancestral to today's Pueblo populations. On the other hand, massive depopulation, European-induced cultural change, and the cultural transformations expectable over the course of several centuries make ethnographic observations of living Pueblo populations a potentially misleading source of information for interpreting Ancestral Pueblo sites.

Through a brief exploration of how archaeologists have used ethnographic data over the past century, I argue first that from the 1920s at least through the 1950s, the analogies that were employed were remarkably free of actual southwestern ethnographic content. Historically, archaeologists have either expressed ambivalence about the utility of ethnographic information, or have relied on "some idealized version" (Cordell and Plog 1979:407) of what they *thought* Pueblo societies were all about. I suggest that the assertions of early archaeologists cannot really be termed ethnographic analogy. It is not the realities of the ethnographic record that curtailed their inferences.

My second point is that once more careful attention was paid to Pueblo ethnography, it became clear that multiple kinds of interpretations of the archaeological record are possible using ethnographic data. My third point concerns the aggregation that began in the thirteenth century. Archaeological data from this period are beginning to substantiate decades-old suggestions by southwestern ethnographers that some aspects of living Pueblos' social and ritual organization have considerable time depth. And finally, the current trends of archaeologists working directly with some Pueblo peoples, and for southwestern Native Americans to become archaeologists, open new and as yet uncharted waters for a different, more nuanced approach to the past. Research designs and interpretations now incorporate Puebloan concepts, histories, and questions due to the direct involvement of Native people in archaeological investigations.

ETHNOGRAPHIC ANALOGY: FACT OR FICTION?

I begin this discussion with the work of Fewkes and other turn-of-the-century archaeologists, which has been well characterized in the preceding chapters by Fowler and Snead. As Fowler notes, ethnographic research by Frank H. Cushing and Jesse W. Fewkes among the Zuni and Hopi led to an understanding of the histories of clan migrations and an interest in determining which archaeological sites corresponded with which named ancestral sites.

Like others of his time, Fewkes also assumed that the people who had lived in the pueblos that he was excavating were not behaviorally different from living Pueblo peoples. The Pueblo Southwest was characterized as culturally homogeneous (Longacre 1970). Fewkes (1909:53) commented, for example, that life at Spruce Tree House on Mesa Verde would have been "practically the same" as that at Walpi.

With the development of the first "New Archaeology" of the early 1900s (Snead, this volume), the assumption that living Pueblo peoples were essentially fossilized versions of the past persisted, but a growing ambivalence developed concerning the ability of Pueblo people to provide reliable information about the past. This disinterest in Pueblo oral tradition was similar to that of contemporary ethnographers, who also discounted the veracity of Native American historical accounts (Anyon et al. 1996:14). In his chapter, for example, Snead (this volume) notes that although Hewett developed close relations with Pueblo peoples, he did not use the information he may have acquired through those relations in interpreting ancestral Tewa sites.

Alfred V. Kidder, on whom I focus here, took a series of contradictory stands concerning the importance of living Pueblos and the interpretation of Ancestral Pueblo sites. On the one hand, he maintained an academic interest in living Pueblos and was particularly hopeful that information on social and ritual organizations would be forthcoming. At the same time, however, he held out little hope for gaining such information from Pueblo people.

Kidder (1924:39) felt that the most characteristic aspect of Puebloan *life* was the architectural construct of the Pueblo village, which of course appeared to persist for hundreds of years into the present. He thus was convinced that Pueblo inhabitants "preserve the ancient culture of the Southwest in almost its aboriginal purity" (Kidder 1924:37–39). He quotes Lummis on the point that due to an assumed lack of cultural change on the part of the Pueblos, it was possible to "catch our archaeology alive" through the study of living Pueblo peoples. He thus expected that the ethnographic research at Jemez, conducted by Elsie Clews Parsons and published as part of the Phillips Academy series, would reveal much about what life had been like at Pecos (Kidder 1924:1). In addition, Carl Guthe's (1925) study of Pueblo pottery making was to provide insights applicable to Pecos because the "Pueblos of today...practice almost exactly the same arts as did their ancestors of a thousand years ago" (Kidder 1925b:1). In his much later publication on Pecos architecture, Kidder (1958:307) expresses regret that he did not come to know southwestern ethnographers as well as he had Mayan ethnographers, presumably because of the insights he expected they would have provided.

At the same time that Kidder was asserting the utility of analogies between the present and the past, and in these same publications, he also expressed strong doubt that modern Pueblos, and especially the Rio Grande Pueblos, would be reliable sources of information. For example, in the preface to Parsons's (1925) Jemez ethnography, he refers to modern Pueblos as "remnants" of prehistoric populations, and asserts that Western Pueblo populations are "more aboriginal" than eastern ones. In the introduction to Guthe's (1925) work Kidder dismisses Pueblo oral history as a source of information. The reluctance of eastern Pueblos to impart information on social and especially religious practices was particularly vexing, because these are precisely the kinds of information Kidder felt would be the most important to derive from living peoples. Later, in his volume on Pecos architecture, Kidder (1958:129, 267) concludes that "Nothing dependable can, I fear, be learned...from any of the living Pueblos, who are notably lacking in historical interest." He was convinced that nothing told to Fewkes, Hewett, and Bandelier about different Pueblo people's pasts was corroborated by the archaeological record.

Thus, after the ethnological immersion of archaeologists like Fewkes at the turn of the century, southwestern archaeology developed remarkably independently from southwestern ethnology, and often in ignorance of what the ethnographic record entailed. In his history of the Pecos Conference, for example, Woodbury (1993:148–150) notes the decades-long debate among the conference's various organizers as to whether ethnologists should be invited to attend. Kidder invited none to the first Pecos Conference, which largely concerned the intricacies of archaeological data, but did invite 10 to the second. Woodbury suggests that the relative lack of ethnological interest in the Pecos Conference stemmed from the fact that it never became a kind of informal meeting place for ethnologists, as it had for archaeologists. In general, some ethnologists did attend the conference over the years, and there were specific sessions for ethnographic reports. Clearly, however, the recurrent debate concerning invitations suggests that archaeologists did not consider ethnologists significant sources of information for the culture histories they were trying to reconstruct.

For the first half of the twentieth century it was ethnographers, more so than archaeologists, who were interested in the relationship between the Ancestral Pueblo record and modern Pueblo society (Longacre 1970). They were the ones formulating possible scenarios as to the antecedents of the peoples they studied. To a person, however, from Elsie Clews Parsons (1925) in the 1920s, to Fred Eggan (1950) in the 1930s and 1940s, to Edward P. Dozier (1958) in the 1950s, each recognized the importance of understanding the ways in which historical processes and events had affected the social structures of Ancestral Pueblo societies. Although they differed substantially in their attribution of the most significant causes of change (Eggan favoring Spanish colonization especially for the eastern Pueblos, and Dozier favoring environmental adaptation), they did not promote direct analogies between the present and the past.

In the late 1960s, when archaeologists such as William A. Longacre and James N. Hill made prehistoric social organization a focus of research, ethnologists were actively sought for their insights. In 1968 Longacre organized a School of American Research symposium on prehistoric Pueblo social organization, and invited two ethnologists (Dozier and David F. Aberle) to participate as discussants. In their concluding chapters to the subsequent volume, the two ethnologists emphasized the problems that variability brought to bear on archaeological use of ethnographic data. Dozier (1970) highlighted the variability in Pueblo social institutions and argued that direct analogies between an archaeological context and a modern Pueblo one would be difficult to draw. Aberle (1970) took a different tack and focused on variability in ethnographic approaches to Puebloan data. He cautioned archaeologists not to be too reliant on a single ethnographer's view of Pueblo social organization. Twenty years later, Elizabeth Brandt (1994) echoed that caution in her paper at the 1990 Southwest Symposium, in which she argued that there was a persistent misunderstanding on the part of archaeologists concerning the nature and functions of clans. Both Longacre (1970) and Brandt (1994) have highlighted the ways in which the adoption of Eggan's Western Pueblo ethnographic model has colored archaeological inferences concerning the past.

Two aspects of archaeologists' early interpretations of Ancestral Pueblo sites illustrate the problems inherent in homogenizing Pueblo society either through idealized versions of what Pueblos were all about, or through generalizing from single ethnographic cases. The first concerns the autonomy of Pueblo villages and the second the primacy of Western Pueblo data in interpreting all Ancestral Pueblo sites.

In 1924 Kidder (1924:41) asserted without reference and without question that each pueblo is a "self-contained, closely-knit, and autonomous unit." Yet Bandelier's (1890) work had already made clear the importance of intercommunity trade and ritual relations. Subsequent ethnographic work in the 1920s and 1930s (Ford 1972) along with clear archaeological evidence supporting the importance of trade among Pueblos that derived from Anna O. Shepard's (1936, 1942) petrographic analyses of Pueblo ceramics should have made clear that assumptions concerning Pueblo village autonomy were unfounded. Kidder in fact noted that Shepard's data should cause southwestern archaeologists to completely rethink their notion of pueblo autonomy:

It has always been assumed that potting was one of the regular household tasks of every Pueblo woman; that each town was in this regard self-sufficient. But if whole classes of pottery such as Glaze I and Biscuit were imported, we must postulate an extraordinary volume of trade and allow for a compensating outward flow of other commodities. Furthermore, we must believe that the production of vessels at the source of supply was much greater than was needed for home consumption, in other words, that rudimentary commercial manufacturing was practiced [Kidder 1936a:xxiii].

In fact, the "extraordinary volume of trade" Shepard documented was not taken into account in Rio Grande archaeology for decades (Snow 1981).

Equally problematic has been the tendency for archaeologists to privilege Western Pueblo ethnography in interpretations of Eastern Pueblo sites. The clan has been viewed as archetypical of Pueblo social systems (e.g., Kidder 1924), despite the fact that Tanoan-speaking Pueblo peoples do not privilege the clan as an organizing principle (Brandt 1994). Residents of Zuni pueblo were relied upon to interpret kiva murals at the site of Kuaua (Dutton 1963) and those from Acoma provided interpretations for Pottery Mound (Hibben 1975).

In sum, well into the 1950s archaeologists' ways of viewing the Ancestral Pueblo record were clearly not constrained by ethnographic analogy, or ethnographic knowledge in general, but by a lack of attention to the degree to which modern Pueblo societies varied, and ethnocentric assumptions about the "archaic" nature of Pueblo cultures.

HIERARCHY

In the late 1970s, some researchers began to challenge the idealized version of egalitarian, autonomous Pueblos that had dominated archaeologists' perspectives on Ancestral Pueblo sociopolitical organization. Cordell and Plog (1979), for example, argued that the consensus-based model of Pueblo political organization was a product of Spanish colonization and did not reflect the reality of earlier centuries. Wilcox (1981), too, maintained that the notion of egalitarian Pueblos derived from purely historic circumstances. He suggested that the protohistoric situation was more complex, involving hierarchical regional systems of confederated pueblos.

As discussed by Stephen Lekson (this volume), Fred Plog developed such an alternative reconstruction of Pueblo IV sociopolitical organization based on his interpretations of the site of Nuvakwewtaqa. He and Steadman Upham (1983; Upham and Plog 1986) used data from Nuvakwewtaqa to argue for the existence of a managerial elite. In particular, they maintained that marked agricultural intensification coupled with a large quantity of trade goods (especially ceramics, shell, and turquoise [Upham and Plog 1986]), reflected the existence of such an elite at the site.

This argument for managerial elites stood in marked contrast to a data-based model developed to describe political organization at another Pueblo IV site, Grasshopper, which lay less than 100 km south of Nuvakwewtaqa. There, the status distinctions that Stephanie M. Whittlesey (1978; Reid and Whittlesey 1990) identified through an analysis of the grave goods were suggested to reflect age and sex distinctions as well as sodality affiliation. Michael Graves and others (1982) maintained that the scale of agricultural production and long-distance exchange were such that centralized management was not necessary and in fact contrast the Grasshopper scenario with Western Pueblo ethnography. Both egalitarian and hierarchical models of late prehistoric Pueblo society have also been proposed for the eastern Pueblos of the Rio Grande (Spielmann 1994; Upham and Reed 1989; Wilcox 1991; but see Graves and Spielmann 2000).

An interesting point about the hierarchical model concerns its ethnographic derivation. At the time that Plog and Upham were developing the hierarchy model for Nuvakwewtaqa, Brandt (1985), an ethnologist and colleague of theirs at Arizona State University, was researching hierarchy among Eastern Pueblo populations. Brandt argued that Pueblo societies were hierarchical rather than egalitarian, and that hierarchy was based on differential access to ritual knowledge. By the late 1980s, Upham (1989) had embraced Brandt's (1985) mechanism, control over ritual knowledge, for the development of hierarchy among Ancestral Pueblo peoples. Thus, the "new" approach to understanding Ancestral Pueblos was perhaps more dependent on ethnographic analogy than the original egalitarian model had been.

As interest in behavior rather than culture history became a focus of North American archaeology in the 1970s, the use of ethnographic analogy expanded. The ethnographic net was cast more widely in search of useful ways of thinking about the Ancestral Pueblo archaeological record. From Douglas W. Schwartz's (1970) use of a diversity of modern cases to understand southwestern migrations, to Michael A. Adler's (1990) cross-cultural survey of ritual structures, Patricia L. Crown's (1994) use of information on historic cults, and Christine Szuter's (2000) work on gender and animal procurement, to name but a few, we have gained a great deal of insight concerning the rationales behind the behaviors we document in the archaeological record.

ORIGINS

In the 1990s, somewhat of a shift occurred from using southwestern ethnographic analogy to interpret the Ancestral Pueblo record to a concern with the deep history of ethnographically documented institutions and practices. The timing and conditions under which these institutions and practices developed among Ancestral Pueblo peoples has become one focus of southwestern archaeological research. Archaeologists have begun to identify thresholds of change in the Ancestral Pueblo record, which appear to be indicative of the origins of different kinds of social and ritual organizations that are documented ethnographically.

One example of this approach is Scott Ortman's (1998, 2000) analysis of grinding bin numbers and locations, which he uses to argue for a change in the cultural metaphor for community, as Pueblo populations aggregated in the late 1200s. Ortman suggests that in the process of aggregation, a more family-based metaphor for community was replaced by the current geographic concept of the village as community. Other archaeologists have concerned themselves with the origins of contemporary ritual organizations, including E. Charles Adams's (1991) work on the Kachina Cult. The transformations documented for Ancestral Pueblo peoples prior to Spanish colonization, however, are not assumed to have remained static over the course of subsequent centuries. Research on historical changes in Pueblo social and ritual organization has also been undertaken, such as Todd Howell's (1994) analysis of Zuni gender roles and Crown's (1994) of Puebloan religious ideology. In the 1960s Ellis (1964) talked of moving from the present backwards by "stripping away" colonial-based relationships to identify ancestral social structures. In practice, archaeologists lately have been moving from the past forward.

COLLABORATION

Finally, southwestern archaeologists are once again working directly with Indian peoples in structuring their research questions and research designs. There are efforts to replace scholar-informant relations with partnerships, as in the case of Robert Preucel's (2000) collaboration with the people of Cochiti Pueblo, and Roger Anyon's and T. J. Ferguson's with Hopi and Zuni peoples (Anyon et al. 1996). Such partnerships require sensitivity about the appropriate use of oral traditions and information on contemporary Pueblo practices. But they also create the possibility for multiple ways of knowing the past that can be communicated to an archaeological public.

Wesley Bernardini's (2002) recent dissertation exemplifies the insights that can be gained from incorporating Pueblo models into "traditional" archaeological research. In his investigation of migrations from ancestral Hopi sites to the Hopi mesas, Bernardini developed expectations based on Hopi traditional knowledge of these migrations. Hopi tradition focuses on the migrating unit, the clan, rather than a particular region. Each clan migrated independently, with a unique series of moves, until it arrived at Hopi. Individual clans often joined or left existing villages, resulting in a complex series of migration pathways (Bernardini 2002:30–35). This complexity stands in contrast to traditional archaeological models of migration, which focus on donor and accepting regions and conceive of migration as a fairly uniform, linear process. Bernardini then evaluated this model with archaeological data from the Anderson Mesa and Homol'ovi areas. His findings support the Hopi model and challenge traditional archaeological assumptions that clusters of pueblos share a common identity.

The fact that increasing numbers of Native Americans are becoming archaeologists also presages a multivocal understanding of the past. That possibility, however exciting, will need more than collaboration to be realized, however. In a recent publication, for example, Ferguson (1999) has noted that tribal archaeological reports, perhaps because they are models of archaeological reporting, rarely contain Native American perspectives in interpreting the archaeological record. It will take not only partnerships and Native American archaeologists, but also a profession more open to the possibilities of multiple understandings, before Pueblo perspectives within archaeology inform our understandings of Ancestral Pueblo peoples.

CONCLUSION

In hindsight, it was not the presence of Puebloan peoples in the Southwest that hampered the interpretation of the Ancestral Pueblo archaeological record, because for the most part archaeologists were relatively ignorant of or uninterested in the realities of the ethnographic record. When the ethnographic record was given a more thorough and careful treatment, however, the efficacy of analogy remained problematic. As became evident during the Grasshopper–Chavez Pass debate and reiterated at the 1990 Southwest Symposium by Brandt (1994) and I (Spielmann 1994), one can find an analogy for almost any kind of behavior one wishes to argue for in the Pueblo ethnographic and ethnohistoric record. At that conference Brandt made the case for a high degree of hierarchical development among Eastern Pueblo peoples, and I for more egalitarian relations, and in many cases we cited the same sources! The recent interest in conflict in the prehispanic Southwest has also illustrated the potential for ethnographic data to support, or call into question, the primacy of warfare among Ancestral Pueblos. The ethnographic record thus cannot be a source of answers for archaeology, but it is a source of ideas about the possible actions of people in the past.

The most exciting current possibilities for a nuanced approach that bridges an understanding of living Pueblo peoples and the Ancestral Pueblo record involves collaborative research between archaeologists and Native Americans and the growing participation of Native American archaeologists in the profession. Increasing attention is being paid to a common ground, which can only enhance the dialogue between ethnography and archaeology as we launch a new century of southwestern archaeology.

14

"The Feeling of Working Completely in the Dark."[1] The Uncertain Foundations of Southwestern Mission Archaeology

James E. Ivey and David Hurst Thomas

Most archaeologists seem to view the Spanish Colonial period in the Southwest as relatively well understood, needing little serious investigation. As two archaeologists with more than a half century of combined experience in excavating missions in the Spanish Borderlands, we question this assumption. The truth is that relatively little archaeology has been done on the missions of the American Southwest: Only a dozen or so seventeenth-century missions have been "excavated" or even minimally "tested." And when we look at the details of this research, it too often comes across as hasty, outdated, and poorly reported.

In this brief paper, we make three simple points: 1) how little is presently known about mission archaeology in the American Southwest; 2) how a priori and unwarranted assumptions continue to distort our understanding of missions as Borderlands institutions; and 3) how up-to-date archaeological investigations could shed significant new light on Hispanic-Pueblo interactions in the mission context, but that research will not be easy.

HISTORY OF INVESTIGATIONS

The earliest missions in the American Southwest in New Mexico were established in the late sixteenth century, and three centuries later, archaeologists (such as Adolph Bandelier) began exploring the ruins. During the 1910s and 1920s, Nels Nelson, Alfred V. Kidder, and Edgar Lee Hewett continued research on the major abandoned mission sites of the Rio Grande area of New Mexico.

Nelson directed the American Museum of Natural History projects at four missions in the Galisteo Basin: San Marcos, San Lázaro, Galisteo, and San Cristóbal (Nelson 1914, 1916). More interested in working out chronological markers for Puebloan cultures than he was in missions, Nelson's brief examinations of the Galisteo Basin missions did little to develop an understanding of these structures.

About the same time, Hewett turned his attention to what he termed the "archaic" missions of the province of New Mexico: Abó, Quarai, Gran Quivira (Las Humanas), Pecos, and Giusewa at Jemez Springs (Hewett 1938:57, 63; Hewett and Mauzy 1940:88). Hewett himself conducted extensive work on the mission churches at Giusewa and Gran Quivira. Several investigators worked at the mission at Jemez, and some useful information from these excavations was recorded and survives in the archaeological archives (Bloom 1923; Bloom and Mitchell 1938; Farwell 1991; Kubler 1940:82–85, 147–148; Scholes 1937). But the data have never been synthesized.

The Works Progress Administration (WPA) began work at Abó and Quarai in the 1930s. No significant records were kept during these excavations, and an overall site report was never prepared. Only brief summary reports appeared, without any detailed presentation of data (e.g., Toulouse 1949); and as Ivey (1988) has noted elsewhere, the dismal quality of work at Quarai probably would not have supported any more detailed discussion anyway. The nearby site of Las Humanas has two churches and two *convento*s. The larger church and convento complex was excavated in the 1920s, again without any significant report being written. The smaller convento and church were excavated in separate projects in the 1950s and 1960s, and relatively well reported (see Hayes et al. 1981; Ivey 1988; Vivian 1979). Although the site of Tabira was well excavated, it was a *visita* church without a convento, and the report was presented only as a journal article (Stubbs 1959; see also Ivey 1988).

Mission San Miguel, in downtown Santa Fe, has been excavated and reported only in a short, rather summary report (Stubbs and

Ellis 1955). At Zuni, the mission of Halona was tested as part of a stabilization project in the 1960s, and the resultant report was not a research-oriented presentation (Caywood 1972).

Adolph Bandelier conducted the initial excavations into the convento at Pecos in the 1880s. Jesse Nusbaum excavated and stabilized the eighteenth-century church in 1915, and Alfred Kidder carried out a few tests within the convento and adjacent buildings over the next 10 years (Kidder 1915:1–47, 1925a:29a–32). WPA excavations within the church and convento were conducted through the second half of the 1930s, ending with the beginning of World War II. After the war, the mission and pueblo were given to the National Park Service in 1965, and further excavations begun in the church and convento as part of the development of the site as a national monument. Extensive work by Jean Pinkley and Alden Hayes probably examined or reexamined virtually every room of the convento. Despite this long series of excavations, only a short interpretive booklet by Alden Hayes was published, and more recent results of archaeomagnetic and materials testing has invalidated many of his conclusions (Eighmy 1994, 1995; Hayes 1974: xii; Morgenstein 1994). Similar narratives could be given about the other National Park Service sites of Abó, Quarai, and Gran Quivira, as well as the state-owned site of Jemez Springs. Today, most of the other abandoned mission sites of New Mexico are owned by Pueblos, private landowners, or conservancies.

It is clear, then, that a number of southwestern missions have been thoroughly cleared of debris and some simple structural outlines have been mapped. But shockingly little useful information has resulted from most of these "excavations." Most of the archaeologists involved were interested primarily in Pueblo culture, not Spanish culture. These investigations tended to confirm, at least in part, the longstanding (if usually tacit) assumption that the Spanish missions and civil settlements in New Mexico were somehow second-rate and substandard relative to comparable institutions elsewhere.

This attitude—the myth of the poverty-stricken frontier—reflects a popularized perception of Hispanic culture in frontier New Mexico as rude and uncivilized, ignorant and isolated. One of us (Ivey 1988:417) has ridiculed this "mission in the wilderness concept," which mistakenly assumes that friars lived alone in their mission conventos, without meaningful interactions with other segments of Spanish society and culture. To some extent, these distortions were based on complaints made by the Spanish participants themselves, especially in official letters back to Mexico; this feeling was also reinforced by the Anglo military forces when they invaded New Mexico in 1846. Even today, local history is commonly taught as if frontier New Mexicans experienced only isolation and squalor, as if they were uninvolved with the larger Spanish Empire. "Archaeologists see what they expect to see, and most archaeologists thought of missions as poverty-stricken places; their quick, rough excavations confirmed these expectations" (Ivey 1988:xv).

Exploring Franciscan Awatovi and Hawikuh

In truth, only two mission sites in the American Southwest have been thoroughly investigated using the best available scientific techniques of the day. Frederick Hodge directed the Museum of the American Indian's Hendricks-Heye expedition at Hawikuh from 1917 to 1923 (reported in Smith et al. 1966); John Otis Brew and his team from the Peabody Museum at Harvard excavated at Awatovi from 1935 to 1939 (Brew 1949:xix; see also Elliott 1995:78–101, 162–187). For decades, these twin excavations have provided the baseline for our current understanding of seventeenth-century life in the missions of the Southwest.

A tremendous amount of information was recovered in each project, but neither of these excavations was specifically aimed at explicating life in a Franciscan convento. Neither principal investigator had significant experience in the American Southwest: the British-born Hodge had been educated in Washington, D.C. (Fowler 2000:370, 378; Elliott 1995:80), and Brew was Boston born and Harvard trained (Elliott 1995:165). Because both archaeologists were unfamiliar with the still-operating missions of the Southwest, they missed clues and insights that could have fruitfully guided their excavation into the seventeenth-century structures.

But to their credit, both project directors drew upon the expertise of others. Hodge brought in the skilled Jesse Nusbaum, who had worked in the Pecos mission with Kidder before undertaking the church and convento at Hawikuh. Nusbaum's detailed notes on the Hawikuh mission were written up by Watson Smith, Richard B. Woodbury, and Nathalie F. S. Woodbury in 1966 (Smith et al. 1966:116). As a result, the Hendricks-Heye excavations of the mission at Hawikuh were interpreted largely on the basis of Brew's research at Awatovi, which took place two decades later.

To understand Franciscan Awatovi, Brew turned to Ross Montgomery, a California-based architect and architectural historian, who
interpreted the southwestern structures in light of his familiarity with
the largely nineteenth-century California missions. These insights
proved so welcome that when Montgomery arrived, Brew commented
wryly that "the feeling of working completely in the dark [has] disap-
peared"(1949:xix).

MISSION ARCHAEOLOGY AND MISSION ARCHITECTURE

The study of mission architecture in the American Southwest proceeded in a rather different direction. Between 1935 and 1939—while
Brew was excavating at Awatovi and Montgomery was formulating his
ideas about life and architecture in the seventeenth-century missions of
New Mexico—a student of architectural history, George Kubler, was
researching and writing "A Critical Study of the Religious Architecture
of New Mexico." Kubler first submitted this study to Yale University in
1936 as a Master of Arts thesis. He rewrote and expanded this thesis
over the next four years, submitting the revision to Yale as his doctoral dissertation. In 1940 the Taylor Museum (in Colorado Springs,
Colorado) published Kubler's dissertation as the now-classic *The Religious Architecture of New Mexico in the Colonial Period and since the
American Occupation.*

Kubler's architectural study received rave reviews. Writing in
the *Hispanic American Historical Review*, Robert C. Smith called it
"a volume which will be the definitive book on the subject" (Smith
1940:619). Decades later, historian John Kessell repeated the refrain,
terming Kubler's dissertation simply "the bible" (Kessell 1980:29). For
the architectural historian Barbara Anderson, the Kubler volume had
become "the basic tool with which historians of the architecture of the
United States were equipped after 1940 to discuss the development of
the Hispanic southwest and western U.S. in relation to contemporane-
ous developments in the East" (Anderson 1990:xiii). In his obituary of
Kubler, Humberto Rodríguez-Camilloni reiterated that *The Religious
Architecture of New Mexico* "remains the definitive work on the subject" (Rodríguez-Camilloni 1997:12–13).

Despite such recognition by historians and architects, it was Montgomery—not George Kubler—who became the patron saint of southwestern mission archaeology. "One of the primary aims of archaeology," claimed Brew,

is to reconstruct conjecturally not only the buildings and industries and arts of a bygone time but also the way of life of the builders of those buildings and the practitioners of those arts.... It is in such speculation that archaeology and anthropology meet and it is by answering these questions that archaeologists justify their labors. Montgomery has provided us...with an anthropological interpretation.... Montgomery has fulfilled our obligation for Franciscan Awatovi [Brew 1949:xx–xxi].

Stressing the uses and regulations that governed church and convento life, Montgomery criticized Kubler's "modernistic preciosity" with regard to church design and construction. Montgomery (1940: 272) carefully distinguished a Kubler-style "[a]rchitecture as one of the fine arts [that] may be interpreted in terms of pure aesthetics, or as an external expression of the builders' creative genius, constrained by factors of tradition, methods, materials, tools and experience" from an architecture "defined as a utilitarian art to serve the pragmatic ends for which it is conceived, the aesthetic definitions of proportion, composition and organic embellishment being relegated to considerations of secondary importance." Montgomery argued that the "mendicants knew nothing of modern aesthetics, and cared less." They were "pragmatists—not patrons of the arts...their architecture in the *Custodia* was simple and utilitarian." According to Montgomery (1940:273–274), Kubler's approach tended to "deduce an esotericism that in fact did not exist."
Kubler defended himself by contrasting the art historian's

detailed inspection and the detailed study of single objects [as] contrary to...anthropologists' procedure of finding groupings and resolving the individuality of the object in the group that has been defined.... So there is a fundamental antipathy of approach of excessive sympathy for the object on the art historians' part and too little understanding of the object on the anthropologists' part [Kubler 1994:17].

To Kubler, the task of the art historian is to identify the "esthetic intent" of the person who designed and built a structure.
Restricting himself to mission architecture within the modern state of New Mexico (not the old province), Kubler excluded the mission at Awatovi from his overview and, of course, did not consider Montgom-

ery's interpretation (which would not be published for another nine years). Not until the fourth edition of *The Religious Architecture of New Mexico,* published in 1972, did Kubler comment on Montgomery's work, remarking that "[t]he western missions were poorly known until the appearance of Ross Montgomery's work on Awatovi.... As an architect and as a specialist on liturgy, Montgomery guided the excavation of the mission buildings, and his parts of the report are a handbook on mission life and building activity" (Kubler 1973:ix). But with regard to Montgomery's interpretation of the Hawikuh excavations, Kubler noted dryly that

> these pages of intricate local detail avoid discussing the relationship of Hawikuh to the rest of Pueblo Mission architecture, by assuming that Montgomery's detailed work on Awatovi had already discharged that obligation. As a monograph this volume belongs among the masterpieces of southwestern archaeological writing [Kubler 1973:ix].

Today, Kubler's comments come across as rather lukewarm (perhaps he had read Montgomery's [1940] review of his own dissertation).

Such comments demonstrate the rather different legacies enjoyed by Kubler and Montomery. Whereas Kubler championed an art historical approach to mission architecture, Montgomery operated more as an archaeologist, stressing the design and actual use of the mission buildings. Today, we believe that strong evidence exists to demonstrate that pragmatic considerations were the dominant design philosophy for the Spanish Borderlands missions, thereby lending support to Montgomery's perspective. Even at the broadest level, it is clear that the design was subordinate to local skills and materials—be they adobe or rough stone in New Mexico, or wattle and daub in east Texas and Spanish Florida. The requirements of these skills and materials dominated the design. Esthetics were clearly relegated to a secondary level.

THE ROLE OF SCHOLES

Given the influence of Montgomery's interpretation of Franciscan Awatovi and Hawikuh, it seems appropriate to examine the roots of his thinking, which take us directly to the research of historian France Scholes (1937, 1942).

An ardent student of documents, Scholes tended to accept Franciscan statements at face value—particularly with regard to the level of dominance and control exerted by the Spanish in New Mexico. As a result, he saw colonial history in New Mexico as involving the nearly complete disruption of Puebloan society. In this view, virtually all Pueblo Indians became Christians and were fully subjugated by Franciscans—except, of course, for a handful of rebels and troublemakers, who protested against the Spanish culture that had absorbed them.

This perspective translated directly into Montgomery's interpretations of mission archaeology. When a kiva was uncovered beneath the altar of Awatovi, for instance, Montgomery attributed its placement to the doctrine of "superposition"—a well-known practice throughout Latin America, in which Catholic churches were deliberately constructed on top of "pagan" places of worship. In so doing, missionaries both literally and symbolically "superimposed" their Christian belief system atop the ideology and architecture of the past. Montgomery imported this doctrine of superposition to the American Southwest, arguing that the Franciscans had symbolically subjugated the people of Awatovi by deliberately placing a Christian altar over the kiva (the sacred ground of the past). So strongly held was this theoretical bias that no alternatives were considered possible for interpreting the archaeological evidence.

The Scholes doctrine regarding the relationship between the Franciscans, the Pueblos, and the civil authorities of New Mexico continues to hold sway in historical archaeological research in New Mexico. In 1974, for instance, Alden Hayes found a kiva inside the convento at Pecos. Because the adobe bricks of the kiva appeared to be the same color as the church, Hayes (1974:23–35) reversed Montgomery's argument of superposition to suggest that the convento kiva must have been built after the Pueblo Revolt of 1680. In this case, liberated Puebloan Indians used bricks from the demolished church to demonstrate their symbolic domination of the Franciscans. Although the artifacts contained within the Pecos kiva place its construction date anytime between about 1620 and perhaps 1720, Hayes downplayed the artifactual evidence in favor of the dominating views of Scholes.

Actually, this overarching paradigm is little more than untested assumption. Scholes "created," in a very real sense, the received view of Spanish colonial history in New Mexico and, given the flow of academic research within the state, Scholes's assumptions have long been accepted without reservation. This may be a serious error.

SOME SUGGESTIONS FROM LA FLORIDA

Scholes's picture of the mission experience in New Mexico is beginning to change. Working from his own documentary research, the historian John Kessell, for example, has published detailed studies of the histories of the missions of Pecos in New Mexico, and Guevavi and Tumacacori in Arizona (Kessell 1970, 1976). More recently, he has summarized his lifetime of historical research in the Spanish Southwest, disclosing a far more critical attitude towards the Franciscans and the claims of total dominance in New Mexico (Kessell 2002).

A resurgence of archaeological research on the missions of Spanish Florida likewise demonstrates the fallacy of a Scholes-like perspective on Franciscan–American Indian interactions. In La Florida, Franciscans boasted of considerable power in their correspondence, but in reality they seem to have accomplished far less than claimed. Recent excavations in the southeastern missions show the persistence of American Indian religious beliefs and demonstrate the degree to which the Hispanic authorities vacillated over whether certain Native practices were compatible with Christianity or not (e.g., Milanich 1999:148–149; Thomas 1988; Worth 1998).

Excavations in the *campo santo* at Mission Santa Catalina de Guale, for instance, show considerable flexibility in mortuary patterns (Thomas 1988, 1993). Conventional Franciscan doctrine held that parishioners should be buried to emulate the burial of Christ; true to form, our excavations show that virtually all of the neophyte Guale Indians were interred in characteristic "Christian" burial posture—in unmarked graves beneath the church floor, heads oriented toward the east, with arms crossed on the chest. But Franciscan dogma likewise called for burial without grave goods and embellishments, and here the neophytes drew the line. For 2,000 years, Native Americans in the American Southeast held the view that specific grave goods were necessary to reflect the sacred and secular beliefs of the now-dead. Faced with this deeply entrenched belief, the friars at Santa Catalina developed a remarkable flexibility with regard to grave furniture. Within the 400–450 Guale graves located inside the church at Santa Catalina, excavators recovered a truly astounding array of associated grave goods, including complete majolica vessels, dozens of projectile points, a rattlesnake shell gorget, glass cruets, two dozen religious medallions (of bronze, gold, and silver), finger rings, copper plaques, and at least 75,000 glass trade beads.

These departures from Franciscan dogma were rationalized by the view that Guale neophytes as not "fully formed" in Christianity, a perspective that granted both friar and convert considerable latitude in the day-to-day practice of the new religion. To the schooled Franciscan mind, this juxtaposition of Christian and pagan was a necessary step in the conversion process. That is, to achieve the outward symbols of conversion (specifically emphasizing burial and baptism records) and to stamp out offensive pagan practices (especially burial mounds and charnel houses), friars "permitted" the Guale Indians to continue their practice of grave goods (despite the fact that this practice directly violated church doctrine). For their part, the Guale clearly maximized their transitional status, simultaneously using the mission system for their own devices while retaining key beliefs from their own traditions.

Similar negotiations took place in the layout and architecture of southeastern missions. At Mission San Luis de Talimali, archaeologists discovered a huge council house measuring 120 ft across, capable of seating 2,000–3,000 people (Shapiro and Hann 1990). Long a mainstay of Indian villages in La Florida, the council house functioned year-round as the seat of Native government, a meeting place for villagers, the locus for interacting with Spanish authorities, and an inn to house the scalps. As the most powerful symbol of Native community, the council house was permitted to survive in the Franciscan missions of Spanish Florida—provided it sported a Christian cross. The council house at San Luis fronted the main mission plaza, symbolizing in architecture the blending of Native and Franciscan beliefs.

Then there is the matter of the ballgame, a centuries-old custom of a game commonly played between competing villages (with 50–100 participants on a side). Games typically lasted half a day, serious injuries were not uncommon, and omens and rituals attended every aspect of the game. During the late seventeenth century, considerable debate raged within the Church about whether or not the ballgame was compatible with Christianity. Was the ballgame a simple athletic contest or a survival of pagan demonic beliefs (Bushnell 1978)? Initially, Spanish authorities supported the ballgame complex. The friars, always on the lookout for ways to promote sedentism among neophytes, recognized that attendance at ballgames translated directly into increased participation in the Mass. The governor of St. Augustine also reluctantly supported the practice, fearing that banning the ballgame would cause the Indians to refuse to work for the Spaniards. In effect, the Franciscans "baptized" this seemingly pagan custom in order to effect conversion.

As a direct result, ball courts became acceptable components within the missions of Spanish Florida.

But through time, the friars reversed their position, concerned over the clearly supernatural aspects of the game, especially the involvement of sun, thunder, and rain deities (which were long-standing components in the harvest rituals—one of the "traditional" religious beliefs that the Franciscans were seeking to stamp out). The Spanish eventually banned the ballgame altogether when some of the "converted" Apalache chiefs admitted that such non-Christian practices should not be permitted among Christianized Indian people (Bushnell 1978).

In short, the archaeological record of Spanish Florida clearly demonstrates a significant give-and-take in the power relationships between Native and Hispanic authorities. The Franciscans friars assigned to the southeastern missions targeted a significant portion of their limited resources toward the most fundamental sacraments of the church—especially baptism, monogamy, participation in the Mass, and Christian burial. But beyond these religious "necessities," the friars made considerable allowances for the sake of conversion. In his monograph on Franciscan Awatovi, J. Franklin Ewing quotes a doctrine of New World mission philosophy: *Abusus non tollat usum* ("the abuse of a thing should be corrected, but it is not a reason for abolishing the proper use of that thing" [Ewing 1949:103]).

Could it be that similar mediating circumstances played out in the American Southwest? Were the Franciscans of New Mexico more accepting of Native practices than their letters to headquarters suggest?

If we admit the possibility of accommodation and negotiation, then perhaps we should revisit conventional interpretations of the archaeological record—such as Hayes's conclusions about the "convento kiva" at Pecos. As it turns out, recent analysis of the bricks and adobe mortar from which the Pecos kiva was made demonstrates that it was constructed from a combination of bricks and mortar employed only during the period from about 1630–1640— squarely during the heyday of Franciscan religion at Pecos (White 1996). If so, then the Hayes interpretation must be incorrect, and other explanations should be entertained.

Ivey (1998) has reexamined similar constructions at other southwestern missions. Like the Pecos kiva, the so-called convento kivas at the missions of Abó and Quarai have long been viewed as the products of reverse superposition: That is, the post-revolt Pueblo Indians built kivas into formerly Franciscan buildings to demonstrate their triumph and dominance over the Spanish religion. But Ivey's reanalysis suggests that these post-revolt convento kivas were likely built during the 1620–1640 period—while the Franciscan mission was still operating. Even Montgomery's interpretation of the kiva beneath the altar at Awatovi comes into question (Ivey 1998).

Ivey believes that such kivalike structures were built under the direct supervision of the Franciscans, creating familiar spaces for use as schoolrooms, to help acculturate Native children and selected adults into the Christian world the Franciscans were trying to create. Although his hypothesis has not met with overwhelming acceptance among southwestern historians and archaeologists (e.g., Liebmann 2002:138, 143), Ivey suggests that instead of invoking contemporary political arguments, critics might wish to concentrate on establishing behaviors from the historic period that could explain the concrete archaeological evidence at hand.

WHERE ARE THE ARTIFACTS?

Despite his detailed and theoretically informed architectural plans, Montgomery's reconstruction of life at Awatovi and Hawikuh ignored the artifacts recovered from the church and convento excavations. We have no idea what artifact groupings were found in the various spaces, and what these discards could tell us about their use. As a result, Montgomery's conclusions about room use and lifeways in both missions remain largely exercises in architectural speculation.

The problem is less severe at Awatovi because little evidence of the Franciscan room occupations survived the Hopi reuse of the convento spaces. According to Brew, other than "a few features in the walls we found nothing which we could attribute authoritatively to pre-Rebellion times" (Montgomery et al. 1949:79). But at Hawikuh, where the Zuni established new floors well above the original Franciscan surfaces, quantities of in situ artifacts seem to have been preserved (e.g., Elliott 1995:178). The Hawikuh report mentions charred fragments of furniture and other woodwork in some rooms and the remains of the wooden altar railings. Published photographs even suggest that burnt fragments of a santo were recovered in front of the main altar (Smith et al. 1966:113–115, Plates 16a, 19c, 19d). It seems likely that the artifacts found in these Franciscan spaces reflect their placement on the day of their destruction in 1672. But the lack of any formal information about artifact contents of individual rooms in both the Awatovi and Hawikuh excavations—plus the absence of subsequent studies in

any southwestern mission excavation demonstrating the direct association between room use and artifact content—leaves a major question
unanswered: Can room use in southwestern missions be identified by
artifact content?

MODERN MISSION RESEARCH

The last major excavation at a southwestern mission ended more than
60 years ago, when Brew and Montgomery stopped work at Awatovi.
But can we assume that our knowledge of southwestern missions was
completely and adequately defined during the 1920–1940 period—
when Scholes in history, Kubler in architecture, and Montgomery in
architectural archaeology did their seminal research?

We think not. We suggest instead that archaeologists and historians
recognize the potential for applying modern excavation and laboratory
techniques to generate new data and reexamine previous conclusions.
Five years ago, the American Museum of Natural History, under our
direction, launched a new, long-term research program at Mission San
Marcos, located about 20 miles south of Santa Fe, New Mexico. The
Mission San Marcos project began with an intensive program of surface and subsurface mapping of the site, with particular emphasis on
ground-penetrating radar and soil resistivity.

The 1999 excavations concentrated on the nave of the mission
church, where we located a large, apparently unfinished altar constructed over an earlier altar platform. At the time, we thought that the
church at Mission San Marcos was being remodeled when the Pueblo
Revolt broke out on August 10, 1680. (We now question this conclusion.) During the summer of 2000, we concentrated on the church
doorway area and nearby rooms inside the Franciscan friary, successfully delimiting the main door of the church and the baptistery.

We then shifted emphasis to the convento interior, which provided
different challenges. When working within the church, we could draw
upon a large body of comparative architecture: the altar should follow
set traditions of form and function, the baptistery should contain a bap-
tismal font, and so forth. But we found ourselves on thinner ice when
attempting to codify a model of Franciscan architectural practice in the
conventos of the northern frontier. To be sure, the presence of ovens
should indicate a kitchen, and built-in benches around the walls and a
large doorway should define a *portería* (the formal entrance room to
the convento). But how would we recognize a friar's cell, especially if it
does not follow a very specific plan seen in some other missions? What

should a storeroom look like? Perhaps there are reliable signatures that would enable us to identify room function from specific criteria of size and/or location. But right now, we are forced to admit how little we know about such patterning in the Southwest.

Perhaps there was no general rule governing Franciscan mission construction. Neverthless, recent work on seventeenth-century mission churches in Florida compared with those in New Mexico suggests strong similarities in religious architecture between the areas. If the architectural plans were consistent for the churches, then perhaps this consistency carried over to the conventos as well. It is likewise possible that eighteenth-century Texas missions (for which the Franciscans prepared detailed inventories) can provide a useful model of room uses and contents. But would such rules apply to the seventeenth century? Since no detailed archaeological record has been kept of excavations into most of these spaces, we lack a usable artifact record to tell us what debris a given use left in a room. California missions of the late eighteenth and early nineteenth centuries may also have something to tell us about seventeenth-century New Mexico missions, but this seems unlikely, since the pattern and plan of California missions had evolved so far from those of New Mexico two centuries earlier.

With these issues in mind, we explored the mission convento at San Marcos during the last two field seasons. We successfully defined the main entry room (portería) into the convento and tested several additional rooms. The convento had been repainted several times, and in several places we discovered several patches of the original convento wall decorations. These striking decorations consist of an alternating series of three-dimensional black-and-red squares, an illusion created by shaded parallelogram sides that create a cascading herringbone pattern. In three cases, a floral design motif had been added, with a six-pointed flower design depicted in fine-line black paint. We stabilized these plaster surfaces in place, using a dilute adhesive solution, then carefully backfilled the area with sand and permeable geocloth fabric.

The floral wall paintings attracted considerable attention in the field, but from a scientific perspective, our most significant discovery involved what we failed to find. If Mission San Marcos had been abandoned with the outbreak of the 1680 Pueblo Revolt—as long assumed from documentary evidence—then the convento floors should be littered with daily debris and smashed Mission period artifacts, such as broken plates and pots, religious items, furniture, and wall decorations. Yet in every convento room examined, we found that the floors had been scrupulously cleaned out before abandonment.

We expected our San Marcos excavations to provide at least pre-liminary patterns of room use and spatial patterning on the Francis-can frontier. Instead, we found mostly new questions, with very few answers. The convento rooms had been extensively remodeled and re-configured, often subdivided with neat walls of formed adobe brick. Documentary records indicate that the Native people of San Marcos permanently abandoned the mission during the first days of the revolt, moving to Santa Fe where they helped drive out the Spanish governor and citizens living there. But if these historic records are accurate, who remodeled the mission?

Did the Native people of San Marcos reoccupy the mission site after the revolt? Did the Franciscans return after the Spanish Recon-quest to resurrect the abandoned Mission San Marcos? Or did a third, unidentified group attempt to rebuild San Marcos? Whatever the even-tual answer, it is clear that historical documents provide only a partial and biased glimpse of life in the Franciscan missions of the American Southwest. We believe that properly conceived archaeological excava-tions have the potential to flesh out a more realistic, less biased under-standing of the past.

The San Marcos research remains a theoretical challenge. We began with the belief that we could clarify Franciscan architectural practice on the northern Spanish frontier. We hoped, ideally, that room use could be associated with artifact content—that is, a room's use could be iden-tified by an artifact presence/absence signature. We expected the San Marcos excavations to offer at least the first suggestions of a pattern of room use and spatial patterning on the Franciscan frontier. Instead, our excavations raised innumerable questions and provided few satisfying answers. As at Awatovi, the rooms contained the partition walls of a Puebloan reoccupation and virtually no artifactual record of Francis-can room use. As a result, our final report will attempt to work out a detailed construction history of the place, but we can say very little of the specifics of daily life in the convento.

Can Franciscan room use be identified by artifact associations? We still do not know. Some elements of room function can be deduced from the architectural plan itself, but the results cannot be carried beyond a fairly basic level. The idea that artifact associations can be used for the attribution of room use may, in fact, be a useless concept. To date, no connection has been demonstrated between the material culture of a mission and the lifeways that were carried out within it; no index of artifacts has been produced that can be associated with specific mission activities except in the most general and generic way. To be sure, considerable information still resides in the unpublished field notes and smaller reports available from southwestern mission sites, and even published excavations can be fruitfully reevaluated in the light of more recent archaeological, historical, and architectural research. There is also much to learn from evaluation of Hispanic period material culture recovered from places like Awatovi and Hawikuh. But, unfortunately, no broad synthesis has been carried out to determine what is known and not known from a century of mission excavations.

The truth is that our present knowledge of Hispanic-Pueblo interactions during this period is heavily one-sided, dominated by paradigms borrowed from elsewhere—from Borderlands historians, art historians, architectural historians, and Franciscan historians. What is missing here is an anthropologically informed archaeology of the Spanish Mission period, an approach that employs well-established, anthropologically based research into lifeways and interactions of the past. For decades, anthropological archaeologists have developed tools for doing this in other contexts and we are advocating that the full range of these research strategies be brought to bear on the Spanish Mission period.

In a real way, Southwest mission archaeology still proceeds in a shadowy darkness not terribly brighter than that commented upon by Professor Brew, when Ross Montgomery began to shed some light into the excavations at Awatovi.

Note

1. The title of this paper derives from Brew (1949:xix).

15

Discussion of Southwest Archaeology in the Twentieth Century

David R. Wilcox

History has many faces, many moods, and many motivations. We see something of that in the essays of this book, which the editors have grouped to tell stories about institutional development and some current themes in southwestern archaeology. All of them are told by professional archaeologists presently doing archaeology in the Southwest, many of us for almost our whole careers. So far as I know, none of us can claim much formal training in the professional disciplines of history, sociology, or philosophy, all of which have been brought to bear to understand the history of other scientific disciplines. In our sister discipline of linguistics, for example, Stephen O. Murray (1994) has a fine book on *Theory Groups and the Study of Language in North America* in which he applies concepts from the sociology of science to analyze the structure of debates in American linguistics and how they have evolved. His book is the sixty-ninth in a series of "Studies in the History of Language Sciences." I know of no comparable series on the history of world archaeology, much less of southwestern archaeology. Why is that? To be sure, the intellectual historians George Stocking (1982) and Curtis Hinsley (1983, 1986, 1994; Hinsley and Wilcox 1995, 1996, 2002) have interested themselves in certain aspects of the history of southwestern archaeology, and their influence can be seen especially in Snead's work (2001, this volume). Cultural anthropologists (Babcock and Parezo 1988; Parezo 1993) and folklorists (Weigle 1989) have also published provocative work relevant to a deeper understanding of southwestern archaeology. It is interesting, is it not, that both

A. V. Kidder and Edgar Lee Hewett helped to train Harvey company employees on what to say to tourists on the "Harvey Tours" (Weigle 1989)?

What more should we desire from histories of southwestern archaeology than the kind of thing found in the essays of this book—all of which are competent, earnest, and informative, if sometimes iconoclastic or self-serving? Let us summarize: Fowler (2000) recounts some of the story of big names who came to the Southwest as agents of outside institutions, while Snead sheds light from archival sources on the formation of local institutions that soon dominated most work done in the Southwest (see Taylor 1954). Reid and Whittlesey praise a famous man (Emil Haury) who did a huge amount to "tell the story" of southwestern archaeology, the culture history story. Mills shows us how Haury and others perpetuated their views by training students in intimate settings (in the field). Kelley and MacWilliams carefully show that south of the border is the other half of the "Southwest" (Northwest, North American Southwest, Greater Southwest,...sorry). Doelle and Phillips give us a firsthand glimpse of how they and others wrested control of the funding for southwestern archaeology from the traditional institutions that Hewett, Haury, and others built. Thought of anything else you would like to know yet?

Nash and Dean provide an intense discussion of the central role environmental studies have played in southwestern archaeology. Huckell ably reviews the first 10,000 years of our subject (good title, that); and Lekson entertains us with an amusing lament about his failure to get outside "big guns" to support his notion that some southwestern societies were "complex." Preucel finds that most discussions by southwestern archaeologists about ethnicity and ethnogenesis are "rarely adequately theorized," something that could be said about his historical analysis. Ivey and Thomas bewail the fact that earlier studies of southwestern missions did not show them how to interpret the San Marcos mission where the Pompeii premise was not realized. Finally, in an excellent appraisal of current institutional issues, Cordell shines light on some of the most difficult challenges that face archaeological practitioners today. Is that all?

Where, hence, the history of southwestern archaeology? What lies ahead and what is it about "how we have come to be as we are" that we still want to know? Are there aspects of the intellectual journey we call southwestern archaeology that are interesting "for their own sake"? Is there anything here of general moment for people with interests in world history, sociology, or philosophy? Sure there is, and we need to do what we can to foster such interest and encourage it. Where we take historical inquiries depends on the questions we ask.

For me, southwestern archaeology has been an opportunity—or a "laboratory" as Fowler (2000) calls it—to study and perhaps to understand the relationship between past and present, to confront how it is that the past is different from the present. Things change; guys like Columbus show up, and we have to deal with the consequences. How can we do this without giving up all we value? Fortunately there is another side to this: the future, too, can be different from the present. Through our acts, if often only in small ways, we can help to bring about a different life that renews or creates an aesthetic that allows us to realize our values. Conflict can result in consensus; stability is possible (Hacking 1992). These are universal themes, which is why I think archaeology intrigues everyone. Let us examine a few questions still worth asking about southwestern archaeology.

Whence have we come: what are the concepts we take for granted, Whorf-like, that affect the way we claim it is worthwhile to spend taxpayer dollars? How *do* we "stand on the shoulders of giants" (Merton 1993) like Emil Haury's, without making a mockery of what he would say today if he knew what we now know, but he did not? The American philosopher Charles Sanders Peirce (Wiener 1958) pointed out that we know ourselves only through inference—so, too, everything. To understand what the Mogollon concept meant to Haury we need to seek for the referents of his language (and humor), allowing for the "multiplicity, patchiness, and heterogeneity" of the intellectual resources he brought to the "space" in which he worked (Pickering 1992:8; see Hacking 1983, 1992; Sargent 1995). Few scientists are automatons, ruled by coherent theories; hence the failure of Preucel's expectations (this volume). Having constructed a model of what Haury thought, we then can examine the difference between us: are our questions the same as his? Do current data support or refute his expectations? Where do we want to go from here? How are we to connect with our audience's knowledge and then conduct them in a direction of our choosing? (For illustrations of this approach, see Wilcox 1981; Wilcox and Shenk 1977.)

A case can be made that modern southwestern archaeology began about 150 years ago with the contributions of Gallatin (1845, 1848) and Squier (1848; see Fowler 2000 and Wilcox and Fowler 2002). By 1902, with the formation of the American Anthropological Association, mechanisms for certifying professionals in archaeology had arisen, following the formation of museums competing for the world's treasures; the World's Columbian Exposition of 1893, which further stimulated that interest; and the beginning of graduate programs (Fowler, this volume). In the Southwest, Charles Lummis and Edgar Lee Hewett sought no less than to create a different style and aesthetic for what it meant to be an American. Against the Eastern Establishment led by Charles Elliott Norton (Turner 1999) and, in anthropology, by Franz Boas (Fowler 1999; Hinsley 1986; Stocking 1982), Hewett and his staff at the Museum of New Mexico created the "Myth of the Santa Fe style" (Stocking 1982; Wilson 1997; see also Morley 1915) with local cultural elements appropriated from Indian and Spanish forms, thus broadening what it meant to be an American and what the "good life" was. This move radically opposed the widespread Anglo attitude of the time derived from General Phil Sheridan's (Hutton 1985) public policy that "the only good Indian is a dead Indian," substituting the proposition that we had much to learn from Indians and Hispanics about how to live well in the arid west. The myth served well, in its day, to create a new social charter for the peaceful relations among New Mexico's diverse ethnic groups (see Malinowski [1926] on myth and Wilson [1997] for a critique). By transforming Pueblo and mission sites into state parks or national monuments, Hewett and company used state sanction to legitimize their aesthetic vision. These moves generated tourism, too, and helped to underwrite the local economy. No adequate study of these initiatives, their aesthetic, or their effect on the trajectory of southwestern archaeology has yet been written—but we are moving in that direction (Snead 2001, this volume).

What connected archaeological institutions to public support in Arizona was more varied than in New Mexico. Harold Sellers and Mary Russell Ferrell Colton brought an aesthetic based on a marriage of science and art (and a family fortune) to the Colorado Plateau at the Museum of Northern Arizona. A professional geologist and ecologist, Colton (1918, 1960) applied his unique experience to devise pioneering models of human ecology. A similar breadth of interest is apparent in the life of William Shirley Fulton, the founder of the Amerind Foundation (Fenner 1977). Dwight and Maie Heard also began supporting both science and art, although the early death of Dwight ended their scientific endeavor (Wilcox 1987). A student of Hewett, Odd Halseth (Wilcox 1993) succeeded in institutionalizing a city museum and the position of city archaeologist in Phoenix. State support for archaeology was assured by the efforts of Byron Cummings at the Arizona

State Museum (ASM) (Wilcox 2001). His student, Emil Haury, having become disillusioned with private patronage (Thompson 1995), when he became director of the ASM in 1938 built on the firm foundation laid by Cummings and through his and his colleagues' efforts at the national level brought about the inclusion of archaeology in federal laws, the history of which has yet to be fully told (but see Wendorf and Thompson 2002; Wilcox 1988b). Because of that success, and the shared values with politicians that brought it about (which had a lot to do with the kind of men Haury and his friends were), the funding environment Doelle and Phillips (this volume) have so well exploited came about. Now that the rules for who can qualify for federal contracts have been broadened to include environmental companies, many from outside the Southwest, it will be interesting to see how well the archaeological companies compete in the future for market share. The aging of the owners of those companies is also a process to watch: will they be able to institutionalize their success through the nonprofit organizations many of them have formed?

Who sets the agenda for southwestern archaeology—or, to put this question another way, how does the agenda get set? Arguably, the "New Archaeology" of Wissler (1917a) in the hands of A. V. Kidder (1927) led to a consensus at the first Pecos Conference among representatives of 14 institutions on what the archaeological agenda in the Southwest should be, and subsequent Pecos conferences kept that consensus alive until recently (Wilcox and Fowler 2002; Woodbury 1993). The "New Archaeology" of the 1960s destroyed that consensus, and nothing comparable has yet emerged. There are now a multiplicity of agendas and voices clamoring to be heard.

How has funding affected agenda? Why are some contributions embraced so that fruitful new knowledge is created by following up on them, while others, perhaps as promising, are dismissed or ignored? How has the trajectory of southwestern archaeology been affected by work that was published and work that was not? What strategies have academic departments followed in their competition for resources, students, and prestige? How has peer review been used to shape the directions in which inquiry is channeled? What has been the role of iconoclasts for good or ill? Will the increased involvement of Indian people in the conduct of archaeology be good for them and good for archaeologists? What form has collaboration taken in the past and what new forms will it take in the future? Asking these questions makes me think that we have only barely scratched the surface of the history of southwestern archaeology.

What themes will be dominant in the future of southwestern archaeology, just as what themes have characterized it so far, depend on who sets the agenda, what support they can muster, and what potential exists in the archaeological record. Can southwestern institutions survive the "curation crisis" (Cordell, this volume)? Will the change in players and their values on museum boards or in university administrations or in federal and state agencies lead to a denigration of the past and a redefinition of what archaeological institutions are about? What effect will such social forces have on the agenda for future archaeology? What can archaeologists do about that? It is time for the present generation to find out the answers to these questions—like it or not. I suggest that a more profound study of the history of southwestern archaeology can help us to cope with these realities. The future history of southwestern archaeology may depend on it.

References

PRIMARY SOURCES CITED IN CHAPTER 3

AIA   Archaeological Institute of America Papers, Stone Science Library, Boston University.

ALK   Alfred Louis Kroeber Papers, Bancroft Library, University of California, Berkeley.

AMNH   Correspondence Files, Archives, Department of Anthropology, American Museum of Natural History, New York.

AMT   Alfred Marston Tozzer Papers, Peabody Museum of Archaeology and Ethnology, Harvard University, Cambridge, Massachusetts.

BSU   Clark Wissler Papers, Department of Anthropology, Ball State University, Muncie, Indiana.

ELH   Edgar Lee Hewett Papers, Fray Angélico Chávez History Library, Palace of the Governors, Santa Fe, New Mexico.

JCM   John Campbell Merriam Papers, Bancroft Library, University of California, Berkeley. C-B 970.

NAA   National Anthropological Archives, National Museum of Natural History, Smithsonian Institution, Washington, D.C.

NCN   Nels C. Nelson Papers, Archives, Department of Anthropology, American Museum of Natural History, New York.

COMBINED REFERENCES

Aberle, David F.
1970   Comments. In *Reconstructing Prehistoric Pueblo Societies*, edited by W. A. Longacre, pp. 214–223. University of New Mexico Press, Albuquerque.

Adams, E. Charles
1991   *The Origin and Development of the Pueblo Katsina Cult.* University of Arizona Press, Tucson.

Adams, E. Charles, and M. Nieves Zedeño
1999   BAE Scholars as Documenters of Diversity and Change at Hopi, 1870–1895. *Journal of the Southwest* 41:311–334.

Adams, William Y.
1951   Archaeology and Culture History of the Navajo Country: Report on Reconnaissance for the Pueblo Ecology Study, 1951. Manuscript on file, Museum of Northern Arizona, Flagstaff.

Adler, Michael A.
1990   *Communities of Soil and Stone: An Archaeological Investigation of Population Aggregation among the Mesa Verde Region Anasazi, A.D. 1000–1300.* Unpublished Ph.D. dissertation, Department of Anthropology, University of Michigan, Ann Arbor.

Adler, Michael A. (editor)

1996   *The Prehistoric Pueblo World*, A.D. *1150–1300*. University of Arizona Press, Tucson.

Adovasio, J. M.

1986   Artifacts and Ethnicity: Basketry as an Indication of Territoriality and Population Movements in the Prehistoric Great Basin. In *Anthropology of the Desert West: Essays in Honor of Jesse D. Jennings,* edited by C. J. Condie and D. D. Fowler, pp. 43–88. Anthropological Papers 110. University of Utah Press, Salt Lake City.

Agenbroad, Larry D.

1982   Geology and Lithic Resources of the Grasshopper Region. In *Multidisciplinary Research at Grasshopper Pueblo,* edited by William A. Longacre, Sally J. Holbrook, and Michael W. Graves, pp. 42–45. Anthropological Papers 40. University of Arizona Press, Tucson.

Ahlstrom, Richard V. N., Carla R. Van West, and Jeffrey S. Dean

1995   Environmental and Chronological Factors in the Mesa Verde–Northern Rio Grande Migration. *Journal of Anthropological Archaeology* 14:125–142.

Alba, R. D. (editor)

1985   *Ethnicity and Race in the U.S.A.: Toward the Twenty-First Century.* Routledge and Kegan Paul, London.

Alessio-Robles, Carmen

1929   *La Region Arqueológica de Casas Grandes, Chihuahua.* Imprenta Núñez, Rep. Salvador, México, D.F.

Amick, Daniel S.

1994   *Folsom Diet Breadth and Land Use in the American Southwest.* Unpublished Ph.D. dissertation, Department of Anthropology, University of New Mexico, Albuquerque.

1996   Regional Patterns of Folsom Mobility and Land Use in the American Southwest. *World Archaeology* 27:411–426.

Amsden, Monroe

1928   *Archaeological Reconnaissance in Sonora.* Southwest Museum Papers 1. Los Angeles.

Anderson, Barbara

1990   Foreword. In *The Religious Architecture of New Mexico in the Colonial Period and Since the American Occupation,* by George Kubler. 5th ed. University of New Mexico Press, Albuquerque.

Anderson, G. C.

1999   *The Indian Southwest, 1580–1830: Ethnogenesis and Reinvention.* University of Oklahoma Press, Norman.

Anderson, Roger Y.

1955   Pollen Analysis, A Research Tool for the Study of Cave Deposits. *American Antiquity* 21:84–85.

Anonymous

1938a   The University of New Mexico and the School of American Research. *New Mexico Anthropologist* 2(3):62.

1938b   Field Sessions in Anthropology of the University of New Mexico. *New Mexico Anthropologist* 2(3):62–63.

1968   New Perspectives in Archaeology: Research Field Program of Field
        Museum of Natural History for High Ability Undergraduate Students,
        June 20–August 29, 1968, An Explanation. Manuscript on file, Field
        Museum of Natural History, Chicago.

Anschuetz, Kurt F.

2000   The Past Is Not a Pickle: Use of Archaeological Resources in Sustaining
        Northern New Mexico Community Traditions. Paper presented at the
        99th Annual Meeting of the American Anthropological Association,
        San Francisco.

Anschuetz, Kurt F., T. J. Ferguson, Harris Francis, Klara B. Kelley, and Cherie L.
        Scheick

2000   "That Place People Talk About": Ethnographic Landscape Literature
        Essays, Petroglyph National Monument. Community and Cultural
        Landscape Contribution 5. Rio Grande Foundation for Communities
        and Cultural Landscape, Santa Fe, New Mexico.

Antevs, Ernst

1935   *Age of the Clovis Lake Clays.* Proceedings of the Academy of the
        Natural Sciences of Philadelphia, Pennsylvania.

1948   Climatic Changes and Pre-white Man. *Bulletin of the University of
        Utah* 38:168–191.

1955a   Geologic-Climatic Methods of Dating. In *Geoarchaeology*, edited by
        T. L. Smiley, pp. 151–169. University of Arizona Press, Tucson.

1955b   Geologic-Climatic Dating in the West. *American Antiquity* 20:
        317–335.

Anyon, Roger, T. J. Ferguson, Loretta Jackson, and Lillie Lane

1996   Native American Oral Traditions and Archaeology. *SAA Bulletin*
        14(2):14–17.

Armillas, Pedro

1969   The Arid Frontier of Mexican Civilization. *Transactions of the New
        York Academy of Sciences* Series II, 31:697–704.

Arnold, B.

1990   The Past as Propaganda: Totalitarian Archaeology in Nazi Germany.
        Antiquity 64:464–478.

Atkins, Victoria M. (editor)

1993   *Anasazi Basketmaker: Papers from the 1990 Wetherill–Grand Gulch
        Symposium.* Bureau of Land Management Cultural Resources Series
        No. 24. Salt Lake City, Utah.

Babcock, Barbara A., and Nancy J. Parezo (editors)

1988   *Daughters of the Desert: Women Anthropologists and the Native
        American Southwest, 1880–1980, An Illustrated Catalogue.* University
        of New Mexico Press, Albuquerque.

Baldwin, S. J.

1985   Room Size Patterns: A Quantitative Method for Approaching Ethnic
        Identification in Architecture. In *Ethnicity and Culture,* edited by
        R. Auger, M. F. Glass, S. MacEachern, and P. H. McCartney, pp. 163–
        174. Archaeological Association of the University of Calgary, Alberta.

Bandelier, Adolph F.
1879   Review (unsigned) of Adolf Bastian's "Die Culturlander des Alten
        Amerika." *The Nation* 28:357–358.
1885   *The Romantic School in American Archaeology*. Trow, New York.
1890–92 *Final Report of Investigations among the Indians of the Southwestern
        United States, Carried on Mainly in the Years from 1880 to 1885*, Parts
        1 and 2. Papers of the Archaeological Institute of America, American
        Series III and IV, Cambridge, Massachusetts.
1890   *The Delight Makers*. Dodd, Mead, New York.
1892   *Final Report of Investigations among the Indians of the Southwestern
        United States, Carried on Mainly in the Years from 1880 to 1885*, Part
        II. Papers of the Archaeological Institute of America, American Series
        IV. Harvard University Press, Cambridge, Massachusetts.
Bannister, Bryant, and William J. Robinson
1986   Archaeology and Dendrochronology. In *Emil L. Haury's Prehistory
        of the American Southwest*, edited by J. Jefferson Reid and David E.
        Doyel, pp. 49–54. University of Arizona Press, Tucson.
Barth, Frederick
1969   Introduction. In *Ethnic Groups and Boundaries: The Social
        Organization of Cultural Difference*, edited by F. Barth, pp. 9–38.
        Little, Brown, Boston.
2000   *Signifying Identities: Anthropological Perspectives on Boundaries and
        Contested Values*. Routledge, London.
Bartlett, John Russell
1854   *Personal Narrative of Exploration and Incidents in Texas, New
        Mexico, California, Sonora, and Chihuahua, connected with the
        United States and Mexican Boundary Commission during the years
        1850, '51, '52, and '53*. 2 vols. D. Appleton, New York.
1965   *Personal Narrative of Explorations and Incidents in Texas, New
        Mexico, California, Sonora and Chihuahua, 1850–1853*. Originally
        published 1854. Rio Grande Press, Chicago.
Beals, Ralph L.
1943   Relations Between Meso America and the Southwest. In *El Norte de
        México y el Sur de los Estados Unidos. Tercera Reunión de Mesa
        Redonda Sobre Problemas Antropológicos de México y Centro
        America*, edited by Rafael Granados Garcia, pp. 245–251. Castillo de
        Chapultepec, México, D.F.
Benavides, O. Hugo
2001   Returning to the Source: Social Archaeology as Latin American
        Philosophy. *Latin American Antiquity* 12:355–370.
Benedict, Ruth
1934   *Patterns of Culture*. Houghton Mifflin, Boston and New York.
Benson, Keith R.
1988   From Museum Research to Laboratory Research: The Transformation
        of Natural History into Academic Biology. In *The American
        Development of Biology*, edited by Ronald Rainger, Keith R. Benson,
        and Jane Maienschein, pp. 49–83. University of Pennsylvania Press,
        Philadelphia.

Bentley, G. C.
1987   Ethnicity and Practice. *Comparative Studies in Society and History*
        29:24–55.
Bernal, Ignacio
1980   *A History of Mexican Archaeology*. Thames and Hudson, London.
Bernardini, W.
2002   *The Gathering of the Clans: Understanding Ancestral Hopi Migration
        and Identity, A.D. 1275–1400.* Unpublished Ph.D. dissertation,
        Department of Anthropology, Arizona State University, Tempe.
Berry, Claudia F., and Michael S. Berry
1986   Chronological and Conceptual Models of the Southwestern Archaic.
        In *Anthropology of the Desert West: Essays in Honor of Jesse D.
        Jennings*, edited by Carol J. Condie and Don D. Fowler, pp. 253–327.
        Anthropological Papers 110. University of Utah Press, Salt Lake City.
Berry, Michael S.
1982   *Time, Space, and Transition in Anasazi Prehistory.* University of Utah
        Press, Salt Lake City.
Betancourt, Julio L., and Thomas R. Van Devender
1981   Holocene Vegetation Change in Chaco Canyon, New Mexico. *Science*
        214:656–658.
Betancourt, Julio L., Thomas R. Van Devender, and Paul S. Martin
1990   Introduction. In *Packrat Middens: The Last 40,000 Years of Biotic
        Change*, edited by Julio L. Betancourt, Thomas R. Van Devender, and
        Paul S. Martin, pp. 2–13. University of Arizona Press, Tucson.
Betancourt, Julio L., Thomas R. Van Devender, and Paul S. Martin (editors)
1990   *Packrat Middens: The Last 40,000 Years of Biotic Change.* University
        of Arizona Press, Tucson.
Binford, Lewis R.
1962   Archaeology as Anthropology. *American Antiquity* 28:217–225.
1980   Willow Smoke and Dogs' Tails: Hunter-Gatherer Settlement Systems
        and Archaeological Site Formation. *American Antiquity* 45:4–20.
1982   The Archaeology of Place. *Journal of Anthropological Archaeology*
        1:5–31.
1994   Systematic Integration of "Fragmentary Oddments": The Challenge
        of Settlement Pattern Approaches. In *Archaic Hunter-Gatherer
        Archaeology in the American Southwest*, edited by B. J. Vierra,
        pp. 527–565. Contributions in Anthropology Vol. 13, No. 1. Eastern
        New Mexico University, Portales.
Blackburn, Fred M., and Ray A. Williamson
1997   *Cowboys and Cave Dwellers: Basketmaker Archaeology in Utah's
        Grand Gulch.* School of American Research Press, Santa Fe, New
        Mexico.
Blair, Mary Ellen, and Laurence Blair
1999   *The Legacy of a Master Potter. Nampeyo and Her Descendants.*
        Treasure Chest Books, Tucson, Arizona.
Bloom, Lansing B.
1923   The Jemez Expedition of the School, Summer of 1922. *El Palacio*
        14:15–20.

1939   Edgar Lee Hewett: His Biography and Writings to Date. In *So Live the Works of Men, Seventieth Anniversary Volume Honoring Edgar Lee Hewett*, edited by Donald D. Brand and Fred E. Harvey, pp. 13–34. University of New Mexico Press, Albuquerque.

Bloom, Lansing B., and Lynn B. Mitchell
1938   The Chapter Elections in 1672. *New Mexico Historical Review* 13: 85–119.

Boas, Franz
1932   *Anthropology and Modern Life*. Rev. ed. Norton, New York.

Bohrer, Vorsila L.
1982   Plant Remains from Rooms at Grasshopper Pueblo. In *Multidisciplinary Research at Grasshopper Pueblo, Arizona*, edited by William A. Longacre, Sally J. Holbrook, and Michael W. Graves, pp. 97–105. Anthropological Papers 40. University of Arizona Press, Tucson.

Boldurian, A. T., and J. L. Cotter
1999   *Clovis Revisited, New Perspectives on Paleoindian Adaptations from Blackwater Draw, New Mexico*. University Museum Monograph 103. University of Pennsylvania, Philadelphia.

Bourdieu, Pierre
1977   *Outline of a Theory of Practice*. Translated by R. Nice. Cambridge University Press, Cambridge.
1990   *The Logic of Practice*. Translated by R. Nice. Stanford University Press, Stanford, California.

Brace, Martha A.
1986   On the Road and in the Field in 1919: The University of Arizona Summer Archaeological Field Season. *Kiva* 51(3):189–200.

Bradford, Richard
1973   *So Far from Heaven*. Lippincott, New York.

Bradley, R. J.
1999   Shell Exchange within the Southwest: The Casas Grandes Interaction Sphere. In *The Casas Grandes World*, edited by C. F. Schaafsma and C. L. Riley, pp. 213–228. University of Utah Press, Salt Lake City.

Brand, Donald D.
1933   *The Historical Geography of Northwestern Chihuahua*. Unpublished Ph.D. dissertation, Department of Geography, University of California, Berkeley.
1935   The Distribution of Pottery Types in Northwest Mexico. *American Anthropologist* n.s. 37:287–395.
1938   Aboriginal Trade Routes for Sea Shells in the Southwest. *Yearbook of the Association of Pacific Coast Geographers* IV:3–10.

Brand, Donald D., Florence M. Hawley, and Frank C. Hibben, et al.
1937   *Tseh So, A Small House Ruin in Chaco Canyon*. University of New Mexico Bulletin 308. University of New Mexico Press, Albuquerque.

Brandt, Elizabeth A.
1985   Internal Stratification in Pueblo Communities. Paper presented at the 84th Annual Meeting of the American Anthropological Association, Washington, D.C.

1994   Egalitarianism, Hierarchy, and Centralization in the Pueblos. In *The Ancient Southwestern Community*, edited by W. H. Wills and Robert D. Leonard, pp. 9–23. University of New Mexico Press, Albuquerque.

Braniff C., Beatriz

1985   La Frontera Protohistórica Pima/Opata en Sonora, México; Proposiciones Arqueológicas Preliminares. Tesis doctoral, Universidad Nacional Autónoma de México.

1995   The Opata-Pima Frontier: Preliminary Notes and Comments. In *The Gran Chichimeca: Essays on the Archaeology and Ethnohistory of Northern Mesoamerica*, edited by Jonathan E. Reyman, pp. 252–268. Worldwide Archaeology Series 12. Avebury Press, Aldershot, United Kingdom.

Braniff C., Beatriz, Linda S. Cordell, María de la Luz Gutiérrez, Elisa Villalpando C., and Marie-Areti Hers

2001   *La Gran Chichimeca, el Lugar de las Rocas Secas.* Conaculta and Jaca Books, Consejo Nacional para La Cultura y las Artes, Mexico.

Breeze, Carla

1990   *Pueblo Deco.* Rizzoli International Publications, New York.

Breternitz, David A.

1959   *Excavations at Nantack Village, Point of Pines, Arizona.* Anthropological Papers 1. University of Arizona Press, Tucson.

Brew, J. O.

1942   Review of *Southwestern Archaeology*, by John C. McGregor. *American Antiquity* 8:191–196.

1949   Introduction. In *Franciscan Awatovi: The Excavation and Conjectural Reconstruction of a 17th-Century Spanish Mission Established at a Hopi Indian Town in Northeastern Arizona,* by Ross Gordon Montgomery, Watson Smith, and John Otis Brew, pp. 1–26. Papers of the Peabody Museum of American Archaeology and Ethnology 36. Harvard University, Cambridge, Massachusetts.

Brewer, Douglas J.

1992   Zooarchaeology: Methods, Theory, and Goals. In *Advances in Archaeological Method and Theory* Vol. 4, pp.195–244. Academic Press, New York.

Brody, J. J.

1977   *Mimbres Painted Pottery.* School of American Research, Santa Fe, and University of New Mexico Press, Albuquerque.

Brody, J. J., Catherine J. Scott, and Steven A. LeBlanc

1983   *Mimbres Pottery. Ancient Art of the American Southwest.* Hudson Hills Press, New York.

Bromley, Yu

1974   The Term *Ethnos* and Its Definition. In *Soviet Ethnology and Anthropology Today*, edited by Yu Bromley, pp. 2–24. Mouton, The Hague.

Browman, David L.

2002a   Frederic Ward Putnam: Contributions to the Development of Anthropological Institutions and Encouragement of Women Practitioners. In *New Perspectives on the Origins of Americanist*

Archaeology, edited by David L. Browman and Stephen Williams, pp. 209–241. University of Alabama Press, Tuscaloosa.

2002b   Origins of Stratigraphic Excavation in North America: The Peabody Museum Method and the Chicago Method. In *New Perspectives on the Origins of Americanist Archaeology,* edited by David L. Browman and Stephen Williams, pp. 242–264. University of Alabama Press, Tuscaloosa.

Browman, David L., and Douglas R. Givens

1996   Stratigraphic Excavation: The First "New Archaeology." *American Anthropologist* 98:80–95.

Bryan, Kirk

1922   Erosion and Sedimentation in the Papago Country, Arizona, with a Sketch of the Geology. In *Contributions to the Geography of the United States,* pp. 19–90. United States Geological Survey Bulletin 730-B.

1940   Erosion in the Valleys of the Southwest. *New Mexico Quarterly* 10:227–232.

1941a   Geological Antiquity of Man in America. *Science* 93(2422):505–514.

1941b   Pre-Columbian Agriculture in the Southwest, as Conditioned by Periods of Alluviation. *Annals of the Association of American Geographers* 31:219–242.

1954   *The Geology of Chaco Canyon, New Mexico in Relation to the Life and Remains of the Prehistoric Peoples of Pueblo Bonito.* Smithsonian Institution Miscellaneous Collections Vol. 122, No. 7. Washington, D.C.

Bryant, Vaughn M., Jr., and Stephen A. Hall.

1993   Archaeological Palynology in the United States: A Critique. *American Antiquity* 58:277–286.

Bullock, Peter Y.

1998   *Deciphering Anasazi Violence.* HRM Books, Santa Fe, New Mexico.

Bunzel, Ruth L.

1929   *The Pueblo Potter: A Study in Creative Imagination in Primitive Art.* Columbia University Press, New York.

Burns, Barney T.

1983   *Simulated Anasazi Storage Behavior Using Crop Yields Reconstructed from Tree-Rings: A.D. 652–1968.* Ph.D. dissertation, University of Arizona, Tucson. University Microfilms, Ann Arbor.

Bushnell, Amy Turner

1978   "That Demonic Game": The Campaign to Stop Indian Pelota Playing in Spanish Florida, 1675–1684. *The Americas* 35:1–19.

Bustard, Wendy

2000   Archaeological Curation in the 21st Century. *CRM* 23(5):10–15.

Butzer, Karl W.

1982   *Archaeology as Human Ecology: Method and Theory for a Contextual Approach.* Cambridge University Press, Cambridge.

Cabrero G., María Teresa

1993   Historia de la Arqueología del Norte de México. In *II Coloquio Pedro Bosch-Gimpera,* edited by María Teresa Cabrero G., pp. 175–194.

Instituto de Investigaciones Antropológicas, Universidad Nacional Autónoma de México, México, D.F.

Callen, Eric O., and Paul S. Martin
1969   Plant Remains in Some Coprolites from Utah. *American Antiquity* 34:329–331.

Cameron, Catherine M.
1995   Migration and the Movement of Southwestern Peoples. *Journal of Anthropological Archaeology* 14:104–124.

Capone, P., and R. W. Preucel
2002   Ceramic Semiotics: Women, Pottery, and Social Meanings at Kotyiti Pueblo. In *Archaeologies of the Pueblo Revolt: Identity, Meaning and Renewal in the Pueblo World,* edited by R. W. Preucel, pp. 99–113. University of New Mexico Press, Albuquerque.

Carey, H. A.
1931   An Analysis of Northwestern Chihuahua Culture. *American Anthropologist* 33:325–374.

Carot, Patricia
2000   Las Rutas del Desierto: De Michoacán a Arizona. In *Nómadas y Sedentarios en el Norte de México: Homenaje a Beatriz Braniff,* pp. 91–112. Universidad Nacional Autónoma de México, Instituto de Investigaciones Antropológicas, Instituto de Investigaciones Estéticas, y Instituto de Investigaciones Históricas, México, D.F.

Carpenter, John P., Guadalupe Sanchez de Carpenter, and Elisa Villalpando C.
1999   Preliminary Investigations at La Playa, Sonora, Mexico. *Archaeology Southwest* 13(1):10–11.

Casteel, Richard W.
1980   National Science Foundation Funding of Domestic Archaeology in the United States: Where the Money Ain't. *American Antiquity* 45:170–180.

Caywood, Louis R.
1972   *The Restored Mission of Nuestra Señora de Guadalupe de Zuni, Zuni, New Mexico.* St. Michaels Press, St. Michaels, Arizona.

Chapman, Kenneth M.
1933–36 *Pueblo Indian Pottery.* 2 vols. Szwedzicki, Nice, France.
1936   *The Pottery of Santo Domingo Pueblo: A Detailed Study of Its Decoration.* Laboratory of Anthropology Memoir 1. Santa Fe, New Mexico.
1970   *The Pottery of San Ildefonso Pueblo.* University of New Mexico Press for the School of American Research, Santa Fe and Albuquerque.

Chauvenet, Beatrice
1983   *Hewett and Friends: A Biography of Santa Fe's Vibrant Era.* Museum of New Mexico Press, Santa Fe.

Childs, S. Terry
1999   Contemplating the Future: Deaccessioning Federal Archaeological Collections. *Museum Anthropology* 23(2):38–45.

Childs, S. Terry (editor)
2004   *Our Collective Responsibility: The Ethics and Practice of Collections Stewardship.* Society of American Archaeology, Washington, D.C.

Chrisman, D., R. S. MacNeish, J. Mavalawa, and H. Savage
1996   Late Pleistocene Human Friction Skin Prints from Pendejo Cave, New Mexico. *American Antiquity* 61:357–376.

Clark, J. J.
2001   *Tracking Prehistoric Migrations: Pueblo Settlers among the Tonto Basin Hohokam*. Anthropological Papers 65. University of Arizona Press, Tucson.

Clisby, K. H., and P. B. Sears
1956   San Augustine Plains—Pleistocene Climatic Changes. *Science* 124: 537–539.

Cohen, A.
1969   *Custom and Politics in Urban Africa: A Study of Hausa Migration in Yoruba Towns*. Routledge and Kegan Paul, London.

Cole, Douglas, and Alex Long
1999   The Boasian Anthropological Survey Tradition: The Role of Franz Boas in North American Anthropological Surveys. In *Surveying the Record: North American Scientific Exploration to 1930*, edited by Edward C. Carter III, pp. 225–249. Memoirs of the American Philosophical Society 231. Philadelphia, Pennsylvania.

Colton, Harold S.
1918   The Geography of Certain Ruins Near the San Francisco Mountains, Arizona. *Bulletin of the Geographical Society of Philadelphia* 16(2):37–60.
1939   *Prehistoric Culture Units and Their Relationships in Northern Arizona*. Museum of Northern Arizona Bulletin 17. Flagstaff.
1946   *The Sinagua: A Summary of the Archaeology of the Region of Flagstaff, Arizona*. Museum of Northern Arizona Bulletin 22. Flagstaff.
1953   *Potsherds: An Introduction to the Study of Prehistoric Southwestern Ceramics and Their Use in Historic Reconstruction*. Northern Arizona Society of Science and Art, Flagstaff.
1960   *Black Sand, Prehistory in Northern Arizona*. University of New Mexico Press, Albuquerque.

Comaroff, John
1987   Of Totemism and Ethnicity: Consciousness, Practice and the Signs of Inequality. *Ethnos* 52:301–323.

Contreras S., Eduardo
1970   Restauraciones en Casas Grandes, 1969–1970. *INAH Boletín* (Junio):4–11.

Cooley, Maurice E.
1962   Late Pleistocene and Recent Erosion and Alluviation in Parts of the Colorado River System, Arizona and Utah. In *Geological Survey Research 1962: Short Papers in Geology, Hydrology, and Topography*, Articles 1–59, pp. 48–50. U.S. Geological Survey Professional Paper 450-B.

Cope, Edward Drinker
1875   Report on the Remains of Population Observed on and near the Eocene Plateau of Northwestern New Mexico. In *Annual Report upon the Geographical Explorations and Surveys West of the One Hundredth*

Meridian, in California, Nevada, Nebraska, Utah, Arizona, Colorado, New Mexico, Wyoming, and Montana, by George M. Wheeler, pp. 166–173. Annual Report of the Chief of Engineers for 1875. U.S. Government Printing Office, Washington, D.C.

Cordell, Linda S.

1979   *Cultural Resources Overview of the Middle Rio Grande Valley, New Mexico.* USDA Forest Service and USDI Bureau of Land Management. Government Printing Office, Washington D.C.

1984   *Prehistory of the Southwest.* Academic Press, New York.

1989a   Durango to Durango: An Overview of the Southwest Heartland. In *Archaeological and Historical Perspectives on the Spanish Borderlands West,* edited by David Hurst Thomas, pp. 17–40. Columbian Consequences, Vol. 1. Smithsonian Institution Press, Washington, D.C.

1989b   Dialogue with the Past: Thoughts on Some University of New Mexico Field Schools. *Journal of Anthropological Research* 45:29–46.

1989c   History and Theory in Reconstructing Southwestern Sociopolitical Organization. In *The Sociopolitical Structure of Prehistoric Southwestern Societies,* edited by Steadman Upham, Kent G. Lightfoot, and Roberta A. Jewett, pp. 33–54. Westview Press, Boulder, Colorado.

1991   Anna O. Shepard and Southwestern Archaeology: Ignoring a Cautious Heretic. In *The Ceramic Legacy of Anna O. Shepard,* edited by Ronald L. Bishop and Frederick W. Lange, pp. 132–153. University Press of Colorado, Niwot.

1994a   *Ancient Pueblo Peoples.* St. Remy Press, Montreal, Quebec.

1994b   The Nature of Explanation in Archaeology. In *Understanding Complexity in the Prehistoric Southwest,* edited by George Gumerman and Murray Gell-Mann, pp. 147–149. Addison-Wesley Press, Reading, Massachusetts.

1997   *Archaeology of the Southwest.* Academic Press, San Diego, California.

1998   *Before Pecos: Settlement Aggregation at Rowe, New Mexico.* Maxwell Museum of Anthropology Anthropological Papers 6. University of New Mexico Press, Albuquerque.

Cordell, Linda S., and George J. Gumerman (editors)

1989   *Dynamics of Southwest Prehistory.* Smithsonian Institution Press, Washington, D.C.

Cordell, Linda S., and Fred Plog

1979   Escaping the Confines of Normative Thought: A Reevaluation of Puebloan Prehistory. *American Antiquity* 44:405–429.

Cordell, Linda S., and V. J. Yannie

1991   Ethnicity, Ethnogenesis, and the Individual: A Processual Approach toward Dialogue. In *Processual and Postprocessual Archaeologies: Multiple Ways of Knowing the Past,* edited by R. W. Preucel, pp. 96–107. Center for Archaeological Investigations Occasional Paper 10. Southern Illinois University Press, Carbondale.

Creamer, Winifred

2001   The Origins of Centralization: Changing Features of Local and Regional Control during the Rio Grande Classic Period, A.D. 1325–1540. In *From Leaders to Rulers,* edited by Jonathan Haas, pp 37–58. Kluwer Academic/Plenum, New York.

Creamer, Winifred, and Jonathan Haas

1998   Less Than Meets the Eye: Evidence for Protohistoric Chiefdoms in
        Northern New Mexico. In *Chiefdoms and Chieftancy in the Americas,*
        edited by Elsa M. Redmond, pp 43–67. University Press of Florida,
        Gainesville.

Crown, Patricia L.

1994   *Ceramics and Ideology: Salado Polychrome Pottery.* University of New
        Mexico Press, Albuquerque.

Crown, Patricia L. (editor)

2000   *Women and Men in the Prehispanic Southwest.* School of American
        Research Press, Santa Fe, New Mexico.

Cruz Antillón, Rafael, Robert D. Leonard, Timothy D. Maxwell, Todd L.
    VanPool, Marcel J. Harmon, Christine S. VanPool, David A. Hindman,
    and Sydney S. Brandwein

2004   Galeana, Villa Ahumada, and Casa Chica: Diverse Sites in the Casas
        Grandes Region. In *Surveying the Archaeology of Northwest Mexico,*
        edited by Gillian E. Newell and Emiliano Gallaga, pp. 149–175.
        University of Utah Press, Salt Lake City.

Cummings, Byron

1940   *Kinishba: A Prehistoric Pueblo of the Great Pueblo Period.* Hohokam
        Museums Association and the University of Arizona, Tucson.

Cushing, Frank H.

1890   Preliminary Notes on the Origins, Working Hypothesis and Primary
        Researches of the Hemenway Southwestern Archaeological Exposition
        [*sic*]. *Congrès International des Américanistes, Compte-rendu de la
        septième session (Berlin, 1888)*:151–194.

Darling, J. Andrew

1999   Mass Inhumation and the Execution of Witches in the American
        Southwest. *American Anthropologist* 100:732–752.

David, Nicholas

1992   The Archaeology of Ideology: Mortuary Practices in the Central
        Mandara Highlands. In *An African Commitment: Papers in Honour
        of Peter Lewis Shinnie,* edited by J. Sterner and N. David, pp. 181–210.
        University of Calgary Press, Calgary, Alberta.

Dean, Jeffrey S.

1969   *Chronological Analysis of Tsegi Phase Sites in Northeastern Arizona.*
        Papers of the Laboratory of Tree-Ring Research 3. University of
        Arizona Press, Tucson.

1988a   A Model of Anasazi Behavioral Adaptation. In *The Anasazi in a
        Changing Environment,* edited by George J. Gumerman, pp. 25–44.
        Cambridge University Press, Cambridge.

1988b   Dendrochronology and Paleoenvironmental Reconstruction on the
        Colorado Plateaus. In *The Anasazi in a Changing Environment,* edited
        by George J. Gumerman, pp. 119–167. Cambridge University Press,
        Cambridge.

1992   Environmental Factors in the Evolution of the Chacoan Sociopolitical
        System. In *Anasazi Regional Organization and the Chaco System,*

edited by David E. Doyel, pp. 35–43. Maxwell Museum of Anthropology Anthropological Papers 5. University of New Mexico Press,
Albuquerque.

1996   Demography, Environment, and Subsistence Stress. In *Evolving
Complexity and Environmental Risk in the Prehistoric Southwest,*
edited by Joseph A. Tainter and Bonnie Bagley Tainter, pp. 25–56.
Santa Fe Institute Studies in the Sciences of Complexity, Proceedings
Vol. 24. Addison-Wesley, Reading, Massachusetts.

Dean, Jeffrey S., and John C. Ravesloot
1993   The Chronology of Cultural Interaction in the Gran Chichimeca. In
Culture and Contact: Charles Di Peso's Gran Chichimeca, edited by
Anne Woosley and John C. Ravesloot, pp. 83–103. Amerind Foundation, Dragoon, Arizona, and University of New Mexico Press, Albuquerque.

Dean, Jeffrey S., and William J. Robinson
1977   *Dendroclimatic Variability in the American Southwest A.D.680 to
1970.* Laboratory of Tree-Ring Research, University of Arizona,
Tucson.

1982   Dendrochronology of Grasshopper Pueblo. In *Multidisciplinary
Research at Grasshopper Pueblo, Arizona,* edited by William A.
Longacre, Sally J. Holbrook, and Michael W. Graves, pp. 46–60.
Anthropological Papers 40. University of Arizona Press, Tucson.

2002   Environment-Behavior Relationships in Southwestern Colorado. In
*Seeking the Center Place: Archaeology and Ancient Communities in
the Mesa Verde Region,* edited by Mark D. Varien and Richard H.
Wilshusen, pp. 81–99. University of Utah Press, Salt Lake City.

Dean, Jeffrey S., William H. Doelle, and Janet D. Orcutt
1994   Adaptive Stress: Environment and Demography. In *Themes in Southwestern Prehistory,* edited by George J. Gumerman, pp. 53–86. School
of American Research Press, Santa Fe, New Mexico.

Dean, Jeffrey S., Robert C. Euler, George J. Gumerman, Fred Plog, Richard H.
Hevly, and Thor N. V. Karlstrom
1985   Human Behavior, Demography, and Paleoenvironment on the Colorado
Plateaus. *American Antiquity* 50:537–554.

Dean, Jeffrey S., George J. Gumerman, Joshua M. Epstein, Robert L. Axtell,
Alan C. Swedlund, Miles T. Parker, and Stephen McCarroll
2000   Understanding Anasazi Culture Change through Agent-Based
Modeling. In *Dynamics in Human and Primate Societies: Agent-Based
Modeling of Social and Spatial Processes,* edited by Timothy A. Kohler
and George J. Gumerman, pp. 179–205. Santa Fe Institute Studies in
the Sciences of Complexity. Oxford University Press, New York.

DeBoer, Warren R.
2001   On- and Off-Again Complexity from South America to the Southwest.
In *Examining the Course of Southwest Archaeology: The Durango
Conference,* edited by David A. Phillips and Lynne Sebastian,
pp. 19–31. Special Publication 3. New Mexico Archaeological Council,
Albuquerque.

Delle, J. A., S. A. Mrozowski, and R. Paynter
2000   *Lines That Divide: Historical Archaeologies of Race, Class, and Gender.* University of Tennessee Press, Knoxville.

Dick, Herbert W.
1965   *Bat Cave.* School of American Research Monograph 27. Santa Fe, New Mexico.

Dietler, M.
1994   "Our Ancestors the Gauls": Archaeology, Ethnic Nationalism, and the Manipulation of Celtic Identity in Modern Europe. *American Anthropologist* 96:584–605.

Dietler, M., and I. Herbich
1998   *Habitus,* Techniques, Style: An Integrated Approach to the Social Understanding of Material Culture and Boundaries. In *The Archaeology of Social Boundaries,* edited by M. Stark, pp. 232–263. Smithsonian Institution Press, Washington, D.C.

Dincauze, Dena F.
2000   *Environmental Archaeology: Principles and Practice.* Cambridge University Press, Cambridge.

Di Peso, Charles
1968   Casas Grandes and the Gran Chichimeca. *El Palacio* 75(4):45–61.
1974   *Casas Grandes: A Fallen Trading Center of the Gran Chichimeca,* Vols. 1–3. Amerind Foundation Publications 9. Dragoon, Arizona.
1976   Gila Polychrome in the Casas Grandes Region. *Kiva* 42(1):57–63.
1983   The Northern Sector of the Mesoamerican World System. In *Forgotten Places and Things, Archaeological Perspectives on American History,* edited by Albert E. Ward, pp. 11–22. Center for Anthropological Studies, Albuquerque, New Mexico.

Di Peso, Charles C., John B. Rinaldo, and Gloria J. Fenner
1974   *Casas Grandes: A Fallen Trading Center of the Gran Chichimeca,* Vols. 4–8. Amerind Foundation Publications 9. Dragoon, Arizona.

Doleman, William H.
1994   Sites, Sampling, and Landscapes: Problems in Defining Assemblages for Analysis. In *Archaic Hunter-Gatherer Archaeology in the American Southwest,* edited by B. J. Vierra, pp. 405–455. Contributions in Anthropology Vol. 13, No. 1. Eastern New Mexico University, Portales.

Dongoske, K., T. J. Ferguson, and L. Jenkins
1993   Understanding the Past through Hopi Oral History. *Native Peoples* 6:24–31.

Dongoske, K., M. Yeatts, R. Anyon, and T. J. Ferguson
1997   Archaeological Culture and Cultural Affiliation: Hopi and Zuni Perspectives in the American Southwest. *American Antiquity* 62:600–608.

Doolittle, William E.
1988   *Pre-Hispanic Occupance in the Valley of Sonora, Mexico: Archaeological Confirmations of Early Spanish Reports.* Anthropological Papers 48. University of Arizona Press, Tucson.
1990   *Canal Irrigation in Prehistoric Mexico.* University of Texas Press, Austin.

Douglas, John E., and César Armando Quijada López
2000   Reconocimiento Arqueológico en los Valles de Bavispe y San
        Bernardino, Sonora. Informe Técnico al Consejo de Arqueología,
        Instituto Nacional de Antropología e Historia, México, D.F.
Douglass, Andrew Ellicott
1914   A Method for Estimating Rainfall by the Growth of Trees. *Carnegie
        Institution of Washington Publication* 192:101–121.
Doyel, David E.
1991   Hohokam Exchange and Interaction. In *Chaco and Hohokam*, edited
        by Patricia L. Crown and W. James Judge, pp. 225–252. School of
        American Research Press, Santa Fe, New Mexico.
Dozier, Edward P.
1958   Ethnological Clues for the Sources of Rio Grande Population. In
        Migrations in New World Culture History, edited by Raymond H.
        Thompson, pp. 21–29. University of Arizona Press, Tucson.
1966   *Hano, a Tewa Indian Community in Arizona*. Holt, Rinehart and
        Winston, New York.
1970   Making Inferences from the Present to the Past. In *Reconstructing
        Prehistoric Pueblo Societies*, edited by W. A. Longacre, pp. 202–213.
        University of New Mexico Press, Albuquerque.
Duff, Andrew I.
2002   *Western Pueblo Identities: Regional Interaction, Migration and
        Transformation*. University of Arizona Press, Tucson.
Dutton, Bertha P.
1938   *Leyit Kin, A Small House Ruin, Chaco Canyon, New Mexico*. School
        of American Research Monograph 7. School of American Research
        Press, Santa Fe, New Mexico.
1963   *Sun Father's Way*. University of New Mexico Press, Albuquerque.
Echo-Hawk, Roger
2000   Ancient History in the New World: Integrating Oral Traditions and the
        Archaeological Record in Deep Time. *American Antiquity* 65:267–290.
Eddy, Frank W.
1966   *Prehistory in the Navajo Reservoir District, Northwestern New
        Mexico*. Papers in Anthropology Vol. 15, No. 1. Museum of New
        Mexico Press, Santa Fe.
Eggan, Fred
1950   *Social Organization of the Western Pueblos*. University of Chicago
        Press, Chicago.
Eighmy, Jeffrey L.
1994   Results of Archaeomagnetic Analysis of Sample LA 625A-1, Area H,
        Room 36, South Wall Fireplace. Colorado State Archaeomagnetic
        Laboratory, Fort Collins.
1995   Results of Archaeomagnetic Analysis of Sample LA 625A-2, Kiva 23,
        Firepit. Colorado State Archaeomagnetic Laboratory, Fort Collins.
2000   Thirty Years of Archaeomagnetic Dating. In *It's about Time: A History
        of Archaeological Dating in North America*, edited by S. E. Nash,
        pp. 105–123. University of Utah Press, Salt Lake City.

Eiseley, Loren C.
1939   Pollen Analysis and Its Bearing upon American Prehistory: A Critique. *American Antiquity* 5:115–139.

Ekholm, Gordon
1939   Results of an Archaeological Survey of Sonora and Northern Sinaloa. *Revista Mexicana de Estudios Antropológicos* 3(1):7–11.

Elliott, Melinda
1987   *The School of American Research, A History: The First Eighty Years.* School of American Research Press, Santa Fe, New Mexico.

1995   *Great Excavations: Tales of Early Southwestern Archaeology, 1888–1939.* School of American Research Press, Santa Fe, New Mexico.

Ellis, Florence Hawley
1951   Pueblo Social Organization and Southwestern Archaeology. *American Antiquity* 17:148–151.

1964   *A Reconstruction of the Basic Jemez Pattern of Social Organization, with Comparison to other Tanoan Social Structures.* University of New Mexico Publications in Anthropology 11. University of New Mexico Press, Albuquerque.

1967   Where Did the Pueblo People Come From? *El Palacio* 74:35–43.

Ellis, Richard
1997   The Changing Image of the Anasazi World in the American Imagination. In *Anasazi Architecture and American Design,* edited by Baker H. Morrow and V. B. Price, pp. 16–23. University of New Mexico Press, Albuquerque.

Elson, Mark D., Miriam T. Stark, and James M. Heidke
1992   Prelude to Salado. In *Proceedings of the Second Salado Conference: Globe, AZ, 1992,* edited by R. C. Lange and S. Germick, pp. 274–285. Occasional Paper 1992. Arizona Archaeological Society, Phoenix.

Eriksen, T. H.
1991   The Cultural Contexts of Ethnic Differences. *Man* 26:127–144.

1993   *Ethnicity and Nationalism: Anthropological Perspectives.* Pluto Press, London.

Euler, Robert C., and George J. Gumerman (editors)
1978   *Investigations of the Southwestern Anthropological Research Group, The Proceedings of the 1976 Conference.* Museum of Northern Arizona, Flagstaff.

Euler, Robert C., George J. Gumerman, Thor N. V. Karlstrom, Jeffrey S. Dean, and Richard H. Hevly.
1979   The Colorado Plateaus: Cultural Dynamics and Paleoenvironment. *Science* 205:1089–1101.

Ewing, J. Franklin
1949   Appendix: The Religious Medals. In *Franciscan Awatovi: The Excavation and Conjectural Reconstruction of a 17th-Century Spanish Mission Established at a Hopi Indian Town in Northeastern Arizona,* by Ross Gordon Montgomery, Watson Smith, and John Otis Brew, pp. 100–106. Papers of the Peabody Museum of American Archaeology and Ethnology 36. Harvard University, Cambridge, Massachusetts.

Farwell, Robin Elizabeth
1991   An Architectural History of the Seventeenth-Century Mission Church of San Jose de Giusewa, Jemez State Monument, New Mexico. Unpublished M.A. thesis, University of New Mexico, Albuquerque.
Feidel, Stuart J.
2000   The Peopling of the New World: Present Evidence, New Theories and Future Directions. *Journal of Archaeological Research* 8:39–103.
Feinman, Gary M.
2000   Corporate/Network: New Perspectives on Models of Political Action and the Puebloan Southwest. In *Social Theory in Archaeology,* edited by Michael B. Schiffer, pp 31–51. University of Utah Press, Salt Lake City.
Feinman, Gary M., Kent G. Lightfoot, and Steadman Upham
2000   Political Hierarchies and Organizational Strategies in the Puebloan Southwest. *American Antiquity* 65:449–470.
Feld, Steven, and Keith Basso (editors)
1996   *Senses of Place.* School of American Research Press, Santa Fe, New Mexico.
Fenner, Gloria
1977   History and Scope of the Amerind Foundation. *Kiva* 42(3–4):317–329.
Fenton, Steve
1999   *Ethnicity, Class and Culture.* Rowan and Littlefield, Lanham, Maryland.
Ferdon, E. N., Jr.
1955   *A Trial Survey of Mexican-Southwestern Architectural Parallels.* School of American Research Monographs 21. Santa Fe, New Mexico.
Ferguson, Bobbie, and Myra Giesen
1999   Accountability in the Management of Federally Associated Archaeological Collections. *Museum Anthropology* 23(2):19–33.
Ferguson, L.
1992   *Uncommon Ground: Archaeology and Early African America, 1650– 1800.* Smithsonian Institution Press, Washington, D.C.
Ferguson, T. J.
1999   NHPA: Changing the Role of Native Americans in the Archaeological Study of the Past. *SAA Bulletin* 17(1):33–37.
Ferguson, T. J., and Micah Lomaomvaya
2001   Nuavutky'ov, Palatsmo, Niqw Wupatki: Hopi History, Culture, and Landscape. Paper presented at the U.S. Route 89 Symposium, 2001 Pecos Conference, Flagstaff, Arizona.
Ferguson, T. J., K. Dongoske, L. Jenkins, M. Yeatts, and E. Polingyouma
1995   Working Together: The Roles of Archaeology and Ethnohistory in Hopi Cultural Preservation. *CRM* 16:27–37.
Fernlund, Kevin J.
2000   *William Henry Holmes and the Rediscovery of the American West.* University of New Mexico Press, Albuquerque.
Fewkes, Jesse W.
1898   Archaeological Expedition to Arizona in 1895. *Seventeenth Annual Report of the Bureau of American Ethnology* Pt. 2, pp. 519–744. Washington, D.C.

1900   Tusayan Migration Traditions. *Nineteenth Annual Report of the Bureau of American Ethnology, 1897–98* Pt. 2, pp. 573–633. Washington, D.C.

1901a   Archaeological Expedition to Arizona in 1895. *Seventeenth Annual Report of the Bureau of American Ethnology, 1895–96* Pt. 2, pp. 519–744. Washington, D.C.

1901b   Dr. Fewkes' Researches. *American Anthropologist* 3:794.

1902   The Pueblo Settlements near El Paso, Texas. *American Anthropologist* 4:57–75.

1904   Two Summers' Work in Pueblo Ruins. *Twenty-second Annual Report of the Bureau of American Ethnology, 1901–02*, pp. 3–195. Washington, D.C.

1907a   The Aborigines of Porto Rico and Neighboring Islands. *Twenty-fifth Annual Report of the Bureau of American Ethnology, 1903–4*, pp. 3–220. Washington, D.C.

1907b   Certain Antiquities of Eastern New Mexico. *Twenty-fifth Annual Report of the Bureau of American Ethnology, 1903–4*, pp. 221–284. Washington, D.C.

1909   *Antiquities of the Mesa Verde National Park: Spruce-Tree House.* Bureau of American Ethnology Bulletin 41. Washington, D.C.

1914   *Archaeology of the Lower Mimbres Valley.* Smithsonian Institution Miscellaneous Collections Vol. 63, No. 10. Washington, D.C.

1919   Designs on Prehistoric Hopi Pottery. *Thirty-third Annual Report of the Bureau of American Ethnology, 1911–1912*, pp. 207–284. Washington, D.C.

1923   Designs on Prehistoric Pottery from the Mimbres Valley. *El Palacio* 15:9–13.

1924   *Additional Designs on Prehistoric Mimbres Pottery.* Smithsonian Institution Miscellaneous Collections Vol. 76, No. 8. Washington, D.C.

1973   *Designs on Prehistoric Hopi Pottery.* Dover, New York.

Figgins, J. D.

1927   The Antiquity of Man in America. *Natural History* 27:229–239.

Fish, Paul R., and Suzanne K. Fish

1991   Hohokam Political and Social Organization. In *Exploring the Hohokam,* edited by George J. Gumerman, pp. 151–175. University of New Mexico Press, Albuquerque.

Fiske, Turbese Lummis, and Keith Lummis

1975   *Charles F. Lummis: The Man and His West.* University of Oklahoma Press, Norman.

Force, Eric, and Wayne Howell

1997   *Holocene Depositional History and Anasazi Occupation in McElmo Canyon, Southwestern Colorado.* Arizona State Museum Archaeological Series 188. University of Arizona Press, Tucson.

Force, Eric. R., R. Gwinn Vivian, Thomas C. Windes, and Jeffrey S. Dean

2002   *Relation of "Bonito" Paleo-Channels and Base Level Variations to Anasazi Occupation, Chaco Canyon, New Mexico.* Arizona State Museum Archaeological Series 194. University of Arizona Press, Tucson.

Ford, Richard I.

1972   Barter, Gift, or Violence: An Analysis of Tewa Intertribal Exchange. In *Social Exchange and Interaction*, edited by E. N. Wilmsen, pp. 21–45. Museum of Anthropology Anthropological Paper 46. University of Michigan Press, Ann Arbor.

1979   Paleoethnobotany. In *Advances in Archaeological Method and Theory* Vol. 2, edited by Michael B. Schiffer, pp. 285–326. Academic Press, New York.

1981   Gardening and Farming before A.D. 1000: Patterns of Prehistoric Cultivation. *Journal of Ethnobiology* 1:6–27.

Ford, Richard I., Albert H. Schroeder, and Stewart L. Peckham

1972   Three Perspectives on Puebloan Prehistory. In *New Perspectives on the Pueblos*, edited by Alfonso A. Ortiz, pp. 22–40. School of American Research Press, Santa Fe, and University of New Mexico Press, Albuquerque.

Foster, Michael S., and Shirley Gorenstein (editors)

2000   *Greater Mesoamerica: The Archaeology of West and Northwest Mexico.* University of Utah Press, Salt Lake City.

Fowler, Andrew, and John R. Stein

2001   The Anasazi Great House in Space, Time, and Paradigm. In *Anasazi Regional Organization and the Chaco System*, edited by David E. Doyel, pp. 101–122. Maxwell Museum of Anthropology Anthropological Papers 5. University of New Mexico Press, Albuquerque.

Fowler, Don D.

1987   The Uses of the Past: Archaeology in the Service of the State. *American Antiquity* 52:229–248.

1992   Models for Southwestern Prehistory, 1840–1914. In *Rediscovering Our Past: Essays in the History of American Archaeology*, edited by Jonathan E. Reyman, pp. 51–66. Avebury Press, Aldershot, United Kingdom.

1999   Harvard vs. Hewett: The Contest for Control of Southwestern Archaeology, 1904–1930. In *Assembling the Past: Studies in the Professionalization of Archaeology*, edited by Alice B. Kehoe and Mary Beth Emmerichs, pp. 165–212. University of New Mexico Press, Albuquerque.

2000   *A Laboratory for Anthropology: Science and Romanticism in the American Southwest, 1846–1930.* University of New Mexico Press, Albuquerque.

2003   E. L. Hewett, J. F. Zimmerman, and the Beginnings of Anthropology at the University of New Mexico, 1927–1946. *Journal of Anthropological Research* 59:305–327.

Fowler, Don D., and David R. Wilcox

1999   From Thomas Jefferson to the Pecos Conference, Changing Anthropological Agendas in the North American Southwest. In *Surveying the Record. North American Scientific Exploration to 1930*, edited by E. C. Carter II, pp. 197–223. American Philosophical Society Memoir 231. Philadelphia, Pennsylvania.

Freed, Stanley A., and Ruth S. Freed
1983   Clark Wissler and the Development of Anthropology in the United
        States. *American Anthropologist* 85:800–825.
1992   Clark Wissler. *Biographical Memoirs, National Academy of Sciences*
        61:469–496.
Fritts, Harold C.
1976   *Tree-Rings and Climate.* Academic Press, New York.
Fritts, Harold C., D. G. Smith, and M. A. Stokes
1965   The Biological Model for Paleoclimatic Interpretation of Mesa
        Verde Tree-Ring Series. In *Contributions of the Wetherill Mesa
        Archaeological Project,* edited by D. Osborne, pp. 101–121. Memoirs of
        the Society for American Archaeology 19. University of Utah Press, Salt
        Lake City.
Futrell, M. E.
1998   Social Boundaries and Interaction: Ceramic Zones in the Northern
        Rio Grande Pueblo IV Period. In *Migration and Reorganization:
        The Pueblo IV Period in the American Southwest,* edited by
        K. A. Spielmann, pp. 285–292. Anthropological Research Papers 51.
        Department of Anthropology, Arizona State University, Tempe.
Gallatin, Albert
1845   Note on the Semi-Civilized Nations of Mexico, Yucatan, and Central-
        America. *American Ethnological Society Transactions* 1:1–352.
1848   Ancient Semi-Civilization of New Mexico. *American Ethnological
        Society Transactions* 2:iii–xcvii.
Geib, Phil R.
1996   *Glen Canyon Revisited.* Anthropological Papers 119. University of
        Utah Press, Salt Lake City.
Gellner, Ernest
1983   *Nations and Nationalism.* Basil Blackwell, Oxford.
Getty, Harry T.
1935   New Dates from Mesa Verde. *Tree-Ring Bulletin* 1(3):21–23.
Giddens, A.
1979   *Central Problems in Social Theory.* University of California Press,
        Berkeley.
1984   *The Constitution of Society.* University of California Press, Berkeley.
Gifford, Carol A., and Elizabeth A. Morris
1985   Digging for Credit: Early Archaeological Field Schools in the American
        Southwest. *American Antiquity* 50:395–411.
Gifford, James C.
1980   *Archaeological Explorations in Caves of the Point of Pines Region,
        Arizona.* Anthropological Papers 36. University of Arizona Press,
        Tucson.
Gilpin, Dennis
1994   Lukachukai and Saline Springs: Late Archaic/Early Basketmaker
        Habitation Sites in the Chinle Valley, Northeastern Arizona. *Kiva*
        60:203–218.
Givens, Douglas R.
1992   *Alfred Vincent Kidder and the Development of Americanist
        Archaeology.* University of New Mexico Press, Albuquerque.

Gladfelter, Bruce G.
1977   Geoarchaeology: The Geomorphologist and Archaeology. *American Antiquity* 42:519–538.
Gladwin, Harold Sterling
1936   Discussion. In *An Archaeological Survey of Chihuahua, Mexico,* by E. B. Sayles, pp. 30–40. Medallion Papers 22. Gila Pueblo, Globe, Arizona.
Gladwin, Winefred, and Harold S. Gladwin
1930   *Some Southwestern Pottery Types: Series 1.* Medallion Papers 8. Gila Pueblo, Globe, Arizona.
1934   *A Method for the Designation of Cultures and their Variations.* Medallion Papers 15. Gila Pueblo, Globe, Arizona.
Glazer, Nathan, and Daniel P. Moynihan
1975   Introduction. In *Ethnicity: Theory and Experience,* edited by N. Glazer and D. Moynihan, pp. 1–28. Harvard University Press, Cambridge, Massachusetts.
Goetzmann, William H.
1966   *Exploration and Empire: The Explorer and the Scientist in the Winning of the American West.* Alfred A. Knopf and Son, New York.
González Arratia, Leticia
1985   The Bolson de Mapimi Archaeological Project: A Research Design. In *The Archaeology of West and Northwest Mesoamerica* Vol. 2, edited by M. S. Foster and P. C. Weigand, pp. 383–391. Westview Press, Boulder, Colorado.
1991   La Mujer Recolectora el la Reproducción Material. *Antropología* 34: 2–21.
Graham, Martha
1993   Settlement Organization and Residential Variability among the Rarámuri. In *Abandonment of Settlements and Regions: Ethnoarchaeological and Archaeological Approaches,* edited by Catherine M. Cameron and Steve A. Tomka, pp. 25–42. Cambridge University Press, Cambridge.
Graves, Laura
1998   *Thomas Varker Keam, Indian Trader.* University of Oklahoma Press, Norman.
Graves, Michael, Sally Holbrook, and William Longacre
1982   Aggregation and Abandonment at Grasshopper Pueblo: Evolutionary Trends in the Late Prehistory of East-Central Arizona. In *Multidisciplinary Research at Grasshopper Pueblo, Arizona,* edited by William Longacre, Sally Holbrook, and Michael Graves, pp. 110–122. Anthropological Papers 40. University of Arizona Press, Tucson.
Graves, William M., and Suzanne L. Eckert
1998   Decorated Ceramic Distributions and Ideological Developments in the Northern and Central Rio Grande Valley, New Mexico. In *Migration and Reorganization: The Pueblo IV Period in the American Southwest,* edited by Katherine A. Spielmann, pp. 263–283. Anthropological Research Papers 51. Department of Anthropology, Arizona State University, Tempe.

Graves, William M., and Katherine A. Spielmann
2000   Leadership, Long-Distance Exchange, and Feasting in the Protohistoric Rio Grande. In *Alternative Leadership Strategies in the Prehispanic Southwest*, edited by Barbara J. Mills, pp. 45–59. University of Arizona Press, Tucson.

Graybill, Donald A., David A. Gregory, Fred L. Nials, Suzanne K. Fish, Robert E. Gasser, Charles H. Miksicek, and Christine R. Szuter
1989   The 1982–1984 Excavations at Las Colinas: Environment and Subsistence. Arizona State Museum Archaeological Series Vol. 162, No. 5. University of Arizona Press, Tucson.

Gregg, Josiah
1954   *Commerce of the Prairies,* edited by Max L. Moorhead. University of Oklahoma Press, Norman.

Gregory, David A.
2000   *Excavations in the Santa Cruz River Floodplain: The Early Agricultural Period Component at Los Pozos.* Anthropological Papers 21. Center for Desert Archaeology, Tucson, Arizona.

Gregory, David A., and David R. Wilcox (editors)
2006   *Zuñi Origins: Anthropological Approaches on Multiple Scales.* Center for Desert Archaeology, Tucson, and Museum of Northern Arizona, Flagstaff, in preparation.

Guevara Sánchez, Arturo
1985   *Apuntes para la Arqueología de Chihuahua.* Instituto Nacional de Antropología e Historia, México, D.F.

Gumerman, George J. (editor)
1971   *The Distribution of Prehistoric Population Aggregates.* Anthropological Reports 1. Prescott College Press, Prescott, Arizona.
1988   *The Anasazi in a Changing Environment.* Cambridge University Press, Cambridge.

Guthe, Carl E.
1925   *Pueblo Pottery Making: A Study at the Village of San Ildefonso.* Phillips Academy Southwestern Expedition Publication 2. Yale University Press, New Haven, Connecticut.

Haas, Jonathan, and Winifred Creamer
1993   *Stress and Warfare among the Kayenta Anasazi of the Thirteenth Century A.D.* Fieldiana Anthropology, n.s. 21. Publication 1450. Field Museum of Natural History, Chicago.

Habicht-Mauche, Judith A.
1993   *The Pottery from Arroyo Hondo Pueblo, New Mexico: Tribalization and Trade in the Northern Rio Grande.* School of American Research Press, Santa Fe, New Mexico.

Hack, John T.
1942   *The Changing Physical Environment of the Hopi Indians of Arizona.* Reports of the Awatovi Expedition, Peabody Museum, Harvard University 1. Harvard University Press, Cambridge, Massachusetts.

Hacking, Ian
1983   *Representing and Intervening.* Cambridge University Press, Cambridge.

1992   The Self-Vindication of the Laboratory Sciences. In *Science as Practice and Culture,* edited by Andrew Pickering, pp. 1–29. University of Chicago Press, Chicago.

Hall, Stephen A.

1977   Late Quaternary Sedimentation and Paleoecologic History of Chaco Canyon, New Mexico. *Geological Society of America Bulletin* 88:1593–1618.

1985   Bibliography of Quaternary Palynology in Arizona, Colorado, New Mexico, and Utah. In *Pollen Records of Late Quaternary North American Sediments,* edited by V. M. Bryant Jr. and R. G. Holloway, pp. 407–423. American Association of Stratigraphic Palynologists Foundation, Dallas, Texas.

Hamilton, Clay

1999   Testimony to the NAGPRA Review Committee. Minutes of the Native American Graves Protection and Repatriation Act (NAGPRA) Review Committee Seventeenth Meeting, May 3–5, 1999, Silver Spring, Maryland. www.cr.nps.gov/nagpra/REVIEW/meetings/RMS017.PDF

Hantman, Jeffrey L., and Michael B. Schiffer

1995   Fred Plog, 1944–1992. *American Antiquity* 60:677–684.

Hard, Robert J., and John R. Roney

1998   A Massive Terraced Village Complex in Chihuahua, Mexico, 3000 Years Before Present. *Science* 279(5337):1661–1664.

Hardy, R. W. H.

1829   *Travels in the Interior of Mexico in 1825, 1826, 1827, & 1828.* H. Colburn and R. Bently, London.

Harrington, John P.

1916   *The Ethnogeography of the Tewa Indians. Twenty-ninth Annual Report of the Bureau of American Ethnology, 1907–08,* pp. 29–618. Washington, D.C.

Haskell, Thomas L.

1977   *The Emergence of Professional Social Science: The American Social Science Association and the Nineteenth-Century Crisis of Authority.* University of Illinois Press, Urbana.

Haury, Emil W.

1936   *The Mogollon Culture of Southwestern New Mexico.* Medallion Papers 20. Gila Pueblo, Globe, Arizona.

1940   *Excavations in the Forestdale Valley, East-Central Arizona.* Social Science Bulletin 12. University of Arizona Bulletin Vol. 11, No. 4. Tucson.

1945   *The Excavation of Los Muertos and Neighboring Ruins in the Salt River Valley, Southern Arizona.* Papers of the Peabody Museum of American Archaeology and Ethnology Vol 24, No. 1. Harvard University Press, Cambridge, Massachusetts.

1950   *The Stratigraphy and Archaeology of Ventana Cave, Arizona.* University of Arizona Press, Tucson, and University of New Mexico Press, Albuquerque.

1953   Artifacts with Mammoth Remains, Naco, Arizona. *American Antiquity* 19:1–14.

1957   An Alluvial Site on the San Carlos Indian Reservation, Arizona. *American Antiquity* 23:2–27.

1958a   Post-Pleistocene Human Occupation of the Southwest. In *Climate and Man in the Southwest*, edited by T. L. Smiley, pp. 69–75. University of Arizona Press, Tucson.

1958b   Evidence at Point of Pines for a Prehistoric Migration from Northern Arizona. In *Migrations in New World Culture History*, edited by Raymond H. Thompson, pp. 1–6. University of Arizona Bulletin 29. University of Arizona Press, Tucson.

1962   The Greater American Southwest. In *Courses toward Urban Life*, edited by Robert J. Braidwood and Gordon R. Willey, pp. 106–131. Viking Fund Publications in Anthropology 32. Wenner-Gren Foundation for Anthropological Research, New York.

1976   *The Hohokam, Desert Farmers and Craftsmen*. University of Arizona Press, Tucson.

1985   *Mogollon Culture in the Forestdale Valley, East-Central Arizona*. University of Arizona Press, Tucson.

1988   Gila Pueblo Archaeological Foundation: A History and Some Personal Notes. *Kiva* 54(1):1–8.

1989   *Point of Pines, Arizona: A History of the University of Arizona Archaeological Field School*. Anthropological Papers 50. University of Arizona Press, Tucson.

Haury, E. W., E. B. Sayles, and W. W. Wasley

1959   The Lehner Mammoth Site, Southeastern Arizona. *American Antiquity* 25:2–30.

Hawley, Florence

1934   *The Significance of the Dated Prehistory of Chetro Ketl, Chaco Canyon, New Mexico*. University of New Mexico Bulletin, Monograph Series Vol. 1, No. 1. University of New Mexico Press, Albuquerque.

Hayden, J. D.

1976   Pre-Altithermal Archaeology in the Sierra Pinacate, Sonora, Mexico. *American Antiquity* 40:274–289.

Hayes, Alden C.

1974   *The Four Churches of Pecos*. University of New Mexico Press, Albuquerque.

Hayes, Alden C., Jon Nathan Young, and A. H. Warren

1981   *Excavation of Mound 7, Gran Quivira National Monument, New Mexico*. Publications in Archeology 16. National Park Service, Washington, D.C.

Haynes, C. Vance, Jr.

1981   Geochronology and Paleoenvironments of the Murray Springs Clovis Site, Arizona. *National Geographic Society Research Reports* 13: 143–251.

1986   Discovering Early Man in Arizona. In *Emil W. Haury's Prehistory of the American Southwest*, edited by J. Jefferson Reid and David E. Doyel, pp. 75–77. University of Arizona Press, Tucson.

1990   The Antevs-Bryan Years and the Legacy for Paleoindian
        Geochronology. In *Establishment of a Geological Framework for
        Paleoanthropology*, edited by L. F. Laporte, pp. 55–68. Geological
        Society of America Special Paper 242. Boulder, Colorado.

1991   Geoarchaeological and Paleohydrological Evidence for a Clovis-Age
        Drought in North America and Its Bearing on Extinction. *Quaternary
        Research* 35:438–450.

1995   Geochronology of Paleoenvironmental Change, Clovis Type Site,
        Blackwater Draw, New Mexico. *Geoarchaeology* 10:317–388.

Hegmon, Michelle

1992   Archaeological Research on Style. *Annual Review of Anthropology*
        21:517–536.

1995   *The Social Dynamics of Pottery Style in the Early Puebloan Southwest.*
        Crow Canyon Archaeological Center Occasional Paper 5. Cortez,
        Colorado.

Hevly, Richard H.

1988   Prehistoric Vegetation and Paleoclimates on the Colorado Plateaus.
        In *The Anasazi in a Changing Environment*, edited by George J.
        Gumerman, pp. 92–118. Cambridge University Press, Cambridge.

Hewett, Edgar L.

1908a   The Excavations at Tyuonyi, New Mexico, in 1908. *American
        Anthropologist* n.s. 11:434–455.

1908b   The Groundwork of American Archeology. *American Anthropologist*
        n.s. 10:591–595.

1908c   Report of the Director. *American Journal of Archaeology* 2nd Series,
        12(Supplement):48–54.

1908d   *Les communautés anciennes dans le désert américain.* Librairie
        Kündig, Geneva.

1909   The Pajaritan Culture. *American Journal of Archaeology* 2nd Series,
        13:334–344.

1923   Anahuac and Aztlan: Retracing the Legendary Footsteps of the Aztecs.
        Art and Archaeology 16(1–2):35–50.

1936   *The Chaco Canyon and Its Monuments.* University of New Mexico
        Press, Albuquerque.

1937   Archaeological Researches on the Distribution and the Social
        Organization of the Ancient Populations in the Southwest of the United
        States and the North of Mexico. Translated by S. Elizabeth Murphey.
        Manuscript on file, Laboratory of Anthropology, Santa Fe, New
        Mexico.

1938   Hispanic Monuments. *El Palacio* 45(9-10).

1943   *Campfire and Trail.* University of New Mexico Press, Albuquerque.

1993   *Ancient Communities in the American Desert.* Translated by Marie
        Rodack, edited by Albert H. Schroeder. Archaeological Society of New
        Mexico Monograph Series 1. Santa Fe.

Hewett, Edgar L., and Wayne L. Mauzy

1940   *Landmarks of New Mexico.* University of New Mexico Press,
        Albuquerque.

Hibben, Frank C.

1941   *Evidences of Early Occupation in Sandia Cave, New Mexico, and Other Sites in the Sandia-Manzano Region.* Smithsonian Institution Miscellaneous Collections Vol. 99, No. 3. Washington, D.C.

1975   *Kiva Art of the Anasazi at Pottery Mound.* K. C. Publications, Las Vegas, Nevada.

Hieb, Louis A., and Susan E. Diggle

2004   A Question of Authorship: A. M. Stephen's Catalogue of the Keam Collection [1884]. *Kiva* 69:401–423.

Hill, James N.

1970   *Broken K Pueblo: Prehistoric Social Organization in the American Southwest.* Anthropological Papers 19. University of Arizona Press, Tucson.

Hill, James N., and Richard Hevly

1968   Pollen Analysis at Broken K Pueblo. *American Antiquity* 33:200–210.

Hinsley, Curtis M., Jr.

1981   *Savages and Scientists: The Smithsonian Institution and the Development of American Anthropology, 1846–1910.* Smithsonian Institution Press, Washington, D.C.

1983   Ethnographic Charisma and Scientific Routine: Cushing and Fewkes in the American Southwest, 1879–1893. In *Observers Observed: Essays on Ethnographic Fieldwork,* edited by George W. Stocking Jr., pp. 53–69. History of Anthropology, Vol. 1. University of Wisconsin Press, Madison.

1986   Edgar Lee Hewett and the School of American Archaeology in Santa Fe, 1906–1912. In *American Archaeology Past and Future,* edited by David J. Meltzer, Don D. Fowler, and Jeremy A. Sabloff, pp. 217–236. Smithsonian Institution Press, Washington, D.C.

1994   *The Smithsonian and the American Indian: Making a Moral Anthropology in Victorian America.* Smithsonian Institution Press, Washington, D.C.

1999   Frederic Ward Putnam. In *Encyclopedia of Archaeology,* Part 1: *The Great Archaeologists,* edited by Tim Murray, pp. 141–174. ABC-Clio, Santa Barbara, California.

Hinsley, Curtis M., Jr., and David R. Wilcox

1995   A Hemenway Portfolio: Voices and Views from the Hemenway Archaeological Expedition, 1886–1889. *Journal of the Southwest* 37(4):519–744.

2000   Arizona's First Sacred Site: The Mystique of Casa Grande, 1848–1889. *The Biennial Review* 25(2):125–145. Arizona State University, Tempe.

Hinsley, Curtis M., Jr., and David R. Wilcox (editors)

1996   *The Southwest in the American Imagination: The Writings of Sylvester Baxter, 1881–1889.* University of Arizona Press, Tucson.

2002   *From Manchester to the Salt River Valley: The Lost Itinerary of Frank Hamilton Cushing, 1886–1887.* University of Arizona Press, Tucson.

Hodder, Ian

1982   *Symbols in Action: Ethnoarchaeological Studies of Material Culture.* Cambridge University Press, Cambridge.

1985   Boundaries as Strategies: An Ethnoarchaeological Study. In *The Archaeology of Frontiers and Boundaries,* edited by S. Green and S. Perlman, pp. 141–159. Academic Press, New York.

Hodge, F. W.

1910   *Handbook of American Indians North of Mexico.* Bureau of American Ethnology Bulletin 30. Washington D.C.

Hofman, J. L., and R. W. Graham

1998   The Paleoindian Cultures of the Great Plains. In *Archaeology on the Great Plains,* edited by W. R. Wood, pp. 87–139. University of Kansas Press, Lawrence.

Holbrook, Sally J.

1982   Prehistoric Environmental Reconstruction by Mammalian Microfaunal Analysis, Grasshopper Pueblo. In *Multidisciplinary Research at Grasshopper Pueblo, Arizona,* edited by William A. Longacre, Sally J. Holbrook, and Michael W. Graves, pp. 73–86. Anthropological Papers 40. University of Arizona Press, Tucson.

Holbrook, Sally J., and Michael W. Graves

1982   Modern Environment of the Grasshopper Region. In *Multidisciplinary Research at Grasshopper Pueblo, Arizona,* edited by William A. Longacre, Sally J. Holbrook, and Michael W. Graves, pp. 5–12. Anthropological Papers 40. University of Arizona Press, Tucson.

Holliday, Vance T.

2000   Vance Haynes and Paleoindian Geoarchaeology and Geochronology of the Great Plains. *Geoarchaeology* 15(6):511–522.

Holmes, William H.

1914   Areas of American Culture Characterization Tentatively Outlined as an Aid in the Study of the Antiquities. *American Anthropologist* 16: 413–446.

Horvath, Steven M.

1979   *The Social and Political Organization of the Genízaros of Plaza de Nuestra Señora de los Dolores de Belén, New Mexico 1740–1812.* Unpublished Ph.D. dissertation, Department of Anthropology, Brown University, Providence, Rhode Island.

Hough, Walter

1897   The Hopi in Relation to Their Environment. *American Anthropologist,* o.s. 10:33–44.

1898   Environmental Interrelations in Arizona. *American Anthropologist,* o.s. 11:133–155.

1903   Archaeological Field Work in Northeastern Arizona. The Museum-Gates Expedition of 1901. *Report of the U.S. National Museum for 1901:* 287–358.

1906   Pueblo Environment. *American Association for the Advancement of Science Proceedings* 55:447–454.

1907   Antiquities of the Upper Gila and Salt River Valleys in Arizona and New Mexico. *Bureau of American Ethnology Bulletin* 35. Washington, D.C.

1914   Culture of the Upper Gila Region, New Mexico and Arizona. Second Museum-Gates Expedition. *U.S. National Museum Bulletin* 87:1–139.

Howard, E. B.

1935   Evidence of Early Man in North America. *Museum Journal* 24(2–3): 61–158.

Howell, Todd

1994   *Leadership at the Ancestral Zuni Village of Hawikku.* Unpublished Ph.D. dissertation, Department of Anthropology, Arizona State University, Tempe.

Huckell, Bruce B.

1984   *The Archaic Occupation of the Rosemont Area, Northern Santa Rita Mountains, Southeastern Arizona.* Arizona State Museum Archaeological Series 147. University of Arizona Press, Tucson.

1995   *Of Marshes and Maize: Preceramic Agricultural Settlements in the Cienega Valley, Southeastern Arizona.* Anthropological Papers 59. University of Arizona Press, Tucson.

1996   The Archaic Prehistory of the North American Southwest. *Journal of World Prehistory* 10:305–373.

Huckleberry, Gary A.

2000   Interdisciplinary and Specialized Geoarchaeology: A Post–Cold War Perspective. *Geoarchaeology* 15(6):523–536.

Huckleberry, Gary A., and Brian R. Billman

2000   Floodwater Farming, Discontinuous Ephemeral Streams, and Puebloan Abandonment in Southwestern Colorado. *American Antiquity* 63: 595–596.

Hutt, Sherry, Elwood W. Jones, and Martin E. McAllister

1992   *Archeological Resource Protection.* Preservation Press, Washington, D.C.

Hutton, Paul Andrew

1985   *Phil Sheridan and His Army.* University of Nebraska Press, Lincoln.

Irwin-Williams, Cynthia

1967   Picosa: The Elementary Southwestern Culture. *American Antiquity* 32:441–457.

1968   The Reconstruction of Archaic Culture in the Southwestern United States. In *Archaic Prehistory in the Western United States*, edited by C. Irwin-Williams, pp. 19–23. Contributions in Anthropology Vol. 1, No. 3. Eastern New Mexico University Press, Portales.

1973   *The Oshara Tradition: Origins of Anasazi Culture.* Contributions in Anthropology Vol. 5, No. 1. Eastern New Mexico University Press, Portales.

1994   The Archaic of the Southwestern United States: Changing Goals and Research Strategies in the Last Twenty-Five Years, 1964–1989. In *Archaic Hunter-Gatherer Archaeology in the American Southwest*, edited by B. J. Vierra, pp. 566–670. Contributions in Anthropology Vol. 13, No. 1. Eastern New Mexico University Press, Portales.

Isaacs, H.

1974   Basic Group Identity: Idols of the Tribe. *Ethnicity* 1:15–41.

Ivey, James E.

1988   In the Midst of a Loneliness: The Structural History of the Salinas Missions. Historic Structure Report, Salinas National Monument, New

Mexico. Professional Paper 15. Southwest Regional Office, National Park Service, Santa Fe, New Mexico.

1998   Convento Kivas in the Missions of New Mexico. *New Mexico Historical Review* 73(2):121–152.

Jennings, Jesse D.
1957   *Danger Cave.* Anthropological Papers 27. University of Utah Press, Salt Lake City.
1966   *Glen Canyon: A Summary.* Anthropological Papers 81, Glen Canyon Series 31. University of Utah Press, Salt Lake City.

Jett, Stephen C.
1992   The Great "Race" to "Discover" Rainbow Natural Bridge in 1909. *Kiva* 58(1):3–66.

Johnson, Alfred E.
1965   *The Development of Western Pueblo Culture.* Unpublished Ph.D. dissertation, Department of Anthropology, University of Arizona, Tucson.

Johnson, Alfred, and Raymond H. Thompson
1963   The Ringo Site, Southeastern Arizona. *American Antiquity* 28: 465–481.

Johnson, Frederick
1961   A Quarter Century of Growth. *American Antiquity* 27:1–6.

Johnson, Gregory A.
1989   Dynamics of Southwestern Prehistory: Far Outside—Looking In. In *Dynamics of Southwest Prehistory,* edited by Linda S. Cordell and George J. Gumerman, pp 371–389. Smithsonian Institution Press, Washington, D.C.

Joiner, Carol
1992   The Boys and Girls of Summer: The University of New Mexico Archaeological Field School in Chaco Canyon. *Journal of Anthropological Research* 48:49–66.

Jones, Sian
1997   *The Archaeology of Ethnicity: Constructing Identities in the Past and Present.* Routledge, London.

Judd, Neil M.
1924   Report on Illegal Excavations in Southwestern Ruins. *American Anthropologist* 26:428–432.
1936   Walter Hough: An Appreciation. *American Anthropologist* 38: 471–481.
1968   *Men Met along the Trail.* University of Oklahoma Press, Norman.

Judge, W. James
1979   The Development of a Complex Cultural Ecosystem in the Chaco Basin, New Mexico. In *Proceedings of the First Conference on Scientific Research in the National Parks* Pt. 3, edited by R. M. Linn, pp. 901–906. National Park Service, Washington, D.C.

Kaldahl, Eric J., and Jeffrey S. Dean
1999   Climate, Vegetation, and Dendrochronology. In *Living on the Edge of the Rim: Excavations and Analysis of the Silver Creek Archaeological Research Project 1993–1998,* edited by Barbara J. Mills, Sarah A.

Herr, and Scott Van Keuren, pp. 11–29. Arizona State Museum Archaeological Series 192. University of Arizona Press, Tucson.

Kantner, John

2002   Complexity. In *Darwin and Archaeology: A Handbook of Key Concepts*, edited by John P. Hart and John Edward Terrell, pp. 89–106. Bergin and Garvey, Westport, Connecticut.

Kantner, John, and Nancy M. Mahoney (editors)

2000   *Great House Communities across the Chacoan Landscape*. University of Arizona Press, Tucson.

Karlstrom, Eric T., and Thor N. V. Karlstrom

1986   Late Quaternary Alluvial Stratigraphy and Soils of the Black Mesa–Little Colorado River Areas, Northern Arizona. In *Geology of Central and Northern Arizona*, edited by J. D. Nations, C. M. Conway, and G. A. Swann, pp. 71–92. Geological Society of America, Rocky Mountain Section Guidebook. Boulder, Colorado.

Karlstrom, Thor N. V.

1988   Alluvial Chronology and Hydrologic Change of Black Mesa and Nearby Regions. In *The Anasazi in a Changing Environment*, edited by George J. Gumerman, pp. 45–91. Cambridge University Press, Cambridge.

Karlstrom, Thor N. V., George J. Gumerman, and Robert C. Euler

1976   Paleoenvironmental and Cultural Correlates in the Black Mesa Region. In *Papers on the Archaeology of Black Mesa, Arizona*, edited by George J. Gumerman and Robert C. Euler, pp 149–161. Southern Illinois University Press, Carbondale.

Kelley, J. Charles

1980   Alta Vista, Chalchihuites: "A Port of Entry" on the Northwestern Frontier of Mesoamerica. In *Rutas de Intercambio en Mesoamerica y el Norte de Mexico* Vol. 2, pp. 53–64. XVI Reunion de Mesa Redonda, Saltillo, Coahuila. Sociedad Mexicana de Antropología, México, D.F.

2000   The Aztatlán Mercantile System: Mobile Traders and the North-westward Expansion of Mesoamerican Civilization. In *Greater Mesoamerica: The Archaeology of West and Northwest Mexico*, edited by Michael S. Foster and Shirley Gorenstein, pp. 137–154. University of Utah Press, Salt Lake City.

Kelley, Jane H., Joe D. Stewart, A. C. MacWilliams, and Loy C. Neff

1999   A West Central Perspective on Chihuahuan Culture. In *The Casas Grandes World*, edited by Curtis F. Schaafsma and Carroll L. Riley, pp. 63–77. University of Utah Press, Salt Lake City.

Kelley, Jane H., and María Elisa Villalpando C.

1996   An Overview of the Mexican Northwest. In *Interpreting Southwestern Diversity: Underlying Principles and Overarching Patterns*, edited by Paul R. Fish and J. Jefferson Reid, pp. 69–77. Anthropological Research Papers 47. Department of Anthropology, Arizona State University, Tempe.

Kelly, Daniel T.

1972   *The Buffalo Head: A Century of Mercantile Pioneering in the Southwest*. Vergara, Santa Fe, New Mexico.

Kelly, Robert L.
1983   Hunter-Gatherer Mobility Strategies. *Journal of Anthropological Research* 39:277–306.
1995   *The Foraging Spectrum, Diversity in Hunter-Gatherer Lifeways.* Smithsonian Institution Press, Washington, D.C.

Kelso, Gerald K.
1982   Two Pollen Profiles from Grasshopper Pueblo. In *Multidisciplinary Research at Grasshopper Pueblo, Arizona*, edited by William A. Longacre, Sally J. Holbrook, and Michael W. Graves, pp. 106–109. Anthropological Papers 40. University of Arizona Press, Tucson.

Kessell, John
1970   *Mission of Sorrows: Jesuit Guevavi and the Pimas, 1691–1767.* University of Arizona Press, Tucson.
1976   *Friars, Soldiers, and Reformers: Hispanic Arizona and the Sonoran Mission Frontier, 1767–1856.* University of Arizona Press, Tucson.
1980   *The Missions of New Mexico, Since 1776.* University of New Mexico Press, Albuquerque.
2002   *Spain in the Southwest: A Narrative History of Colonial New Mexico, Arizona, Texas, and California.* University of Oklahoma Press, Norman.

Kidder, Alfred V.
1915   1915—Daily Record. Kidder Files, Pecos National Historical Park, New Mexico.
1916   The Pottery of the Casas Grandes District, Chihuahua. In *Holmes Anniversary Volume Anthropological Essays*, pp. 253–268. Washington, D.C.
1920   Ruins of the Historic Period in the Upper San Juan Valley, New Mexico. *American Anthropologist* 22:322–329.
1924   *An Introduction to the Study of Southwestern Archaeology.* Yale University Press, New Haven, Connecticut.
1925a   Field Notes, 1925. Kidder Files, Pecos National Historical Park, New Mexico.
1925b   Introduction. *Pueblo Pottery Making: A Study at the Village of San Ildefonso.* Phillips Academy Southwestern Expedition Publication 2. Yale University Press, New Haven, Connecticut.
1927   Southwestern Archaeological Conference. *Science* 66:489–491.
1936a   Introduction. In *The Pottery of Pecos* Vol. 2, edited by A. V. Kidder and Anna O. Shepard, pp. xvii–xxxi. Papers of the Phillips Academy Southwestern Expedition 7. Yale University Press, New Haven, Connecticut.
1936b   Speculations on New World Prehistory. In *Essays in Anthropology Presented to A. L. Kroeber*, edited by Robert H. Lowie, pp. 143–152. University of California Press, Berkeley.
1939   Review of *Starkweather Ruin*, by Paul H. Nesbitt. *American Anthropologist* 41:314–316.
1957   Unpublished Memoirs. 3 vols. Peabody Museum Archives, Harvard University, Cambridge, Massachusetts.
1958   *Pecos, New Mexico: Archaeological Notes.* Papers of the Robert S. Peabody Foundation for Archaeology 5. Andover, Massachusetts.

1960   Reminiscences in Southwestern Archaeology: 1. *Kiva* 25(4):1–32.

Kidwell, Clara Sue

1999   Every Last Dishcloth: The Prodigious Collecting of George Gustav
        Heye. In *Collecting Native America, 1870–1960,* edited by Shepard
        Krech III and Barbara A. Hail, pp. 232–258. Smithsonian Institution
        Press, Washington, D.C.

King, Thomas F., Patricia Parker Hickman, and Gary Berg

1977   *Anthropology in Historic Preservation: Caring for Culture's Clutter.*
        Academic Press, New York.

Kirchhoff, Paul

1954   Gatherers and Farmers in the Greater Southwest: A Problem in
        Classification. *American Anthropologist* 56:529–550.

Klein, Richard, and Kathryn Cruz-Uribe

1984   *The Analysis of Animal Bones from Archaeological Sites.* University of
        Chicago Press, Chicago.

Kluckhohn, Clyde

1939   Discussion. In *Preliminary Report on the 1937 Excavations: Bc
        50–51, Chaco Canyon, New Mexico,* edited by Clyde Kluckhohn
        and Paul Reiter, pp. 151–162. University of New Mexico Bulletin 345.
        Anthropological Series Vol. 3, No. 2. University of New Mexico Press,
        Albuquerque.

1940   The Conceptual Structure in Middle American Studies. In *The Maya
        and Their Neighbors,* edited by Clarence L. Hay, Samuel K. Lothrop,
        Ralph L. Linton, Harry L. Shapiro, and George C. Vaillant, pp. 44–51.
        D. Appleton Century, New York.

Koepping, Klaus-Peter

1983   *Adolf Bastian and the Psychic Unity of Mankind.* University of
        Queensland Press, Brisbane, Australia.

Kohler, Timothy A., and Carla R. Van West

1996   The Calculus of Self-Interest in the Development of Cooperation:
        Sociopolitical Development and Risk among the Northern Anasazi.
        In *Evolving Complexity and Environmental Risk in the Prehistoric
        Southwest,* edited by Joseph Tainter and Bonnie Bagley-Tainter,
        pp. 169–196. Addison-Wesley, Reading, Massachusetts.

Kohler, Timothy A., James Kresl, Carla R. Van West, Eric Carr, and Richard H.
        Wilshusen

2000   Be There Then: A Modeling Approach to Settlement Determinants and
        Spatial Efficiency among Late Ancestral Pueblo Populations of the Mesa
        Verde Region, U.S. Southwest. In *Dynamics in Human and Primate
        Societies: Agent-Based Modeling of Social and Spatial Processes,* edited
        by Timothy A. Kohler and George J. Gumerman, pp. 145–178. Santa Fe
        Institute Studies in the Sciences of Complexity. Oxford University Press,
        New York.

Kottlowski, Frank E., Maurice E. Cooley, and Robert V. Rushe

1965   Quaternary Geology of the Southwest. In *The Quaternary of the
        United States,* edited by H. E. Wright Jr. and David G. Frey, pp. 287–
        298. Princeton University Press, Princeton, New Jersey.

Kramer, Barbara
1996   *Nampeyo and Her Pottery.* University of New Mexico Press, Albuquerque.

Kroeber, Alfred L.
1916   *Zuñi Potsherds.* Anthropological Papers of the American Museum of Natural History Vol. 18, No. 1. New York.
1917   *Zuñi Kin and Clan.* Anthropological Papers of the American Museum of Natural History Vol. 18, No. 2. New York.
1939   *Cultural and Natural Areas of Native North America.* University of California Publications in American Archaeology and Ethnology 38. Berkeley.

Kubler, George
1940   *The Religious Architecture of New Mexico in the Colonial Period and since the American Occupation.* University of New Mexico Press, Albuquerque.
1973   *Religious Architecture of New Mexico in the Colonial Period and since the American Occupation.* 4th ed. University of New Mexico Press, Albuquerque.
1994   Art Historian George A. Kubler, Oral History Transcript, 1991 (University of California, Los Angeles and J. Paul Getty Trust). Manuscript No. 300/411 on file in Department of Special Collections, Charles E. Young Research Library, University of California, Los Angeles.

Kuhn, Thomas S.
1962   *The Structure of Scientific Revolutions.* University of Chicago Press, Chicago.

Lange, Charles H.
1959   *Cochiti: A New Mexican Pueblo, Past and Present.* University of Texas Press, Austin.

Lange, Charles H., and Carroll L. Riley
1996   *Bandelier: The Life and Times of Adolph Bandelier.* University of Utah Press, Salt Lake City.

Laudermilk, J. D., and P. A. Munz
1934   Plants in the Dung of *Nothrotherium* from Gypsum Cave, Nevada. *Carnegie Institution of Washington Publication* 453:29–37.

LeBlanc, Steven A.
1999   *Prehistoric Warfare in the American Southwest.* University of Utah Press, Salt Lake City.

Lee, Ronald F.
1970   *The Antiquities Act of 1906.* U.S. Department of the Interior, National Park Service, Washington, D.C.

Lekson, Stephen H.
1991   Settlement Patterns and the Chaco Region. In *Chaco and Hohokam: Prehistoric Regional Systems in the American Southwest,* edited by Patricia L. Crown and W. James Judge, pp. 31–55. School of American Research Press, Santa Fe, New Mexico.

1999   *Chaco Meridian: Centers of Political Power in the Ancient Southwest.*
        Altamira Press, Walnut Creek, California.
2002   War in the Southwest, War in the World. *American Antiquity* 67:
        607–624.
Lekson, Stephen H. (editor)
2005   *The Archaeology of Chaco Canyon. An Eleventh-Century Pueblo
        Regional Center.* School of American Research Press, Santa Fe, New
        Mexico.
Lekson, Stephen H., and Catherine Cameron M.
1995   The Abandonment of Chaco Canyon, the Mesa Verde Migrations and
        the Reorganization of the Pueblo World. *Journal of Anthropological
        Archaeology* 14:184–202.
LeTourneau, P. D.
2000   *Folsom Tool Stone Procurement in the Southwest and Southern
        Plains.* Unpublished Ph.D. dissertation, Department of Anthropology,
        University of New Mexico, Albuquerque.
Lewenstein, Suzanne, and Fabiola Sánchez B.
1991   Proyecto Arqueológica-Etnoarqueológico Sierra Tarahumara. *Boletín,
        Consejo de Arqueología* 1:167–171.
Liebmann, Mathew J.
2002   Signs of Power and Resistance: The (Re)Creation of Christian Imagery
        and Identities in the Pueblo Revolt Era. In *Archaeologies of the Pueblo
        Revolt: Identity, Meaning, and Renewal in the Pueblo World,* edited
        by Robert W. Preucel, pp. 132–144. University of New Mexico Press,
        Albuquerque.
Lincoln, T. R.
2000   A Brief History of Salado Archaeology. In *Salado,* edited by Jeffrey S.
        Dean, pp. 17–25. Amerind Foundation Publication, University of New
        Mexico Press, Albuquerque.
Lipe, William D.
1999   History of Archaeology. In *Colorado Prehistory: A Context for the
        Southern Colorado River Basin,* edited by William D. Lipe, Mark
        D. Varien, and Richard Wilshusen, pp. 51–94. Colorado Council of
        Professional Archaeologists, Denver.
Lipe, William D., Mark D. Varien, and Richard Wilshusen (editors)
1999   *Colorado Prehistory: A Context for the Southern Colorado River
        Basin.* Colorado Council of Professional Archaeologists, Denver.
Lister, Robert H.
1958   *Archaeological Investigations in the Northern Sierra Madre
        Occidental, Chihuahua and Sonora, Mexico,* with reports by Paul C.
        Mangelsdorf and Kate Peck Kent. University of Colorado Studies, Series
        in Anthropology 7. University Press of Colorado, Boulder.
1961   Twenty-Five Years of Archaeology in the Greater Southwest. *American
        Antiquity* 27:39–45.
Lister, Robert H., and Florence C. Lister
1968   *Earl Morris and Southwestern Archaeology.* University of New Mexico
        Press, Albuquerque.

1981   *Chaco Canyon: Archaeology and Archaeologists.* University of New
        Mexico Press, Albuquerque.
1990   *Aztec Ruins National Monument: Administrative History of an
        Archaeological Preserve.* Southwest Cultural Resources Center,
        Professional Papers 24. National Park Service, Santa Fe, New Mexico.

Lomatuway'ma, Michael, Lorena Lomatuway'ma, and Sidney Namingha Jr.
1993   *Hopi Ruin Legends, Kiqotutwutsi,* collected and edited by Ekkehart
        Malotki. Northern Arizona University Press, Flagstaff, and University
        of Nebraska Press, Lincoln.

Longacre, William A.
1964   A Synthesis of Upper Little Colorado Prehistory, Eastern Arizona. In
        Chapters in the Prehistory of Eastern Arizona Vol. 2, pp. 201–215.
        Fieldiana Anthropology 55. Field Museum of Natural History, Chicago.
1970   A Historical Review. In *Reconstructing Prehistoric Pueblo Societies,*
        edited by W. A. Longacre, pp. 1–10. University of New Mexico Press,
        Albuquerque.
1973   Current Directions in Southwestern Archaeology. *Annual Review of
        Anthropology* 2:201–209.

Longacre, William A., and J. Jefferson Reid
1974   The University of Arizona Archaeological Field School at Grasshopper:
        Eleven Years of Multidisciplinary Research and Teaching. *Kiva* 40
        (1–2):3–38.

Longacre, William A., Sally J. Holbrook, and Michael W. Graves (editors)
1982   *Multidisciplinary Research at Grasshopper Pueblo, Arizona.*
        Anthropological Papers 40. University of Arizona Press, Tucson.

Lorenzo, José L.
1981   Archaeology South of the Rio Grande. *World Archaeology* 13(2):
        190–208.

Lorenzo, J. L., A. Pérez-Elías, and J. García-Bárcena
1976   *Hacia una Arqueología Social: Reunión de Teotihuacan.* Instituto
        Nacional de Antropología, México, D.F.

Love, David Waxham
1980   *Quaternary Geology of Chaco Canyon Northwestern New Mexico.*
        Unpublished Ph.D. dissertation, Department of Geology, University of
        New Mexico, Albuquerque.

Lowell, Julie C.
1991   *Prehistoric Households at Turkey Creek Pueblo.* Anthropological
        Papers 54. University of Arizona Press, Tucson.

Lowie, Robert H.
1915   Oral Tradition and History. *American Anthropologist* 17:597–599.

Lumholtz, Carl
1902   *Unknown México.* 2 vols. Charles Schribner's Sons, New York.

Lyman, R. Lee, Michael J. O'Brien, and Robert C. Dunnell
1997   *The Rise and Fall of Culture History.* Plenum Press, New York.

Mabry, J.
2002   The Role of Irrigation in the Transition to Agriculture and Sedentism in
        the Southwest. In *Traditions, Transitions, and Technologies, Themes*

in Southwestern Archaeology, edited by S. H. Schlanger, pp. 178–199. University Press of Colorado, Boulder.

Mabry, J. (editor)

1998   *Archaeological Investigations of Early Village Sites in the Middle Santa Cruz Valley.* Anthropological Papers 19. Center for Desert Archaeology, Tucson, Arizona.

MacDonald, William K.

1976   Introduction: Archaeology and the Profits of Research. In *Digging for Gold: Papers on Archaeology for Profit*, edited by William K. MacDonald, pp. vii–xii. Technical Reports No. 5, Research Reports in Archaeology Contribution 2. Museum of Anthropology, University of Michigan Press, Ann Arbor.

MacWilliams, A. C.

2001   *La Cruz Sites in West Central Chihuahua.* Unpublished Ph.D. dissertation, Department of Anthropology, University of Arizona, Tucson.

McClung de Tapia, Emily

1999   Cultural Patrimony in Mexico: Proposal for a New Law to Replace the 1972 Legislation. *SAA Bulletin* 17(5):28–29.

McGregor, John C.

1941   *Southwestern Archaeology.* John Wiley and Sons, New York.

1965   *Southwestern Archaeology.* 2nd ed. University of Illinois Press, Urbana.

McGuire, Randall H.

1992   *A Marxist Archaeology.* Academic Press, San Diego, California.

1993   Charles Di Peso and the Mesoamerican Connection. In *Culture and Contact: Charles C. Di Peso's Gran Chichimeca*, edited by Anne I. Woosley and John C. Ravesloot, pp. 23–38. New World Studies Series 2. Amerind Foundation, Dragoon, Arizona.

2001   Ideologies of Death and Power in the Hohokam Community of La Cuidad. In *Ancient Burial Practices in the American Southwest*, edited by Douglas R. Mitchell and Judy L. Brunson-Hadley, pp. 27–44. University of New Mexico Press, Albuquerque.

2002   The Meaning and Limits of the Southwest/Northwest: A Perspective from Northern Mexico. In *Boundaries and Territories: Prehistory of the U.S. Southwest and Northern Mexico,* edited by M. Elisa Villalpando, pp. 173–183. Anthropological Research Papers 54. Department of Anthropology, Arizona State University, Tempe.

McGuire, Randall H., and Dean J. Saitta

1996   Although They Have Petty Captains, They Obey Them Badly: The Dialectics of Prehispanic Western Pueblo Social Organization. *American Antiquity* 61:197–216.

McGuire, Randall H., and Elisa Villalpando

1989   Prehistory and the Making of History in Sonora. In *Archaeological and Historical Perspectives on the Spanish Borderlands West,* edited by David Hurst Thomas, pp. 159–177. Columbian Consequences, Vol. 1. Smithsonian Institution Press, Washington D.C.

McGuire, Randall H., E. Charles Adams, Ben A. Nelson, and Katherine A. Spielmann
1994 Drawing the Southwest to Scale: Perspectives on Macroregional Relations. In *Themes in Southwest Prehistory*, edited by George J. Gumerman, pp. 239–265. School of American Research Press, Santa Fe, New Mexico.

McIntosh, Roderick J., Joseph A. Tainter, and Susan Keech McIntosh
2000 *The Way the Wind Blows: Climate History and Human Action*. Columbia University Press, New York.

McKusick, Charmion R.
1982 Avifauna from Grasshopper Pueblo. In *Multidisciplinary Research at Grasshopper Pueblo, Arizona*, edited by William A. Longacre, Sally J. Holbrook, and Michael W. Graves, pp. 73–86. Anthropological Papers 40. University of Arizona Press, Tucson.

Malina, J., and Z. Vasícek
1990 *Archaeology Yesterday and Today: The Development of Archaeology in the Sciences and Humanities*. Cambridge University Press, Cambridge.

Malinowski, Bronislaw
1926 *Myth in Primitive Psychology*. Paul Kegan, London.

Márquez-Alameda, Arturo
1990 Hacia una Síntesis de la Arqueología del Noroeste de México. *Actas del Primer Congreso de Historia General Comparada*: 23–32. Universidad Autónoma de Ciudad Juárez, Mexico.

Martin, Paul Schultz
1963a Early Man in Arizona: The Pollen Evidence. *American Antiquity* 29:67–73.
1963b *The Last 10,000 Years: A Fossil Pollen Record of the American Southwest*. University of Arizona Press, Tucson.
1964 Pollen Analysis of Prehistoric Human Feces: A New Approach to Ethnobotany. *American Antiquity* 30:168–180.
1967 Prehistoric Overkill. In *Pleistocene Extinctions, The Search for a Cause*, edited by P. Schultz Martin and H. E. Wright Jr., pp. 75–120. Yale University Press, New Haven, Connecticut.

Martin, Paul Schultz, and William Byers
1965 Pollen and Archaeology at Wetherill Mesa. In *Contributions of the Wetherill Mesa Archeological Project*, assembled by Douglas Osborne, pp. 122–135. Memoirs of the Society for American Archaeology 19. University of Utah Press, Salt Lake City.

Martin, Paul Schultz, and Peter J. Mehringer
1965 Pleistocene Pollen Analysis and Biogeography of the Southwest. In *The Quaternary of the United States*, edited by H. E. Wright Jr. and David G. Frey, pp. 433–451. Princeton University Press, Princeton, New Jersey.

Martin, Paul Sidney
1937 Review of *The Mogollon Culture of Southwestern New Mexico*, by Emil W. Haury. *American Antiquity* 2:233–234.
1974 Early Development in Mogollon Research. In *Archaeological Researches in Retrospect*, edited by G. R. Willey, pp. 3–29. Winthrop, Cambridge, Massachusetts.

1975a   Philosophy of Education at Vernon Field Station. In *Chapters in the Prehistory of Eastern Arizona* Vol. 4, edited by Paul S. Martin, Ezra B. W. Zubrow, Daniel C. Bowman, David A. Gregory, John A. Hanson, Michael B. Schiffer, and David R. Wilcox, pp. 3–11. Fieldiana Anthropology 65. Field Museum of Natural History, Chicago.

1975b   Introduction. In *Chapters in the Prehistory of Eastern Arizona* Vol. 4, edited by Paul S. Martin, Ezra B. W. Zubrow, Daniel C. Bowman, David A. Gregory, John A. Hanson, Michael B. Schiffer, and David R. Wilcox, pp. 1–2. Fieldiana Anthropology 65. Field Museum of Natural History, Chicago.

Martin, Paul S., and Fred T. Plog

1969   New Perspectives in Archaeology: Research Field Program of Field Museum of Natural History for High Ability Undergraduate Students, June 19–August 28, 1969, An Explanation. Manuscript on file, Field Museum of Natural History, Chicago.

Martin, Paul S., and John B. Rinaldo

1950a   *Turkey Foot Ridge Site: A Mogollon Village, Pine Lawn Valley, Western New Mexico*, pp. 237–396. Fieldiana Anthropology 38(2). Field Museum of Natural History, Chicago.

1950b   *Sites of the Reserve Phase, Pine Lawn Valley, Western New Mexico*, pp. 403–577. Fieldiana Anthropology 38(3). Field Museum of Natural History, Chicago.

Martin, Paul S., John B. Rinaldo, and Ernst Antevs

1949   *Cochise and Mogollon Sites, Pine Lawn Valley, Western New Mexico*, pp. 1–234. Fieldiana Anthropology 38(1). Field Museum of Natural History, Chicago.

Martin, Paul S., John B. Rinaldo, and Elaine Bluhm

1954   *Caves of the Reserve Area*. Fieldiana Anthropology 42. Field Museum of Natural History, Chicago.

Martin, Paul S., John B. Rinaldo, Elaine Bluhm, Hugh C. Cutler, and Roger Grange Jr.

1952   *Mogollon Cultural Continuity and Change: The Stratigraphic Analysis of Tularosa and Cordova Caves*. Fieldiana Anthropology 40. Field Museum of Natural History, Chicago.

Martin, Paul S., John B. Rinaldo, William A. Longacre, Constance Cronin, Leslie G. Freeman Jr., and James Schoenwetter

1962   *Chapters in the Prehistory of Eastern Arizona* Vol. 1, pp. 1–244. Fieldiana Anthropology 53(1). Field Museum of Natural History, Chicago.

Martin, Paul S., John B. Rinaldo, William A. Longacre, Leslie G. Freeman Jr., James A. Brown, Richard H. Hevly, and M. E. Cooley

1964   *Chapters in the Prehistory of Arizona* Vol. 2, pp. 1–261. Fieldiana Anthropology 55(1). Field Museum of Natural History, Chicago.

Martin, Paul S., William A. Longacre, and James N. Hill

1967   *Chapters in the Prehistory of Eastern Arizona* Vol. 3, pp. 1–249. Fieldiana Anthropology 57(1). Field Museum of Natural History, Chicago.

Mathien, Frances Joan

1992   Women of Chaco: Then and Now. In *Rediscovering Our Past: Essays on the History of American Archaeology,* edited by Jonathan E. Reyman, pp. 103–130. Avebury Press, Aldershot, United Kingdom.

2001   Anthropology and Archaeology in Chaco Canyon: The Hyde Exploring Expedition. In *Following Through: Papers in Honor of Phyllis S. Davis,* edited by Regge N. Wiseman, Thomas C. O'Laughlin, and Cordelia T. Snow, pp. 103–114. Papers of the Archaeological Society of New Mexico 27. Santa Fe.

Mathien, Joan, and Randall H. McGuire (editors)

1986   *Ripples in the Chichimec Sea: New Considerations of Southwestern-Mesoamerican Interactions.* Southern Illinois University Press, Carbondale.

Matson, R. G.

1991   *The Origins of Southwestern Agriculture.* University of Arizona Press, Tucson.

Meltzer, David J.

1983   The Antiquity of Man and the Development of American Archaeology. *Advances in Archaeological Method and Theory* 6:1–51.

1993   Is There a Clovis Adaptation? In *From Kostenki to Clovis, Upper Paleolithic–Paleo-Indian Adaptations,* edited by O. Soffer and N. D. Praslov, pp. 293–310. Plenum Press, New York.

1994   The Discovery of Deep Time: A History of Views on the Peopling of the Americas. In *Method and Theory for Investigating the Peopling of the Americas,* edited by R. Bonnichsen and D. Gentry Steele, pp. 7–26. Center for the Study of the First Americans, Oregon State University, Corvallis.

Mendiola Galván, Francisco

1997   La Definición de los Estilos del Arte Rupestre en Chihuahua. In *Prehistory of the Borderlands: Recent Research in the Archaeology of Northern Mexico and the Southern Southwest,* edited by John Carpenter and Guadalupe Sanchez, pp. 10–20. Arizona State Museum Archaeological Series 186. University of Arizona Press, Tucson.

Mera, Harry P.

1935   *Ceramic Clues to the Prehistory of North Central New Mexico.* Technical Series, Bulletin 8. Laboratory of Anthropology, Santa Fe, New Mexico.

Merriam, C. Hart, and Leonhard Stejneger

1890   *Results of a Biological Survey of the San Francisco Mountain Region and Desert of the Little Colorado, Arizona.* North American Fauna 3. U.S. Government Printing Office, Washington, D.C.

Merton, Robert K.

1993   *On the Shoulders of Giants.* University of Chicago Press, Chicago.

Meskell, Lynn

1999   *Archaeologies of Social Life: Age, Sex, Class et cetera in Ancient Egypt.* Basil Blackwell, Oxford.

266   REFERENCES

Milanich, Jerald T.
1999   *Laboring in the Fields of the Lord: Spanish Missions and Southeastern Indians.* Smithsonian Institution Press, Washington, D.C.

Mills, Barbara J.
1999a   Ceramic Ware and Type Systematics. In *Living on the Edge of the Rim. Excavations and Analysis of the Silver Creek Archaeological Research Project 1993–1998,* edited by Barbara J. Mills, S. A. Herr, and Scott Van Kueren, pp. 243–268. Arizona State Museum Archaeological Series 192. University of Arizona Press, Tucson.
1999b   The Research Setting. In *Living on the Edge of the Rim. Excavations and Analysis of the Silver Creek Archaeological Research Project 1993–1998,* edited by Barbara J. Mills, Scott A. Herr, and Scott Van Keuren, pp. 1–10. Arizona State Museum Archaeological Series 192. University of Arizona Press, Tucson.
2000a   The Archaeological Field School in the 1990s: Collaboration in Research and Training. In *Working Together: Native Americans and Archaeologists,* edited by Kurt E. Dongoske, Mark Aldenderfer, and Karen Doehner, pp. 121–128. Society for American Archaeology, Washington, D.C.
2000b   Alternative Models, Alternative Strategies: Leadership in the Prehispanic Southwest. In *Alternative Leadership Strategies in the Prehispanic Southwest,* edited by Barbara J. Mills, pp. 1–18. University of Arizona Press, Tucson.

Mills, Barbara J. (editor)
2000   *Alternative Leadership Strategies in the Prehispanic Southwest.* University of Arizona Press, Tucson.

Mills, Barbara J., and Patricia L. Crown (editors)
1995   *Ceramic Production in the American Southwest.* University of Arizona Press, Tucson.

Mills, Barbara J., and Sarah A. Herr
1999   Chronology of the Mogollon Rim Region. In *Living on the Edge of the Rim. Excavations and Analysis of the Silver Creek Archaeological Research Project 1993–1998,* edited by Barbara J. Mills, S. A. Herr, and Scott Van Kueren, pp. 295–324. Arizona State Museum Archaeological Series 192. University of Arizona Press, Tucson.

Mindeleff, Cosmos
1900   Localization of Tusayan Clans. *Nineteenth Annual Report of the Bureau of American Ethnology,* 1897–97 Pt. 2, pp. 635–653. Washington, D.C.

Mindeleff, Victor
1891   A Study of Pueblo Architecture: Tusayan and Cibola. *Eighth Annual Report of the Bureau of American Ethnology, 1886–87,* pp. 3-228. Washington, D.C.

Minnis, Paul E.
1985   Domesticating People and Plants in the Greater American Southwest. In *Prehistoric Food Production in North America,* edited by R. I. Ford, pp. 309–340. Anthropological Papers 75. Museum of Anthropology, University of Michigan Press, Ann Arbor.

1989   The Casas Grandes Polity in the International Four Corners. In *The Sociopolitical Structure of Prehistoric Southwestern Societies*, edited by Steadman Upham, Kent G. Lightfoot, and Roberta A. Jewett, pp. 269–305. Westview Press, Boulder, Colorado.

Montgomery, Ross G.

1940   Review of *The Religious Architecture of New Mexico in the Colonial Period and since the American Occupation*, by George Kubler. *New Mexico Quarterly* 10(4):272.

Montgomery, Ross Gordon, Watson Smith, and John Otis Brew

1949   *Franciscan Awatovi: The Excavation and Conjectural Reconstruction of a 17th-Century Spanish Mission Established at a Hopi Indian Town in Northeastern Arizona*. Papers of the Peabody Museum of American Archaeology and Ethnology 36. Harvard University, Cambridge, Massachusetts.

Montúfar López, Aurora, and María Luisa Reyes Landa

1995   Estudio de los Restos Botánicos de la Cueva de la Olla, Chihuahua. In *Investigaciones Recientes en Paleobotánica y Palinología*, edited by Aurora Montúfar López, pp. 29–36. Instituto Nacional de Antropología e Historia, México, D.F.

Morgan, Lewis H.

1870   *Systems of Consanguinity and Affinity of the Human Family*. Smithsonian Contributions to Knowledge Vol. 17. Washington, D.C.

1877   *Ancient Society*. Henry Holt, New York.

1880   A Study of the Houses of the American Aborigines. *First Annual Report of the Archaeological Institute of America*, pp. 29–80. Cambridge, Massachusetts.

1881   *Houses and House Life of the American Aborigines*. Contributions to North American Ethnology 4. Washington, D.C.

1965   *Houses and House-life of the American Aborigines*. University of Chicago Press, Chicago.

Morgenstein, Maury

1994   Petrographic Analysis of Adobe and Mortar Samples, Pecos National Historic Park, Pecos, New Mexico. Geosciences Management Institute, Boulder City, Nevada.

Morley, Sylvaneus

1915   Santa Fe Architecture. *Old Santa Fe* 2(3):278–301.

Morris, Don P.

1970   Walnut Creek Village: A Ninth-Century Hohokam-Anasazi Settlement in the Mountains of Central Arizona. *American Antiquity* 35:49–61.

Murray, Stephen O.

1994   *Theory Groups and the Study of Language in North America: A Social History*. John Benjamins, Philadelphia, Pennsylvania.

Naranjo, Tessie

1995   Thoughts on Migration by Santa Clara Pueblo. *Journal of Anthropological Archaeology* 14:247–250.

Nash, Stephen E.

1998   Time for Collaboration: A. E. Douglass, Archaeologists, and the Establishment of Tree-Ring Dating in the American Southwest. *Journal of the Southwest* 40(3):261–306.

1999   *Time, Trees, and Prehistory: Tree-Ring Dating and the Development of North American Archaeology 1914–1950.* University of Utah Press, Salt Lake City.

2000   Seven Decades of Archaeological Tree-Ring Dating. In *It's About Time: A History of Archaeological Dating in North America,* edited by S. E. Nash, pp. 60–83. University of Utah Press, Salt Lake City.

Nash, Stephen E., and Gary M. Feinman

2003   Introduction: A Glorious Foundation: 109 Years of Anthropology at the Field Museum of Natural History. In *Curators, Collections, and Contexts: Anthropology at the Field Museum, 1893–2002,* edited by Stephen E. Nash and Gary M. Feinman, pp. 5–8. Fieldiana Anthropology n.s. 36. Field Museum of Natural History, Chicago.

Nelson, Ben A.

1995   Complexity, Hierarchy, and Scale: A Controlled Comparison between Chaco Canyon, New Mexico, and La Quemada, Zacatecas. *American Antiquity* 60:597–618.

Nelson, Margaret C.

1991   The Study of Technological Organization. In *Archaeological Method and Theory* Vol. 3, edited by Michael B. Schiffer, pp. 57–100. University of Arizona Press, Tucson.

Nelson, Nels

1914   *Pueblo Ruins of the Galisteo Basin.* Anthropological Papers of the American Museum of Natural History Vol. 15, No. 1. New York.

1916   Chronology of the Tano Ruins. *American Anthropologist* 18:159–180.

Nesbitt, Paul

1938   *Starkweather Ruin.* Publications in Anthropology 6. Logan Museum, Beloit, Wisconsin.

Noguera, Eduardo

1930   Ruinas Arqueológicas del Norte de México. In *Dirección de Monumentos Prehispánicos, Publicaciones de la Secretaría de Educación Pública,* pp. 5–27. Tallares Gráficos de la Nación, México, D.F.

Novick, Andrea Lee

1980   Symposium on the Curation of Archaeological Collections. *Curator* 23(1):5–6.

Olsen, John W.

1982   Prehistoric Environmental Reconstruction by Vertebrate Faunal Analysis, Grasshopper Pueblo. In *Multidisciplinary Research at Grasshopper Pueblo, Arizona,* edited by William A. Longacre, Sally J. Holbrook, and Michael W. Graves, pp. 63–72. Anthropological Papers 40. University of Arizona Press, Tucson.

Olsen, Stanley J.

1982   Water Resources and Aquatic Fauna at Grasshopper Pueblo. In *Multidisciplinary Research at Grasshopper Pueblo, Arizona,* edited by William A. Longacre, Sally J. Holbrook, and Michael W. Graves, pp. 61–62. Anthropological Papers 40. University of Arizona Press, Tucson.

Orcutt, Janet D.

1991   Environmental Variability and Settlement Changes on the Pajarito Plateau, New Mexico. *American Antiquity* 56:315–332.

Ortiz, Simon J.
1992   *Woven Stone*. University of Arizona Press, Tucson.
Ortman, Scott G.
1998   Corn Grinding and Community Organization in the Pueblo Southwest, A.D. 1150–1550. In *Migration and Reorganization: The Pueblo IV Period in the American Southwest*, edited by K. A. Spielmann, pp. 165–192. Anthropological Research Papers 51. Department of Anthropology, Arizona State University, Tempe.
2000   Conceptual Metaphor in the Archaeological Record: Methods and an Example from the American Southwest. *American Antiquity* 65: 613–645.
Oyuela-Caycedo, Augusto, Armando Anaya, Carlos G. Elera, and Lidio M. Valdez
1997   Social Archaeology in Latin America? Comments to T. C. Patterson. *American Antiquity* 62:365–374.
Pailes, Richard A.
1980   The Upper Río Sonora Valley in Prehistoric Trade. *Transactions of the Illinois Academy of Science* 72(4):20–39.
1990   Elite Formation and Interregional Exchanges in Peripheries. In *Perspectives in Southwestern Prehistory*, edited by Paul Minnis and Charles Redman, pp. 213–228. Westview Press, Boulder, Colorado.
Pailes, Richard A., and Daniel T. Reff
1985   Colonial Exchange Systems and the Decline of Paquimé. In *The Archaeology of West and Northwest Mesoamerica*, edited by Michael S. Foster and Phil C. Weigand, pp. 353–363. Westview Press, Boulder, Colorado.
Parezo, Nancy J.
1986   Now Is the Time to Collect. *Masterkey* 59(4):1–18.
1987   The Formation of Ethnographic Collections: The Smithsonian Institution in the American Southwest. *Advances in Archaeological Method and Theory* 10:1–46.
Parezo, Nancy J. (editor)
1993   *Hidden Scholars: Women Anthropologists and the Native American Southwest*. University of New Mexico Press, Albuquerque.
Parsons, Elsie Clews
1925   *The Pueblo of Jemez*. Papers of the Phillips Academy Southwestern Expedition 3. Yale University Press, New Haven, Connecticut.
1932   Isleta, New Mexico. *Forty-seventh Annual Report of the Bureau of American Ethnology*, pp. 193–466. Washington, D.C.
Patterson, Alex
1994   *Hopi Pottery Symbols*. Johnson Books, Boulder, Colorado.
Patterson, Thomas C.
1994   Social Archaeology in Latin America: An Appreciation. *American Antiquity* 59:531–537.
Pauly, Philip J.
1988   Summer Resort and Scientific Discipline: Woods Hole and the Structure of American Biology, 1882–1925. In *The American Development of Biology*, edited by Ronald Rainger, Keith Benson,

and Jane Maienschein, pp. 121–150. University of Pennsylvania Press, Philadelphia.

Pavesic, Max G.

1999   Reflections on the United States National Museum Gates Expeditions to the American Southwest, 1901 and 1905. *Journal of California and Great Basin Anthropology* 21(1):136–145.

Pearson, David, and Fernando Sánchez Martínez

1990   Casas-Acantilado en Chihuahua. Nueva Evidencia en la Sierra Madre Occidental. *Arqueología* 4:41–58.

Peckham, Stewart

1990   *From This Earth. The Ancient Art of Pueblo Pottery.* Museum of New Mexico Press, Santa Fe.

Pepper, George H.

1909   The Excavation of a Burial Room in Pueblo Bonito, New Mexico. In *Putnam Anniversary Volume, Anthropological Essays Presented to Frederic Ward Putnam in Honor of His Seventieth Birthday*, pp. 196–252. G. E. Stechert, New York.

1920   *Pueblo Bonito.* Anthropological Papers of the American Museum of Natural History 27. New York.

Peregrine, Peter N., and Gary M. Feinman (editors)

1996   *Pre-Columbian World-Systems.* Prehistory Press, Madison, Wisconsin.

Peru, D. V.

1984   *New River: A Lithic Industry in Maricopa County, Arizona.* Arizona Archaeological Society Occasional Paper 1. Phoenix.

Petersen, Kenneth L.

1988   *Climate and the Dolores River Anasazi.* Anthropological Papers 113. University of Utah Press, Salt Lake City.

Péwé, Troy L.

1954   The Geological Approach to Dating Archaeological Sites. *American Antiquity* 20:51–61.

Phillips, Arthur M., III

1984   Shasta Ground Sloth Extinction: Fossil Packrat Midden Evidence from the Western Grand Canyon. In *Quaternary Extinctions: A Prehistoric Revolution*, edited by Paul Schultz Martin and Richard G. Klein, pp. 148–158. University of Arizona Press, Tucson.

Phillips, David A., Jr.

2002   Mesoamerican-Southwestern Relationships: An Intellectual History. In *Culture and Environment in the Southwest: Essays in Honor of Robert C. Euler*, edited by David A. Phillips Jr. and John A. Ware, pp. 177–195. SWCA Anthropology Research Paper 8. SWCA Environmental Consultants, Phoenix, Arizona.

Pickering, Andrew

1992   *Science as Practice and Culture.* University of Chicago Press, Chicago.

Pilles, Peter J., Jr.

1996   The Pueblo III Period along the Mogollon Rim: The Honanki, Elden and Turkey Hill Phases of the Sinagua. In *The Prehistoric Pueblo World A.D. 1150–1350*, edited by M. A. Adler, pp. 59–72. University of Arizona Press, Tucson.

Plog, Fred
1983   Political and Economic Alliances on the Colorado Plateaus, A.D. 400–
1450. *Advances in World Archaeology* 2:289–330.
Plog, Fred, and Steadman Upham
1983   The Analysis of Prehistoric Political Organization. In *Development of
Political Organization in Native North America*, edited by
E. Tooker and M. Fried, pp. 199–213. American Ethnological Society,
Washington, D.C.
Plog, Fred, George J. Gumerman, Robert C. Euler, Jeffrey S. Dean, Richard H.
Hevly, and Thor N. V. Karlstrom
1988   Anasazi Adaptive Strategies: The Model, Predictions, and Results.
In *The Anasazi in a Changing Environment*, edited by George J.
Gumerman, pp. 230–276. Cambridge University Press, Cambridge.
Plog, Stephen
1980   *Stylistic Variation in Prehistoric Ceramics: Design Analysis in the
American Southwest.* Cambridge University Press, Cambridge.
1983   Analysis of Style in Artifacts. *Annual Review of Anthropology* 12:
125–142.
1990   Sociopolitical Implications of Stylistic Variation in the American
Southwest. In *The Uses of Style in Archaeology*, edited by M. Conkey
and C. Hastorf, pp. 61–72. Cambridge University Press, Cambridge.
1995   Equality and Hierarchy: Holistic Approaches to Understanding
Social Dynamics in the Pueblo Southwest. In *Foundations of Social
Inequality*, edited by T. Douglas Price and Gary M. Feinman, pp. 189–
206. Plenum, New York.
Polaco, Oscar J., and Ana Fabiola Guzmán
1997   Archaeological Occurrence of the Meadow Vole, *Microtus pennsylvani-
cus*, in Chihuahua, México. *Southwestern Naturalist* 42(1):101–102.
Politis, Gustavo G.
1995   The Socio-Politics of the Development of Archaeology in Hispanic
South America. In *Theory in Archaeology: A World Perspective*, edited
by Peter J. Ucko, pp. 197–235. Routledge, London.
2003   The Theoretical Landscape and the Methodological Development of
Archaeology in Latin America. *American Antiquity* 68:245–272.
Powell, John W.
1895–96 Introduction. *Seventeenth Annual Report of the Bureau of American
Ethnology*, pp. xxvii–lxxiii. Washington, D.C.
Powers, Robert P., William B. Gillespie, and Stephen H. Lekson
1983   *The Outlier Survey: A Regional View of Settlement in the San Juan
Basin.* Reports of the Chaco Center 3. Division of Cultural Research,
National Park Service, Albuquerque, New Mexico.
Praetzellis, Adrian
1993   The Limits of Arbitrary Excavation. In *Practices of Archaeological
Stratigraphy*, edited by Edward C. Harris, Marley R. Brown III, and
Gregory J. Brown, pp. 68–86. Academic Press, San Diego, California.
Prescott, William H.
1843   *History of the Conquest of Mexico, with a Preliminary View of the
Ancient Mexican Civilization and the Life of the Conqueror, Hernando
Cortés.* Harper Bros., New York.

Preucel, Robert W.

1997   *The Kotyiti Research Project Report of the 1996 Field Season*. USDA Forest Service, Southwest District, Santa Fe, New Mexico.

2000   Making Pueblo Identities: Architectural Discourse at Kotyiti, New Mexico. In *An Archaeology of Communities in the Americas*, edited by J. Yaeger and M. Canuto, pp. 58–77. Routledge, London.

Preucel, Robert W., Loa P. Traxler, and Michael V. Wilcox

2002   "Now the Gods of the Spanish are Dead": Pueblo Ethnogenesis and Community Formation in the Aftermath of the Pueblo Revolt of 1680. In *Traditions, Transitions, and Technologies: Themes in Southwestern Archaeology in the Year 2000*, edited by S. Schlanger, pp. 71–94. University Press of Colorado, Boulder.

Radding, C.

1998   The Colonial Pact and Changing Ethnic Frontiers in Highland Sonora, 1740–1840. In *Contested Ground: Comparative Frontiers on Northern and Southern Edges of the Spanish Empire*, edited by D. J. Guy and T. E. Sheridan, pp. 52–66. University of Arizona Press, Tucson.

Ranger, T.

1991   Missionaries, Migrants and the Manyika: The Invention of Ethnicity in Zimbabwe. In *The Creation of Tribalism in Southern Africa*, edited by L. Vail, pp. 118–150. University of California Press, Berkeley.

Rapp, George, Jr., and Christopher L. Hill

1998   *Geoarchaeology: The Earth-Science Approach to Archaeological Interpretation*. Yale University Press, New Haven, Connecticut.

Redman, Charles L.

1993   *People of the Tonto Rim: Archaeological Discovery in Prehistoric Arizona*. Smithsonian Institution Press, Washington, D.C.

Reed, Erik K.

1949   Sources of Upper Rio Grande Pueblo Culture and Population. *El Palacio* 56:163–184.

1951   Cultural Areas of the Pre-Hispanic Southwest. *New Mexico Quarterly* 21:428–439.

1964   The Greater Southwest. In *Prehistoric Man in the New World*, edited by Jesse D. Jennings and Edward Norbeck, pp. 175–193. University of Chicago Press, Chicago.

Reed, James S.

1980   *Clark Wissler: A Forgotten Influence in American Anthropology*. Unpublished Ph.D. dissertation, Department of Anthropology, Ball State University, Muncie, Indiana.

Reid, J. Jefferson

1986   Historical Perspective on the Concept of Mogollon. In *Mogollon Variability*, edited by C. Benson and S. Upham, pp. 1–8. University Museum Occasional Papers 15. New Mexico State University Press, Las Cruces.

1989   A Grasshopper Perspective on the Mogollon of the Arizona Mountains. In *Dynamics of Southwest Prehistory*, edited by L. Cordell and G. Gumerman, pp. 65–97. Smithsonian Institution Press, Washington, D.C.

1999   The Grasshopper–Chavez Pass Debate: Existential Dilemmas and Archaeological Discourse. In *Sixty Years of Mogollon Archaeology: Papers from the Ninth Magollon Conference, Silver City, New Mexico,* edited by S. M. Whittlesey, pp. 13–22. SRI Press, Tucson, Arizona.

Reid, J. Jefferson, and David E. Doyel
1986   *Emil W. Haury's Prehistory of the American Southwest.* University of Arizona Press, Tucson.

Reid, J. Jefferson, and Stephanie M. Whittlesey
1990   The Complicated and the Complex: Observations on the Archaeological Record of Large Pueblos. In *Perspectives on Southwestern Prehistory,* edited by P. E. Minnis and C. L. Redman, pp. 184–195. Westview Press, Boulder, Colorado.

1997   *The Archaeology of Ancient Arizona.* University of Arizona Press, Tucson.

1999   *Grasshopper Pueblo: A Story of Archaeology and Ancient Life.* University of Arizona Press, Tucson.

Reinhard, Karl J., and Vaughn M. Bryant Jr.
1992   Coprolite Analysis: A Biological Perspective on Archaeology. *Archaeological Method and Theory* 4:245–288.

Renaud, E. B.
1931   Prehistoric Flaked Points from Colorado and Neighboring Districts. *Proceedings of the Colorado Museum of Natural History* 10:6–21.

Renfrew, Colin
2001   Production and Consumption in a Sacred Economy: The Material Correlates of High Devotional Expression at Chaco Canyon. *American Antiquity* 66:14–25.

Rex, John
1986   *Race and Ethnicity.* Open University Press, Milton Keynes, London.

Reyman, Jonathan E.
1989   The History of Archaeology and the Archaeological History of Chaco Canyon, New Mexico. In *Tracing Archaeology's Past. The Historiography of Archaeology,* edited by Andrew L. Christenson, pp. 41–53. Southern Illinois University Press, Carbondale and Edwardsville.

Reyman, Jonathan E. (editor)
1995   *The Gran Chichimeca: Essays on the Archaeology and Ethnohistory of Northern Mesoamerica.* Avebury Press, Aldershot, United Kingdom.

Rice, Glen E.
1990   An Intellectual History of the Salado Concept. In *A Design for Salado Research,* edited by G. E. Rice, pp. 21–30. Roosevelt Monograph Series 1, Anthropological Field Studies 22. Arizona State University, Tempe.

Rice, Glen E., John C. Ravesloot, and Christy G. Turner II
1992   Salado Ethnic Identity and Social Complexity: The Biocultural Approach. Paper presented at the 57th Annual Meeting of the Society for American Archaeology, Pittsburgh, Pennsylvania.

Riley, Carroll L.
1985   Spanish Contact and the Collapse of the Sonoran Statelets. In *The Archaeology of West and Northwest Mesoamerica,* edited by M. S.

Foster and P. C. Weigand, pp. 419–430. Westview Press, Boulder, Colorado.

1987   *The Frontier People, The Greater Southwest in the Protohistoric Period.* Rev. ed. University of New Mexico Press, Albuquerque.

Robbins, Wilfred W., John P. Harrington, and Barbara Freire-Marreco

1914   *Ethnobotany of the Tewa Indians.* Bureau of American Ethnology Bulletin 55. Washington, D.C.

Roberts, Frank H. H., Jr.

1935a   A Survey of Southwestern Archaeology. *American Anthropologist* 37:1–35.

1935b   *A Folsom Complex: Preliminary Report on Investigations at the Lindenmeier Site in Northern Colorado.* Smithsonian Institution Miscellaneous Collections 49. Washington, D.C.

1936   *Additional Information on the Folsom Complex: Report on the Second Season's Investigations at the Lindenmeier Site in Northern Colorado.* Smithsonian Institution Miscellaneous Collections Vol. 95, No. 10. Washington, D.C.

1940   Developments in the Problem of the Paleo-Indian. In *Essays in Historical Anthropology of North America*, pp.51–116. Smithsonian Institution Miscellaneous Collections 100. Washington, D.C.

Rodríguez-Camilloni, Humberto

1997   Obituary, George Kubler. *Newsletter of the Society of Architectural Historians* 41(3):12–13.

Rose, Martin, J. S. Dean, and William J. Robinson

1981   *The Past Climate of Arroyo Hondo, New Mexico, Reconstructed from Tree Rings.* Arroyo Hondo Archaeological Series 4. School of American Research Press, Santa Fe, New Mexico.

Rose, Martin R., William J. Robinson, and Jeffrey S. Dean

1982   Dendroclimatic Reconstruction for the Southeastern Colorado Plateau. Report submitted to the Dolores Archaeological Project, the Chaco Center, and Eastern New Mexico University. Manuscript on file, Laboratory of Tree-Ring Research, University of Arizona, Tucson.

Roth, B. J., and B. B. Huckell

1988   Cortaro Points and the Archaic of Southern Arizona. *Kiva* 57:353–370.

Rothman, Hal

1988   *Bandelier National Monument: An Administrative History.* Southwest Cultural Resources Center Professional Papers 14. National Park Service, Santa Fe, New Mexico.

1989   *Preserving Different Pasts: The American National Monuments.* University of Illinois Press, Urbana.

1992   *Navajo National Monument: A Place and Its People, an Administrative History.* Southwest Cultural Resources Center, Professional Papers 40. National Park Service, Santa Fe, New Mexico.

Rowe, John Howland

1954   *Max Uhle, 1856–1944: A Memoir of the Father of Peruvian Archaeology.* Publications in American Archaeology and Ethnology Vol. 46, No. 1. University of California, Berkeley.

Runte, Alfred
1987   *National Parks: The American Experience.* University of Nebraska
        Press, Lincoln.
Russell, Frank
1908   The Pima Indians. *Twenty-sixth Annual Report of the Bureau of
        American Ethnology, 1904–5,* pp. 3–389. Washington, D.C.
Sackett, James
1985   Style and Ethnicity in the Kalahari: A Reply to Weissner. *American
        Antiquity* 50:154–159.
Saitta, Dean J.
1997   Power, Labor, and the Dynamics of Change in Chacoan Political
        Economy. *American Antiquity* 62:7–26.
Sargent, Rose-Mary
1995   *The Diffident Naturalist, Robert Boyle and the Philosophy of
        Experiment.* University of Chicago Press, Chicago.
Sauer, Carl O., and Donald D. Brand
1931   *Prehistoric Settlements of Sonora with Special Reference to Cerro de
        Trincheras.* University of California Publications in Geography 3,
        pp. 425–458. Berkeley.
Sayles, E. B.
1933   Field Records and Correspondence. Arizona State Museum Archives.
        University of Arizona, Tucson.
1936   *An Archaeological Survey of Chihuahua.* Medallion Papers 10. Gila
        Pueblo, Globe, Arizona.
Sayles, E. B., and Ernst Antevs
1941   *The Cochise Culture.* Medallion Papers 29. Gila Pueblo, Globe,
        Arizona.
Schaafsma, Polly
1997   *Rock Art Sites in Chihuahua, Mexico.* Archaeology Notes 171. Office
        of Archaeological Research, Museum of New Mexico, Santa Fe.
2000   *Warrior, Shield and Star: Imagery and Ideology of Pueblo Warfare.*
        Western Edge Press, Santa Fe, New Mexico.
Schelberg, John D.
1984   Analogy, Complexity, and Regionally Based Perspectives. In *Recent
        Research on Chaco Prehistory,* edited by W. James Judge and John
        D. Schelberg, pp 5–21. Reports of the Chaco Center 8. National Park
        Service, Albuquerque, New Mexico.
Schiffer, Michael B.
1987   *Formation Processes of the Archaeological Record.* University of New
        Mexico Press, Albuquerque.
Schoenwetter, James
1961   The Pollen Analysis of Eighteen Archaeological Sites in Arizona and
        New Mexico. In *Chapters in the Prehistory of Arizona* Vol. 1, edited by
        Paul S. Martin, pp. 168–209. Fieldiana Anthropology. Field Museum of
        Natural History, Chicago.
1970   Archaeological Pollen Studies of the Colorado Plateau. *American
        Antiquity* 35:35–48.

Schoenwetter, James, and Alfred E. Dittert Jr.
1968   An Ecological Interpretation of Anasazi Settlement Patterns. In *Anthropological Archaeology in the Americas*, edited by Betty J. Meggars, pp. 41–66. Anthropological Society of Washington, Washington, D.C.

Schoenwetter, James, and Frank W. Eddy
1964   Alluvial and Palynological Reconstruction of Environments: Navajo Reservoir District. Papers in Anthropology 13. Museum of New Mexico Press, Santa Fe.

Scholes, France V.
1937   *Church and State in New Mexico, 1610–1650*. Publications in History 7, Historical Society of New Mexico. University of New Mexico Press, Albuquerque.
1942   *Troublous Times in New Mexico, 1659–1670*. Publications in History 11, Historical Society of New Mexico. University of New Mexico Press, Albuquerque.

Schuchert, Charles
1928   Memorial of Frank Springer. *Bulletin of the Geological Society of New Mexico* 39:65–80.

Schulman, Edmund
1956   *Dendroclimatic Changes in Semi-Arid America*. University of Arizona Press, Tucson.

Schwartz, Douglas W.
1970   The Postmigration Culture: A Basis for Archaeological Inference. In *Reconstructing Prehistoric Pueblo Societies*, edited by W. A. Longacre, pp. 175–193. University of New Mexico Press, Albuquerque.
1981   Four Exceptional Men: The Foundations of Rio Grande Archaeology. *Papers of the Archaeological Society of New Mexico* 6:251–273.

Sears, Paul B.
1932   The Archaeology of Environment in Eastern North America. *American Anthropologist* 34:610–622.
1937   Pollen Analysis as an Aid in Dating Cultural Deposits in the United States. In *Early Man*, edited by G. MacCurdy, pp. 61–66. Lippincott, London.

Sears, Paul B., and K. H. Clisby
1952   Two Long Climatic Records. *Science* 116:176–178.

Sebastian, Lynne
1992   *The Chaco Anasazi: Sociopolitical Evolution in the Prehistoric Southwest*. Cambridge University Press, Cambridge.

Sellards, E. H.
1940   Early Man in America. *Bulletin of the Geological Society of America* 51:373–432.
1952   *Early Man in America*. University of Texas Press, Austin.

Shackley, M. S.
1988   Sources of Archaeological Obsidian in the Southwest: An Archaeological, Petrological, and Geochemical Study. *American Antiquity* 43:752–772.

1996   Range and Mobility in the Early Hunter-Gatherer Southwest. In *Early Formative Adaptations in the Southern Southwest*, edited by B. J. Roth, pp. 5–16. Monographs in World Archaeology 25. Prehistory Press, Madison, Wisconsin.

Shapiro, Gary N., and John H. Hann

1990   The Documentary Image of the Council Houses of Spanish Florida Tested by Excavations at the Mission of San Luis de Talimali. In *Archaeological and Historical Perspectives on the Spanish Borderlands East*, edited by David Hurst Thomas, pp. 511–526. Columbian Consequences, Vol. 2. Smithsonian Institution Press, Washington, D.C.

Shaul, David L., and Jane H. Hill

1998   Tepimans, Yumans, and Other Hohokam. *American Antiquity* 63: 375–396.

Shennan, S. J. (editor)

1989   *Archaeological Approaches to Cultural Identity*. Unwin Hyman, London.

Shepard, Anna O.

1936   The Technology of Pecos Pottery. In *The Pottery of Pecos* Vol. 2, by Alfred V. Kidder and Anna O. Shepard, pp. 389–587. Papers of the Phillips Academy Southwestern Expedition 7. Yale University Press, New Haven, Connecticut.

1942   *Rio Grande Glaze Paint Ware: A Study Illustrating the Place of Ceramic Technological Analysis in Archaeological Research*. Contributions to American Anthropology and History 39, Publication 528. Carnegie Institution of Washington, Washington, D.C.

Simmons, Allan H.

1989a   Early Man in the Southwest—The Paleoindians. In *Human Adaptations and Cultural Change in the Greater Southwest*, edited by A. H. Simmons, A. L. W. Stodder, D. D. Dykeman, and P. A. Hicks, pp. 21–38. Arkansas Archeological Survey Research Series 32. Fayetteville.

1989b   The Unknown Archaeology of the Southwest—The Archaic. In *Human Adaptations and Cultural Change in the Greater Southwest*, edited by A. H. Simmons, A. L. W. Stodder, D. D. Dykeman, and P. A. Hicks, pp. 39–74. Arkansas Archeological Survey Research Series 32. Fayetteville.

Smith, Robert C.

1940   Review of *The Religious Architecture of New Mexico in the Colonial Period and since the American Occupation*, by George Kubler. *Hispanic American Historical Review* 20(4):619.

Smith, Watson

1971   *Painted Ceramics of the Western Mound at Awatovi*. Papers of the Peabody Museum of Archaeology and Ethnology 38. Harvard University Press, Cambridge, Massachusetts.

1987   Emil Haury's Southwest: A Pisgah View. *Journal of the Southwest* 29:107–120.

Smith, Watson, Richard B. Woodbury, and Nathalie F. S. Woodbury

1966   *The Excavation of Hawikuh by Frederick Webb Hodge: Report of the Hendricks-Hodge Expedition, 1917–1923*. Contribution from the Museum of the American Indian 20. New York.

Snead, James E.

1999   Science, Commerce, and Control: Patronage and the Development
        of Anthropological Archaeology in the Americas. *American
        Anthropologist* 101:256–271.

2001   *Ruins and Rivals: The Making of Southwestern Archaeology.*
        University of Arizona Press, Tucson.

2002a   The "Western Idea": Local Societies and American Archaeology. In
        *Excavating Our Past: Perspectives on the History of the Archaeological
        Institute of America,* edited by Susan Heuck Allen, pp. 123–140.
        Archaeological Institute of America, Colloquia and Conference
        Papers 5. Boston, Massachusetts.

2002b   Lessons of the Ages: Archaeology and the Construction of Cultural
        Identity in the American Southwest. *Journal of the Southwest* 44(1):
        17–34.

2006   "Treasures of Primitive Empires Revealed": Building an Audience for
        Archaeology in the North American Southwest. In *The Fabric of the
        Past: Historical Perspectives on the Material Culture of Archaeology,*
        edited by Nathan Schlanger. Berghan Press, New York, in preparation.

Snow, David H.

1981   Protohistoric Rio Grande Economics: A Review of Trends. In
        The Protohistoric Period in the North American Southwest,
        A.D. 1450–1700, edited by D. R. Wilcox and W. B. Masse, pp.
        354–377. Anthropological Research Papers 24. Department of
        Anthropology, Arizona State University, Tempe.

Speth, John D.

1988   Do We Need Concepts Like "Mogollon," "Anasazi," and "Hohokam"
        Today? A Cultural Anthropological Perspective. *Kiva* 53:201–204.

Spielmann, Katherine A.

1994   Clustered Confederacies: Sociopolitical Organization in the
        Protohistoric Rio Grande. In *The Ancient Southwestern Community,*
        edited by W. H. Wills and R. D. Leonard, pp. 45–54. University of New
        Mexico Press, Albuquerque.

1998   The Pueblo IV Period: History of Research. In *Migration and
        Reorganization: The Pueblo IV Period in the American Southwest,*
        edited by Katherine A. Spielmann, pp. 1–30. Anthropological Research
        Papers 51. Department of Anthropology, Arizona State University,
        Tempe.

Spier, Leslie

1917   An Outline for a Chronology of Zuni Ruins. *Anthropological Papers of
        the American Museum of Natural History* 18:207–332.

Springer, Frank

1910a   The Field Session of the School of American Archaeology. *Science,* n.s.
        23(827):622–624.

1910b   The Summer Session of the School of American Archaeology. *Santa Fe
        New Mexican* 24(September):5.

1917   Address of the Hon. Frank Springer. *El Palacio* 4(4):1–18.

Squier, E. G.
1848   New Mexico and California. *The American Review, Devoted to Politics and Literature* 11(5):503–528.

Stark, M. T., J. J. Clark, and M. D. Elson
1995   Social Boundaries and Cultural Identity in the Tonto Basin. In *The Roosevelt Community Development Study: New Perspectives on Tonto Basin Prehistory*, edited by M. D. Elson, M. T. Stark, and D. A. Gregory, pp. 343–368. Anthropological Papers 15. Center for Desert Archaeology, Tucson, Arizona.

Stephen, Alexander M.
1936   *Hopi Journals of Alexander M. Stephen*, edited by E. C. Parsons. 2 vols. Columbia University Contributions to Anthropology 23. Columbia University Press, New York.

Steward, Julian H.
1937   Ecological Aspects of Southwestern Society. *Anthropos* 32:87–104.
1955   *Theory of Culture Change*. University of Illinois Press, Urbana.

Stock, Chester
1938   John Campbell Merriam as Scientist and Philosopher. In *Cooperation and Research by Staff Members and Research Associates, the Carnegie Institution of Washington*, pp. 765–778. Carnegie Institution of Washington Publication 501. Carnegie Institution of Washington, Washington, D.C.

Stocking, George W.
1982   The Santa Fe Style in American Anthropology: Regional Interest, Academic Initiative, and Philanthropic Policy in the First Two Decades of the Laboratory of Anthropology, Inc. *Journal of the History of Behavioral Sciences* 18:3–19.

Streuver, Martha H.
2001   *Painted Perfection*. In *The Pottery of Dextra Quotskuyva*. Wheelwright Museum of the American Indian, Santa Fe, New Mexico.

Stuart, David E.
2000   *Anasazi America*. University of New Mexico Press, Albuquerque.

Stuart, David E., and Rory P. Gauthier
1981   *Prehistoric New Mexico: Background for Survey*. New Mexico Historic Preservation Bureau, Santa Fe.

Stubbs, Stanley A.
1959   "New" Old Churches found at Quarai and Tabira (Pueblo Blanco). *El Palacio* 66:162–169.

Stubbs, Stanley A., and Bruce T. Ellis
1955   *Archaeological Investigations at the Chapel of San Miguel and the Site of La Castrense, Santa Fe, New Mexico*. Monographs of the School of American Research 20. Laboratory of Anthropology, Museum of New Mexico, Santa Fe.

Swanton, John R., and Frank H. H. Roberts Jr.
1931   Jesse Walter Fewkes. *Annual Report of the Smithsonian Institution for 1930*, pp. 609–616. Washington, D.C.

Szuter, Christine
2000   Gender and Animals: Hunting Technology, Ritual, and Subsistence in the Greater Southwest. In *Women and Men in the Prehispanic Southwest*, edited by P. L. Crown, pp. 197–220. School of American Research Press, Santa Fe, New Mexico.

Tainter, Joseph A.
1988   *The Collapse of Complex Societies.* Cambridge University Press, Cambridge.

Tainter, Joseph A., and Fred Plog
1994   Strong and Weak Patterning in Southwestern Prehistory: The Formation of Puebloan Archaeology. In *Themes in Southwest Prehistory*, edited by G. J. Gumerman, pp. 165–181. School of American Research Press, Santa Fe, New Mexico.

Tanner, Clara Lee
1954   Byron Cummings, 1860–1954. *Kiva* 20(1):1–20.

Taylor, Walter W.
1948   *A Study of Archaeology.* Memoirs of the American Anthropological Association 69. Menasha, Wisconsin.
1954   Southwestern Archaeology, Its History and Theory. *American Anthropologist* 56:561–575.

Teague, Lynn S.
1993   Prehistory and the Traditions of the O'Odham and Hopi. *Kiva* 58(4):435–454.

Thomas, David Hurst
1988   Saints and Soldiers at Santa Catalina: Hispanic Designs for Colonial America. In *The Recovery of Meaning in Historical Archaeology*, edited by Mark P. Leone and Parker B. Potter Jr., pp. 73–140. Smithsonian Institution Press, Washington, D.C.
1993   The Archaeology of Mission Santa Catalina de Guale: Our First Fifteen Years. In *The Missions of La Florida*, edited by Bonnie G. McEwan, pp. 1–34. University of Florida Press, Gainesville.

Thomas, Jeffery Allen
1999   *Promoting the Southwest: Edgar L. Hewett, Anthropology, Archaeology, and the Santa Fe Style.* Unpublished Ph.D. dissertation, Department of History, Texas Tech University, Lubbock.

Thompson, Raymond H.
1991   Shepard, Kidder, and Carnegie. In *The Ceramic Legacy of Anna O. Shepard,* edited by Ronald L. Bishop and Frederick W. Lange, pp. 11–41. University Press of Colorado, Niwot.
1995   Emil W. Haury and the Definition of Southwestern Archaeology. *American Antiquity* 60:640–660.
2000a   An Old and Reliable Authority. An Act for the Preservation of American Antiquities. *Journal of the Southwest* 42(2).
2000b   Edgar Lee Hewett and the Political Process. *Journal of the Southwest* 42(2):271–318.
2000c   The Crisis in Archaeological Collection Management. *CRM* 23(5):4–6.
2006   An Informal History of the Department of Anthropology at the University of Arizona: The First 75 Years, 1915–1991. University of Arizona Press, Tucson, in preparation.

Thompson, Raymond H., and William A. Longacre
1966   The University of Arizona Archaeological Field School at Grasshopper,
        East Central Arizona. *Kiva* 31(4):255–275.
Thompson, R. S., C. Whitlock, P. J. Bartlein, S. P. Harrison, and W. G.
        Spaulding
1993   Climatic Changes in the Western United States Since 18,000 years
        B.P. In *Global Climates since the Last Glacial Maximum*, edited by
        H. E. Wright, J. E. Kutzbach, F. A. Street-Perrott, and P. J. Bartlein,
        pp. 468–513. University of Minnesota Press, Minneapolis.
Toulouse, Joseph H., Jr.
1949   *The Mission of San Gregorio de Abo: A Report on the Excavation and
        Repair of a Seventeenth-Century New Mexico Mission.* Monographs
        of the School of American Research 13. University of New Mexico
        Press, Albuquerque.
Towner, Ronald H., and J. S. Dean
1996   Questions and Problems in Pre–Fort Sumner Navajo Archaeology. In
        The Archaeology of Navajo Origins, edited by Ronald H. Towner,
        pp. 3–18. University of Utah Press, Salt Lake City.
Trigger, Bruce G.
1989   *A History of Archaeological Thought.* Cambridge University Press,
        Cambridge.
Turner, Christy G., II, and Jacqueline A. Turner
1999   *Man Corn: Cannibalism and Violence in the Prehistoric American
        Southwest.* University of Utah Press, Salt Lake City.
Turner, James
1999   *The Liberal Education of Charles Eliot Norton.* Johns Hopkins
        University Press, Baltimore.
Upham, Steadman
1982   *Polities and Power: An Economic and Political History of the Western
        Pueblos.* Academic Press, New York.
1987   The Tyranny of Ethnographic Analogy in Southwestern Archaeology.
        In *Coasts, Plains and Deserts: Essays in Honor of Reynold J. Ruppe,*
        edited by S. W. Gaines, pp. 265–281. Anthropological Research
        Papers 38. Department of Anthropology, Arizona State University,
        Tempe.
1989   East Meets West: Hierarchy and Elites in Pueblo Society. In *The
        Sociopolitical Structure of Prehistoric Southwestern Societies,* edited by
        Steadman Upham, Kent Lightfoot, and Roberta A. Jewett, pp. 77–102.
        Westview Press, Boulder, Colorado.
Upham, Steadman, and Fred Plog
1986   The Interpretation of Prehistoric Political Complexity. *Journal of Field
        Archaeology* 12:223–238.
Upham, Steadman, and Lori Reed
1989   Regional Systems in the Central and Northern Southwest: Demography,
        Economy and Sociopolitics Preceding Contact. In *Archaeological and
        Historical Perspectives on the Spanish Borderlands West,* edited by
        David Hurst Thomas, pp. 17–40. Columbian Consequences, Vol. 1.
        Smithsonian Institution Press, Washington, D.C.

Upham, Steadman, Patricia L. Crown, and Stephen Plog
1994   Alliance Formation and Cultural Identity in the American Southwest.
        In *Themes in Southwest Prehistory,* edited by George J. Gumerman,
        pp. 183–210. School of American Research Press, Santa Fe, New
        Mexico.
VanPool, Christine S.
2002   Flight of the Shaman. *Archaeology* 55(1):40–43.
Van West, Carla R.
1990   *Modeling Prehistoric Climatic Variability and Agricultural Production
        in Southwestern Colorado.* Ph.D. dissertation, Washington State
        University. University Microfilms, Ann Arbor.
1994a   *Modeling Prehistoric Agricultural Productivity in Southwestern
        Colorado: A GIS Approach.* Reports of Investigations 67. Department
        of Anthropology, Washington State University, Pullman, and Crow
        Canyon Archaeological Center, Cortez, Colorado.
1994b   Reconstructing Paleoenvironment in the Middle Little Colorado River
        Area and Modeling Human Responses. In *River, Rain, or Ruin:
        Intermittent Prehistoric Land Use along the Middle Little Colorado
        River,* edited by Carla R. Van West, pp. 213–238. SRI Press, Tucson,
        Arizona.
1996   Agricultural Potential and Carrying Capacity in Southwestern
        Colorado, A.D. 901 to 1300. In *The Prehistoric Pueblo World,
        A.D. 1150–1350,* edited by Michael A. Adler, pp. 214–227. University of
        Arizona Press, Tucson.
Van West, Carla R., and Jeffrey S. Dean
2000   Environmental Characteristics of the A.D. 900–1300 Period in the
        Central Mesa Verde Region. *Kiva* 66:19–44.
Vargas, Victoria D.
1995   *Copper Bell Trade Patterns in the Prehispanic U.S. Southwest and
        Northwest México.* Arizona State Museum Archaeological Series 187.
        University of Arizona Press, Tucson.
Vasquez León, Luis
1994   Mexico: The Institutionalization of Archaeology. In *History of Latin
        American Archaeology,* edited by Augusto Oyuela-Caycedo, pp.69–89.
        Avebury Press, Aldershot, United Kingdom.
Veit, U.
1989   Ethnic Concepts in German Prehistory: A Case Study on the
        Relationship between Cultural Identity and Archaeological Objectivity.
        In *Archaeological Approaches to Cultural Identity,* edited by
        S. Shennan, pp. 36–56. Unwin Hyman, London.
Vermeulen, H., and C. Grovers (editors)
1994   *The Anthropology of Ethnicity.* Het Spinhuis, Amsterdam.
Vierra, Bradley J.
1994   Archaic Hunter-Gatherer Mobility Strategies in Northwestern New
        Mexico. In *Archaic Hunter-Gatherer Archaeology in the American
        Southwest,* edited by B. J. Vierra, pp. 121–154. Contributions in
        Anthropology Vol. 13, No. 1. Eastern New Mexico University, Portales.

Vierra, Bradley J. (editor)
1994   *Archaic Hunter-Gatherer Archaeology in the American Southwest.*
       Contributions in Anthropology Vol. 13, No. 1. Eastern New Mexico
       University, Portales.

Villalpando, M. Elisa
1988   Rutas de Intercambio y Objectos de Concha en el Noroeste de México.
       Cuilcuilco 21:77–81.

Vivian, Gordon
1979   *Gran Quivira: Excavations in a Seventeenth-century Jumano Pueblo.*
       National Park Service Archaeological Research Series 8. Washington,
       D.C.

Vivian, Gordon, and Tom W. Mathews
1965   *Kin Kletso: A Pueblo III Community in Chaco Canyon, New Mexico.*
       Southwestern Monuments Association Technical Series Vol. 6, No. 1–2.
       Globe, Arizona.

Vivian, Gordon, and Paul Reiter
1965   *The Great Kivas of Chaco Canyon and Their Relationships.* School
       of American Research Monograph 22. School of American Research
       Press, Santa Fe, New Mexico.

Vivian, R. Gwinn
1990   *The Chacoan Prehistory of the San Juan Basin.* Academic Press,
       New York.

Vroman, Adam C.
1961   *Photographer of the Southwest. Adam Clark Vroman, 1856–1916,*
       edited by R. I. Mahood. Ward Ritchie Press, Los Angeles.

Wade, Edwin L., and Lea McChesney
1980   *America's Great Lost Collection: The Thomas V. Keam Collection of
       Hopi Pottery from the Second Hemenway Expedition, 1890–1894.*
       Heard Museum, Phoenix, Arizona.
1981   *Historic Hopi Ceramics: The Thomas V. Keam Collection of the
       Peabody Museum of Archaeology and Ethnology, Harvard University.*
       Peabody Museum Press, Cambridge, Massachusetts.

Wallace, H. D., and W. H. Doelle
2001   Classic Period Warfare in Southern Arizona. In *Deadly Landscapes:
       Case Studies in Prehistoric Southwestern Warfare,* edited by G. E. Rice
       and S. A. LeBlanc, pp. 239–287. University of Utah Press, Salt Lake City.

Ware, John A.
2001   Chaco Social Organization: A Peripheral View. In *Chaco Society and
       Polity: Papers from the 1999 Conference,* edited by Linda S. Cordell,
       W. James Judge, and June-el Piper, pp 79–93. Special Publication 4.
       New Mexico Archaeological Council, Albuquerque.

Warrior, Claire
2003   "A Small Collection from New Mexico and Arizona": Barbara Freire-
       Marreco in the Southwestern United States, 1910–13. *Journal of
       Museum Ethnography* 15:115–130.

Washburn, Dorothy K.
1977   *A Symmetry Analysis of Upper Gila Area Ceramic Design.* Papers
       of the Peabody Museum of Archaeology and Ethnology 68. Harvard
       University Press, Cambridge, Massachusetts.

Wasley, William W.
1957   Highway Salvage Archaeology in Arizona. *Kiva* 23(2):4–7.
Waters, Michael R.
1986   *The Geoarchaeology of Whitewater Draw, Arizona.* Anthropological
        Papers 45. University of Arizona Press, Tucson.
1988   Holocene Alluvial Geology and Geoarchaeology of the San Xavier
        Reach of the Santa Cruz River, Arizona. *Geological Society of America
        Bulletin* 100:479–491.
1998   Geoarchaeological Investigations in the Tonto Basin. In *Environment
        and Subsistence in the Classic Period Tonto Basin: The Roosevelt
        Archaeology Studies,* edited by Katherine E. Spielmann, pp. 7–47.
        Anthropological Field Studies 39, Roosevelt Monograph Series 10.
        Arizona State University Office of Cultural Resource Management,
        Tempe.
Waters, Michael R., and John C. Ravesloot
2000   Late Quaternary Geology of the Middle Gila River, Gila River Indian
        Reservation, Arizona. *Quaternary Research* 54:49–57.
Watkins, Joe
2000   *Indigenous Archaeology: American Indian Values and Scientific
        Practice.* Altamira Press, Walnut Creek, California.
Watson, Patty Jo
1995   Archaeology, Anthropology, and the Culture Concept. *American
        Anthropologist* 97:683–694.
Wauchope, Robert
1962   *Lost Tribes and Sunken Continents: Myth and Method in the Study of
        American Indians.* University of Chicago Press, Chicago.
Webb, William, and Robert A. Weinstein
1973   *Dwellers at the Source. Southwestern Indian Photographs of
        A. C. Vroman, 1895–1904.* Grossman, New York.
Weigand, Phil C., and Acelia García de Weigand
2000   Dinámica Socioeconómica de la Frontera Prehispánica de Mesoamérica.
        In *Nómadas y Sedentarios en el Norte de México: Homenaja a Beatriz
        Braniff,* edited by Phil C. Weigand and Acelia García de Weigand,
        pp. 113–124. Universidad Nacional Autónoma de México, Instituto de
        Investigaciones Antropológicas, Estéticas, y Históricas, México, D.F.
Weigle, Marta
1989   From Desert to Disney World: The Santa Fe Railway and the
        Fred Harvey Company Display the Indian Southwest. *Journal of
        Anthropological Research* 45:115–137.
Wendorf, Fred
1950   *A Report on the Excavation of a Small Ruin near Point of Pines, East
        Central Arizona.* Social Science Bulletin 19. University of Arizona
        Bulletin Vol. 21, No. 3. Tucson.
1954   A Reconstruction of Northern Rio Grande Prehistory. *American
        Anthropologist* 56:200–227.
Wendorf, Fred, and Erik K. Reed
1955   An Alternative Reconstruction of Northern Rio Grande Prehistory.
        El Palacio 62:131–173.

Wendorf, Fred, and Raymond H. Thompson
2002 The Committee for the Recovery of Archaeological Remains: Three Decades of Service to the Archaeological Profession. *American Antiquity* 76:317–330.

Whalen, Michael E., and Paul E. Minnis
2001 *Casas Grandes and Its Hinterland*. University of Arizona Press, Tucson.

Wheat, Joe Ben
1953 *A Study of the Mogollon Culture Prior to A.D. 1000*. Unpublished Ph.D. dissertation, Department of Anthropology, University of Arizona. Tucson.
1954a Southwestern Cultural Interrelationships and the Question of Area Co-tradition. *American Anthropologist* 56:576–586.
1954b *Crooked Ridge Village (Arizona W:10:15)*. Social Science Bulletin 24. University of Arizona Bulletin Vol. 21, No. 3. Tucson.
1955 *Mogollon Culture prior to A.D. 1000*. American Anthropological Association Memoir 82. Society for American Archaeology Memoir 10. Menasha, Wisconsin.

White, Courtney
1996 Adobe Typology and Site Chronology: A Case Study from Pecos National Historical Park. *Kiva* 61(4):347–364.

White, Leslie A.
1935 *The Pueblo of Santo Domingo*. American Anthropological Association Memoir 43. Menasha, Wisconsin.
1940 *Pioneers in American Anthropology: The Bandelier-Morgan Letters, 1873–1883*. 2 vols. University of New Mexico Press, Albuquerque.

Whiteley, Peter M.
2002 Archaeology and Oral Tradition: The Scientific Importance of Dialogue. *American Antiquity* 67:405–415.

Whittlesey, Stephanie M.
1978 Status and Death at Grasshopper Pueblo: Experiments Toward an Archaeological Theory of Correlates. Unpublished Ph.D. dissertation, Department of Anthropology, University of Arizona, Tucson.
1999 Preface. In *Sixty Years of Mogollon Archaeology: Papers from the Ninth Mogollon Conference, Silver City, New Mexico, 1996*, edited by Stephanie M. Whittlesey, pp. vii–xiv. SRI Press, Tucson, Arizona.

Whittlesey, Stephanie M., Eric Arnould, and William Reynolds
1982 Archaeological Sediments: Discourse, Experiment, and Application. In *Multidisciplinary Research at Grasshopper Pueblo, Arizona*, edited by William A. Longacre, Sally J. Holbrook, and Michael W. Graves, pp. 28–35. Anthropological Papers 40. University of Arizona Press, Tucson.

Wiener, Philip P. (editor)
1958 *Charles S. Peirce: Selected Writings (Values in a Universe of Chance)*. Dover, New York.

Wiessner, Polly
1985 Style or Isochrestic Variation? A Reply to Sackett. *American Antiquity* 50:160–166.

Wilcox, David R.

1981   The Entry of Athapaskan Speakers into the American Southwest: The Problem Today. In *The Protohistoric Period in the North American Southwest, A.D. 1450–1700*, edited by David R. Wilcox and W. Bruce Masse, pp. 213–256. Anthropological Research Papers 24. Department of Anthropology, Arizona State University, Tempe.

1984   Multi-ethnic Division of Labor in the Protohistoric Southwest. *Papers of the Archaeological Society of New Mexico* 9:141–156.

1986   A Historical Analysis of the Problem of Mesoamerican-Southwestern Interaction. In *Ripples in the Chichimec Sea: New Considerations of Southwestern-Mesoamerican Interactions*, edited by F. J. Mathien and R. H. McGuire, pp. 2–44. Southern Illinois University Press, Carbondale.

1987   *Frank Midvale's Investigation of La Ciudad*. Anthropological Field Studies 19. Arizona State University Office of Cultural Resource Management, Tempe.

1988a   Rethinking the Mogollon Concept. *Kiva* 53:205–209.

1988b   The Changing Context of Support for Archaeology and the Work of Erich F. Schmidt. In *Erich F. Schmidt's Investigations of Salado Sites in Central Arizona,* by John W. Hohmann and Linda Kelley, pp. 11–28. Museum of Northern Arizona Bulletin 56. Flagstaff.

1991   Changing Contexts of Pueblo Adaptation. In *Farmers, Hunters, and Colonists: Interaction between the Southwest and the Southern Plains,* edited by Katherine Spielmann, pp. 128–154. University of Arizona Press, Tucson.

1993   Pueblo Grande as Phoenix: Odd Halseth's Vision of a City Museum. In *Archaeology of the Pueblo Grande Platform Mound and Surrounding Features, Introduction to the Archival Project and History of Research,* edited by Christian E. Downum and Todd W. Bostwick, pp. 97–138. Pueblo Grande Museum Anthropological Papers 1. Phoenix, Arizona.

1996   The Diversity of Regional and Macroregional Systems in the American Southwest. In *Debating Complexity,* edited by Daniel A. Meyer, Peter C. Dawson, and Donald T. Hanna, pp. 375–390. Archaeological Association of the University of Calgary, Calgary, Alberta.

2001   Creating a Firm Foundation: The Early Years of the Arizona State Museum. Paper presented at the 100th Annual Meeting of the American Anthropological Association, Washington, D.C.

Wilcox, David R., and Don D. Fowler

2002   The Beginnings of Anthropological Archaeology in the North American Southwest: From Thomas Jefferson to the Pecos Conference. *Journal of the Southwest* 44(2):121–234.

Wilcox, David R., and Lynette O. Shenk

1977   *The Architecture of the Casa Grande and Its Interpretation*. Arizona State Museum Archaeological Series 115. University of Arizona Press, Tucson.

Wilcox, David R., and Charles Sternberg

1983   *Hohokam Ballcourts and Their Interpretation*. Arizona State Museum Archaeological Series 115. University of Arizona Press, Tucson.

Willey, Gordon R., and Phillip Phillips
1958   *Method and Theory in American Archaeology.* University of Chicago
        Press, Chicago.
Willey, Gordon R., and Jeremy A. Sabloff
1980   *A History of American Archaeology.* 2nd ed. W. H. Freeman, San
        Francisco.
Wills, Wirt H.
1988   *Early Prehistoric Agriculture in the American Southwest.* School of
        American Research Press, Santa Fe, New Mexico.
2000   Political Leadership and Construction of Chacoan Great Houses,
        A.D. 1020–1140. In *Alternative Leadership Strategies in the
        Prehispanic Southwest,* edited by Barbara J. Mills, pp. 19–44.
        University of Arizona Press, Tucson.
Wills, Wirt H., and Bruce B. Huckell
1994   Economic Implications of Changing Land-use Patterns in the Late
        Archaic. In *Themes in Southwest Prehistory,* edited by George J.
        Gumerman, pp. 33–52. School of American Research Press, Santa Fe,
        New Mexico.
Wilmsen, Edwin N., and Frank H. H. Roberts Jr.
1978   *Lindenmeier, 1934–1974: Concluding Report on Investigations.*
        Smithsonian Contributions to Anthropology 24. Smithsonian
        Institution Press, Washington, D.C.
Wilson, Chris
1997   *The Myth of Santa Fe: Creating a Modern Regional Tradition.*
        University of New Mexico Press, Albuquerque.
Wilson, C.
1999   Testimony to the NAGPRA Review Committee. Minutes of the Native
        American Graves Protection and Repatriation Act (NAGPRA) Review
        Committee Seventeenth Meeting, May 3–5, 1999, Silver Spring,
        Maryland. www.cr.nps.gov/nagpra/REVIEW/meetings/RMS017.PDF
Winterhalder, B., and C. Goland
1997   An Evolutionary Perspective on Diet Choice, Risk, and Plant
        Domestication. In *People, Plants, and Landscapes: Studies in
        Paleoethnobotany,* edited by K. J. Gremillion, pp. 123–160. University
        of Alabama Press, Tuscaloosa.
Wissler, Clark
1917a   The New Archaeology. *The American Museum Journal* 17(2):100–101.
1917b   *The American Indian.* D. C. McMurtrie, New York.
1926   *The Relation of Nature to Man in Aboriginal America.* Oxford
        University Press, New York.
Wobst, H. M.
1977   Stylistic Behavior and Information Exchange. In *Papers for the
        Director: Research Essays in Honor of James B. Griffin,* edited by
        C. Cleland, pp. 317–342. Anthropological Papers 61. University of
        Michigan Press, Ann Arbor.
Wood, J. S.
2000   Vale of Tiers Palimpsest: Salado Settlement and Internal Relationships
        in the Tonto Basin Area. In *Salado,* edited by J. S. Dean, pp. 107–141.

Amerind Foundation, Dragoon, Arizona, and University of New Mexico Press, Albuquerque.

Woodbury, Richard B.

1989   Foreword. In *Point of Pines, Arizona: A History of the University of Arizona Archaeological Field School,* by Emil W. Haury, pp. xi–xiii. Anthropological Papers 50. University of Arizona Press, Tucson.

1990   Watson Smith and Southwestern Archaeology. In *When Is a Kiva? and Other Questions about Southwestern Archaeology,* edited by Raymond H. Thompson, pp. 5–30. University of Arizona Press, Tucson.

1993   *Sixty Years of Southwestern Archaeology: A History of the Pecos Conference.* University of New Mexico Press, Albuquerque.

Wormington, H. M.

1957   *Ancient Man in North America.* 5th ed. Denver Museum of Natural History, Popular Series 4. Denver, Colorado.

Worth, John E.

1998   *The Timucuan Chiefdoms of Spanish Florida,* Vol. 1: *Assimilation.* University Press of Florida, Gainesville.

Wright, H. E., Jr. and David G. Frey (editors)

1965   *The Quaternary of the United States.* Princeton University Press, Princeton, New Jersey.

Yellen, John E., and Mary W. Greene

1985   Archaeology and the National Science Foundation. *American Antiquity* 50:332–341.

Yoffee, Norman

2001   The Chaco "Rituality" Revisited. In *Chaco Society and Polity: Papers from the 1999 Conference,* edited by Linda S. Cordell, W. James Judge, and June-el Piper, pp 63–78. Special Publication 4. New Mexico Archaeological Council, Albuquerque.

Yoffee, Norman, Suzanne K. Fish, and George Milner

1999   Communidades, Ritualities, Chiefdoms: Social Evolution in the American Southwest and Southeast. In *Great Towns and Regional Polities,* edited by Jill E. Neitzel, pp 261–271. University of New Mexico Press, Albuquerque.

Young, M. Jane

1988   *Signs from the Ancestors: Zuni Cultural Symbolism and Perceptions of Rock Art.* University of New Mexico Press, Albuquerque.

Zedeño, M. N.

1994   *Sourcing Prehistoric Ceramics at Chodistaas Pueblo, Arizona.* Anthropological Papers 58. University of Arizona Press, Tucson.

Zeder, Melinda A.

1997   *The American Archaeologist, A Profile.* AltaMira Press, Walnut Creek, California.

Contributors

Linda S. Cordell is director of the Museum of Natural History, University of Colorado, Boulder, and professor of anthropology, University of Colorado, Boulder.

Jeffrey S. Dean is professor of dendrochronology, Laboratory of Tree-Ring Research; professor of anthropology, Department of Anthropology; and curator of archaeology, Arizona State Museum, University of Arizona, Tucson.

William H. Doelle is president of Desert Archaeology, Inc., Tucson, Arizona.

Don D. Fowler is Mamie Kleberg Professor of Historic Preservation and Anthropology, Emeritus, University of Nevada, Reno.

Bruce Huckell is professor of anthropology, University of New Mexico, Albuquerque.

John Ivey is historian with the National Park Service in Santa Fe, New Mexico.

Jane H. Kelley is Professor of Archaeology Emerita, Department of Archaeology, University of Calgary, Alberta, Canada.

Stephen H. Lekson is curator of anthropology, Museum of Natural History, University of Colorado, Boulder.

Arthur MacWilliams is adjunct assistant professor, Department of Archaeology, University of Calgary, Alberta, Canada.

Barbara Mills is professor of anthropology, University of Arizona, Tucson.

Stephen E. Nash is head of collections, Department of Anthropology, Field Museum of Natural History, Chicago, Illinois.

David A. Phillips Jr. is curator of archaeology, Maxwell Museum of Anthropology, University of New Mexico, Albuquerque.

Robert Preucel is Gregory Annenberg Weingarten Associate Curator of North American Archaeology, University of Pennsylvania Museum of Archaeology and Anthropology; and associate professor of anthropology, University of Pennsylvania.

J. Jefferson Reid is professor of anthropology, University of Arizona, Tucson.

James E. Snead is assistant professor of anthropology, George Mason University, Alexandria, Virginia.

Katherine A. Spielmann is professor of anthropology, Arizona State University, Tempe.

David Hurst Thomas is curator, Division of Anthropology, American Museum of Natural History, New York.

Stephanie Whittlesey is chief research officer and senior principal investigator, Statistical Research, Inc., Tucson, Arizona.

David R. Wilcox is curator of anthropology, Museum of Northern Arizona, Flagstaff.

Index